Ellen Axson Wilson

*"Apple Orchard," painted by Ellen Axson Wilson
in May 1911 at Old Lyme, Connecticut.
Courtesy of* The Papers of Woodrow Wilson

First Lady Between Two Worlds

Ellen Axson Wilson

by Frances Wright Saunders

The University of North Carolina Press
Chapel Hill and London

Library of Congress Cataloging in Publication Data

Saunders, Frances Wright, 1920–
Ellen Axson Wilson: first lady between two worlds.

(Supplementary volumes to The papers of Woodrow Wilson)
Bibliography: p.
Includes index.
1. Wilson, Ellen Axson. 2. Wilson, Woodrow, 1856–
1924—Family. 3. Presidents—United States—Wives—
Biography. 4. Presidents—United States—Biography.
I. Title. II. Series.
E767.3.W64S28   1985   973.91'3'0924 [B]   84-20812

ISBN 0-8078-1641-8

Designed by Naomi P. Slifkin

For Monica, whose life was too brief,
and to my mother, who gave us roots and wings

Contents

Part Five · 1902–1906

Part Six · 1906–1910

Part Seven · 1910–1912

Part Eight · 1913–1914

Illustrations

Acknowledgments

Ellen Axson Wilson, while playing an essential role in Woodrow Wilson's private and professional life, manifestly expanded the expected Victorian woman's role beyond the bounds of domesticity. Editor, counselor, teacher, politician, artist, landscape designer, and latent feminist, she read widely in the classics, literature, art, philosophy, history, and political topics. Facile in languages, she translated German monographs for Wilson to use in his scholarly writings, and she broadened his cultural background. While she helped her husband politically, she pursued her own career as an artist. She insisted that her three daughters be trained to earn a living rather than be dependent upon a husband for financial security.

I hope that this biography will help to solve one of the problems of contemporary historians: how to make women, or the family, a "truly integral part of history" which "old" historians see as "consisting (not exclusively, but essentially) of the unfolding of great events, in which 'great men' . . . play a conspicuous part."*

I wish to thank Arthur S. Link, a scholar who recognized early in his work the significance of Ellen Axson, for his unfailing trust and for his invaluable editorial advice on the final draft of the manuscript. The counsel, interest, and friendship of David W. Hirst, senior associate editor of *The Papers of Woodrow Wilson*, have lightened the tasks of research immeasurably. The suggestion that I write a biography of Ellen Axson Wilson was first made by Link and Hirst. These two editors and their staff, through their superbly edited and annotated volumes of *The Papers*, have provided easy access to a wealth of information. These volumes, the Woodrow Wilson Papers in the Library of Congress, and the Woodrow Wilson Collection at Princeton University contain hundreds of letters which passed between Ellen Wilson, her husband, her friends, and her family. The Ray Stannard Baker Collection in the Library of Congress contains valuable material. John Mul-

---

*Gertrude Himmelfarb, *New York Times Book Review*, Aug. 17, 1980, p. 3.

der's scholarly book, *Woodrow Wilson: The Years of Preparation*, has afforded useful insights, and Eleanor Wilson McAdoo's *The Woodrow Wilsons* has been helpful.

In addition to these sources of material, the three children of Jessie Wilson Sayre allowed me to examine and copy nearly three hundred intimate family letters and a number of photographs never before made public. Without the support and encouragement of Francis Bowes Sayre, Jr., Eleanor Axson Sayre, and Woodrow Wilson Sayre, my research would have been far less rewarding and the returns considerably leaner. I owe a special debt of gratitude to Frank and Harriet Sayre for their gracious hospitality even while I ransacked the family archives.

Several other caches of material have turned up in such unusual ways that Ellen Wilson herself would have ascribed the results to "a kind Providence." One group of fifty-six Axson family letters, dating from 1837 to 1882, was preserved by Jean Van Houten in her Princeton home as a trust from Margaret Axson Elliott. I am grateful, indeed, to Mrs. Van Houten for her belief that the right person to make use of the letters would, in due course, appear, and that I was that person. I wish to thank Arthur P. Morgan of the Princeton Bank and Trust Company, who provided the first clues which led me to the Van Houten collection, and A. Perry Morgan for allowing me to examine the papers of Junius Spencer Morgan.

Marjorie Brown King, a cousin of Ellen Wilson's, has shared events from her amazing memory, as well as family letters which she, too, had saved for the use of someone who "might" be interested. Mrs. King also contributed information which led to the discovery of the Wilson-McAdoo Collection at the University of California, Santa Barbara. Another preserver of letters, Catherine Williams Bayliss, allowed me to see the correspondence between her aunt, the artist Adele Williams, and Ellen Wilson. Two other packets of letters written by Ellen came to light, one in the Fondren Library, Rice University, the other in the Macbeth Gallery Papers in the Archives of American Art. A single important letter was found in the possession of Margaret Brady Lovejoy of Pinehurst, North Carolina.

I am indebted to two of Ellen's cousins, Ben Palmer Axson and Dr. William Dana Hoyt, himself a historian, for information about their families and for their constant help and enthusiasm; both have become warm friends.

No biographer could survive without that special breed of person—

the archivist—who can lighten one's day with a fragment of a manuscript or a clue which leads to the unraveling of a textual puzzle. Earle Coleman, archivist at the Seeley Mudd Library, Princeton University, is one of those rare human beings who combines patience, wit, and enthusiasm with an encyclopedic mind. Others who have cheerfully located material are William G. Allman, Curatorial Assistant, Office of the Curator, The White House; Andrea P. Brown and Professor Martha Stoops, St. Mary's College, Raleigh, North Carolina; Lawrence Campbell and Tom Hall, Art Students League; Henry G. Fulmer, Manuscripts Division, South Caroliniana Library, University of South Carolina; Dolores Lescure, President, the Woodrow Wilson Birthplace, Staunton, Virginia; Barbara McAdams, Curator, Florence Griswold Museum, Old Lyme, Connecticut; William McNaught and Judy Throm, Archives of American Art; Sybil McRay, Chestatee Regional Library, Gainesville, Georgia; Beatrice Millican, Curator of the Henderson Room, Carnegie Library, Rome, Georgia; Gertrude Mignery, Archives Supervisor, Jessie Ball duPont Library, the University of the South, Sewanee, Tennessee; Janis Richardson, Special Collections Assistant, the Woodson Research Center, Rice University; Dr. Ruth See, Research Historian, The Historical Foundation of the Presbyterian and Reformed Churches, Montreat, North Carolina; Catherine Stover, the Pennsylvania Academy of the Fine Arts; and Arthur Walworth and the staff of the Manuscripts Room, Yale University Library.

I would also like to thank the staff of Firestone Library, Princeton University, and in particular, Carol Hazen, Eleanor Weld, and the late Louise Anderson of the Reference Department; Ann Van Arsdale and Charles Green of Rare Books and Manuscripts; and Mary Ann Jensen, Curator of the Theater Collection.

I am grateful for the assistance of the Art Institute of Chicago; the Cleveland Museum of Art; the staffs of the First Presbyterian Churches of Athens and Rome, Georgia; University of Georgia Libraries, Athens, Georgia; the Georgia Historical Society, Savannah; Goucher College, the Maryland Historical Society, and the Peabody Conservatory of Music, Baltimore; the Indianapolis Museum of Art; the Institute of Living, Hartford, Connecticut; the National Academy of Design, New York; Free Library of Philadelphia; St. Paul's Church, Augusta, Georgia; and Martha Sullivan Sword, Alumni Secretary, Princeton Day School.

Among a host of Georgians to whom I am indebted are: Roger

Aycock, Roy E. Bottoms, Martha Clarke, Sara Fahy, Martha Gilbert, Ellis Hale, Wade Cothran Hoyt, Sadie Langston, and Judy Summerbell, all of Rome; also, E. H. Armor, Caroline C. Hunt, Robert Stephens, Mrs. Thomas Wheeling, and Emma Stephens Wilson. I wish especially to thank Ellen Jervis of Rome; Frances and Tharpe Sanders of Monroe, Georgia; and Sigrid and Paul Watson of Cambridge, Massachusetts, in whose homes I spent happy and fruitful hours.

From among the many other helpful individuals, I should like to list a few: Alice and Wallace Alston, Virginia J. Coates, Eleanor Marquand Delanoy, Selma H. Diggle, Jane Griffin Dix, Ruth Daniel Dye, Lila N. Eisberg, Sam J. Ervin, Jr., Elizabeth Erwin Hutchins, Dorothy K. MacDowell, Irma J. Murray, Helen W. Saunders, Margaret B. Selby, Glen Stice, Denise Thompson, Anne Venzon, and Jasper E. and Rebecca F. Wright.

To Margaret Douglas Link, Julia F. Metzger, Allan F. Saunders, and Ann W. Waldron, who read early versions of parts of the manuscript, I am deeply grateful. Teri Betros worked long hours at typing many drafts of each chapter; and Susannah Jones delivered a labor of love in reading, making editorial suggestions, and typing the first completed draft. I am grateful to the New Jersey Historical Commission for a research grant awarded in 1980.

Lastly, I wish to thank my husband, David R. Saunders, for his constant support and his skills with a word processor, and my two sons, Eric and Jon, who were unwavering in their optimism that the book would be completed.

Part One

1860–1883

Ellen Louise Axson, c. 1866.
Courtesy of the Very Reverend Francis B. Sayre.

Chapter 1

Meeting

On April 8, 1883, Ellen Louise Axson attended worship as usual in the First Presbyterian Church of Rome, Georgia. The service, a solemn one with Holy Communion, was led by her father, the Reverend Samuel Edward Axson, pastor of the church. Still in mourning for her mother, the twenty-two-year-old Miss Axson was dressed in black with a heavy crepe veil over her hair. She was unaware that, diagonally behind her, a visitor had noticed her and was distracted from the sacred ritual. Instead of meditating piously, the young man sat thinking to himself: "What a bright, pretty face; what splendid, mischievous, laughing eyes! I'll lay a wager that this demure little lady has lots of life and fun in her!" When the service was over, Ellen Axson moved up the aisle speaking to friends, oblivious that the man was watching her.[1]

His name was Woodrow Wilson. A novice lawyer from Atlanta in Rome on legal business for his mother, he was staying with his uncle, James W. Bones, an elder in Edward Axson's church. That Woodrow wanted to make an early afternoon call at the minister's home appeared to the Bones family to be a thoughtful gesture, because they knew that Axson and Woodrow's father, the Reverend Dr. Joseph Ruggles Wilson, were old friends and colleagues.

When Woodrow arrived at the Axson residence, the pastor ushered him into the parlor. As the conversation droned on between the two men, Woodrow realized that Axson had no inkling of the true mission of this visit. In desperation, he pointedly asked after the pastor's daughter's "health"; Axson, obviously surprised, summoned her to join them.[2] There stood "a slip of a girl," about five feet, three inches tall and weighing no more than 115 pounds. Her silky, bronze-blonde hair, swept up in a braided knot at the back, fell in front in a few tendrils over a high forehead; the mouth suggested a faint pout. Her dark-brown, deep-set eyes were hypnotic.[3] After the introductions were made, and with Ellen's sparkling health altogether evident, Axson turned to his guest to ask: "Why have night congregations grown so small?" Woodrow stumbled through an answer, uneasy with both the minister's question and his daughter's presence.[4]

If the confrontation in the parlor was love at first sight, neither Ellen nor Woodrow admitted it as such. But by the time that he returned to his law office in Atlanta later in the week of April 8, he knew that he was in love. To win Ellen became a consuming challenge for the next few months.[5] More deliberate in allowing herself to fall in love, Ellen nevertheless sensed something commanding about this young man. Physically, he was not unusual: he was slim, five feet, eleven inches tall, and had straight brown hair, heavy eyebrows, a flowing mustache, and a prominent lower jaw. His most arresting feature by far was the compelling intensity of his blue-gray eyes that were framed by long dark eyelashes.[6] The composite picture was unquestionably patrician.

Before Woodrow Wilson came on the scene, Ellen had discouraged other men, some of whom could not believe that she was serious in declining their proposals of marriage or overlooking their "intentions." When she was eighteen, Joe Walker of Darien, Georgia, proposed to her and continued to pursue her for four years after she had firmly turned him down. The possessive attentions of a Mr. Williams, from Savannah, only disgusted her; James Wright, of Rome, suffered from "wounded pride," although she tried "very hard" to manage so that he would not feel "humiliated"; and she "gave the gate" to another Roman, Charles Thornwell, whose mother was abetting the son's efforts. She was not at all tempted by an offer of marriage from a young missionary who wanted to take her to China.[7] After she had told one of her closest woman friends that, if she ever loved a man, it would be against her will,[8] she was known as "Ellie, the Man Hater," a title which she still held when Woodrow arrived in town.[9]

One simple explanation of her attitude is that none of the men in her life fulfilled the requirements which she had set down at age seventeen: "good, nice, handsome, splendid, delightful, intelligent and interesting."[10] Yet evidence appears later in her life which suggests that there were more complex reasons for her reluctance to become entangled. Meanwhile, she began to see more and more of "Mr. Wilson."

Thomas Woodrow Wilson was born on December 28 / 29, 1856,[11] in the Presbyterian manse in Staunton, Virginia, the third child and first son of Joseph Ruggles Wilson and Janet (Jessie) Woodrow Wilson. Woodrow Wilson, like Ellen Axson, was a child and grandchild of

Presbyterian divines. His boyhood was spent in Augusta, Georgia, where his father was pastor of the First Presbyterian Church from 1858 to 1870. From Georgia, Joseph Wilson went to Columbia, South Carolina, to join the faculty of the Columbia Theological Seminary and, for a time, he supplied the pulpit of the First Presbyterian Church. In September 1873, Woodrow went to Davidson College in North Carolina, but dropped out after one year. The family moved in 1874 to Wilmington, North Carolina, and, in September 1875, Woodrow left to attend the College of New Jersey (now Princeton University). He graduated in 1879, and that fall entered the University of Virginia Law School. Abandoning his formal studies a year and a half later, he went home to Wilmington, where he read law for an additional eighteen months. In June 1882, he and his father chose Atlanta, a fast-growing postwar city, as a promising location for a fledgling attorney. He opened an office there with Edward Ireland Renick, also a law graduate of the University of Virginia; in October 1882, he was admitted to the bar. The firm of Renick and Wilson experienced an austere first year, largely because Atlanta was oversupplied with aspiring young lawyers. Wilson was disappointed financially, and the practice of the law itself bored him. By the time that he met Ellen Axson, he was disenchanted with both law and the burgeoning New South. He wanted to lead an intellectual life and to have social intercourse with persons whose minds stretched his own. To this end, he decided to study at The Johns Hopkins University, an institution in ferment with stimulus from German scholarship in history and social science. He planned graduate work in preparation for college teaching.[12]

These changes and choices were heavily on his mind when he returned to Rome in late May 1883 to resume work on the legal matters which had brought him there initially. More important, however, was his plan to court Ellen Axson. He stayed in East Rome with his first cousin, Jessie Bones (Mrs. Abraham Thew H.) Brower, at her home, Oakdene. From there, on May 28, 1883, he wrote his first letter to the woman he hoped would become his wife:

> Miss Axson, East Rome   Monday morning
>   I write to beg that you will gratify me by taking a drive with me this afternoon. I shall call at 5 o'clock if that hour will suit your convenience. If you have any previous engagement for this after-

noon, I hope that you will vouchsafe me the pleasure of riding with you tomorrow at the same hour.

> Very Respty Yours, Woodrow Wilson[13]

She replied on the same day:

> Mr. Wilson,   Monday
> I have no engagement for this afternoon, and it will afford me pleasure to take the drive. I will be ready at the appointed hour.
> Very sincerely, Ellen L. Axson.[14]

By mid-June, Woodrow had told his mother that he was in love with Ellen Axson and intended to ask her to marry him. After a quick trip to Atlanta to arrange to have his worldly goods moved to his parents' home in Wilmington, he was back again in Rome. This time, he stayed a fortnight and pursued Ellen as ardently as he dared.

Jessie Brower arranged a picnic for the young people on Friday, June 29, the day before Woodrow was to leave Rome, an event that marked an important turn in the courtship. Rome historians tell us that the picnic was held east of Lindale near a spring which forms part of the headwaters of Silver Creek, that the young people rode out in a wagon furnished with side seats and filled with straw, that Woodrow and Ellen sat alone in the back and dangled their feet as the wagon bumped along, and that the two of them left the group to hunt four-leaf clovers. Woodrow, himself, later commented on riding home from the picnic in a wagon.[15]

When he left the next day, Ellen had only promised to correspond with him. She assured her dearest friend, Rosalie Anderson, in a letter surely written that same evening, that she was *not* engaged.[16] Discreet letters ("My dear Miss Axson," "Dear Mr. Wilson," and "your sincere friend") passed between Rome and Wilmington during July. In August, Woodrow went with his mother and his sister, Annie (Mrs. George, Jr.) Howe, to Flat Rock in the North Carolina mountains near Asheville for a vacation; meanwhile, Ellen left Rome to visit friends in nearby Morganton, North Carolina.

It is impossible to disagree with the Wilson scholar who said, "The peculiar sequence of events that culminated in Woodrow Wilson's engagement to Ellen Axson tempts one to believe that they were later right in ascribing the result to a kind Providence."[17] Among the coincidental events were her visit to Morganton while Woodrow was vaca-

Woodrow Wilson, 1883, at the time of his engagement to Ellen Louise Axson.
Princeton University Library.

tioning with his family nearby; the fact that Woodrow's family unexpectedly changed resorts from Flat Rock to Arden, south of Asheville, so that a crucial letter which Ellen sent to him "wandered"; and that *his* wish to visit her in Morganton was aborted because Ellen was summoned home due to her father's illness. Knowing that Woodrow planned to leave North Carolina for Baltimore on or about Friday, September 14, Ellen wrote from Morganton on the twelfth that their meeting appeared to be doomed, for "by the next train—the same which carries this note," she was leaving for Rome because her father needed her. However, this note did not reach Arden until Saturday, and on Friday Woodrow went into Asheville for the day. For unknown reasons, Ellen's own departure from Morganton was delayed until that same Friday, September 14, when she arrived in Asheville, probably in the late morning, to make train connections for Rome. Apparently unable to get a suitable train before evening, she took a room at the Eagle Hotel. Woodrow walked down the street in Asheville past the Eagle Hotel and recognized Ellen in the window of her second-floor room by the arrangement of her hair.[18]

The events of the next two days can be pieced together from their later letters. Woodrow persuaded her to postpone her departure until Sunday, when he would leave for Baltimore. Probably on Saturday, a decidedly nervous Miss Axson was driven to Arden to meet his mother, sister, and younger brother, Joseph. On Saturday night he took a room at the Eagle Hotel, but he was too excited either to sleep or eat. Shortly before he was to board his train on Sunday, and still unsure of Ellen's feelings, Woodrow professed his love and asked her to marry him. Ellen was dazed, tongue-tied, and wretched because he was leaving. Yet she knew that she was "letting those few precious moments slip away unused," and she said "yes." Painfully aware that they were in the public hallway of the Eagle Hotel, they sealed their pledge with a kiss. Woodrow left for the station, but before he was out of sight, he realized that he did not know the size of her ring finger. He rushed back to the hotel, borrowed one of her rings, and dashed for his train.[19]

When Ellen returned to Rome, she found the Axson grandparents with her father, who was in bed overcome by nervous exhaustion and insomnia. The only person with whom she shared her secret was her sixteen-year-old brother, Stockton. She told him that her fiancé was "the greatest man in the world and the best."[20] On the afternoon of October 2, Ellen received a diamond ring in the mail, "a perfect beauty in every respect." The setting, she said, was "extremely chaste" and the ring was "in exquisite taste."[21]

Chapter 2

Heritage and Childhood

Most of Ellen Axson's forebears had been well established in New England and New Jersey before they migrated to Georgia and South Carolina.[1] One colonial ancestor, John Hoyt, came from Curry Rivel, Somersetshire, England, to Salem, Massachusetts in 1629. John's great-great-grandson, and Ellen's great-great-grandfather, Winthrop Hoyt, born in 1739, was a soldier in the French and Indian War when he was not yet eighteen years old, and later served with Ethan Allen and his Green Mountain Boys when they captured Fort Ticonderoga from the British in 1775.[2]

Winthrop's grandson, Nathan Hoyt, Ellen Axson's maternal grandfather, was born in Gilmanton, New Hampshire, in 1793. A self-educated man, he studied theology privately to prepare for his ordination to the Presbyterian ministry. In 1826, he married Margaret Bliss, of Springfield, Massachusetts, and the following year they moved to Beech Island, South Carolina. He was pastor of the Presbyterian Church of Beech Island for two years, briefly served a pulpit in Washington, Georgia, and, in 1830, accepted a call to the First Presbyterian Church in Athens, Georgia, where he remained the rest of his life. It was in this church that Ellen's parents were married in 1858.[3]

Margaret Jane ("Janie"), Ellen's mother, was born in Athens on September 8, 1838, the sixth and last child of Nathan and Margaret Bliss Hoyt. The five older siblings were Thomas Alexander, born January 31, 1828, who became a prominent Presbyterian clergyman; Louisa Cunningham, born January 22, 1830, who married a Georgia businessman, Warren A. Brown; William Dearing, born November 11, 1831, who became a physician; Henry Francis, born October 27, 1833, also a Presbyterian minister; and Robert T. Hoyt, born December 24, 1835, who became a pharmacist.[4]

When she was fifteen, Janie Hoyt enrolled at the Greensboro Female College, Greensboro, Georgia, a school established by the Presbyterian Synod of Georgia for daughters of the Old South that they might become "as corner stones polished after the similitude of a Palace."[5]

Janie's father, Nathan, was a part-time faculty member, and Ellen's paternal grandfather, the Reverend Isaac Stockton Keith Axson ("the Great Axson"), was president of the college.

Born in 1813 in Charleston, Axson was descended from settlers who had come to South Carolina in 1684 from England by way of Bermuda. Isaac's father, Samuel Edward Axson, died young and his mother, Sarah Ann Palmer Axson, reared and educated her two sons, Forster, who became a physician in New Orleans, and Isaac.[6] After graduating from the College of Charleston, Isaac completed his theological studies in May 1834 at the Columbia Theological Seminary, Columbia, South Carolina, and, in October, married Rebecca Longstreet Randolph.

Rebecca's father, Isaac Fitz Randolph, had migrated to the South from Princeton, New Jersey, shortly after the American Revolution, settled in Columbia, and dropped the "Fitz" from his name. A prosperous businessman who owned stagecoach lines to Camden, Charleston, and Augusta, Georgia, Randolph entertained the Marquis de Lafayette when he visited Columbia in 1825. Rebecca, then ten years old, later described the occasion to her granddaughter, Ellen Louise Axson.[7]

In the spring of 1836, Isaac and Rebecca Axson moved to Liberty County, Georgia, where he had accepted a call as copastor of the Midway Presbyterian Church. He became the senior pastor in 1849, and served there for seventeen years altogether. Three children were born at Waltourville in Liberty County: Ellen's father, Samuel Edward (known as "Edward") on December 23, 1836; Randolph, on October 1, 1838; and Sarah Ellen, on May 8, 1841. A son, John Leighton Wilson, born in Dorchester, South Carolina, in 1835 had died in infancy.[8] In 1853, I. S. K. Axson left the Midway Church to become president of the Greensboro Female College.[9] The next year, his son Edward entered Oglethorpe College as a declared candidate for the ministry.[10]

It is not surprising that Edward Axson's mother, on surveying the young women at the Greensboro Female College, decided that Janie Hoyt was her choice to be Edward's wife.[11] Janie was extremely bright and "devastatingly beautiful," with "great lustrous gray eyes, redbrown hair rippling back from a Madonna-like forehead, and a slim body instinct with grace."[12] A lover of books, Janie said that one of her "greatest temptations" was to read. She would often become "so absorbed in a book or paper" that her *work* remained undone.[13] In the summer of 1856, after Edward Axson had completed his first year at the Columbia Theological Seminary, he and Janie Hoyt became engaged.[14]

Isaac Stockton Keith Axson, c. 1834, "the Great Axson,"
paternal grandfather of Ellen Axson Wilson. From an oil painting
done by an unknown Charleston artist. Courtesy of Ben Palmer Axson.

Janie won so many academic honors at Greensboro that her brother, William, then a student at the Jefferson Medical College in Philadelphia, wrote in jest that she was "too grand with collegiate honors" to correspond with him. Immediately after her graduation in 1856, Janie became a teacher at the college.[15]

In the late fall of 1857, I. S. K. Axson left Greensboro to accept a call to the prestigious Independent Presbyterian Church of Savannah. For several months Janie was the guest of her future in-laws in Savannah while her fiancé completed his theological studies.[16] Janie's daughter said many years later that Grandmother Axson "literally *made* Mama come to stay with them."[17]

Janie and Edward were married in Athens on November 23, 1858, with both minister-fathers participating in the ceremony.[18] On "Sabbath, May 22, 1859," Edward was ordained to his first pastorate in the Presbyterian Church of Beech Island, South Carolina,[19] where he began his first full-time ministry. The young Axsons boarded in a private home until the birth of their daughter, Ellen Louise, on May 15, 1860. Named after her Aunt Ellen Axson and her Aunt Louisa Hoyt, Ellen was born in the northwest second-floor bedroom of the Presbyterian manse in Savannah, the home of her Axson grandparents.[20] Sometime between late January and February 9, 1861, when Edward left the Beech Island church, Ellen was baptized there either by her grandfather Hoyt or her own father.[21]

The year of their daughter's birth marked a pinnacle of happiness for Edward and Janie Axson. By the time that Ellen was a year old, Georgia had seceded to become a part of the Confederacy, and the Civil War had begun. For the next four years, mother and daughter were exposed to increasing instability as hostilities spread through most of the state which to Janie was "the garden spot of the earth."[22]

During the war years, Edward Axson was often separated from his wife and child. Janie, who divided her time between the Hoyts in Athens and the Axsons in Savannah, kept Edward informed about their daughter who was "spirited," "merry," and showed a strong willpower.[23] As a toddler Ellen "dictated" a letter to her father, then serving as chaplain of the First Regiment, Georgia Infantry: "My dear little Papa, Dis is a bad 'ittle dirl, she hollow and ty [cry], and steam [scream]."[24]

Edward Axson left his military post in December 1863 because he was "gravely" ill (with what is unclear)[25] and, sometime in 1864, he returned to the pastorate in the Madison Presbyterian Church, Madison, Georgia. According to incomplete records, he remained there until shortly after the war. In addition to his ministerial duties, he taught in the Madison Male and Female Academy, a community-supported school held in the Axson home on Porter Street, where Ellen, now in her fifth year, had her first formal education.[26]

Late in 1865, Edward Axson was invited to preach at the First Presbyterian Church of Rome, Georgia. The town, located seventy miles northwest of Atlanta, had had a population of about four thousand in 1860, depleted to about half that number in late 1865.[27] When Edward arrived, the city and the church were in shambles.[28]

The Presbyterian church then, as now, had a standard form for issuing ministerial calls which clearly stated the conditions of employment such as specific duties, arrangements for housing, salary, and the like. The call sent to Edward Axson is historic in its departure from protocol:

> Dear Sir:
> We have returned to our desolated homes. While trying to reconstruct our fortunes, we wish to take steps to reconstruct our church also. Will you come and help us? If we succeed in our enterprise, you will be taken care of. If we fail, you must suffer with us. Will you come? These are times that we must have faith in men as well as in God.[29]

Edward accepted. In March 1866, he began his pastorate in Rome. Janie, who had been in Athens with her parents during the illness and death of her father, joined her husband a few months later. When the family moved into "half of a large house" owned by Nicholas Omberg at 615 West First Street,[30] this became the first stable home that Ellen Louise Axson had known. On June 6, 1867, Ellen's brother, Isaac Stockton Keith Axson (to be called "Stockton") was born, and not long afterward, Margaret Bliss Hoyt came to live with her daughter and son-in-law.[31]

The Axson family stayed in the Omberg house for about a year and then briefly occupied two other dwellings, both apparently owned at least partially by the Presbyterian church. (Whether they actually lived in the last of these is questionable.) In 1871, Edward and Janie bought a lot, reputedly a gift of I. S. K. Axson, at 402 East Third Avenue (at the corner of the present-day East Fourth Street and Third Avenue) on which they built their own house and where the family lived for their remaining years in Rome.[32]

Edward's ministry, which began with so little promise, gradually prospered. From a ragged band of "forty or fifty" members, out of 186 before the war, by 1871 the congregation had grown to 151, and the pastor's annual salary, from $750 to $1,431.[33] The Sabbath School had 100 children enrolled, one of whom was Ellen Louise Axson. The session minutes of July 8, 1871, state: "Ella Lou Axson presented herself for membership and upon examination having given satisfactory evidence of knowledge and piety[,] was received."[34]

Although churches, government, and businesses began to function again in Rome, there were still no public schools. Before the war the Presbyterian church had established the Rome Female College, which eventually became privately owned by its two founders, the Reverend John McKnitt Madison Caldwell and his wife, Caroline Elizabeth Livy (Libbey) Caldwell. Closed during the war, the Female College reopened in September 1871 with training offered in four departments: primary, preparatory, novian, and college.[35]

The eleven-year-old Ellen, who became a student that fall, likely entered as a novian, for she had been tutored during her early years by her competent mother. College records were destroyed by fire in 1886,[36] but it can be deduced from family letters that Ellen was studying algebra, philosophy, logic, natural history, and botany, and that she was an outstanding student in French, English literature, and composition.[37] According to a Hoyt cousin, Ellen took geometry and then taught herself trigonometry during one summer.[38] Unquestionably, she had exceptional talent in art. During her five years at the college, two glorious worlds opened to her: the world of intimate friendships with her peers and the world of art. Out of a number of pleasant Rome associations, four women would provide life-long friendships: Rosalie Anderson, Elizabeth Leith Adams, Anna Harris, and Agnes Beville Vaughn. Other companions, all of whom attended the Rome Female College, were Sara Jonas and Annie Lester of Rome, and Janie Porter, whose father, Dr. David H. Porter, was pastor of the First Presbyterian Church in Savannah.

Chapter 3

Growing Up and Friendships

Ellen's first and dearest friend was Rosalie Anderson. Their relationship, strong from early childhood, was disrupted only by death. Rosalie, born in Rome in 1860, moved with her family in 1871 to Sewanee, Tennessee. Ellen and Rosalie, playmates from ages six to eleven, agonized over this separation, but shortly thereafter a correspondence began between them which continued for more than forty years.[1] We first learn of Ellen's interest in art through Rosalie's letters. (Ellen's letters to Rosalie were apparently destroyed in a fire.) In the fall of 1875, Rosalie returned to Rome as a boarding student at the Female College, from which she graduated in the class of 1876 with Ellen Axson.

After graduation, Ellen continued her drawing lessons with the college's Helen F. Fairchild, who, from 1871 to 1875, had studied in New York at the National Academy of Design.[2] In 1878, Miss Fairchild ("who has so largely contributed to . . . my happiness") had submitted a portfolio from her students to be judged in the Paris International Exposition. One item, a drawing of a "school scene" executed by Ellen Louise Axson, won a bronze medal for excellence in freehand drawing.[3]

Education at the Rome Female College did not satisfy Ellen's thirst for knowledge. She wanted to know "everything."[4] With Rosalie, she made plans to enter the Normal Department of Nashville University, an institution which required applicants to pass proficiency examinations. Ellen passed brilliantly (Rosalie did not), but Edward Axson could not afford to send his daughter away to college. This outraged Rosalie, who wrote with uncanny prescience: "You my sweetness . . . will be something wonderful before you are done. . . . You shain't settle down to a humdrum everyday life in some unheard of place."[5]

Ellen grew up surrounded by books, for which she had "an unreasoning love." As a child, she often went with her mother on parish calls and, while the adults talked, she read any book she could find. In February 1879, several Romans started the Young Men's Library Asso-

Ellen Louise Axson, 1876. Courtesy of Sara Fahy.

ciation, a subscription facility which was frequented day and evening by both sexes. Ellen and her brother, Stockton, were constant users.[6] In addition to extensive reading, Ellen enrolled as a postgraduate student at the Rome Female College where she took German, advanced courses in French, and art. In her eighteenth year, she began to charge a small fee for crayon portraits which she usually drew from photographs. She

Rosalie Anderson DuBose, 1876. Courtesy of Sara Fahy.

was soon doing well enough to support herself,[7] and she and Rosalie now dared to talk about studying art in New York City.[8] If Ellen carried out this plan, however, she would have to earn her own way. In March 1876, her second brother, Edward William Axson, had been added to the family, and her father had become uneasy about his professional effectiveness.

In the summer of 1875, when Edward Axson had served the Rome church for nearly ten years, he believed that his pastorate had not brought a harvest commensurate with his faithful efforts "to sow the seed." Reluctant to trouble his father, Edward wrote to Joseph Ruggles Wilson: "The burden becomes very heavy when after [ten] years of toil and ceaseless anxiety, one feels that the best he can say touching the result is that he has succeeded in staying the perpetual tendency of things to go to pieces."[9] Dr. Wilson counseled Edward to continue his labors in the Rome congregation.

Five years later, Edward received two calls: one to a church in Salem, South Carolina, where the town and salary were smaller, the other to a more prosperous congregation in Galveston, Texas. He turned down the latter as not a healthful place to live; he vacillated over the former for many weeks, or until the Rome parishioners virtually decided for him that *he* could not leave *them*. Even though the issue was resolved, the tensions were such that Edward suffered a breakdown. In the summer of 1880, he went alone to Janie's sister, Louisa H. (Mrs. Warren A.) Brown, in Gainesville, Georgia, for an extended rest. When he returned to Rome in mid-August, his father came from Savannah to preach at the Sunday morning services and to relieve him of pastoral duties for a month.[10] By late September of 1880, the Axson household was relatively stable again. The Rome congregation, with 183 members now on the roll, paid their pastor a yearly salary of $1,751.[11]

The qualities of intellectual independence and a keen critical sense, which appeared early in Ellen Louise Axson, displeased her father, who thought his daughter "obstreperous" and "entirely too much inclined to have her own opinions" and to make her own decisions.[12]

In the spring of 1878, when Ellen visited her Axson grandparents in Savannah for several months, she criticized a discourse delivered by a clergyman who had been brought in to rouse the spiritual fervor of a local congregation. The speaker developed his "catchy" topic, "The Siege of Gibraltar," Ellen wrote to her parents, with an emotional diatribe on the battles, bloodshed, and brave deeds which were part of the rock's history, and she thought that he would be a "more useful and powerful preacher if he kept his literary and historical addresses in one role and his sermons in another."[13] (Edward Axson's reaction to his seventeen-year-old daughter's critique is not known.)

Also while she was in Savannah, Ellen sent three samples of fabric to her mother from which to choose one for a new "best" dress. If Janie

Samuel Edward Axson, 1879, father of Ellen Axson Wilson.
Courtesy of Ben Palmer Axson.

wanted a "handsome church dress," Ellen advised, then she should select the "newer and stylish shade of green," not a *neutral* shade. Grandmother Axson expected enthusiasm when she gave Ellen "a lot of pretty little things" appropriate for most teenagers, but the grand-daughter would have preferred to have "*one* nice thing like the 'Library of Poetry and Song' or a writing desk."[14] As a small girl, Ellen had had a confrontation with Grandmother Axson who was trying to change Ellen's mind. "Grandmama" doesn't do that, and "*Mama*" doesn't do that, and "Little Auntie" doesn't, Mrs. Axson coaxed. "Yes, but *I* do," the tot replied.[15]

Ellen continued to work at her drawing in Savannah and Rome and gained a "considerable reputation" among "the best people of Geor-gia."[16] Her artistic interests were kept in perspective by a strain of Hoyt toughness. In April 1878, at Uncle Henry Hoyt's in Darien, Ellen plunged into a round of physical activity which included rowing and shooting. She wrote to her mother: "We had an oyster shell fastened upon a board [as target] and would you believe it, I cut it in two! I was the only one who touched it." A sailboat trip was almost postponed because of predicted high winds, but she went anyway, and found it "perfectly delightful as the boat fairly danced on the water." Also in Darien, despite Ellen's evasive tactics, a "Mr. Joe Walker" fell in love with her and asked her to marry him. Persistent to the last hour, Walker only annoyed her. She felt sorry for him because he was "so desperately in earnest," but, as she told Janie, "he isn't strong enough in the upper extremity to be a very dangerous character to me."[17]

When Ellen returned home from Darien and Savannah in the late summer of 1878, she received the first of many letters from her close friend, Elizabeth ("Beth") Adams, with whom she had visited on her way home.[18] The middle child of Mr. and Mrs. Lawrence Augustus Adams, Beth was born December 10, 1860. After Mrs. Adams's death in 1864 from tuberculosis, the children were brought up by relatives. Known as "Lizzie" to her family, Beth had come to the Rome Female College from "Summer Hill," her home in Edgefield County, South Carolina, sometime after 1876, when Ellen was a postgraduate stu-dent.[19] Shortly after Beth returned to Summer Hill in 1878, she and Ellen began to correspond in an intensely affectionate manner that continued for three years. Although only Beth's letters have survived, she frequently quotes from Ellen's letters to her. In one of her early letters to Ellen, Beth wrote:

You ask if I do not remember people with their special surroundings, I always do. Now I will tell you [of two instances]
when I oftenest think of you: that evening, or afternoon rather,
spent in the Parlour with my head on your lap, with my eyes looking straight up in your face[,] seeing nothing there to lead to distrust, only all that was loving and sincere. If *any one* were to tell
me that the love you then expressed for me was not sincere love
they could never convince me of it. I know that you enjoyed just
as much as I did that sweet confidential talk. I can understand
easily, dear, how I could have fallen so idiotically in love with you,
but why did you fancy me? . . . You are the only girl I have ever
seen who I think understands me. . . .

The next picture [of you] is one evening lying down in Carrie's
room [at the Rome Female College] resting[.] Do you remember
Mamie's disgust at our "sickening ways" because we exchanged
one single kiss. Then I remember looking so straight into your
eyes as I kissed you goodbye and your steadfast earnest gaze in
return.[20]

During the early spring of 1880, when Edward Axson was considering the move to Salem, South Carolina, Ellen did not write Beth for
several months. Her silence probably indicated her trepidation at the
thought of leaving Rome, a veritable metropolis compared to Salem.
Beth consoled herself by reading all of Ellen's old letters. She then
wrote to Ellen:

What a throng of loving memories . . . came over me; so overwhelming do they become that I must write and give expression
to them. You who are at once my second nature, even you, can
scarcely guess how great the love is given you by one who . . . calls
herself your friend. . . . I loved you while with you [but] it was
nothing like this . . . which has . . . grown so entirely a part of myself, that it would be like tearing asunder my heart strings to
[w]rest it from me now and I do not intend to part with it even
though it at times gives me pain as well as pleasure; do not think
my dear love that I for one instant *doubt* your love—No Thank
God![21]

At this time Ellen proposed a pact between them: she and Beth
would set up "a hall" for unmarried women, Beth to be the manager

and housekeeper, while Ellen supported the place with money made from her drawing and painting.[22] Beth approved, but the waiting was painful. She wrote: "You must make no more suggestions of how we would spend our time together because it makes me so long for it and . . . longing which brings restlessness in its train is . . . only terrible . . . [to one] who [is] one day to live on the fruits of that brush or pencil."[23] Beth ended her letters with "I love you, I love you, I love you" and in yet another: "[These] last two lines are filled with loving kisses for you."[24]

Ellen had expressed a restless desire to be with Beth, a restlessness which Beth understood well. "There is nothing on earth I care for except a look into your earnest, sweet face," Beth wrote, "and my hardest trial has always been—since knowing you[,] my separation from you." Beth had dreamed that Ellen was beside her in bed and that she had turned and looked into Ellen's eyes. "Why is it," Beth asked, "that your *eyes* I so often dream of and oftener think of. Your mouth is sweeter and yet it is always those eyes . . . and I feel that if I could get one *long* look into them *I* would find 'Nirvana.'" She urged Ellen to plan to visit in Augusta in the summer (of 1881). She could promise little in the way of entertainment, but some of the loveliest views, some of the most beautiful sunsets, "and *last*—but I know to you *first* dear heart—some of the most loving kisses that in your short life you were ever in receipt of."[25]

They were now nineteen and both had beaus, but neither girl up to that time had found compelling friendships with men. Beth was sorry for "Mr. Williams," a beau scorned by Ellen. Beth explained that if she loved Ellen and "could not get one spark of love in return knowing what a sweet thing that love is," she would feel abused. "Yet I must confess . . . that I am glad Mr. W. does not possess [your love] as I do not care to have my territory in your heart invaded."[26]

Ellen warned Beth, who was being ardently courted by an Augusta beau: "Use all your faculties before *beginning* to yield to a man's fascinations." Beth answered: "I could never love this man and be happy— and what do I want with his, or any man's love when I am rich, oh so rich in the love of my darling. . . . God grant that it may be years to come before I have to share your heart of hearts with anyone but when that time comes, as come it will I fear sooner or later, in spite of our plans to the contrary—I suppose I will have to love him too, or rather make him love me."[27]

A lonely, sensitive girl, Beth was, like Ellen, a voracious reader. The novelist they liked best was George Eliot, from among whose books they preferred *Middlemarch*. They read Laurence Sterne and Thomas Hardy (whose *Far from the Madding Crowd* and *Return of the Native* had been published by 1878). Ellen, at least, had read Henry James's new novel, *Portrait of a Lady*, and Dante. They devoured Shakespeare, Scott, Dickens, Ruskin, Emerson, Macaulay's *History of England*, and Carlyle's essays. Both had studied Macaulay's essays on Milton and Burns and both had read Emanuel Swedenborg. They were au courant with lesser works, such as *The Light of Asia*, by Edwin Arnold, a poem about the life and teaching of Buddha, and they discussed a novel, *Endymion* ("it is all the rage now") written by Benjamin Disraeli in his seventy-sixth year. The works of the romantic poets, and Wordsworth in particular, were favorites, but hardly more so than Elizabeth Barrett Browning's *Aurora Leigh* and *Sonnets from the Portuguese*. Perhaps Ellen was a step ahead of Beth in the matter of literary taste, but Beth was quicker to acquire the latest books, which she often bought and sent to Ellen.[28]

In their correspondence from 1878 to 1881, the two friends constantly discussed literature and art. Neither girl had met a man who could share these intellectual interests. Indeed, Ellen regarded most of the men she had met as complete bores. Beth had declined a proposal from "Mr. Boatright," but then confessed "a fearful attraction" to another admirer, "an infidel," who read all the things he should *not* read, such as the Koran, Talmud, and essays on Buddhism. Another male friend cautioned Beth in February 1881 that her attachment for Ellen Axson would be "the misfortune of your life." He had never seen any woman feel toward another woman as Beth did toward Ellen. The niche in Beth's heart which was obviously filled by Ellen should be the province of a man, and *no man* would be content to have second place in Beth's affections. The friend admonished Beth that her life would never be perfected unless she loved and married a man.[29] The warning goaded her far more than she realized at the time. We cannot be sure what Ellen thought of this, but we do know that she had accused Beth, a short time earlier, of trying to find a "loophole" for escape from their plans. But if Beth ever did "turn traitor," Ellen cautioned, she must instantly tell Ellen—who would instantly forgive her.[30]

In the spring of 1881, Ellen invited Beth to come to Rome that June. Beth was ecstatic. "Darling, darling," she wrote to Ellen, "can there be

Elizabeth Leith Adams, 1881.
Courtesy of the Very Reverend Francis B. Sayre.

happiness so perfect . . . [as] the happiness of again putting my arms about you, and feeling that you are mine."[31]

The three-year separation ended on June 1, when Beth arrived in Rome to stay almost two months. Together they attended the commencement exercises of the Rome Female College in the First Presbyterian Church, where they heard the Reverend David Willis, a Presbyterian clergyman then serving as chaplain in the United States Army, give an address on "The Ideal of a Woman." Willis cautioned the graduating class about forsaking the role established by the Almighty for women; woman's sphere was clearly marked, and if she assumed duties beyond her true sphere, she lost her femininity and "became no help-meet to man." Moreover, he went on, when a woman abdicated her true station as "ministering angel around the hearthstone," or assumed a masculine role—as some were doing—she invited contempt. This was true, in particular, of women who advocated going to the polls with the vulgar crowd. The clergyman praised fat women as the hope of the nation, because they were healthier and happier.[32]

After the commencement exercises, a grand concert took place in Rome's Nevin Opera House, which had opened in October 1880.[33] The two friends also saw an art exhibit which included drawings by Ellen, Janie Porter, and Annie Lester, a Rome woman who would later study art in New York with Ellen.[34]

In August, Beth went on to Morganton, North Carolina, to "take the mountain air" and visit relatives. Less than a month later, she wrote to Ellen that she had fallen in love with a Morganton man, Hamilton Erwin, and, pending her father's approval, she planned to marry him. The news was so upsetting to Ellen that, even with Beth's express permission, she could not bring herself to share the news with Janie Axson. Ellen wrote a long, reasoned letter to Beth which evoked a point-by-point response. Ellen was gravely concerned about "congeniality of mind" and marriage as a mutual process of self-improvement; she feared that Beth would "never know just how much I love you." Ellen concluded: "I suppose if you love him, I must *let you go* with God speed." Beth defended Erwin, who lacked intellectual interests and was a stranger to books. Someday, Beth vowed, she and her fiancé would take time for "mutual improvement." This new love was an emotion which Beth would never be able to explain and one which Ellen had to take on faith. Ellen tried to do so for her friend's sake. She sent a conciliatory letter delivered at the church door just after Beth and Hamilton were married on January 11, 1882.[35] The newlyweds went immediately to Morganton, where Beth would spend the rest of her short life. Meanwhile, events in Rome affected Ellen's future far more drastically than a curtailed friendship.

Chapter 4

Transition

Janie Axson, now in her forty-third year, was expecting her fourth baby in October 1881. Ellen was twenty-one, Stockton, fourteen, and Eddie, five. By reasonable predictions, the family should have been complete. With her mother's confinement due in mid-October, Ellen went to Sewanee to visit Rosalie in the interim.

Several of Ellen's letters to her mother that have been saved from this period show a girlish lightheartedness that never reappeared in her future correspondence. "I have an announcement to make that . . . will fill your heart with joy. . . . Since the boys [students at Sewanee University] are obliged to be in their rooms by 10, they leave about 9:45, and I, with my usual perversity always more disposed to behave myself when no one tells me I ought, retire immediately. . . . Don't tell on me, but I think the whole crowd of Sewanee boys an abominable nuisance. They try too hard to be funny." And, she went on, "to me who has been accustomed to sit down to easel or [sewing] machine in the morning and stay there until dark drove me away, it seems quite odd to be flitting in this butterfly fashion from one thing to another."[1]

In a letter of September 30, 1881, the last that Ellen would write to her mother, she described a friend of Rosalie's: "I wish you could see the exquisite contours of the girl's face—the delicious curves of chin and throat and cheek. She has the lovliest mouth I ever saw with perfect teeth and exquisite complexion. The face . . . [has] such a bright, innocent, happy expression. If I wanted to paint a young madonna, I would have her just so." She added, "I haven't seen one [boy] yet who deserves description."[2]

Ellen was still in Sewanee on October 10, the day on which her sister, Margaret Randolph ("Madge"), was born. When Ellen returned to Rome soon afterward, she found her mother suffering with puerperal fever, and, on November 4, Janie Axson died. Louisa Hoyt Brown, living in Gainesville, Georgia, took the infant to raise.[3]

In losing her mother, Ellen felt as if "from the sun itself the glory seem[s] to have passed away forever." She said later, "I think I would

Margaret Jane Hoyt Axson, 1879, mother of Ellen Axson Wilson.
Courtesy of Ben Palmer Axson.

give half of my life to be with her, to feel her sympathy, for one short hour."[4] Janie Axson had loved Ellen unselfishly and with rare understanding. More than once, she had denied herself pleasure to give "extras" to her daughter. When the nineteen-year-old Ellen went with her father to Savannah for Christmas and to attend a family wedding, she wept on the train en route "thinking of you, Mama, there alone, . . . the very one who *should* have been on the way."[5] When Ellen was invited the following year by "the Wrights" (probably the family of Judge Augustus R. Wright) to go with them to Canada and Niagara Falls, she wrote to her mother: "I can't feel grateful enough for this trip. I feel so much more self-reliant than when I left Rome. As Uncle Will said once about my going to Savannah alone, 'it will be worth two years at school.' "[6]

Janie was sensitive to Ellen's needs both for companionship and time to be alone. When a teenage Ellen disregarded her health by reading "far, far into the night" and by eating barely enough "to keep a bird alive," Janie fretted.[7] Nevertheless, the mother provided time for the young artist to read and to work. Janie encouraged the visits to and from Rosalie and, at Ellen's suggestion, invited Janie Porter, a friend from Savannah, to live with the Axsons and attend the Rome Female College for two years.[8] During the first six years of Ellen's life, her mother was the parent who provided constant nurture and, later, Ellen was "everything" to Janie Axson.[9] At first, Ellen reacted to her mother's death by vowing that she would never again touch "brush or pencil."[10] By June 1882, however, she had resumed her artwork enough to exhibit a crayon still life for the benefit of the Young Men's Christian Association in Atlanta.[11] Now surrogate mother to her two younger brothers and hostess for her father, Ellen gradually learned to live in a home without Janie Axson.

Edward Axson was shattered by his wife's death. Shortly after the Christmas of 1881, spent in Savannah, he wrote to Louisa that the sense of "loss and loneliness" was almost more than "the flesh can bear." He struggled through the next few months trying to be a pastor when his own life had lost its meaning. Less and less able to cope, and on the verge of a total breakdown, he went again to Louisa Brown's in the summer of 1882 for the rest and care which his sister-in-law so ably provided.[12]

Late in that same summer, Ellen went to New York and New England for two months. It is not clear who arranged this trip, but it was most likely Uncle Will Hoyt ("my second father,—always"), who kept in touch with his mother's relatives whom Ellen was to visit. Going first to New York City, she stayed with her cousin, Benjamin K. Bliss, a widower who lived on East Thirty-fifth Street, and his daughter, Clara, six years older than Ellen. She surely looked in on the Art Students

League at 38 West Fourteenth Street, where for several years she had wanted to study. Accompanied by Cousin Ben, she visited other Bliss kin in New Hampshire and in Springfield, Massachusetts.[13]

Home on October 5, Ellen was teased by Janie Porter: "I'm afraid old lady, you'll hardly know your poor friends whose aspirations are no higher than *North* Georgia. Just think of where you have been and what you have seen since we parted."[14] Ellen did think of what she had seen. The contrast was painfully obvious between that other world and Rome, where indigence and family responsibilities were overlaid by a nagging uneasiness about her father.

As the Christmas season approached, the family again went to Savannah for the holidays. Back in Rome, Edward Axson was again ill and once more his father came to help out with the pastoral duties. Ellen had a party for Eddie on March 1, his seventh birthday (his sixth, coming so soon as it did after his mother's death, had hardly been noticed). March drifted into April; it was in April 1883 that Ellen Axson met Woodrow Wilson.

When Woodrow had encountered Ellen in Asheville the following September, she was on her way back to Rome from Beth Erwin's home in Morganton. Ellen told Beth first, Rosalie second, and other friends in turn about her engagement. Beth was overjoyed until she saw a photograph of Woodrow. "You have always had pretty much your own way," she wrote to Ellen, "and now will this will of yours bend to his easily?—for bend it must to that *chin!*" A cousin of Beth's had pronounced that, if Ellen Axson ever did marry, the man would probably be "insignificant" because bright women rarely married men who were their intellectual equals.[15]

Now engaged to McNeeley DuBose, a student in the Episcopal Seminary in Sewanee, Rosalie was "intensely amused" and "more than gratified" that Ellen had succumbed. What had become, Rosalie wondered, of that "grand institution . . . which was to instill into the feminine part of the coming race, contempt of the men, and entire independence?"[16] Janie Porter, who had announced her engagement to Samuel Chandler of Decatur, Georgia, celebrated the news by doing a wild war dance accompanied by shrieks of triumph over Ellen's downfall.[17] Agnes Vaughn, recently married to a young widower, Arthur W. Tedcastle, was tastefully charmed, but Anna Harris was horrified.

Anna had also graduated from the Rome Female College in the class of 1876. A Rome native, she was plain, unsentimental, stable, and loyal,

Anna Harris, 1876. Courtesy of Sara Fahy.

with a tenacious, analytical mind that was "masculine." Known as "old Anna," the brightest student in the college, she had very little use for men, who did not exactly flock to her. Now, about this man Wilson, Anna wanted to know,—had Ellen actually committed herself, had she *given herself away without reserve*? Anna concluded that Ellen was "perfectly crazy" for not waiting until she knew Mr. Wilson with whom she now had barely more than a speaking acquaintance.[18]

Another Rome woman important in Ellen's life and affections was Uncle Will's oldest daughter, Mary Eloise Hoyt. Awestruck when she learned of her adored cousin's engagement, Mary began immediately to take a deep interest in this man named Woodrow Wilson.[19]

When Woodrow arrived in Baltimore from Asheville late on September 17, he found his father, en route to Wilmington, North Carolina, from a vacation in Saratoga Springs, New York, waiting at the train station. On hearing about his son's engagement, Joseph Ruggles Wilson could hardly have been more pleased with Woodrow's choice. He sent Ellen his "warmest love," and his assurance that he would love her as much as she could wish.[20] Woodrow's mother, distressed in June that her twenty-seven-year-old son "should be involved in any way just yet," still thought that there was not "a purer, sweeter girl" than "Ellie Lou."[21] But it was not until December that Jessie Wilson wrote directly to her prospective daughter-in-law: "It has not been my privilege to see much of you . . . but I know enough to make me sure that your love will be his comfort and happiness. I will try not to tell you what I think of *him*—what he is to me—who has never given me an anxious thought —who has always been a comfort to me—without any drawback— always so unselfish, so thoughtful, so tender. I will not try to tell you of what you will soon find out for yourself."[22]

Edward Axson learned about his daughter's engagement through a letter from Woodrow. Ellen knew that her fiancé had written, and she had tried to intercept the letter for fear that its contents would unduly upset her father, whom she had assured over and over that she would *never* become engaged. Incredulous about Ellen's sudden decision, Edward nevertheless wrote a brief, cordial note to his prospective son-in-law.[23]

From the time of their engagement until their marriage two years later, Ellen Axson and Woodrow Wilson wrote hundreds of letters to each other. In the genre of love letters, few if any of those known have surpassed this correspondence in clarity, vigor, and beauty. It reveals their interacting personalities, particular modes of thought, opinions on a variety of issues, and the details of their daily lives.

Part Two

1883–1885

Ellen Louise Axson, 1884, at the time of her engagement to Woodrow Wilson. Courtesy of the New York Times.

Chapter 5

Getting Acquainted

In his first letter to Ellen written after their engagement, Woodrow told her that no love like his could be a mistaken love. It had brought a "deep sense of joy and peace" like nothing he had ever imagined. He gently reminded her that *she* had not actually said that she, too, loved him, and he was longing to hear those words.[1] Her answer was unambiguous:

> And to think that, after all I have said, I should decide such a question without even waiting "to sleep over it"! But that was'nt my fault; it was only because there was *no* "tomorrow." You were going away,—and that is the secret of it all. Ah well, I suppose most theories are constructed only to be toppled over again, or slowly undermined, and it seems one *can* find one's self out, very completely, between the asking of a question and it's answer! I had no smallest idea how much I loved you until I found how wretched I was made at the thought of your leaving. . . . But the joy of a sudden meeting and the pain of an imminent parting, turning a strong light on one's heart, will reveal things which whole months of ordinary comings and goings would not have discovered. But however the sweet lesson was taught me, one thing at least is *sure*—I *know* it now, right well. You would have me say the words? Then, dearest, I know that *I love you entirely*, now and always "with the smiles, tears, breath of all my life, and if God choose I shall but love you better after death."[2]

Ellen sensed that she had pledged herself to a brilliant and intense man, a commitment that in the beginning made her uneasy for fear that she could not measure up to what she perceived as his needs in a wife. (Her mother had had the same qualms about marriage to Edward twenty-five years earlier.) She was concerned about her "badly regulated energy and concentration," a fault that made it virtually impossible for her to divide a day into units of work as other women did. "I must do one thing all day long . . . [and] I want to *go on* to the end. . . .

I am altogether too one-idead, and it is a terrible quality for a woman. I imagine it would be rather useful for a man. I used often to wish myself a man just on account of it. . . . I am not without hope of learning some self-control in this matter."[3] Woodrow, who had not the least doubt about her virtues, reminded her that it was Ellen the whole person whom he loved.[4] When he was "so agonizingly trying" to win her, he had learned that there was nothing which he could "urge," but it was altogether a question of where Ellen "would be pleased to bestow."[5] In turn, when she learned about his "various gifts and the high, pure and noble purposes" to which they were dedicated, she felt "a quiet little glow and thrill of admiration" to her "very finger-tips." She was "quite too awfully proud" of this young man upon whom she had bestowed her gift of love.[6]

Not unlike many of his contemporaries, Woodrow believed that a woman could love a man only for "qualities of heart and traits of character," and *not* for his intellectual qualities.[7] He was pleasantly surprised to find that, in addition to her many "feminine" virtues, Ellen provided intellectual companionship, something he had once been willing to forego.[8] The discovery was mildly disconcerting. "I hope you don't know much about the Constitution of the United States," he told her, "for I know marvelously little about art and if you know *both* subjects how am I to be head of the house?"[9] When Ellen disagreed with him, or set aside his "conclusions as overwrought or foolish," he confessed to "a wee drop of jealousy."[10] She continued, however, to state her own opinions to him on a variety of subjects. (One was the matter of her name. "You are quite welcome to call me anything you please [even Eileen] *except* Ellie *Lou*. I have a decided dislike to that name—indeed, to all compound names.")[11] Woodrow discovered that for the first time in Ellen's life, she had met a man who was intellectually stimulating and, indeed, she had been initially attracted to him because of this.[12]

During the next three trying months in Rome, Woodrow's frequent, fervent letters helped Ellen to maintain her equilibrium. After recovering somewhat from his illness in September 1883, Edward Axson went to Louisa Brown's home in Gainesville for further rest while Ellen and Eddie stayed in Rome with Agnes and Arthur Tedcastle. Stockton, now sixteen, had entered Fort Mill College,[13] a Presbyterian boarding school in Fort Mill, South Carolina. Edward Axson vacillated about returning to Rome from Gainesville, but once at home he demanded all of his daughter's attention. More nervous than usual because he had submitted his resignation to the congregation in Rome, he could not bear to have Ellen out of his sight for an instant.[14] The church turned down his first request to dissolve the pastoral relationship, and offered him a three-month furlough instead. A week later, the congregation met and heard a second communication in which Edward insisted that his resignation be accepted. This time his wishes were granted, and a unanimous resolution of gratitude was voted to the "shepherd, who has watched over us so vigilantly, guided us so wisely, and fed us so richly for the past seventeen years."[15]

Edward decided that he, Ellen, and Eddie would go to his parents' home in Savannah to live. During the next three weeks, Ellen found her father to be intractable. She schemed with the Tedcastles to have him stay with them for several days to spare him from the turmoil of packing, a chore which she preferred to do without his distracting presence. Ellen tried to humor him, but she desperately wanted to get him out of Rome and away from painful associations. When she agreed that they should stay in Rome, he immediately opted for leaving—and vice versa. She kept her poise by regarding his erratic moods as an amusing game. In November, the anniversary of Janie's death left Edward in a frenzy of nervousness aggravated by bouts of insomnia. With a sense of relief, Ellen shepherded the family to Savannah on November 28.[16] Back in the house where she had been born twenty-three years before, she could now turn to the support and care of her grandparents.

Besides Rebecca and I. S. K. Axson, others living in the commodious manse on Whitaker Street were Randolph Axson, his wife, Ella Law Axson, and their five children: Leila, sixteen; Ben Palmer, twelve; Randolph, ten; Ellen, nine; and Carrie Belle, four. Edward Axson, Ellen, and Eddie brought the family number to twelve.[17] Although Stockton was away at boarding school, the grandparents' house had become his home also.

Family life at the manse was disrupted shortly after the Christmas holidays when Edward Axson, apparently after becoming violent, was committed on January 13 to the Georgia State Mental Hospital at Milledgeville. Ellen was mortified for her fiancé's sake. Woodrow reacted to the news by going to Savannah almost immediately—after he had borrowed money for his railroad fare from a fellow student, Charles H. Shinn.[18]

Although Woodrow was in Georgia for a week, he and Ellen could scarcely have had much time alone, for the manse overflowed with Axson relatives, none of whom he had met. The love and concern which he showed in making the long journey, however, stirred her heart. "I thought I already loved you as much as possible," she told him, "[but] . . . I had only begun to know you, my great-hearted friend—tender and true! There are many noble uses of adversity, and among them is the power . . . of knitting soul to soul."[19]

In the days that followed her father's hospitalization, Ellen questioned whether her happiness in Woodrow's love was inappropriate while her parent declined in the asylum. Woodrow gently reasoned with her that it was right to be happy—that she was given a "sunny, hopeful disposition" to be just what she had been, "an aid and comfort and joy" to those about her.[20] Even as she tried to accept Woodrow's counsel, she cried out: "What future is there for one who, at best *has been* the inmate of an insane asylum?" She desperately wanted to believe, as Woodrow did, that a wise and loving God had ordained it all "for His own great and good purposes"; yet, she could not blindly accept this view.[21]

In February, Rosalie Anderson came to Savannah to visit with Ellen and help to lift her spirits. Confident that there had never been a man in Rome good enough for Ellen, Rose was now eager to compare notes on their respective fiancés. Woodrow passed![22] Together, the two women took lessons in "art needlework," painted, shopped, and read. (Rose, who had just finished *Ben Hur*, gave it a rave review. Ellen thought it "peculiarly adapted to the tastes and needs of young church women who had the slight tinge of the devotee about them.")[23] Grandfather Axson, "with the face of a martyr," went with Ellen and Rosalie to hear an "address by a *woman*!"[24] The speaker was none other than Hannah Whitall Smith, whose book, *The Christian's Secret of a Happy Life*, had just been published.

Rosalie left Savannah in late March with a faithful promise from Ellen to come to Sewanee in June. After this restful interlude with her friend, Ellen's thoughts turned again to serious family matters. Now that her parental home was gone and her father's income terminated, she felt a financial responsibility for Stockton and Eddie. To help with their support, she wanted to get a teaching post in art. She had heard that there was such an opening at the Rome Female College, and she also thought that something might be available through a teacher's agency in New York City.[25]

Woodrow, too, felt a sense of responsibility for Ellen's younger brothers. To this end, he wrote to Ellen that he was thinking of leaving The Johns Hopkins University to take a teaching job himself, so that they could be married forthwith. Their home would belong to Eddie and Stockton, whom Woodrow would "love and care for . . . as if they were blood brothers." He had heard in mid-April of a possible opening at the Arkansas Industrial University in Fayetteville. The position was, however, dependent on the creation of a new professorship, a matter which the trustees would not decide upon until June.[26]

Ellen kept a level head about this possibility. "Would the . . . University expect to take you *now*, or wait 'till they can get you!—that is, until you finish your course at Baltimore? . . . I hav'nt much to *say* on the subject—have only like yourself, to *wait* and *hear* more of the facts." Woodrow was concerned that if he went to Arkansas his studies at the Hopkins would not be completed, and he would sorely miss Baltimore's splendid libraries, but the most trying thing, he wrote to Ellen, would be passing his first year among strangers. He would have no fears about that, however, if *she* were with him.[27]

Ellen told him that if she had only herself to think of, she would not hesitate to do anything he wished; yet the "terrible suspense" about her father, and the needs of Stockton and Eddie, were a part of her responsibility. She knew, too, that Woodrow would be miserable in an environment lacking the best research facilities. He was already at work on an essay ("History of American Political Economy") to be part of a collaborative book and he was working at the same time on a projected volume of his own.[28]

On May 6, Ellen went to Rome to stay with the Tedcastles while she began to look for a job. This move upset Woodrow, who, although he would "oppose nothing" that seemed wise to Ellen and her family, said that further postponement of their marriage would be "like a consignment to a prison-cell for a twelve-month!"[29] Ellen admonished him not to get too exercised over the question of her taking a job, and she promised him that she would make no binding decision until they could discuss the matter when Woodrow came to Georgia after his classes were over in May.[30]

Woodrow's motives in trying to provide a home for Eddie and

Stockton were not totally selfless. He desperately wanted to be married and, unknown to Ellen, he had tried to enlist his father's financial help. Although it pained him to say so, Dr. Wilson believed that Woodrow would be unwise to contract a marriage which would cause Ellen to be dependent upon her in-laws for support. If, however, Woodrow did decide to marry, Dr. Wilson assured his son that the couple would be welcome in his home.[31]

Before the spring semester was over, Woodrow learned that he had been awarded a fellowship of five hundred dollars for a second year of study at the Hopkins.[32] He had not told Ellen that he was a candidate for this stipend for fear of disappointing her if he was unsuccessful. Ellen wrote:

> I am *so* glad so *very* glad, and *proud*, my darling. . . . Certainly, your year in Baltimore has been a complete triumph. . . . Are you *very sure* that you are wise to think of going elsewhere next year? Of course I can't pretend to judge . . . since I can't know *all* the circumstances, but the first thought which strikes me, . . . is that it would be "such a pity" for you to give them all up so soon. . . . You have made a place for yourself there,—have gained distinction. Is it well for you to drop out of it *now*, and go so far away, where you would be . . . only the echo of a voice.

She urged him not to consider her in making his decision, for she had a positive offer of a place as art teacher to which she must reply within a few days.[33] Her decision was postponed and eventually became moot because of a change in her father's condition.

Samuel Edward Axson

Placing Edward Axson in a mental hospital had been painful for both Ellen and her grandparents, who would have cared for him at home under any circumstances of physical disability. In mid-February, Ellen was encouraged when she received several letters from her father, the first he had been able to write. He was lucid and affectionate but his handwriting, which had gradually deteriorated, looked by early March as if it came from a stranger's hand. His normally precise, flowing script had become a stiff, awkward backhand with shakily formed letters.[1]

Edward's erratic health, a recurrent theme through much of his adulthood, certainly anticipated his mental breakdown. During the war years and his frequent separations from Janie, he was intermittently ill. When his mother-in-law was near death in the fall of 1872, he was in Savannah to take an extended rest because of poor health. He was unhappy and depressed in 1875, a time when he told his old mentor, Joseph R. Wilson: "I am often weary, and it would be with a sigh of relief that I would lay the burden down."[2] In the summer of 1880, after vacillating for weeks over whether or not to accept another pastorate, he had a breakdown and, in August 1881, when Janie's confinement approached, he was again unwell. Sustained by his wife and her sister, Louisa, and by the constant support of his parents, Edward had always recovered. Janie's death, however, removed the strongest stabilizing influence in his life.

His breakdown might have been moderated had it been possible to divert or amuse him, something Ellen tried unsuccessfully to do after her mother's death. Her father took almost no interest in anything outside of his pastoral work, not even in the conventional hobbies of light literature and sports.[3] The demands of his profession consumed so much energy that he had no reserves. His sermons, painstakingly written, were models of biblical exegesis and rarely tainted with anecdotes or levity.[4] He was generally regarded as the "gentle, mild, and quiet" clergyman, yet medical records describe him as "always a very nervous man, easily excited."[5] Edward was more "feminine" than "masculine" in the traditional definition of these roles, and the Civil War took its toll on his sensitive nature. In the aftermath of the war, he regarded the fall of the Confederacy as "the saddest of failures." Looking back at the South's "hopes and expectations and costly outlay of treasure and blood," and contrasting "the bright fancies of the past with the gloomy realizations of the dark present," Edward pondered the question: "Why is it that we have failed?" He attributed the failure largely to corruption in the Confederate government and people. Their *cause* remained noble. He believed that in due course the North would receive a richly deserved punishment at the hands of a "justly incensed God." The "sudden and absolute emancipation policy," which had "ruined one race and doomed another" to "unmeasured misery and eventual annihilation," was incomprehensible to him.[6]

Ellen tried as best she could to fill the place of her mother, but her efforts sometimes irritated rather than soothed her father. Before she went to Morganton in September 1883, Ellen had written to Woodrow that because her father was "very unwell," she was determined not to visit Beth Erwin at all. Yet Edward Axson insisted that his daughter's presence aggravated his "nervous complaint."[7] However, when Edward's distress later increased to an almost "unbearable level," he did not want Ellen out of his sight.

Although there was never any question of Ellen's loyalty to her father, she apparently regarded him more highly as a parent than as a man. Before she was twelve years old, she made a revealing comment to Rosalie during a heart-to-heart talk about what they would do when they grew up. In Rosalie's future, there was always a prince charming on a white horse, something Ellen regarded as just plain silly. Then what *should* Ellen's sweetheart be, Rose wanted to know, a preacher? *ELLEN*: "No." *ROSE*: "Why?" *ELLEN*: "Because." *ROSE*: "Because *what*?" *ELLEN*: "Well, just *because*."[8]

Three compositions which Ellen wrote during her junior and senior years at the Rome Female College survive.[9] In context, they are suggestive. "Somebody's Child," dated November 16, 1875, focuses on one character, an orphan boy. He steadily improves his frugal lot, only to be murdered. "The Old Maid," written in April 1876, tells about Elsie, "beautiful, noble, and selfless." Elsie's parents are introduced as the father who gives "fostering care" and the mother "tender love." As the narrative proceeds, Elsie's father, her fiancé, and her sister's husband all die. Elsie, who never marries, gets satisfaction from life by taking care of, first, her younger sister, and, later, her sister's children. The third composition, "The Raindrop's Story," also written in 1876, is clearly a projection of Ellen's own longings. The raindrop makes five global journeys, always maintaining its identity and always doing "much good" along the way. In the end, it has changed from "inexperienced" to "experienced" and has acquired stores of knowledge about the world.

In 1876, barely past her sixteenth birthday, Ellen snapped about a young man, "People say of him that he is as good and pure as a girl; though that is rather an equivocal compliment."[10] Her ability to think for herself and to want her own firsthand experiences led to conflict with her father. She resented the impression with which she grew up that "it is *always* wrong to do what one *wants* to do." Even though she had the spunk to protest, this did not destroy the impression itself, a conditioning which caused her "torment" well into adulthood.[11] She had her father in mind when she said, "I believe our good Presbyterian ancestors make a mistake in insisting so strongly on the duty of *self-examination*. It is apt to become a morbid habit—to make the conscience *too* sensitive."[12]

Edward Axson was the male model that Ellen knew best. She admired and loved Uncle Will and her Grandfather Axson, but her father's image was first and constant. Her antipathy toward men, unusual as it was for a southern woman in the 1880s, had to have an origin, and the logical origin was her own father. At eleven years old, she implicitly rejected the idea of a "preacher-husband"; at fifteen and sixteen, she wrote stories in which the male characters were methodically killed off; at twenty, she proposed the pact with Beth which eliminated men from their lives and projected a future of professional and financial independence; and from eighteen to twenty-three, she preferred the close companionship of women friends. During those years she discouraged suitors, declined several proposals of marriage, and frequently assured her father that she would never become engaged. A Savannah friend of her Axson grandparents believed that Ellen would never marry because she "never saw a girl who seemed to shrink so from all that sort of thing."[13]

Ellen's adamant belief that marriage should be for mutual self-improvement suggests that she did not regard her parents' relationship as mutually fulfilling. Certainly when her mother died after childbirth, Ellen's antimale feelings were reinforced. In the light of her observations and perceptions, Ellen said that she expected marriage to bring "the common woman's fate,—to give much and receive little—after perhaps a few weeks . . . of blind, unreasonable, infatuation!"[14]

Woodrow wondered whether she fell in love with him because she admired him. "Not exactly that," she told him, "for we don't fall in love with everyone whom we admire; and yet I could not love anyone whom I did not admire and look up to and believe in *wholly*. . . . And the admiration, of course, came before love for I admired you extremely the first day I met you; you seemed to me even then 'a Saul, than your fellows taller and stronger,' and I certainly had not fallen in love with you *then*."[15]

On March 6, 1884, Edward Axson wrote one last letter to Ellen. It was coherent, but almost illegible. His closing message was: "It is dark now, but He can make it all light about us. Let us pray for one another with ever increasing faith and earnestness. Will He not hear us? Don't grow weary in prayer my darling with love for all, tender and infinite."[16] He remained physically well for the next few weeks, but on May 28, he died suddenly in the Milledgeville Hospital. He was forty-six years old.

Too upset to write even Woodrow, Ellen asked Mary Hoyt to let him know. Mary did so in a brief note on May 29.[17] The Savannah family (except Edward's prostrate mother who had lost her firstborn child and whose daughter, Ellen, had died in childbirth) and Stockton came to Rome for the funeral services held in the First Presbyterian Church where, seven months before, Edward had resigned as pastor. He was buried in Myrtle Hill Cemetery beside his dear Janie.[18]

Among the many messages of condolence Ellen received, one of unusual interest came from the Reverend Benjamin Morgan Palmer, her cousin in New Orleans: "I cherish the warmest love for all of the Axson name . . . and I cannot forbear expressing my sympathy with you, perhaps in some respects the deepest mourner in the family group. As the oldest of the children, and with those sensibilities which are keenest in a daughter, the loss of such a father comes with overwhelming force upon a heart that has not recovered from the loss of such a mother as yours. . . . *The place and manner* of your father's death are inexpressibly sad. . . . It was a dark cloud which had settled upon his reason."[19]

Palmer's statement about the "place and manner," strongly suggests that Edward Axson took his own life. There is nothing in the records to contradict this, and much that would be difficult to account for in any other way. During his last two months in Milledgeville, Edward was terribly depressed, and, in view of his generally sound physical health, his death was sudden. The medical records from Milledgeville state: "Slight suicidal tendency. Is disposed to be violent occasionally. . . . Has been in the habit of taking chloral at night."[20]

The session minutes of the First Presbyterian Church in Rome, although duly noting Janie Axson's death, make no mention of Edward's. However, two Presbyterian elders who died in Rome a few months after Edward are eulogized in elaborate statements "spread upon the minutes." The Synod of Georgia, which met annually in the fall, did not memorialize Edward until October 1885. The Reverend David Lyman Buttolph, appointed chairman of the synod committee to prepare and present Edward's eulogy, himself had had a daughter in the Milledgeville State Hospital in 1882.[21]

When Woodrow's father wrote a letter of condolence to Ellen in June 1884, he tactfully sidestepped the issue of suicide, considered then to be a mortal sin. Dr. Wilson reiterated his love for Edward and rejoiced that Ellen's father was now "united with his Lord, whom he so faithfully preached and so sweetly served." In closing, he added, "Will you excuse me if I conclude with expressions of cordial affection such as are due to my own daughter?"[22]

Had Woodrow Wilson not been so important in Ellen's life during her father's final illness and death, she would have been more deeply scarred. She accepted the theological tenet that God had been merciful to deliver Edward Axson from his trials, but this did not make the loss "much easier" for her. "What an end to such a life!" she told Woodrow.[23] In one anguished outburst to her fiancé, Ellen expressed the strain of the last few months. "I sometimes wish I could go to sleep and never, never wake again."[24]

When Woodrow arrived in Rome on June 9, he found Ellen and Stockton, whom he met for the first time, still at the Tedcastles. (He again stayed with his cousin, Jessie Bones Brower, at Oakdene.) He came to comfort her, and was heartbroken when Ellen, because of the doctrinal disgrace related to her father's death, tried to break their engagement. Only Woodrow's ardent importunities "overrode her scruples."[25]

After Woodrow had spent a fortnight with Ellen, she was lifted to a pinnacle of happiness and strength which, in the circumstances, she had never dreamed to be possible: "The joy it gives me 'to love and be loved by you' is too deep and entire to be affected, *beyond measure*, by accident of time and place."[26]

_____ *Chapter 7* _____

From Rome to New York

Edward Axson left an estate of approximately twelve thousand dollars in the form of cash (largely from a life insurance policy), stocks and bonds, and real estate (the Rome property), a sum equivalent to about one hundred thousand dollars in 1980.[1] After Uncle Randolph, Edward's executor and the children's guardian, told Ellen about the inheritance, she said to Stockton, with unabashed enthusiasm, "Now that we are *rich*, you can go to college and I can go to the Art League."[2] Through the sorrow, she and Stockton could see the future with unexpected clarity. In a sense, she was freed by her father's death.

With Ellen's attendance now assured at the Art Students League, and with Woodrow the recipient of a fellowship, their immediate dilemmas were resolved. Stockton was enrolled at Davidson College in North Carolina, and Eddie was to stay with Uncle Henry Hoyt, now in Maysville, Georgia, about fifteen miles east of Gainesville, where Madge lived with Aunt Louisa.

After Ellen and Stockton finished the task of sorting and packing the family possessions, she planned to make the promised visit to Rosalie, and from Sewanee, to go to Gainesville where she, Stockton, Eddie, Madge, and the Axson grandparents would have a reunion at Aunt Louisa's. From Gainesville, en route to New York City, she would go to Wilmington to spend time with her fiancé and future in-laws, a stopover arranged through a correspondence between a reluctant Grandmother Axson and Woodrow's mother that was just short of angry.[3]

Ellen did not include a visit to Beth in her itinerary and had not answered Beth's prompt letter of condolence written in June. Beth was hurt. Already in Gainesville when she finally did write in early September, Ellen did not mention the visit with Rosalie, but she did tell Beth about the plans to go to New York. Expecting her second baby in November, and "too nervous even to write," Beth thought Ellen's plan charming but urged her to visit Morganton before going so far away. Ellen did not write again until December.[4]

When Ellen Axson said goodbye to Rome, Georgia, on July 24, 1884,

Stockton, Mary Hoyt, and Mary's sister, Florence Stevens Hoyt, went with her as far as Lookout Mountain, Tennessee. At sunrise the next morning, they saw at the "Point" a view "magnificent . . . beyond description." When the others returned to Rome, Ellen went on to Sewanee, where she arrived at teatime on the twenty-fifth. The changes in her life since her visit to "the mountain" three years before were staggering.[5]

Ellen spent four weeks with Rosalie and even then found it difficult to break away. They both knew that these were the "last times," and that in many ways the old order was about to give way to the new. Rose would be married the next year and leave Sewanee, Ellen was going to New York, and the two women had eighteen years of stored memories and friendship to savor. Near the end of her visit, Ellen and Rosalie spent one day ("*so* delicious that we felt as though we couldn't spend any of it *indoors*") at a spot on the mountain called "Morgan Steep." They stayed there until sunset, reading *Aurora Leigh*, talking, and absorbing the scenery.[6]

Impatient to see his fiancée, Woodrow had been jealous of Ellen's time with Rosalie, but it was a period of rest that Ellen sorely needed. "Even if I cared to try," she wrote him, "it would be impossible for me to make you understand, dear, the great and constant pressure which I have been under for many months." She was very, *very* sorry that she had been the cause of his being unhappy or depressed.[7] Woodrow's letters—and his impatience—subsided when Ellen reached Wilmington on September 16, the anniversary of their engagement. He presented her with a writing portfolio that he hoped would remind her of the love of "your own Woodrow."[8]

On Wednesday, October 1, Ellen and Woodrow took the train from Wilmington to Washington, where they had hotel accommodations for one night. They spent Thursday sight-seeing, a tour that included the Corcoran Gallery of Art, and that evening they boarded a sleeper for New York. On Friday morning, Woodrow accompanied her to 60 Clinton Place (now Eighth Street), a boarding house for women where two Rome friends, Annie Lester and Florence Young, were already established. Woodrow visited with some college friends and returned to Baltimore later the same day.[9]

The three women shared a first-floor room that, with board, cost each of them five dollars a week. Their room, none too pleasant, was soon overcrowded by the addition of a fourth friend, Eva McNulty, from Savannah. On October 16, ten days after her work began at the Art Students League, Ellen moved to Mrs. Elizabeth Beatty's boarding house at 120 West Eleventh Street. Mrs. Beatty's establishment, where there were only fifteen boarders (eight ladies and seven gentlemen) was "strictly first-class," with "no working girls and no retail clerks." For the "ruinous cost of *eleven* dollars per week," Ellen had found a charming place which would be her home until May.[10]

The Art Students League allowed a freedom of expression that Ellen had not experienced at the Rome Female College or with Helen Fairchild ("the Academy and Miss Fairchild had but one rule").[11] Founded in 1875, the League, with an enrollment in 1884 of nearly five hundred students, had progressed to its third location in three upper floors at 38 West Fourteenth Street. From its inception, the League was regarded as radical, based as it was upon a student-run, nonauthoritarian society with equal status accorded to women and men. Any applicant of "sound character" who had submitted acceptable drawings in two categories was admissible. Besides a nominal tuition payment, fees were charged by the month for each individual course. A student could enroll in as many classes as she or he could manage, although admission to some of the more advanced ones was contingent upon demonstrated proficiency. The League's faculty was made up largely of young artists who had studied abroad and who had brought with them the thorough training of Munich and the academic influence of Paris. Showing a disregard for the older, established American genre painters, the teachers preferred to give their students "facility of expression" and to create a new and vigorous interest in art.[12]

In the portrait class, taught by George DeForest Brush, charcoal was used entirely, a material handled far differently from the crayon to which Ellen was accustomed.[13] Thomas W. Dewing was her instructor in the antique department, a course which enabled students to draw copies of antique sculpture. After a successful tryout, she was admitted to the sketch class in which each member, in an elaborate costume of her own choosing, posed in turn for the rest of the group. (Ellen wore a Kate Greenaway outfit when it was her turn to model.) Once a week, she attended Frederick Dielman's lectures on perspective, a subject which she found tiresome.[14]

George DeForest Brush, a young instructor who joined the faculty that fall, appealed to Ellen both as a teacher and a person. She admired his face, which "lights up so finely with intellect and genius." Brush liked her work, terming it "first-rate," showing "great feeling" and "understanding . . . *very strong* and yet delicate"; in fact, he "quite" took her "breath away" with his praise. He admonished his students to haunt the galleries and educate their "*feeling*" as well as their "fingers." Too much work, he believed, dulled the senses.[15]

The most coveted achievement was admission to the life class in which live models were used. A student could enroll in this class only after successful competition in drawing, but Ellen refused to try out because she knew that only one entering student had been good enough to win a place. During her first month at the League, she drew a head of Homer for "the antique" that was so exquisite her peers urged her to enter it in the life class competition. She refused. Unknown to Ellen, another woman student filled out an entry blank and submitted the Homer in Miss Axson's name. The ruse worked, and, in November, Ellen was admitted to the class. "When you remember that none of these girls or boys were 'in' themselves, or had any hope of being admitted soon," she wrote Woodrow, "you will begin to see why I think the League is delightful."[16]

The life class was disappointing, however, because of the instructor, Frederick Warren Freer. If George DeForest Brush was one of the best teachers Ellen had ever seen, Freer was one of the poorest. Freer was "a comical looking man, a very large blonde, bald headed, spectacled, and exceedingly awkward. He looks like a big school boy when he comes into the room; his arms are always slightly crooked and held away from his sides, as though he had paint on his hands and was afraid of soiling his clothes, and he always sits down as though he had'nt the least idea whether it was a high stool, a low stool, or the floor, that he was going to strike. But he has a pleasant, bright smile . . . [and] he is *very* deaf . . . which of course makes matters a great deal worse."[17]

Fortunately, there was an opening in Julian Alden Weir's afternoon section to which Ellen transferred. Weir was "pleasant though brusque in his manner." Germanic with a "big rough head, . . . a big round body . . . and a smoothly shaven face with very 'cleanly' cut lips," Weir bore a close resemblance to a likeness Ellen had seen of the young Martin Luther.[18]

For the first time in her art study, Ellen could sketch live models, some nude and some draped. (Separate sections were conducted for men and women.) While she drew, Ellen constantly wondered, and speculated, about the models' thoughts and feelings and tried to comprehend their characters and fates.[19]

Involvement in four fine-arts courses and one lecture class did not deter Ellen from following the advice of Brush to educate her feeling. New York, with its relative sophistication in art, provided a plethora of galleries but no first-rate museum. The Metropolitan Museum of Art, founded in 1870 and installed nine years later in its present location at Fifth Avenue and Central Park, had a limited but growing collection. Ellen, who studied the Metropolitan's changing loan exhibits, was enchanted by the works of an English artist, George Frederic Watts. The Watts show, made up of more than fifty paintings, most of which were portraits of famous people, lured her again and again, and, before the exhibit closed, she had taken Woodrow to see this, "the greatest art treat" he would likely have outside of Europe.[20]

She also visited the Gustav Reichard Gallery, the Goupil Gallery of Paintings, the National Academy of Design, Tiffany's, the American Art Gallery, and the studio of William Merritt Chase, an American landscape and portrait painter who had studied abroad and was now on the faculty of the Art Students League. She spent most of an afternoon in the studio of William Trost Richards, famous for his ability to depict the "wettest water ever painted." (When she and Woodrow had visited the Corcoran Gallery in Washington, they had seen Richards's *On the Coast of New Jersey*, a painting commissioned in 1883 by the Corcoran.)[21]

Arthur Goodrich, one of the "seven gentlemen" at Ellen's boarding house and a sales representative of the Boston publishers Houghton, Mifflin & Company, took her to see an exhibit of the original drawings which Elihu Vedder had executed for the 1884 edition of Edward Fitzgerald's translation of *The Rubaiyat of Omar Khayyam*. Ellen believed that Vedder had more genius than any other American artist, but it seemed to her a pity that "such noble work should be expended on such a heathenish poem."[22]

Her life in the city was not limited to art. Theater, lectures, social events, and church occupied her time. At the Star Theater, she saw Ellen Terry and Henry Irving in *The Merchant of Venice, Hamlet, Twelfth Night*, and *Much Ado About Nothing*. She was wild about Edwin Booth, whom she saw at the Fifth Avenue Theater in *Macbeth, Othello* (as Iago), and in *Hamlet*.[23]

Despite Woodrow's misgivings, she began to attend evening lectures unescorted. To allay his apprehensions, she explained that everybody— some of them "first families"—regarded her with unmitigated wonder and amusement when she hesitated about going out at night, and it would certainly be a pity to miss all the lectures (at the Art League) because of a three-minute walk over brilliantly lighted streets. The first time she ventured out with only other women, she was not afraid, but she did feel "*awfully* ashamed."[24] She told Woodrow: "Oh, . . . how I *do love* fine speaking, and good lectures! . . . That is one great advantage . . . in being a man—one can hear so much more of it!" She resub- scribed to *The Nation* in order to keep informed about politics, which "quite exercised" her.[25]

Her social life was far from dull: she shopped ("I bought a love of a cloak"); attended her cousin Clara Bliss's wedding at the fashionable Episcopal Church of the Holy Communion (her first experience "of a city wedding"); toured an ocean liner at its Hudson River pier; had Thanksgiving dinner at the St. James Hotel with Uncle Thomas and Aunt Sadie Hoyt; went out with two of Woodrow's college friends, Charles H. Shinn (Hopkins) and Robert Bridges (Princeton); and a Yankee gentleman fell madly in love with her.[26]

The man was none other than Arthur Goodrich. When Goodrich first met Ellen, probably at the dinner table on the evening of October 16 at their boarding house, he was immediately smitten. At that time, she wore Woodrow's diamond ring, not on the traditional third finger, but on her forefinger, so that her engagement could not be deduced from that clue. Two eligible men, Shinn and Bridges, both then living in New York, had called on her. Shinn, who took her out several times, once sent flowers.[27] To Goodrich, this single woman studying on her own in the city appeared to be fair game; and Ellen did not discourage his attentions. He shared with her an interest in literature, art, and the theater. It was he who took her to see Terry and Irving in *Hamlet*—after she had determined that he was "a thorough gentleman, . . . of good old Massachusetts Puritan stock, & one who had been most carefully trained up in the way he should go." A recent Andover graduate, he was younger than Ellen, "fresh, unspoiled, intelligent and entertain- ing," and "oh base consideration! he is so *convenient*!" Their three- month friendship ended when Goodrich, even after finding out about her engagement, lost his head and made an open declaration of his love. Ellen, assuming a pose of great shock, laid on Goodrich the responsibility for matters having got so far out of hand. At best, she was naive to believe that they were "running the platonic schedule." Her attempts to be "just friends" with southern men had been unsuccessful, but she was sure that a cool-headed New Englander would be different. At worst, she was disingenuous.[28]

All through the friendship with Goodrich, she was frank with Woodrow; in fact, in her letters during this period, she mentioned Goodrich forty-eight times. Woodrow at first ignored the accumulating evidence, but in mid-January his patience wore thin. He insisted that "just friends" would no longer do. When Ellen thought to taper off the friendship gradually so as not to hurt Goodrich's feelings, Woodrow remarked that, "to go with him to the theatre on Monday, to prayer-meeting on Wednesday, and to the theatre again next week is scarcely discouraging his attentions—is it, little lady?"[29] Poor Goodrich, unable to eat or sleep, finally accepted the inevitable—but only after some painful confrontations with Ellen.[30]

She was more discreet in establishing her church ties. For the first time in her life, Ellen worshipped in denominations other than Presbyterian. At the Church of the Heavenly Rest, a Protestant Episcopal Church at 551 Fifth Avenue, she came away in "a rapturous state of mind" because of the magnificent choral music. Her basic religious orthodoxy was jolted, however, by the Ethical Culture Society to which not a few of the Art Leaguers belonged. This "no faith" was bad enough for the men, she thought, but for a young *woman* to adopt it was unconscionable.[31] On a bright Sunday morning in November, she and her southern friends walked across the newly opened Brooklyn Bridge to the Plymouth Congregational Church to hear Henry Ward Beecher. She had vowed to do this at least once even in the face of warnings that to listen to Beecher on Sunday would be a sin.[32]

Not until January did she finally decide on the Scotch Presbyterian Church at 53 West Fourteenth Street, where she took a six-month sitting for ten dollars. She joined the morning Bible class, taught by Peter Carter, "a beautiful old man." Within a week's time, Carter asked her to help him and his two daughters teach on Sunday afternoons in the Spring Street Mission School, a city mission to black children located over a barroom. Ellen consented, although she thought that this sort of work was of little value unless one could follow up on the children in their homes. When Woodrow questioned the wisdom of her doing this and especially the setting in which she worked, she argued that to think first of any small risk or unpleasantness connected with the teaching was not quite right, and the possibility should not keep her from *trying* to do something. She continued to help at Spring Street until she left New York in late May.[33]

Because of her art studies, her constant participation in the excitements of New York, and her daily letters to Woodrow, Ellen had no time to write to her old friends and relatives in the South. Almost everyone was angry with her except Aunt Louisa, "the kindest and most sensible of women,"[34] and Uncle Will, who advised her to "see everything worth seeing, hear everything worth hearing and go everywhere worth going." Time, he said, is never going to come back so "make the most of it while you have got it."[35] Rosalie, who had hoped to join Ellen for the spring semester to study decorative art, now wrote that, because of family finances, there was not "a shadow of a chance" of her coming.[36] Beth, on the other hand, who had to get Ellen's address from Jessie Brower in Rome, wondered if Ellen, in all the rush and interest of her work, had time even to "think of me and love me as of old." Ellen then wrote a letter which arrived in Morganton the day before the birth, on December 12, of Beth's second child and first son, Marcus Erwin.[37] After scolding Ellen for her long silence, Mary Hoyt wrote to her "darling cousin and sweetest friend," that Ellen was the "one girl in the world" who really understood Mary—the woman who had also had to put aside her "dreams and ideals for duty." Mary, who would soon be twenty-one and still knew "absolutely nothing,"[38] wanted, like Ellen, to get an education—and Ellen would not forget.

As the holiday season approached—the first that she had ever spent outside Georgia—Uncle Tom invited her, and he added lamely, "I suppose Mr. Wilson," to come to Philadelphia for Christmas.[39] Ellen thought it would be "infinitely more satisfactory" for Woodrow to come to New York, a change accepted after she promised to go to her uncle's for the New Year's weekend.[40]

She and Woodrow spent their first Christmas and his twenty-eighth birthday together in New York. Woodrow had asked Robert Bridges to send him the address of a place near West Eleventh Street where he could get a week's board at reasonable rates since he could not afford a hotel.[41] Other than their brief stop in Washington en route north, these were the first leisurely days that they had had alone during the fifteen-month engagement. Their privacy during this week together is shielded by the absence of correspondence; but back in Baltimore on

January 2, Woodrow wrote to her that the past eight days had been the happiest he had ever spent. "[Your] caresses teach me that I have found what I need more than wealth or power or opportunity," he said.[42]

Ellen stole a few minutes at Uncle Tom's to write him a note that ended, "Goodnight, my darling, I love you more, a thousand times more than life; there is no standard great enough to measure my love."[43]

Chapter 8

Marriage

While Ellen progressed with her art studies, Woodrow was making his own mark at The Johns Hopkins University. During the fall term of 1884, he finished writing his book, *Congressional Government*, and, on October 7 sent the manuscript to Houghton, Mifflin. In late November, he received word that it was accepted for publication and, near the end of January 1885, the volume appeared in print. Highly acclaimed at the time, *Congressional Government* put Woodrow Wilson, not yet thirty years old, in the forefront of promising young scholars.[1]

When Woodrow mailed a copy to Ellen, he had difficulty composing the inscription because what he wanted to say would be "out of place on the public face of a book. . . . As your love runs through this my first book, so it must be the *enobling power* in all that I may write hereafter."[2]

The success of *Congressional Government* stimulated Woodrow to confide in Ellen that his early ambition was "to become a public servant and actively participate in the direction of affairs." Since that ambition had been "shut out" because he had no independent means, his goal now was to become a guide of public thought and policy through his writing.[3]

Ellen was troubled by his use of a phrase so strong as "shut out." Was this first ambition only a youthful desire, or was it still one of his secret yearnings, she wanted to know. She wondered whether he preferred active participation in directing public affairs to writing books of permanent value. "Of all the world's workers," she wrote to him, "those which to my mind take by far the highest rank are the writers of noble books. . . . Men of letters are constantly going into public life in England,—why not in America too, if it seemed good to them." But these were questions for the years alone to answer, she counseled, and no man of twenty-eight needed to talk of disappointed ambitions. She was sure that his destiny would work itself out *"all in good time."*[4]

Woodrow regretted that he had been unable to "strike out" toward "a *statesman's* career," he told Ellen, but this was now nothing *more* than a regret. To be content with the "sober methods of the scholar and man of letters" had required stringent discipline on his part, and, if Ellen continued to love him as she did at that moment, he would stop short of nothing of which his powers were capable. He accepted her judgment that a writer's career was "the highest."[5] He was sure that with Ellen as his wife, he could do *anything*. She had "sweetened" his ambition so that he now strove for success because of her. Even so, he stood in absolute need of "constant outpourings" of her love and sympathy. He wanted to share *everything* with her.[6] Ellen recognized that this brilliant and highly strung man needed the kind of intellectual and emotional nurture that she could provide. To her alone was he able to confess his weaknesses, his needs, and ambitions. Her understanding and love were therapy to his low moods and intermittent headaches at Hopkins.[7] But even she could not solve his immediate problem of too many academic commitments.

During the second semester of his graduate work (January 1884) Woodrow had begun to write *Congressional Government*; a month later he was invited by one of his instructors, Dr. Richard T. Ely, to write one-third of a proposed history of political economy in the United States. Woodrow considered the curricular requirements restrictive, and this opportunity to delve freely into research was irresistible. He had begun to work seriously on the Ely project in the fall of 1884, simultaneously reading for the Ph.D. examinations and carrying the normal load of academic subjects. As the pressure mounted, he realized that the cramming was killing him by inches. After a conference with his major professor, Dr. Herbert Baxter Adams, he decided to finish the class work and his commitment to Ely and, after a year in a teaching position, to return to take his doctoral examinations. He would submit *Congressional Government* for his dissertation.[8]

With some of the academic pressure relieved, Woodrow's health improved, but he still longed for Ellen. "Nothing ever makes me so ill so soon as a heart-want," he told her, "and nothing ever cures me of all ailments so surely as the satisfaction of my heart needs. . . . Oh my darling, you cannot love me more than I *need* to be loved. . . . Without love I should die."[9]

Her promise was unequivocal: "You shall never want for wifely love and faith and sympathy, my darling, or for anything that love can give."[10] They made a pact never to withhold confidences, and to be one "in hopes and plans and anxieties and sorrows and joys."[11] Ellen told him that only a man of his stature "could have so stirred my nature to its utmost depths. . . . Your love has changed me in many ways, either by infusing something new into my nature or developing what was latent there, or by crowding out some things that were best away."[12]

She remembered the time when she thought to be a woman "a rather sad fate," but *his* love had given new meaning to "womanhood."[13] In New York she heard "a great deal" about "a woman's right to live her own life," but this right, she believed, would provide little satisfaction unless one was sure that "said life is worth living!" She thought that women's work, absorbing as it was to some, might "prove to be after all but a pretty plaything."[14]

The flush of excitement that accompanied the sensual and intellectual experiences of her first months in New York had begun to fade as Woodrow's star ascended. Her life at the Art Students League where she did her *own* work all day long, was, she now thought, "selfish." "True love" to be "perfect" should become a "*service* of love." She wanted to take care of Woodrow, and "yes, darling, I want to be taken care of *by* you!" For Ellen Louise Axson, with her "foolish pride and sensitiveness and independence," this was quite an admission, she thought.[15] Yet, she had not "surrendered" her "right of private judgment" she told her fiancé, and he was not to "flatter" himself too much, because he had never made her "say or do anything *against*" her will.

Although she was later reputed to be "the most unambitious of women,"[16] Ellen said something decidedly different about herself. She told Woodrow: "Ah! but I *am* ambitious! And the best of it is that *mine* is *gratified* ambition, for I am ambitious for *you*—and for *myself*, too, dearest, I hardly dare too [*sic*] say how *great* is my ambition."[17] The woman who had once been an advocate of independence, and of having her own profession, had resolved these issues by deciding to invest her own considerable talents and ambition in Woodrow Wilson, a man of such promise that she felt confident about the returns. It was an investment from which she never retreated and from which evolved a formidable and determined team.

Ellen's latest ideas about her destiny went unchallenged until a new friend, Antoinette Farnsworth, from "the West," enrolled at the Art Students League. Early in April, Antoinette moved in with Ellen at 120 West Eleventh Street, and on May 1, the two of them took a less expensive room at 95 Seventh Avenue. At about the same time, Ellen won a coveted place in the League's advanced painting class which enabled her to drop a less demanding one at the Metropolitan.[18]

This new roommate was free and easy in manner, warmhearted, impulsive, and intelligent. The two women could talk "on matters of deeper interest than either books or art"; yet Antoinette was disturbed by Ellen's hard work and her enthusiasm for something that was to be given up almost immediately. She accused Ellen of being an incorrigible little southerner without a grain of ambition and "too much in love to have any sense." An avowed bohemian, Antoinette argued warmly with Ellen over a woman's duty which, she declared, was *not* to be a homebody. *Her* art should always come first. If Ellen recognized Antoinette's views as an echo of her own pronouncements to Beth four years earlier, she ignored the coincidence. She related her arguments with Antoinette to Woodrow, then dismissed them with "I have positively refused ever to be drawn into the subject again."[19]

The liberal opinions of Ellen's friends did not trouble Woodrow, but her talent in art did. When she casually mentioned having won a place in the advanced painting class, he told her that he believed she could do some "really *great* work" in portraiture, and that he was just as much interested in her work as she was in his. That their marriage would, of course, curtail her chances for a career in art made him feel "guiltily selfish." He wanted to know what her wishes were "about it all."[20]

In a stunningly reasoned letter, virtually a fifteen-hundred-word position paper, Ellen responded to his concerns. "Suppose for the sake of argument, it were as great a sacrifice [to give up my art] as even you imagine; my darling *must* know that it would be a pitiable price to pay for such a love as his, . . . for the wonderful happiness with which he has filled my life to overflowing." She did have talent, she said, even above the average art student, and it was possible that, after years of steady, hard work, she might win a place in the first rank of American artists. At some future time, she would like to take lessons in landscape painting, and she wanted to continue to do crayon portraits. She told Woodrow that she would never give him "a divided allegiance," and she assured him that she had never felt the slightest pang of regret for what she was allegedly giving up. "My darling, it would not be a sacrifice to *die* for you," she wrote, "how can it then be one to live for you?"[21]

Woodrow was transported. He did not understand this "marvelous woman's love," but he would simply accept it with "boundless joy and gratitude." If he and Ellen were not ready for marriage, then "who ever was?" he asked her.[22]

They were, indeed, ready for marriage. Only two matters of importance intervened, and one of those, a teaching position for Woodrow, was now settled. The other, when and where they were to be married and what would comprise a suitable honeymoon, were questions tossed back and forth between New York and Baltimore until the end of their spring terms in late May.

The position that Woodrow accepted, at an annual salary of fifteen hundred dollars, was associate in history at Bryn Mawr College,[23] a school recently established near Philadelphia by Quakers for the higher education of women. The dean, Martha Carey Thomas, daughter of a trustee of The Johns Hopkins University, had, after graduation in 1877 from Cornell, taken a Ph.D. degree, *summa cum laude*, in November 1882 from the University of Zurich, a feat so unusual that it brought her notoriety both at home and abroad. A brilliant, attractive woman exactly Woodrow's age, Carey Thomas was totally committed to excellence in higher education for women. With this goal in mind, she helped to select a distinguished faculty for the new college. Eight of the nine appointees had doctorates, most of them from German universities, and some had teaching experience of two and three years. The one exception was Woodrow Wilson who was considered nevertheless to be a highly promising young scholar.[24]

To be confronted by a woman equal or even superior in professional status was a new and discomfiting experience for Woodrow, who would, of course, "*prefer* to teach young men."[25] Ellen wondered if her fiancé would be content to "serve in that sort of institution" (in her limited experience, female institutions afforded neither challenge nor selectivity) and she was skeptical about his ability to cooperate with the strong-minded Carey Thomas.[26] Ellen was also concerned for fear that marriage would place an unfair financial burden upon Woodrow, who would need money for professional expenses (e.g., books and travel) that a salary of fifteen hundred dollars could not provide. "My only *comforting* thought is that I too can work, and will," she offered.[27] Certain that they could manage adequately, Woodrow believed that it was his duty to support *her*; he wanted, however, to leave her "absolutely free" to make her own decision.[28]

When Ellen first suggested that their marriage in Savannah take place in early September, Woodrow was disappointed. Ellen knew that to make the necessary preparations for a proper wedding, and to assemble even a modest trousseau, would require time, matters beyond her fiancé's ken. He continued to plead so fervently for June that she relented and named the twenty-fourth as a firm date.[29] This would allow only three weeks, after she left New York, to work with Aunt Ella, an elderly Grandmother Axson, and the seamstress.

Ellen, too, had not forgotten a promise made to herself the summer before, soon after her father's death. She had determined, when in New York, where women doctors were available, to have a thorough physical examination, and if she were "not quite sound" to break the engagement. She asked Woodrow, "What do we girls know about ourselves?—Why absolutely nothing!" Even though Ellen perceived her constitution to be like Grandfather Axson's—"india rubber"—she knew that, because of the terrible strain of that last fall and winter in Rome, she could not bear as much as she once could.[30] Marriage to Ellen was for Woodrow "a matter of life and death." He reminded her of his own erratic health, and, in the light of that fact, he asked her what right *he* had to beg her to marry *him*.[31] She suggested that neither of them should ever raise such questions again.[32] Conditioned by the history of her immediate family's health, Ellen's misgivings about her constitution were not unreasonable. Stockton, about whom she had been anxious for some time, would later prove her concerns to be justified.[33]

Her last weeks in New York were a mad whirl of saying goodbye to people and to art exhibits, interspersed with shopping and visits to the dressmaker. On May 30, with many regrets at leaving the "Leaguers,"[34] Ellen boarded a steamer, the *City of Savannah*, for Georgia. The voyage, a time of sweet stillness after the bustle and noise of New York, would always seem to her a radiant dream in which she was borne to Woodrow.[35]

In early June, Woodrow joined his parents for three weeks in Columbia, South Carolina, at the home of his sister, Annie Howe.[36] Following his father's advice, Woodrow indulged in a complete physical rest and led a "mere animal life"—sleeping, lounging, and staying away from books. During those days of waiting, he wrote to Ellen that he wanted to hear from her own sweet lips of her readiness "for that act which is to crown our lives with a happiness such as we are now waiting for."[37] She answered promptly and promised that, before the ceremony, he would, indeed, hear from her lips that she was ready "for that act which will make me *all yours*."[38]

On June 23, the Wilson and Howe families arrived in Savannah and moved into the Screven Hotel "nearest the church." The next evening, shortly before seven o'clock, the families assembled in the double parlors of the manse. Present from the Axson side of the house were Uncle Randolph, Aunt Ella, their five children, Stockton, and Eddie. Young Palmer Axson excited over this, his fourteenth birthday, kept his poise, but nine-year-old Eddie Axson did not. He found a convenient matter of disagreement with the groom's nephew, Wilson Howe, and the two boys tried to settle their differences with a vigorous fistfight. Woodrow was amused, but Ellen was appalled.[39]

The couple stood together in the double doorway between the front and back parlors while they took their vows. Ellen wore a simple white summer dress which she had designed with a plain long skirt looped up on one side to show a lace short skirt. On her hair was draped an exquisite lace veil worn by Janie Hoyt at her marriage to Edward Axson in 1858. She carried no flowers, and there was no music. Grandfather Axson and Woodrow's father shared in performing the ceremony in the presence of the immediate families and a few close friends.[40]

Mary was the only Hoyt present. Uncle Will, unable to come because he was "pinch broke" wrote, "I love you Elly . . . you are as dear to me . . . as if you were my own."[41] Rosalie, who could not afford the rail fare to Savannah, was absent.[42] (The two friends would meet again, in due course, but only twice.) An elderly friend of the Axsons, Mrs. Louisa Gilmer, lamented, "What a pity for such a beautiful girl to throw herself away on an unknown lawyer from Atlanta."[43]

Accompanied by the Howes and the Wilsons, the bride and groom left Savannah that same evening for Columbia, where they were the guests of Woodrow's sister until July 1. En route to Arden, North Carolina, for a six-week honeymoon,[44] Woodrow stopped for most of a day in Augusta, Georgia, to show his wife the scenes of his boyhood.[45] In Arden, undisturbed by any contact with the outside world other than letters, they read, they studied German, and Woodrow prepared for his classes at Bryn Mawr.[46] On their way north, they visited Beth and Hamilton Erwin at their home, "Maplewood," in Morganton.[47] From North Carolina, the newlyweds joined the senior Wilsons, who were in New York City briefly before Joseph Ruggles Wilson would begin a new teaching position at the Southwestern Presbyterian University in Clarksville, Tennessee.[48] By the time that Ellen and Woodrow arrived in Bryn Mawr in mid-September, she was two months pregnant.

Part Three

1885–1894

Ellen Axson Wilson, 1892.
Courtesy of William D. Hoyt

Bryn Mawr

During their first month in Pennsylvania, Ellen and Woodrow lived in Haverford and boarded with Miss Addie Wildgoss. Finding these accommodations unsatisfactory, they moved in mid-October to rooms in a small frame cottage, Yarrow Hall, built by college authorities on the Bryn Mawr grounds for rental to faculty members. Yarrow Hall, the "Betweenery," was situated between the "Deanery," residence of Dean Carey Thomas, and Kelserhof, the "Greenery," across the way with a view. A cook-housekeeper was provided for each establishment, a fortunate circumstance because Ellen was unwell.[1] Early in her pregnancy, she had become miserably nauseated, and remained so for nearly four months.

Uncle Will sent words of encouragement—"It is always so at first [and] this is the worst part."[2] Although Mary Hoyt offered to leave her teaching position in Rome to take care of Ellen,[3] Aunt Louisa advised generously on prenatal care: Ellen must take fresh air every day, keep her system relaxed, and be "calm and cheerful." She must not become constipated, not wear her corset after the fifth month, nor use the sewing machine "very fast" or for long periods. Nervous feelings, pains in the limbs, bad dreams, anxious forebodings, and swollen feet were to be expected during pregnancy and were no cause for alarm.[4]

Rosalie, whose wedding would be in Sewanee in December,[5] was bitterly disappointed that Ellen would now be unable to come. At first distrustful because of Ellen's long silence, Beth, married for three years, was apologetic because she had intended to "stand in place" of Ellen's mother and talk "of things" which Ellen should know about, but she had kept "putting it off."[6] "It seems North Carolina is determined to claim Mr. Wilson," Beth informed Ellen. "In an article the other day I saw his name mentioned as one of several great intellects that North Carolina had let escape from the state."[7]

Antoinette, still the bohemian in New York City, wrote to Ellen that she was now engaged. "But *I* shall not give up art. Not one bit. It will be useless to tell you so but I *can* and *will* show you. I don't agree with you anymore than I did on a woman's duty. . . . Do you remember how we used to argue that question [of jealousy]? Well, I put into practice my theory." Antoinette went places with men just as she had done before her engagement, except for two evenings a week which she kept for her fiancé. "Now you darling little home girl," she wrote Ellen, "tell me all about yourself."[8] If Ellen and Antoinette had further correspondence, none has survived.

By January, Ellen had tentatively decided that she would go either to Aunt Louisa's or to Uncle Will's for her confinement. Rome was abruptly eliminated when word came that Uncle Robert Hoyt, who had been in miserable health for two years, had taken his own life. The burden of this family sorrow (Robert left a wife and five children) was carried largely by Uncle Will.[9] Aunt Louisa, who had made "a life-time study" of postnatal care, offered to teach Ellen how to take care of both herself and the baby. She cautioned Ellen to come to Gainesville no later than the first week in April, even though the baby was not due until the end of the month.[10]

Woodrow's mother was aghast that her son was sending his "little wife away,"[11] but, in truth, the plan was largely Ellen's idea. She knew that in Bryn Mawr Woodrow could not afford to pay for the kind of medical and nursing care which would be necessary, a problem she solved by convincing him that she wanted her baby to be born in the South.[12] Ellen knew, too, that her confinement and postnatal recovery would be disruptive to Woodrow's teaching and studying. Their small quarters at the Betweenery, adequate for bride and groom, afforded little privacy for a family. At the end of May, Woodrow would face the written examinations for his unfinished Ph.D. degree. To prepare for these, he would need a period of intensive, uninterrupted reading.

On April 14, Woodrow accompanied Ellen to Washington, where he helped her to change to the train which would carry her through to Gainesville that same evening. On April 16, at 11:30 A.M., in Aunt Louisa's home, Margaret Woodrow Wilson arrived. Named after her two grandmothers, she was "finely developed" and looked "as bright as a month old baby." Aunt Louisa informed the shocked young father by telegram of Margaret's arrival.[13]

Not until the twenty-first was Ellen permitted to write a brief note to her husband. "Ah sweetheart, it seemed impossible for anything else to bring us closer than we were, but what a wonderful bond of union is this precious little life! *Our* baby *your* baby! I love it twice as well because it is yours, and I *love* you, oh! I *love you infinitely*, my husband."[14]

The radiance of motherhood was dimmed because the baby was not a boy, who would, when he came, Ellen said, "excite more the paternal *pride* and *hope*."[15] Woodrow promptly reassured her: "I *know* that no [little] 'Woodrow'—especially if he be like me—can ever take the place of that dear little girl . . . especially if she be like you!"[16] Woodrow was less concerned over the sex of his child than over the demands which pregnancy made on Ellen's health. This "fate" need never attend his wife any more, he vowed, even though he would give "half" of all he expected to "win in the world, and *more*" for a son.[17]

For Ellen's twenty-sixth birthday Woodrow sent her a sewing "work-box." Selecting a gift for his baby daughter remained a problem, even after he wandered "bashfully and helplessly" through the infants' department at Wanamaker's in Philadelphia and inspected the plentiful goods displayed there.[18]

Woodrow's mind now turned to preparation for his written examinations at the Johns Hopkins, the first of which would be on May 21. He passed "by no means brilliantly [but] about in accordance with the standard of five days' preparation."[19] The second were finished on Friday, May 28; he had his final oral on Saturday. He wrote Ellen immediately: "Hurrah—a thousand times hurrah—*I'm through, I'm through*—the degree is actually secured!"[20] He had won the doctorate for *her*, he said.[21] Ellen was "very glad" about the degree which would assure better working conditions for Woodrow. As for herself, she would be content with "an attic and a crust and *you*"—as long as he was happy and free to write.[22]

In Gainesville, Ellen was occupied with relatives. Madge Axson, now four and a half, was not a little upset because overnight this infant had usurped her star role in Aunt Louisa's household. Stockton arrived from Savannah, where he had spent the past year in the cotton brokerage business with Uncle Randolph. Eddie Axson, now ten, came over from Maysville on May 5 to stay at Aunt Louisa's while his sister was there. Ellen was appalled at the condition of his wardrobe ("he is actually in *rags*"), which Uncle Henry's wife was unable to repair because of arthritic hands. Ellen began immediately to sew both for him and for herself ("I have . . . been trying on my dresses and not one of them will meet across the bust by several inches!"). Much more distressing than Eddie's wardrobe was his stammering, which had become "dreadful" during his year with Uncle Henry and Aunt Emma.[23] Ellen knew that Eddie needed a stable, loving home, but she also knew that she and Woodrow could not house him in the small Betweenery.

Woodrow was now impatient to see his wife and baby, and Ellen was unabashedly hungry for his presence. Every sentence of her letters to him were written, she said, in his arms and punctuated with his kisses. "I am just *wearying* for you . . . [oh] *won't* I make love to you in our holiday time! and oh *how* I love you now."[24] Their separation ended on June 12, when Woodrow arrived in Gainesville. After visits to Rome and to the Hoyt cousins in Nashville, they spent the rest of the summer with the senior Wilsons in Clarksville, Tennessee, except for a week that Woodrow spent with his sister Marion (Mrs. J. Ross, Jr.) Kennedy, in Little Rock.[25]

The Wilson family returned to Bryn Mawr on September 16 for the start of Woodrow's second year of teaching women. As Ellen suspected, her husband did not relish the prospect. Woodrow had in mind yet another book, a magnum opus on comparative politics, eventually referred to as "P.O.P.," or "Philosophy of Politics,"[26] which would require considerable reading of scholarly monographs in German. To understand his scholarly pursuits, Ellen read books in history, political economy, and political philosophy, and she soon learned how to discriminate between excellent and inferior political writers. More facile in languages than her husband, Ellen began an intensive study of German so that she could translate and digest some of the background material needed from German monographs. By doing this "toilsome drudgery" (Stockton's words), she saved Woodrow's time and energy for the more creative work of interpreting and synthesizing ideas. She engaged a part-time nurse for Margaret, who was soon weaned to a bottle.[27]

Ellen's skills in German would also be needed if Woodrow carried out his plan to take the family abroad while he studied for a year in Berlin. To finance this venture, Ellen had proposed that they use the balance of her inheritance from her father's estate, which now amounted to $1,462.82.[28]

Woodrow's father, ever ambitious for this brilliant son, was touched by "dear Ellie's generous proposal." He advised Woodrow's family to sail early in July, "and may God bless her and you in carrying your . . .

purpose to the desired end!"[29] Irrespective of their intent to be away for a year, the Wilsons had united with the Presbyterian Church of Bryn Mawr on December 29, 1886, she, by letter of transfer from Rome, he, from the First Church of Wilmington.[30]

Early in January, the European plans had to be canceled because Ellen was again pregnant and the nausea had struck early and acutely. Woodrow wrote for guidance to Beth Erwin who sent pills and capsules from her physician in Morganton. The medicines had no effect on Ellen, who was ill and weak for the next two months.[31] Aunt Louisa took her usual pragmatic approach: "I feared you would 'get into trouble' again when you wrote [that] Margaret had weaned herself. I am not surprised though I am very sorry to hear it: But you must not grieve about it . . . for such things will happen and you are not alone."[32]

In April, the Wilsons leased an unfurnished eleven-room house (the "parsonage") in a wooded area on Gulph Road. Ellen now dipped liberally into her inheritance to buy furniture for the house. They moved their possessions into the parsonage in June, but only so tenants could sublease for the summer.[33] Shocked at their apparent extravagance, Woodrow's mother warned him that too many spare rooms would be an embarrassment;[34] but Jessie Wilson did not know that her daughter-in-law had definite purposes in mind for the space. Ellen's first priority was to bring Eddie from Georgia in the fall to be a part of the Wilson family;[35] her second, to invite Mary Hoyt to live with them and attend Bryn Mawr.

Mary, restless, bright, and unable to afford college, told Ellen that "surely to be an ambitious girl is the worst of fates." A graduate of Shorter College, a Baptist institution begun in Rome in 1877, Mary's education was approximately equivalent to that of a boarding school. With this training, she was teaching first grade in the Rome public schools, and she was helping to educate her younger sister, Florence, at Shorter. "Ellen, darling," Mary wrote: "You know how I long to be educated . . . [and] I thank you for the sweet love that planned it all. . . . And Cousin Woodrow, too, please thank him. I do not believe one man in a thousand would be so good to his own cousin even— much less [to] his wife's."[36]

In mid-June, the family went to Gainesville—Ellen to be near Aunt Louisa for her second confinement in August, and Woodrow to spend the time writing. They roomed and boarded first with Mrs. S. A. Langston and, later, at the Piedmont Hotel, owned and operated by the Confederate general, James Longstreet.[37]

When Ellen arrived in Gainesville, she found that Madge, Eddie, and Stockton were all there. Aunt Louisa, who had had Eddie with her for the Christmas holidays, had insisted on keeping him for the rest of the year. Eddie was certainly happier, and Henry Hoyt was relieved to share this obligation of an orphaned nephew with Louisa.[38] During his year in Savannah in the cotton brokerage business, Stockton had continued his education informally by reading Latin and Greek with a tutor. By the spring of 1887, he was restless for several reasons: the climate in Savannah was apparently affecting his health, the world of business was not challenging, and he and his first cousin, Leila Axson, had fallen in love. Both were nearly twenty, had similar tastes and sympathies, and were constantly thrown together in the Savannah household. Although first cousins in the South not infrequently married each other, the idea of this match between two so closely related people was unnerving to the family. No longer comfortable in Savannah, Stockton's dilemma was solved temporarily by big-hearted Aunt Louisa, who took him into her home in April "to take charge of her garden."[39] (The Reverend I. S. K. Axson, now pastor emeritus after nearly thirty years at the Independent Presbyterian Church, had moved from the manse to 166 Hall Street, where his son, Randolph, had bought a house.)[40] Stockton's health and humor improved, but what he most wanted was to be near Ellen and her husband, two people whom he loved and admired and who, he thought, understood him.

After the Wilsons arrived in Gainesville, Woodrow soon left the five—Ellen, Stockton, Eddie, Madge, and baby Margaret—to get reacquainted, as it were, while he went to Columbia to see his sister's family and his mother, who was visiting Annie Howe. With a nurse to help care for Margaret, Ellen had free time to rest and read while Woodrow was away. She delved into Dickens and reread five of Shakespeare's plays. The heat in Gainesville, almost unbearable at ninety-eight degrees, both night and day, sapped Ellen's energy and afflicted Margaret with a fever and heat rash. Ellen successfully persuaded Woodrow to extend his stay in Columbia where the accommodations, the people, and the weather were more agreeable. She believed that for her husband's scholarly work it was important that his summer change

Stockton Axson, c. 1888. Courtesy of William D. Hoyt.

should be advantageous, and if he were in Gainesville he would take all her "aches and pains to heart."[41]

As the time drew near for her confinement, Ellen longed for her mother with whom she wanted to *share* her happiness. Sometimes she allowed herself to imagine that she was going home to her mother and taking Woodrow and the little ones.[42] In her mind, the second little one was, of course, a boy. Jessie Woodrow, a healthy girl baby, was born on August 28, 1887, in the Piedmont Hotel. Joseph Ruggles Wilson sent his love and congratulations, but he "could have wished for the advent of a *boy*." He also sent half of a sum of money which Woodrow had requested for a loan, yet he was grieved that his son had to borrow money "to eke out a living."[43] The son was back in Bryn Mawr on September 29, but Ellen and the babies stayed in the South for three more weeks of Aunt Louisa's care.

Grandfather Axson came from Savannah to visit and to baptize little Jessie, his second great-grandchild. (Grandmother Rebecca Axson, whose mind and body had been failing for more than a year, had died on September 22.)[44]

The summer in Gainesville brought Ellen closer to Stockton. He told Ellen that, on the last evening he ever spent alone with their father, Edward Axson had confided to Stockton that there could be no better model of the man whom he, Edward, wanted Stockton to follow than young Woodrow Wilson. After long, searching talks, Ellen convinced her brother that he should return to college. Ambivalent about a career, Stockton had decided against business; briefly, he considered law and journalism, and for a very brief time, indeed, he thought of the ministry. Like his sister, he loved books and was an avid reader. Still uncertain of his goals, he subsequently enrolled for the fall term of 1887 at the University of Georgia as an elective student.[45]

On October 12, Ellen, with Mary Hoyt, Eddie, and the two babies, left Georgia for Bryn Mawr. Eddie's departure had involved a battle of wills among Stockton, who was adamant that Eddie should be with Ellen, Uncle Randolph, Uncle Henry, and Grandfather Axson. The others thought he should probably stay in the South. Eddie wept uncontrollably at the thought of not going with his sister and settled the matter with the power of his tears.[46]

As the academic year progressed, Woodrow was increasingly restless at Bryn Mawr. To enhance his income, now two thousand dollars per year, he had contracted with The Johns Hopkins University for a three-year lecture series at five hundred dollars per year. He would deliver twenty-five lectures, two a week, for thirteen successive weeks beginning in February 1888. The assistant in history promised by the college authorities had not materialized, and he continued to be the only teacher in the history department. When Woodrow wrote Robert Bridges that he almost feared a breakdown in health if he stayed at Bryn Mawr another year, Bridges began a discreet campaign to find a place for Woodrow on the faculty at Princeton.[47] Any positive feelings that Woodrow now had for Bryn Mawr, he said, derived from the fact that Ellen was a woman; otherwise, he hated the place "very cordially."[48] Ellen kept him steady, cured his morbidness by being "herself incapable of it," and looked his "ugly moods out of countenance."[49] She was convinced that he would, in due course, find another position, but her immediate concern was the lack of time for his book, *The State*.

Ellen had weaned Jessie to a bottle at six weeks, a process that Ellen thought at times would cause the baby and herself "to kill each other,"[50] but she had more freedom for herself and Woodrow. Two afternoons a week, she went into Philadelphia to the cooking school of Mrs. S. T. Rorer, who gave a glorified home economics course. Although the Wilsons had a cook, in addition to a house servant, Ellen wanted to learn the skills of household management.[51] Preparation for Woodrow's Hopkins lectures consumed many evenings at the parsonage, evenings which Ellen spent with him, listening, reading, or sewing. The Hopkins lectures were barely over in the spring of 1888 when Woodrow's mother died suddenly. With his "precious mother" gone, he told Ellen that she was now his "*whole* earthly stay and support," and that he would need her to love him "more than ever."[52]

As Ellen had predicted, Woodrow would escape from Bryn Mawr. In late June, Wesleyan University, in Middletown, Connecticut, proffered a chair in political science and history at a salary of twenty-five hundred dollars. Morally committed by a contract made with Bryn Mawr in March to remain three more years as associate professor of history and political science, Woodrow nevertheless found the Wesleyan offer irresistible. Believing that Bryn Mawr had invalidated the contract by not providing the promised assistant in history, he submitted his resignation on June 29. The board of trustees acquiesced but not entirely in Quaker silence.[53] Woodrow would at last have his male students who would, he thought, be more drawn to political science and who would not suffer from "a painful *absenteeism* of mind."[54]

In July, Ellen and Woodrow leased a large dwelling in Middletown at 106 High Street which would be their home for the next two years. A hectic August followed with packing and houseguests. Stockton, Joseph R. Wilson, Jr. ("Josie"), and Grandfather Axson, whom Ellen had persuaded to venture north, all came to Bryn Mawr. Although he lived until March 1891, the "Great Axson" would not see his dearest grand-daughter again.[55]

In Gainesville, Aunt Louisa was doing her bit to help clothe Eddie Axson for a Connecticut winter without herself cluttering her niece's household. After more than a reasonable wait, she wanted Ellen to let her know whether "the bundle of drawers" arrived safely.

> I bought the cloth for E[ddie]'s drawers from Mr. Evans[;] it took 18 yds: it was 8½ cents per yd, 20[cts] for thread and buttons, 25[cts] for [express] postage . . . 6 pairs at 30[cts] per pair, $1.80 is what you owe . . . the woman for making them. . . . I would give dear little Eddie the making of the garments but we have met with so many losses. . . . Our valuable cow died in April and our horse died in May.[56]

On September 1, 1888, the family of five left Bryn Mawr for Middletown, where Ellen looked forward to a period of better health.[57]

Chapter 10

Wesleyan

Ellen had thought that northerners were "cold," but she found the opposite to be true. The Reverend Azel Washburn Hazen, pastor of the First Congregational Church, and his wife, Mary Butler Thompson Hazen, became close friends. The Wilsons transferred their membership to this church in November.[1] John Monroe Van Vleck, acting president of Wesleyan, took a personal interest in the Wilsons' housing needs. On Thanksgiving Day "these good New England folk" provided dinner for the family (probably at the Hazens').[2] Determined to be more involved in "social intercourse" than at Bryn Mawr, Ellen began the required calling and returning calls. One day she managed seven, and on another afternoon, four. John Franklin Jameson, then a professor at Brown University, who spent a November weekend with the Wilsons, was "greatly obliged" for so delightful an addition "as Mrs. Woodrow Wilson" to his circle of friends. He sent her a copy of George Washington Cable's liberal tract, *The Negro Question*, which he thought Ellen would like to read.[3]

Still in touch with friends, Ellen learned that Beth, now pregnant for the fourth time, had christened her third child "Ellen Woodrow Erwin." Beth had kept boarders during the previous summer to ease her precarious finances,[4] and, at Christmastime, Ellen packed and sent a huge box of toys and clothing to Beth's children.[5] Rosalie had spent a restful summer in Sewanee with new baby daughter, Margaret;[6] Janie Porter Chandler, who had moved with her husband to San Diego because of Janie's weak lungs, had improved so rapidly that she hoped to regain the health and strength which she had enjoyed before her marriage.[7]

Mary Hoyt had made a splendid first-year record at Bryn Mawr and was back for her second year. Florence Hoyt, now teaching in public school in Rome, was taking her turn at helping Mary with college expenses. Ellen invited Mary to Middletown for the Christmas holidays, a visit made possible when Uncle Tom, pleading lack of space in his Philadelphia house, donated Mary's rail ticket.[8] Stockton, at the University of Georgia for a second year, stayed in Athens for the holidays. His bruised heart was recovering with the help of a young lady from Atlanta, but choosing a career continued to be a dilemma. "In 4½ months, I will be out in the world," he wrote Ellen at Christmas, "and I am beginning to feel a little shaky as I have literally nothing in prospect."[9]

When Woodrow left Middletown in February 1889 to deliver his second series of lectures at Johns Hopkins, Ellen was again pregnant. As the nausea and nervousness intensified, she sought medical care from Dr. Florence Taft, a local physician. Woodrow's qualms about a woman doctor were temporarily allayed in the hope that she could provide relief to Ellen, "wholly or in part."[10] Overwhelmed by the intensity of her illness, Ellen was convinced that her married life was a failure, that she, for most of it, had been a dead weight on Woodrow. In a rare mood of depression she spilled over to him:

> Oh this last year! What a shameful record it has been! I have been your *tormentor* instead of your helpmeet. Not the smallest thing has gone wrong but that *you* have been . . . worried with seeing me go "all to pieces" over it. . . . Oh I am not fit to live! What *has* happened to me? What curse has fallen on me? And to think before I married my most striking characteristic as every one said was my singular *serenity* of disposition. . . . How easy it is for young girls—and men—to be philosophical—for *anybody*, indeed, whose nerves have not been racked and tortured by long weary months of *steady* suffering.[11]

This outburst not only brought Woodrow to Middletown for the weekend; he offered to cancel the lectures at Hopkins and stay by her side. The visit helped to calm Ellen's nerves, but not the nausea. Woodrow then sent for their old nurse from Bryn Mawr so that Ellen could have needed rest.[12] In her daydreams, Ellen fancied that the baby had arrived and that the doctor had announced that it was a "fine boy." If this could be true, she was more than willing to undergo all the prenatal torture, a price she "paid *most gladly*" if the cost did not include her "being a nervous wreck for life."[13] In a moment of prescience, Woodrow wrote that he was as glad at the thought of "having another little girl—almost—as at the thought of having a boy." Whatever the outcome of this third pregnancy, he had resolved that this would be the end of Ellen's childbearing.[14]

Back in Baltimore, Woodrow took to heart every domestic detail, from Margaret and Ellen's constipation and Eddie's mumps to Ellen's request for more books to read. She had finished "a dose of Balzac," the English essayist Philip Gilbert Hamerton's *Human Intercourse*, Turgenev's *On the Eve*, and a "stack of trash" brought in by one of the Middletown ladies.[15] In March, Woodrow crowded his remaining lectures in back to back so that he could come home a week early, a gesture about which Ellen had mixed feelings. She thought that it was better for him to be in the pleasant, stimulating atmosphere at the Hopkins than in "this atmosphere of *nausea!*"[16]

Relieved that his manuscript for *The State* was almost completed, Woodrow wrote to Ellen: "Since I have been here, a distinct *feeling* of maturity . . . has come over me, . . . the feeling . . . that I need no longer hesitate . . . to assert myself and my opinions in the presence of and against the selves and opinions of . . . 'my elders.' . . . I am coming to the maturity of my powers."[17] Her "mission in life," Ellen had told a friend, was to give Woodrow faith in himself and confidence in his "own powers,"[18] a mission which was well on the way to achievement. She rejoiced that the "frolic" was still in him, and she hoped that he would never outgrow that.[19]

When Woodrow returned to Middletown, one of his and Ellen's first tasks was to discuss Stockton's vocational dilemma. That he would make a competent teacher of English, the Wilsons agreed, and the logical place to prepare was at Wesleyan on whose faculty was one of the foremost teachers of English literature in the United States, Caleb Thomas Winchester. This idea appealed to Stockton. At Ellen's suggestion, he planned to come to Middletown in the summer to study German with her to remove his deficiency in that subject. "I owe you . . . a debt of gratitude which I will never be able to pay," Stockton wrote to Ellen and Woodrow, "not even by making a scholar of whom you will think with some pride." He added a cautionary postscript which was eerie in the light of a tragedy which would occur in Eddie's life sixteen years later: "Remembering Ed's love of the water, and your proximity to the [Connecticut] river I am afraid he may get off with a crowd of boys and go in unless he is warned [about drowning]."[20]

Shortly before Stockton arrived, Woodrow sent to his publisher the finished manuscript of *The State*, dedicated to Ellen. With a relatively light heart, he then set off for Princeton to attend his tenth reunion and to talk with the college's recently elected president, Francis Landey Patton. Robert Bridges continued to work for Woodrow's appointment to the faculty of their alma mater. The idea was not unattractive to Woodrow, who, although far happier at Wesleyan than at Bryn Mawr, admitted that his students were "very inferior" in preparation and came from a parentage for the most part of "narrow circumstances" and "narrow thought."[21]

Late in the summer of 1889, Ellen developed alarming symptoms in the seventh month of pregnancy; severe headaches and accompanying eye trouble (probably caused by edema) plagued her. Analysis of a urine specimen showed the presence of albumin, a harbinger of the kidney disease which would eventually develop.[22] Uneasy over this turn of events, Woodrow wrote to his brother-in-law, Dr. George Howe, Jr., for an opinion about women doctors. Howe responded with masculine objectivity: "I am one of those who believe that there is one drawback to women doctors, namely that the nervousness which most of them suffer from at their menstrual periods, unfits them for some of the emergencies arising in the practice of medicine. Aside from this, I see no reason why the woman should not be quite as efficient as the man in the medical profession."[23] Reassured about the general competence of women physicians, Woodrow left Ellen to the whimsy of Dr. Florence Taft's hormones while he took a week's vacation with Robert Bridges.

On October 16, with Dr. Taft in attendance, Ellen gave birth to Eleanor Randolph Wilson. When told that she had another daughter, Ellen wept. Woodrow's father sent congratulations and invoked God's blessing even as he confessed that he had unreasoningly hoped for a boy. Uncle Tom also wished it had been a boy; and Beth, now the mother of two girls and two boys, lamented its sex. Ellen had neglected to tell either the Savannah kin or Aunt Louisa that she was expecting a third baby. Uncle Randolph was "simply not prepared for the news," and a surprised Aunt Louisa hoped that the three little girls would grow up to be as lovely as their mother.[24]

Autumn turned into winter, and the time inevitably came for Woodrow to leave for Baltimore, his third year of lecturing at The Johns Hopkins University. He was there on February 18 when the board of trustees at Princeton unanimously elected him to the Chair of Political

Economy and Jurisprudence. Two days later, he accepted the position, to begin in September 1890, at a salary of three thousand dollars.[25]

Only one year before, Ellen had made the despondent appraisal of her "shameful record" in marriage. Unfounded at the time, her record was now demonstrably outstanding. She and Woodrow had three healthy, bright daughters and a virtual son in Eddie. They had helped two promising young southerners, Stockton and Mary, on their way to successful teaching careers. Woodrow's second book, *The State*, had appeared in September to largely positive reviews and was immediately selected as a textbook at Harvard.[26] Before *The State* was off the press, he had agreed to write yet another volume, to be called "Division and Reunion," as part of a series entitled *Epochs of American History*, edited by Albert Bushnell Hart of Harvard.[27] Wake Forest College in North Carolina had awarded him an honorary degree *in absentia*, and he had declined a professorship at Williams College.[28] With barely five years of teaching behind him, he was now joining the faculty of one of the most outstanding institutions in the country. The thirty-three-year-old professor told his wife: "It would be hard to say in what part of my life & character you have *not* been a supreme and beneficent influence. You are all-powerful in my development."[29]

With Woodrow in Baltimore, the fates seemed determined to decree unsound health for Ellen. When instructing a new cook, Ellen upset a pan of boiling lard on her feet, causing burns so severe that she was unable to walk for more than three months.[30] Ellen spent part of her enforced leisure in searching for some means to help Eddie with his stammering. The answer seemed to be a reputable speech therapist in Philadelphia, where Eddie went in April to stay at Uncle Tom's home. Six weeks later he bragged: "You just ought to hear me talk now Sister and see what improvement I have made."[31] By early June, Eddie had not stammered on a single word for about two weeks, and he vowed that he did not ever intend to again. Uncle Tom thought his restoration phenomenal, but Eddie's recovery would prove to be transient.[32]

Ellen was further absorbed in planning the decor for their house in Princeton. They had decided to rent a large frame dwelling at 48 Steadman Street (now 72 Library Place) which belonged to Dr. John Dale McGill of Jersey City. Woodrow had seen the place on his way from Baltimore to Middletown and had evidently provided Ellen with a floor plan. Dr. McGill agreed to put the house in first-class condition and to allow Ellen to redecorate throughout.[33]

In September, Stockton left to enter graduate school at The Johns Hopkins University, and Eddie went south to the Bingham School in Mebaneville, North Carolina, where Joseph Wilson, Jr., had gone. Mary Hoyt was, of course, back at Bryn Mawr.[34] For the first time in three years, the family comprised only Ellen, Woodrow, and their own children.

Chapter II

Early Princeton

In the fall of 1890, the Wilsons began a residency of nearly twenty-three years in Princeton, longer than they had lived, or ever would live, in any other place. Rich in colonial history, the town, or borough, with a population of thirty-four hundred, was located about forty-five miles equidistant from New York to the northeast and Philadelphia to the south. The college, around which the borough had grown, had an enrollment of 873 (105 were graduate students), a faculty of forty-nine, and eight administrators. Society centered around the activities of the school year, with its intercollegiate ball games, public lectures, student debates, faculty dinner parties, receptions, and commencements. The elite of the town, generally associated with the college and the Theological Seminary, were mostly Presbyterian, a fact of life not unfamiliar to the Wilsons.

When Ellen, Woodrow, and the three children arrived in Princeton in September, the McGill house was still not ready for occupancy. Their first few weeks in town were spent in the Nassau Hotel, where George McLean Harper, a young instructor in French at the college, met the family one evening "still at dinner." Harper later recalled that Ellen looked "so young, so happy and so beautiful" that he could hardly tell for a moment which was mother or which daughters. (He could hardly have been mistaken at the time because Margaret, Jessie, and Eleanor were four, three, and one, respectively.)

Later a frequent visitor to the Wilson home, Harper supposed that, "with three children to bring up and with a husband breaking ground in a new position," Ellen Wilson would have had enough to do; but it soon became apparent that their household was to be continually enlarged by relatives from both sides of the family.[1]

The first of the relatives to visit after Ellen had the house in order was Woodrow's sister, Annie Howe, whom he had urged to come. (His other sister, thirty-nine-year-old Marion, and her husband, the Reverend J. Ross Kennedy, Jr., had died the previous summer only a few months apart, both apparently from tuberculosis.)[2] Unwell, and pregnant with a "mid-life" baby, Annie was afraid that her condition might embarrass her brother and sister-in-law. Ellen wrote a kind and sympathetic letter, urging Annie to come immediately for a rest and change. Arriving in time for Thanksgiving, Annie stayed a fortnight, the first of many long visits she would make to the Wilsons' home.[3] Annie was scarcely on her way back to South Carolina before Woodrow's lonely, grieving father arrived, joined for the Christmas holidays by Mary Hoyt and Stockton.

In January, when Woodrow resumed his six-week lecture series at Johns Hopkins, Ellen and the children accompanied him to Baltimore. They took rooms in Miss Mary Jane Ashton's boarding house at 909 North McCulloh Street near the university and close to Stockton. Engrossed in his lectures and his family, Woodrow atypically neglected to write his father. The older Wilson grumbled, "Of course I know you are hurried and worried, and our dear Ellie would of course never think of writing when you cannot! But maybe she is lecturing too!"[4]

Joseph Ruggles Wilson, now sixty-nine, faced retirement from Southwestern Presbyterian University. His deteriorating health was adversely affected by the prospect of inactivity and by the loss of the constant ministrations of his wife. He suggested to Woodrow and Ellen that he and they buy or build a house in Princeton together, and for that purpose, he would "get together a few thousand dollars."[5] Consequently, in May 1891, Woodrow's father contributed fifteen hundred dollars toward the purchase, for three thousand dollars, of a large lot located on the present Washington Road between Ivy Lane and Prospect Street. This was the first step toward realizing their dream house— one which Ellen would design and decorate.

The Wilsons spent the summer of 1891 in Princeton while Woodrow completed about two thirds of *Division and Reunion*. This pace caused Dr. George Howe, who had sent a prescription for Woodrow's eyes, to warn that he was afraid Woodrow was "abusing" his health.[6] The Wilsons' only houseguests during the summer were Stockton, Woodrow's father, Uncle Randolph Axson, and his fourteen-year-old daughter, Ellen. Mary Hoyt had ventured far afield to spend the summer at Hull House in Chicago.[7]

Through his brother-in-law's mediations, Stockton had acquired a summer job in New York on the *Review of Reviews* edited by Woodrow's friend, Albert Shaw. At summer's end, Stockton returned to Wesleyan University to take a master's degree in English literature with Professor

Winchester rather than return to Hopkins where the focus was on linguistics. Eddie would again be at the Bingham School.[8]

The first year in Princeton was decidedly pleasant for the Wilsons. Professionally, the young pedagogue was a "brilliant & unqualified success," so much so, in fact, that President Patton was afraid of losing him. Columbia College (now University) had a covetous eye on him, a threat which Patton countered by suggesting that several affluent alumni might increase Woodrow's salary to thirty-four hundred dollars, a move discussed, but not brought about immediately.[9]

When 1892 began, Ellen was excited about plans to accompany Woodrow to Baltimore in late January, and then, when he had finished his lectures in March, she and the children would visit Savannah and Rome.[10] She had not been to Georgia for five years, and most of the relatives had seen neither Jessie nor Eleanor. When she arrived at Uncle Randolph and Aunt Ella's new home at 166 Hall Street on March 4, it was her first visit to Savannah since her marriage.

At the old manse on Whitaker Street, Ellen took tea with her grandfather's successor, the Reverend J. Frederick Dripps, and his wife. In the familiar parlors, she felt strange as she stood in the same spot where she and Woodrow Wilson had made their vows to each other seven years earlier.[11] The weather in Savannah was "glorious," the children, a sensation, and everybody thought that Ellen looked *better* than when she was first married.[12]

While his wife socialized, Woodrow was in Princeton staying at the Nassau Hotel, tormented by the strong possibility that, because of his "selfish self-indulgence," Ellen was pregnant.[13] He requested that she send him a cipher telegram when, and if, her menstrual period began, although it was not due for ten days.[14] The suspense, her absence, and his temporary celibacy contributed to his anguish. Fear of offending Ellen's taste restrained Woodrow from writing the things which his intensely passionate nature impelled him to write. He was not ashamed of the way in which he loved her, he said, but only of the way that his sometimes "rude demonstrations of . . . man-like love" must often pain her.[15] "What fools those very perspicacious people have been," he said, "who have judged me by my cold exterior and have imagined my feelings as temperate as my reason."[16] "Sometimes I am afraid of myself, my little wife. I can tell you so because you have *so much sense* and know that what I say . . . argues not one whit of real infidelity to you—is anatomical and not of the heart."[17] He tried to console himself by translating, from the French, the lascivious boudoir scene in Théophile Gautier's *Mademoiselle de Maupin*.[18]

In reaction to his obvious discomfort, Ellen asked Woodrow if *he* remembered when her period was due. He sent her the precise date. In distressing detail, she described to him the last weeks in the life of Rosalie's older sister, Julie, whose death was "due entirely to that awful nausea" in pregnancy. Ellen added casually, "But it is a *shame* to fill my letter with so sad a subject."[19] When Woodrow eventually received word from her that "all was well," his relief was effusive.[20]

Now in Rome, Ellen attended to a long overdue task. For her father, who had lain in Myrtle Hill Cemetery in an unmarked grave for eight years, she now ordered a headstone. After consultation with Stockton, Woodrow, and Uncle Randolph, she chose this inscription:

> In Memory of Rev. S. E. Axson
> who departed this life May 28, 1884
> aged 47 years 5 months,
> For seventeen years pastor of the Rome Presbyterian Church.
> While yet in the noonday of life
> In the heat of a well-fought fight
> the Master called him to his exceeding great reward.[21]

(In 1887, when the interior of the Rome church was renovated, the congregation had placed a handsome marble tablet in the sanctuary to Edward's memory.)[22]

Ellen now continued her visit with a lighter heart. At Uncle Will's the disorder and confusion were "so stupendous," she supposed that she should be glad not to "lose the children."[23] Agnes and Arthur Tedcastle entertained her delightfully in their "great [new] mansion" situated on a high point which afforded a panorama of views. Ellen would *almost* be willing to live in Rome for the sake of such a feast as Agnes had spread before her.[24] On Sunday, in her father's former church, she looked with "longing eyes" at the Axson pew "where we used to sit." When the services were over, all three girls were greatly admired, but Jessie received the supreme compliment as the one who looked like her grandmother, Janie Hoyt Axson.[25]

Retracing the old Rome paths refreshed Ellen's intense admiration for her husband. She did not simply *believe* it, she *knew* that the combination of qualities found in him were the "rarest, finest, noblest, *grandest*" of which human nature was capable, and which, if put "in all its naked truth would be censured by every critic as impossible." He was ineffably tender, unselfish and thoughtful "in things great and small," and "exquisitely gifted in power of sympathy." In addition to these lover's traits, she recognized in him all of those gifts which "go to make a born leader of men." In short, he was clearly a *genius* for whom she knew many honors lay yet ahead. His critics, she said, would never know the "beautiful things" of which he was capable.[26] She had learned to release her anger at those who did not fully appreciate her husband by a "passion of lovemaking" that would fill him with a "mad, uncontrollable joy."[27]

Their separation, now more than a month, was frustrating to both of them, but Ellen had yet to visit Aunt Louisa and Madge. If she did not stay in Gainesville at least two weeks, feelings would be hurt. Ellen was homesick for Princeton not solely because of Woodrow. Her seven years spent in the enlightened academic circles of the North had given her a different perspective on the small Georgia towns of her girlhood. In Gainesville, she was really "roughing it" among "these good southern relatives of mine." She was concerned about Madge, a spoiled ten-year-old, who had acquired "all the dreadful Gainesville peculiarities of speech." Ellen wanted to take her sister to Princeton for the summer, a subject which Aunt Louisa found too painful even to discuss. The Browns were planning, however, to move in the fall to the college town of Athens, Georgia, so that Madge could attend a better school.[28]

On April 22, with the threat of pregnancy no longer a problem, Ellen went to Columbia to visit the Howes, after which she planned to make brief stops in Morganton and Asheville with Beth and Rosalie.[29] The week allotted to Columbia turned into nearly three weeks when Jessie fell and broke her collarbone.[30] With the trip to North Carolina now canceled, Ellen was happily surprised when Rosalie, Mac, and their three children, Margaret, Julia, and McNeeley DuBose, Jr., appeared in Columbia to visit Mac's only brother, Dr. Theodore DuBose, a physician who lived near the Howes. The reunion of the two friends, the first since their respective marriages, was poignant.[31]

The presence of the DuBoses made the time pass more happily for Ellen whose loyalty to Annie Howe was due more to family ties than to compatibility. Woodrow, who had urged Ellen to go to Columbia, was sure that, after Annie's loving welcome, Ellen would not need to feel that she had gone only in compliance with his wishes.[32] Ellen found another diversion in the Howes' second son, George, a bright, ambitious teenager, who wanted to follow his Uncle Woodrow's example and become a professor. Ellen suggested that Woodrow try to help George to get a scholarship at the Lawrenceville School near Princeton, in order to increase his chances of admission to one of the best colleges. Eddie Axson was already enrolled as a scholarship student at Lawrenceville, a matter in which Woodrow had successfully wielded influence. Too late in applying for financial aid, George was admitted anyway for the fall of 1892.[33]

While Ellen was still in Columbia, Woodrow wrote to her about another educational matter that promised excitement for the Wilsons. The University of Illinois had invited him to become its president at an annual salary of six thousand dollars.[34] Ellen bombarded Woodrow with astute questions. Is the salary *just* six thousand dollars, or that plus perquisites such as house, grounds, staff, and traveling expenses? How large is the faculty and how many students? What sort of endowment? Enough to compete with the University of Chicago? What is, and has been, the spirit of the legislature toward it? What sort of place is Urbana? She counseled that the most important question was which position (i.e., Princeton or Illinois) would give him the most time for original work, a matter "we" will want to consider *very* carefully.[35]

Ellen was thoroughly annoyed with the Princeton administration, still too timid to raise Woodrow's salary despite his increasing prominence in the world of scholars, for fear of offense to other faculty members. "I do not see why even if the *College* raised your salary any of those other men would have the *remotest* cause to resent it until *they* too had $6000 offers," she wrote. The Illinois offer, she believed, was just as much a crisis for Princeton as for Professor and Mrs. Wilson. The administration had to decide forthwith whether "they" would continue as the College of New Jersey, or become a great university. Princeton could not achieve this status, she said, without a concerted effort to get and to keep "the best men, in open market on equal terms." "If I were you," she urged Woodrow, "I would push this issue unhesitatingly to the end *for the good of the college* no less than for my own."[36]

If Woodrow might have been lured to Illinois before Ellen's tough advice, the chances were now decidedly diminished. The more he thought about the matter, the less appealing the idea of a college presidency became,[37] and he concurred with Ellen's final assessment. "I *think*," she said, "it will probably be best for you to decline—yet *not in too great a hurry*." She wanted to keep the Princeton trustees "in the hottest kind of water" on her husband's account until they were "shaken out of their selfish lethargy" in the matter of salaries.[38] In declining the Illinois offer, Woodrow apparently used it as a lever to secure a five-hundred-dollar housing allowance and to persuade Dr. Patton to appoint immediately a man in political economy.[39]

The Wilsons spent the summer of 1892 in Princeton, except for a quick trip which Woodrow made to Columbia in June to be with the Howes, his father, and his brother, Joseph, Jr., now married and managing editor of the Clarksville, Tennessee, *Progress-Democrat*. "Old Anna" Harris came all the way to Princeton for commencement festivities and to visit with Ellen while Woodrow was away. The two friends read aloud Elizabeth Gaskell's *Cranford*, with Anna often reading while Ellen sewed. They attended worship at the First Presbyterian Church to hear "an intolerably smug" looking preacher whose every word sounded to Ellen like cant. Eddie, now home for summer vacation, went with Ellen and Anna to the Jersey shore at Long Branch to give Anna her first look at the ocean.[40] The Princeton heat was overwhelming in July and August, a discomfort which the Wilsons resolved never to bear again. Through the sweltering weeks, Ellen guarded Woodrow's study door while he finished writing *Division and Reunion*.[41]

When the academic term began in the fall of 1892, Eddie Axson and George Howe were at nearby Lawrenceville; Stockton, who had spent the summer in Cambridge, Massachusetts, studying French and German, had won an interim teaching appointment at the University of Vermont.[42] Despite the usual influx of relatives, Woodrow found time to proofread the galleys of *Division and Reunion*, which appeared in print in early March.[43]

During the school year, the Wilsons made time for informal intercourse with students, and, in particular, those from the South. According to Stockton, it was through conversations with a few of these southerners who were invited into the Wilsons' home that Ellen learned about the cheating habits of some of the Princeton men.[44] Outraged, she began to work with a group of concerned upperclassmen (among whose leaders were allegedly James M. Brodnax, a junior from Mason, Tennessee, and Charles W. Ottley, a senior from Atlanta)[45] whom she urged to work in turn with other students to establish an honor system. She then prodded Woodrow to press for the reform at faculty meetings. On January 13, 1893, a strong editorial calling for the change appeared in *The Daily Princetonian*, and, on the following Wednesday, at the faculty meeting, a resolution to establish an honor system was passed. Before the vote was taken, Woodrow gave an eloquent plea in favor of the resolution, which had been presented by Dean James O. Murray. The plan was inaugurated at midyear examinations in February 1893.[46]

In January, when Woodrow went to Baltimore for his sixth year of Hopkins lectures, he again took Ellen and the children. They returned to Mary Jane Ashton's boarding house where they had stayed two years before. At home in March, Ellen and Woodrow began a concerted campaign to help Stockton find a permanent teaching position, but Stockton's popularity at Vermont had spurred the authorities there to raise funds to keep him for a second year.[47]

After Woodrow finished his academic commitments for 1892–1893, the Wilsons left Princeton for a month's vacation on Long Island. They boarded at Sagaponock, near Bridgehampton, with Mrs. S. S. Topping.[48] Late in July, while the family remained at the seashore, Woodrow went to Chicago to address the International Congress of Education, a meeting organized by the great Columbian Exposition which had opened in May in Jackson Park. The congress conferred a singular honor on the young professor at Princeton by choosing him to be one of the featured speakers before this distinguished group.[49]

August found the Wilsons back at Steadman Street more relaxed and rested than for several years, and ready to receive visits from "our southern relatives." An overflow of Hoyts, Howes, and Axsons caused Ellen (and probably Woodrow) to have to sleep in the nursery to provide space for guests.[50]

Before the academic year began, Ellen made her own visit to the Columbian Exposition. Mary Hoyt, who had graduated from Bryn Mawr in June, planned to spend a few days in Chicago en route to a teaching position at the Mary Institute in St. Louis. With Mary, and Mary's friend, Alice Gould, Ellen left Philadelphia on September 6 for her first trip west of the Alleghenies.[51]

For the first time in the annals of world's fairs, a special building had been constructed to house a women's department. A national competition held among women for the structure's design was won by Sophia G. Hayden, a graduate of the Massachusetts Institute of Technology's School of Architecture. It was to this building that Ellen went at once,

Mary Eloise Hoyt, 1893.
Courtesy of the Very Reverend Francis B. Sayre.

and, in its rooftop restaurant, she, Mary, and Alice had dinner during their first evening in Chicago.[52] The concept of a "woman's building" stirred memories of Ellen's own girlhood plans to establish a woman's hall, to be run by women, for women only, yet nothing in her limited experiences as an eighteen-year-old remotely approached the grandeur of what she now saw. The entire edifice, planned, decorated, and designed by women, displayed sculpture, art, and crafts by women only. Surrounding the art gallery was a broad frieze on which names of outstanding women of history were inscribed.[53] For seven years, Ellen had barely touched her own painting, and these works by other women artists were indeed rewarding. She saw yet another unique exhibit (the "Loan collection") by a group of artists called "French Impressionists," whose work would indirectly influence her in the future.[54]

Before her visit to the exposition was over, she had dined on international cuisine, inspected the horticultural, mining, and anthropological exhibits, and walked through the Court of Honor. After several exhausting days, she hired a chair to ride down the Midway Plaisance late in the evening "to stir the Bohemian" in her. These exotic diversions made her hungry for "my darling's arms," and she also missed her "babies."[55]

Florence Hoyt, in Princeton to help Woodrow with the children and household, kept things going smoothly, but Woodrow missed his wife and yearned for her as always when they were separated. When Ellen returned to Princeton on September 14, his days of "existing provisionally" came to an end.[56]

The fall of 1893 brought new responsibilities. Eddie Axson and George Howe, both freshmen at Princeton, lived with the Wilsons; Helen Woodrow Bones, Woodrow's teenage first cousin, had come as a boarding student to Princeton's Evelyn College for girls. She, Ed, and George looked to Ellen as surrogate mother.[57] Woodrow had contracted with the Brooklyn Institute of Arts and Sciences to give six lectures on constitutional government in November and December. These were in addition to his seventh annual commitment to The Johns Hopkins University and, for the second consecutive year, his lectures at the New York Law School. All of this, his other public addresses (many for the university), his teaching, and his writing, made an incredibly heavy professional load.[58] Before he submitted his essays, book reviews, and longer scholarly works to publishers, Woodrow read them to Ellen, whose mind, he said, had "educated and liberalized" him.[59] He appreciated her ability to listen, without interruption, until the end—her "speaking silence."[60]

Despite Woodrow's schedule, Ellen maintained a home life of calm and continuity. From a diary kept by Eddie Axson in 1893–1894, one gets an intimate look at the Wilson household. It was a very busy place indeed, but the pervading mood was, nevertheless, one of unadulterated happiness. Eddie, George Howe, and Helen Bones, clearly unin-

Florence Stevens Hoyt, 1898.
Courtesy of the Very Reverend Francis B. Sayre.

hibited young people, indulged in card games, pillow fights, and on occasion, "Whiskey Poker," in which the loser ostensibly paid off in drinks. They had heart-to-heart sessions in Eddie's room and often took their evening meals there when Ellen and Woodrow were having dinner parties.

The Christmas holidays were uproarious in 1893. Florence Hoyt (Mary was in St. Louis), Stockton, Eddie, Helen, and George participated in festivities which began on Saturday, December 23. Woodrow and Ellen joined the young people in an afternoon of parlor games. Ellen devised a game that involved drawing historical pictures which had to be identified. Eddie's favorite game, "Twenty Questions," was a singular triumph when Woodrow, unable to guess "the North Pole," "almost flunked." On Sunday evening, December 24, the family attended services at the First Presbyterian Church. After the children went to bed, Eddie, Ellen, and Woodrow filled the stockings. As bedtime approached for the grown-ups, they were involved in conspiracy intermingled with laughter. Christmas morning was one grand eruption when the children, followed by sleepy adults, came down to open their presents around the tree. Finding oranges and candy in his stocking, Eddie pretended great surprise at Santa's generosity, while Margaret and Jessie, who had put them there, jumped up and down in excited approval. Woodrow gave Eddie the *Epochs of American History* series, and Ellen, two throw pillows and a chair for his room.

On Christmas night, Woodrow and Stockton, the two professorial types, retreated for political and philosophical talk. Florence Hoyt studied, Ellen went into the parlor to read, and the young people played cards. Eddie added some unexpected levity by passing out small Cuban cigarettes; and his sister, Ellen, convulsed him by puffing away on one. Stockton, in a holiday mood, served whiskey to Helen Bones—this, surely, without his sister's knowledge.[61]

Woodrow's departure for Baltimore in January made him feel abruptly cut off from this affectionate family circle. He could hardly put together a letter to Ellen because it was still so short a time since he was in her arms.[62] He needed time alone in Baltimore to write and study, yet no professional duty took priority over the least favor he could do for his wife. At the Decorative Art Society in Baltimore, where he went to have Ellen's "square of fine cashmir" stamped to make a shawl, he was puzzled about how she wanted it done—and made a second trip downtown after writing her "in haste and ignorance" for instructions. Ellen decided, after Woodrow had deposited an armful of her dresses at a Baltimore dry cleaner, that she wanted "the skirt to the white flannel ripped from the band" *before* cleaning. He rushed down again to the shop to see that her wishes were carried out. She sent a piece of jewelry with him to be repaired and returned forthwith, which he attended to promptly.[63]

These mundane chores were but a small way to reduce the irreducible: his debt of love to her. "This attachment of yours . . . seems part of the force of my mind," he wrote to Ellen. "It is the source of the imaginative colour that has come into my writing of late years. . . . Your mind [that] burns with such a soft and warming flame sacrifices nothing to brilliancy. . . . I should never have come within hailing distance of literature, if I had married anyone else."[64]

Their love, which seemed to Ellen only to magnify, was a marvel. She questioned whether it was wrong to worship her husband as she did, but she felt that she might as well ask if it were wrong to *breathe*; both were inevitable if she was "to *live* at all."[65]

The Extended Family

*Ellen believed that the important training of children was a parental re-*sponsibility, and she planned in the fall of 1894 to conduct school at home for the two older girls. She asked Woodrow, while in Baltimore, to select and send specimen copies of books suitable to use in teaching—arithmetic, geography, history, and spelling books.[1]

Woodrow played with his "sweet little chicks," sang and read to them, but Ellen was the parent who answered questions, soothed pain, and settled the inevitable nursery disputes. When it was necessary, she spanked the children (and invariably cried afterward), episodes in discipline usually kept from Woodrow.[2] She introduced a custom of celebrating birthdays by giving presents to each child instead of heaping gifts on one alone, a custom which she regarded as conducive to selfishness.[3]

Like good Presbyterian parents of their generation, the Wilsons were strict in observance of the Sabbath and would not permit games, charades, or even songs on that day. No unnecessary work of any sort was done, nor were servants required to perform duties. Ellen taught the children the Shorter Catechism and their "Sunday-school lessons" rather than send them to the local church school. Later, when they could read, she provided them with religious books chosen carefully to improve their "minds and characters."[4]

Margaret and Jessie, the two blondes, were near in age and close in relationship; Eleanor (Nell), the dark-haired, sensitive baby, was often the brunt of her sisters' teasing. A favorite bait of the older girls was to accuse Nell, born in Connecticut, of being a "Yankee." She did not understand what it meant, but their intentions were unmistakably belittling.[5] Margaret, the natural leader of the three, took seriously her role of oldest sister. She mothered the younger ones, sometimes ferociously, when taunting neighborhood boys had to be dealt with. She climbed and explored like a kitten and could be disarmingly literal.[6] When she was about seven years old, she had an upsetting dream that a "bull cow" had eaten them all up. Attempts to point out her sexual confusion were

Left to right: Jessie, Eleanor, and Margaret Wilson, 1893.
Courtesy of the Very Reverend Francis B. Sayre.

in vain. "I don't care," Margaret said indignantly, "I *dreamt* a bull cow! I can't tell a lie!"[7] Jessie, the classic beauty, was like her mother, compassionate and gentle. Extremely bright, she, like Ellen Wilson, had extraordinary powers of concentration; she was able to read even while her sisters pulled her long hair! Nell liked her own world of imagination, somewhat in defense of her fledgling psyche threatened by two strong, older sisters. One game which they often played was "dividing things." Sometimes they distributed the Greek gods and goddesses, or the world, or their house. Jessie, quick with new ideas, would take first choice, usually Juno or Jupiter, America, or the Wilsons' parlor; Margaret had second draw, and Eleanor, in tears, got what was left.[8]

During her daughters' early years, Ellen made and designed their clothes. She tended to ignore the latest fashion in lieu of her own creations in color and form, and these homemade dresses were later a source of embarrassment to a preteen Nell, who often suffered the double jeopardy of hand-me-downs.[9] However, the three children were far more accustomed to security and love than to embarrassments or denials. Besides doting parents and nurse, they received a large measure of affection from their young uncle, Eddie Axson. To have him in the house again in 1893–1894 was a source of pleasure to everyone in the family.

Eddie, now nearly eighteen, was an especially winning lad. Games of pretend (he was a popular guest at his small nieces' doll tea parties), clever pranks, and laughter came naturally to him. His scientific and mechanical abilities were unique in a household that was all humanities and thumbs. He could repair anything, and he was willing to be helpful. Bicycles, toys, typewriters, sewing machines—all came under his care. He designed and installed an electric bell in the dining room to summon servants, and another at the front door. Woodrow said that Ed was "worth his weight in gold."[10] One day in February (Woodrow was in Baltimore), the two servants were on the verge of hysterics because of a strange and terrible noise in the basement. Armed with his air rifle, Eddie went down the dark stairs to defend the six females in his care. The dragon, which turned out to be an enormous rat thrashing around in a paper bag, was dispatched by Eddie with a few well-placed shots.[11]

Like his three siblings, Eddie was unusually intelligent; like Ellen, he was adaptable, affectionate, and creative. Between this older sister and himself there was an unshakable bond of love. Eddie was also fond of Stockton ("the best brother a fellow ever had"). From his meager salary, Stockton would send his younger brother extra spending money, which Eddie recognized as "dear Stock denying himself for me."[12]

As a Princeton freshman, Eddie's life was smooth and happy except for the problem with his stammering. His achievements on the proficiency examinations in October had placed him in the first division in every subject,[13] so that he was expected to recite—and recite well. These performances, extremely painful at times, were eased somewhat when Professor Bliss Perry arranged to give him private lessons in rhetoric. Once, when talking with Helen Bones, Eddie stammered so dreadfully that he would have given up trying to overcome his impediment had it not been for Ellen and Stockton. For them, he would keep fighting to "get entire control of this vile trouble."[14]

During his second winter in Vermont, Stockton's health appeared to be affected adversely by the climate in Burlington. Ellen was disturbed enough to ask Woodrow to scout the Baltimore area for something that might be suitable for Stockton. Consequently, Woodrow made inquiries which led, in the fall of 1894, to a staff lectureship for his brother-in-law with the American Society for the Extension of University Teaching of Philadelphia. At the end of the Vermont term, Stockton moved to Princeton, from where he could travel to his various teaching assignments.[15]

Ellen and Woodrow wanted to make Joseph Ruggles Wilson's last years "bright and full of love," and, in 1894, to that end, they urged "dear father" to establish himself in the Princeton household. Ellen went a step further and suggested that some rewarding occupation be found "to help anchor him and make him happy again."[16] Their urgings were appreciated but unheeded.

In addition to the trials of an aging father, Woodrow and Ellen recognized the need for Madge to escape from the limitations of Aunt Louisa's household. The Warren Browns had moved to Athens where better educational facilities were available, but, even as Ellen, Stockton, Eddie, Helen Bones, and the two Hoyt cousins had had to leave the South to acquire an education, so, too, would Madge. Ellen was finally able to persuade Aunt Louisa to let Madge spend the summer of 1894 in Princeton.[17]

A tomboyish twelve-year-old girl of untamed spirit, Madge discovered that her sister's ménage was far different from Aunt Louisa's old-fashioned household. In Princeton, humorous and stimulating table conversation, in which everyone took part, required some mental adjustment. Subjects and book titles, all foreign to Madge, rolled off Yankee-sounding tongues. (Yet another visitor suggested that a revolving bookcase for handy reference should be installed in the Wilsons' dining room.) Not only were they waited on by white servants, but dinner was served at *night*, a practice which Aunt Louisa abhorred as certain to give Madge dyspepsia. Madge's three nieces seemed to wear "Sunday" clothes even on weekdays, and neighboring houses stood behind clipped and forbidding hedges. But the crowning blow came when Madge discovered that her big sister was not "Ellie Lou" of Gainesville, Georgia, but simply "Ellen." Madge's onset of weariness and aches, which pointed to a bad case of homesickness, was soon diagnosed as malaria. She spent the next two weeks in bed.[18] These were not the most propitious circumstances for winning this young rebel to the advantage of living in the North in a house which over-flowed with people who came and went in shifts.

Madge's impressions were not unsound. Before permanently absorb-ing a teenage sister and a seventy-two-year-old father into the family, Ellen and Woodrow planned to build a large house. To help pay for it, Woodrow agreed to deliver three addresses in July at the School of Applied Ethics in Plymouth, Massachusetts, and, later in the summer, a series of lectures, to be delivered in July and August, at the Colorado College Summer School in Colorado Springs.[19]

While Woodrow was in the West, Ellen, again with Eddie's help, took the children and a wan Madge to the Jersey shore, where they boarded in a place as adequate, but not as pleasant, as their Long Island retreat of 1893. Margaret, Jessie, and Nell were immediately stricken with digestive problems. Ellen, who saw no point in wasting money on a place that caused misery to the children, returned to Princeton. She left Eddie and Madge, unaffected by the shore cuisine, to finish out the month. The August heat in Princeton turned out to be fierce.[20] On sultry afternoons, Ellen searched in the college library for books that might provide attractive house plans. She found one which showed architectural styles to her liking, and, from this, she began to develop her own design.[21]

Woodrow fared considerably better in Colorado Springs. Since his six lectures were virtually the same as those he had given in November and December at the Brooklyn Institute of Arts and Sciences,[22] he had time to sightsee and relax. He stayed at 1109 North Weber Street with his first cousin, Harriet Woodrow Welles and her husband, Edward, from whose home he enjoyed a view of Pike's Peak. Woodrow found the Rocky Mountain scenery awesome.[23] After an expedition into the mountains, he lectured at a woman's club in Denver, a beautiful city, he observed, full of elegant residences of every conceivable architectural style such as the Columbian Exposition might have erected had there been space enough.[24] He wanted Ellen, caught in New Jersey's heat wave, to be with him to share every new sight and sensation; she insisted that he not feel guilty about the children and herself in the torrid East while he enjoyed the Rocky Mountain air. His presence in the West, she said, would not only help the college (Princeton) but it would extend her husband's professional reputation.[25]

Not long after Woodrow was home from Colorado, he and Ellen had a spat—about what they did not reveal—and it was so upsetting that he called it "that afternoon of unhappiness." The effects left both of them so wretched that he apologized for causing her even a single moment of pain.[26]

While Woodrow addressed the meeting of the American Bar Association in Saratoga Springs, Ellen fulfilled a promise to him to begin the required business of "calling." "Such a bore to put on one's best things, —and *gloves*,—actually!" she said. Her level of tolerance for pretentious people was no higher than Woodrow's. She declined an invitation from one Princeton couple, pseudointellectuals patently not to her taste, and hoped "the poor things" would not trouble to ask again.[27]

Part Four

1895–1902

Ellen Axson Wilson, 1899. Courtesy of William D. Hoyt.

Chapter 13

The House on Library Place

In October 1894, the Wilsons bought a lot for three thousand dollars on Steadman Street (now 82 Library Place) adjacent to the McGill property which they had rented for four years. Edward Southwick Child, an architect from the New York firm of Child & de Goll, had reworked in considerable detail Ellen's preliminary house plans, and rendered an estimate of seventy-four hundred dollars on the eleven-room house.[1] Joseph Ruggles Wilson sent the two thousand dollars which he had earlier promised his son, and, for the remainder of the costs, Woodrow planned to borrow seven thousand dollars from the wealthy Princeton trustee, Moses Taylor Pyne.[2] Child's estimate shocked Woodrow, who had set a limit of seven thousand dollars for everything,[3] and he was further dismayed to discover through an intermediary, Cornelius Cuyler Cuyler, that Pyne intended to charge the customary interest rate of $5\frac{1}{2}$ percent rather than the $4\frac{1}{2}$ percent which Cuyler had led Woodrow to expect.[4] Woodrow cancelled all building plans, even as he went on his "knees" to pray that his wife might be able to bear the disappointment.[5] Astonished that Woodrow might find her lacking in "sense or self-possession," Ellen not only agreed that his decision was sensible, but she was relieved that they would not be so encumbered financially.[6]

Ellen's largesse renewed Woodrow's determination to provide the house that she wanted. He said that he was even willing to scrap his plans for two scholarly works, one, a history of the American people, the other, "Philosophy of Politics," and write solely for money. But striving for mercenary goals would kill him, he told Ellen, an outcome that would not be "serving" her.[7]

In January and February, while Woodrow was lecturing at Hopkins, a blizzard in Princeton, followed by several days of extremely cold weather, made the McGill house so uncomfortable that Ellen complained.[8] The inadequacy of this rented property and the sudden death from peritonitis of Annie Howe's husband, Dr. George Howe, Jr., revived Woodrow's determination to build a commodious, comfortable home. Now surrogate father to Annie's children, he wanted living quarters that would accommodate the Wilsons' immediate and extended family.

Cornelius Cuyler, renewing his role as intermediary, had persuaded Pyne to reduce to 4½ percent the needed loan. Cuyler advised Woodrow to close the matter by accepting the new terms so that "you may soon have a home in which you may live to end your days in Princeton for we could never spare you from the old town." But Woodrow, still offended, declined the offer.[9] Instead, he sold the land on Washington Road for thirty-six hundred dollars, and secured a mortgage for seven thousand dollars from the Mutual Life Insurance Company of New York.[10]

Ellen began to work again with Child to sketch a house with the same basic exterior, but more shallow. She eliminated such extras as a back staircase, a bay window in the sitting room, a "cemented" terrace, and a wide overhang at the back.[11] On about June 10, 1895, ground was broken for a two-story, half-timbered Tudor house, with an overhanging upper story and full basement. The third floor, to be finished later, would provide space for extra bedrooms and storage. When the final bids came in with an estimate of almost fourteen thousand dollars, Ellen wanted to postpone the building—but her husband was not to be turned back.[12]

To meet these burgeoning expenses, Woodrow agreed to give three series of five lectures, at $250 a series, for the American Society for the Extension of University Teaching. The first would be delivered in July, the second and third in the fall. The editor of *Harper's Magazine* invited him to write six essays on the life of George Washington to be published in installments beginning in early 1896. For these, Woodrow would be paid a total of $1,800.[13]

There was no vacation in the summer of 1895 while Woodrow assembled and organized the material for *George Washington*. Ellen, who protected him from interruptions,[14] was also his "critic and mentor." He was abashed, he told her, to do his work under her constant scrutiny, to keep his mind constantly under her eye, "with its *in*sight." "My defence is that you are a woman, and *loyal* beyond all words!"[15] The "loyal woman" attended to her own intellectual nurture through books. On her reading list for 1895–1896 were Plato, Homer, and Herodotus; Walter Bagehot (probably his *Physics and Politics*); John Richard

Green's *A Short History of the English People*; William Milligan Sloane's *Life of Napoleon Bonaparte*; Mariana Griswold Van Rensselaer's essays on English cathedrals; the literary critic Charles Mills Gayley; American short-story writer Mary Wilkins Freeman; and, always, her favorites—Shakespeare, Milton, Coleridge, Keats, and the Brownings. She frequently quoted from the lesser-known English poets, Francis Quarles, Robert Herrick, Richard Lovelace, and John Dryden.[16] Years later, Nell said that she had never known "a woman with more versatile literary taste or one who was better read" than her mother—poetry and philosophy, history, religion, the great novels, and "every book on art she could get her hands on."[17]

By the time that classes began in the fall, Woodrow was exhausted. In October, he was in bed for a week, which delayed the completion of the first installment of *George Washington*. His six lectures scheduled to begin at the Brooklyn Institute of Arts and Sciences were postponed until October 10. By the end of November, with the third installment on Washington due at *Harper's Magazine*, he was again on his back with "a sharp attack of indigestion."[18] By December 30, however, essay number three was finished, and, on January 22, he went to Baltimore to begin his ninth year of lectures at Johns Hopkins, an interregnum which Ellen now called her "annual widowhood."[19]

After Woodrow left for Baltimore, Ellen was in bed for two weeks with "nausea, indigestion, and a low grade fever." Her sickroom, "a bower of flowers, chiefly exquisite roses," was further brightened by daily visits from Jenny Hibben who showed the solicitude of a sister.[20] Woodrow slipped up to Princeton to see her on the weekend of January 31, even though he, himself, felt far from robust.

Once on her feet again, Ellen was engrossed in the details of the rapidly evolving house. She bombarded Woodrow with frequent reports, not all of which were encouraging. February 12, 1896: "The post of the staircase [designed by the architectural firm] . . . is rather ugly and queer looking. . . . However, it will do well enough."[21] A day later: "The mill-man has . . . an appointment with the architect . . . to see about the storm doors. They haven't been made and the man doesn't understand about them. I regret to say that your window-seat is not made either. He says it was not ordered and is not on his plans. . . . It is now an 'extra' and will cost us eight dollars. . . . The stained glass [for the sliding doors to the dining room] is going to be a great deal less than we feared" ($36.00 rather than $75.00).[22] On February 14: "[The contractor] says . . . the side walls of the third floor ought to be lathed because children playing up there would certainly run or fall over the edges. . . . The whole thing . . . would cost us less than ten dollars." She asked Woodrow to shop in Baltimore for window shades. A local estimate was "shocking."[23] February 15: "I can cut down the shade bill . . . by using the old ones in the kitchen etc. etc. . . . The stair-builders have disappointed us. They were to have come the first of the week but they are not here yet. . . . It has delayed the carpenters who today have had to quit work until the stair builders are through."[24] February 19: "The stair-builders came Monday and will soon be through. . . . In fact the whole house is getting to look so elegant that it is hard to believe it is really ours!"[25]

While the carpenters were finishing upstairs, the pipes in the northeast corner of the basement froze and burst, but to wrap them in "mineral wool" would cost another fifteen dollars.[26] Ellen also asked Woodrow for money so that she could shop for fabrics and some furnishings at the spring sales.[27]

He responded painstakingly to her every concern. By all means do the lathing; have the pipes properly insulated; order *all* new window shades of the best quality, but to save time, would she not write the order herself? As for her shopping, he apologized for not having sent her a check before. He found it "incredible" that she had managed so long on the small sum he had left with her.[28]

During his spare time in Baltimore, Woodrow had concentrated on completing the last chapters of *George Washington*. Despite Ellen's continual reports on the problems with the house, he had fewer distractions than he had had in the fall of 1895 in Princeton. Annie Howe had moved to Philadelphia to live with her son, Wilson, who was employed there. This did not relieve Woodrow of his responsibility to advise and counsel—and in due course, to contribute substantially to Annie's support—but he could easily visit and reassure her en route to and from Baltimore.[29] Shortly before Woodrow returned to Princeton, Ellen informed him that the house, virtually finished, was "a dream."[30]

By mid-March, the Wilsons were in their new home. Ellen devised an ingenious scheme for organizing the move: she hired "ten movers for one day rather than one mover for ten days," and, almost overnight, the house was in order.[31] Before she squandered money on the work-

The Woodrow Wilson home, 82 Library Place, Princeton, N.J.
Photograph by Jon W. Saunders.

ers, Ellen had planned in her sketch pad where the furniture should be placed.[32] Margaret, Jessie, and Nell moved their own precious possessions—a canary and a fat, white cat named "Puffin." On their first night in the new dwelling, Joseph Ruggles Wilson was there to pray a blessing on the new home while all of the family knelt together.[33]

Chapter 14

New Friends, Old Patterns

During most of the spring in Baltimore, Woodrow had not been well. He attributed his ailments to digestive disturbances, but he was clearly worn to a frazzle. Sensing his need for a complete change, Ellen urged him to take the advice of his classmate, Dr. Charles Wellman Mitchell of Baltimore, and spend the summer of 1896 in England and Scotland. Woodrow resisted the idea because it meant another painful separation from Ellen; but she assured her husband that she could love him as "profoundly and as proudly," could take the same deep joy in him, as if he were in Princeton, and she wanted him to have the "mental refreshment."[1]

Woodrow had admitted to Howard Pyle, his illustrator for *George Washington*, that he was exhausted, with barely enough strength to take care of the "alarming arrears" in his work at Princeton.[2] Ellen's well-executed move to their own home helped Woodrow to tend to his classroom duties and to finish the two final installments of *George Washington* with a minimum of disruption. Harper and Brothers contracted with him in May to publish the six installments in book form, a volume which appeared later in the year.[3] It was dedicated to "E.A.W. without whose sympathy and counsel literary work would lack inspiration." About the same time, Woodrow arranged with Houghton, Mifflin to publish a second collection of essays entitled *Mere Literature and Other Essays*, a small volume dedicated to Stockton Axson: "By every gift of mind a critic, and lover of letters, By every gift of heart a friend."[4]

Woodrow now relented and followed Ellen's advice to book passage abroad for what he now recognized as "an imperatively needed rest."[5] In addition to Ellen's persuasiveness, unexpected support had come in the form of a check from a Princeton friend, Mrs. Susan Dod Brown, a wealthy widow who lived around the corner from the Wilsons. In 1890 and 1891, Mrs. Brown had given funds to erect two dormitories, Dod and Brown halls, named for her brother and her husband. The college was important to her, and Woodrow Wilson was important to the college. He was inclined at first to refuse the financial help, but Ellen was adamant.[6] Her concerns about his health were justified when not long before Woodrow sailed, he suffered an attack of pain in his right arm and severe "writer's cramp" in his right hand. Although he would assure Ellen five weeks later that his arm was "getting well as calmly and steadily as you please" and gave him "scarcely a twinge," he would write all of his letters to her from England with "this poor old [clumsy] left hand, . . . such a painfully slow process."[7]

On Saturday, May 30, 1896, Ellen went to New York with her husband to see him off on the S.S. *Ethiopia* for his first ocean voyage. This separation, the longest since their marriage, would last for fifteen weeks. After Woodrow boarded ship, Ellen spent the afternoon at the Metropolitan Museum of Art, her first visit there since she was at the Art Students League. When she got home to the children, Margaret, in particular, insisted on knowing exactly *where* in the ocean her father was, something Ellen would like to have known herself.[8]

While Woodrow toured Scotland and England, Ellen devoted the summer to her relatives, art, and her children. Stockton, now in fine spirits after a brief bout of midwinter depression, had accepted a position for the fall as full professor of English at Adelphi College in Brooklyn. Before his new teaching assignment began, he planned to spend August relaxing in the Finger Lakes region of New York.[9] Eddie, who had made "first" in every single subject during his junior year at Princeton, was asked by William Francis Magie, professor of physics, to assist during the summer in rewriting an elementary physics textbook. In addition to his competency in science, Ed had learned both shorthand and typing, a combination of skills which Magie found highly attractive in this young assistant.[10] On June 16, Madge arrived from Athens, Georgia, for the summer. A second-year student at the Lucy Cobb School, she had taken "first honour" in everything, the only person in her class to do so.[11] Woodrow's father was spending the summer in Richmond, Virginia. Florence Hoyt, who had finished her junior year at Bryn Mawr, came to Princeton for a vacation but left soon to join Mary in Rome, Georgia, to be with their terminally ill mother. Uncle Tom Hoyt appeared unannounced and stayed three days. The tasteful new home of his niece was in itself a lure for the Reverend Dr. Hoyt, whose pomposity Ellen could tolerate only in small doses. He raved about Madge, whom he had never seen before; found Eddie "a perfect wonder, so strong and complete in mind, body

Margaret Randolph Axson, 1896.
Courtesy of the Very Reverend Francis B. Sayre.

and character"; there was "never such a young man" as Stockton; and, as for Ellen, his praises were so effusive that she dismissed them as nonsense.[12]

This was the same Uncle Tom, who, when visiting the Wilsons overnight in Middletown, had left his muddy boots outside his bedroom door to be cleaned and polished. Not considered an appropriate job for the two female servants, the bootblack's chore was done by Woodrow, who left the boots ready for Hoyt when he got up the next morning.[13] This uncle of Ellen's had managed more skillfully than any other of her relatives to look after his own interests; he had even avoided the disruption of his career by the Civil War. (Joseph Ruggles Wilson allegedly described him as "a wolf in sheep's clothing," and Woodrow had once said, "There is unquestionably an odd contradiction in 'Uncle Tom's' character.")[14] Unlike his philanthropic brother, Dr. Will Hoyt, Tom had remained relatively aloof from sister Janie's children, his orphaned nieces and nephews. Ellen's marriage to Woodrow Wilson, which now brought prestige to the family, was a source of considerable satisfaction to him. He savored the honor of being three times the guest preacher at the chapel services at the College of New Jersey and Princeton University.[15]

While Woodrow was abroad, Ellen resumed her artwork for the first time in ten summers. She completed four landscapes in watercolor, one of which was to be hung in the parlor. From the college's art collection, she copied a large English landscape etched by French artist Alfred-Louis Brunet-Debaines. She had drawn crayon enlargements of George Washington, Daniel Webster, William Gladstone, Edmund Burke, and Walter Bagehot, and a splendid likeness of Joseph Ruggles Wilson, all portraits to be hung in Woodrow's study.[16] About this time, she copied from a loan exhibit at Princeton an oil painting of a Madonna by the French artist Guillaume-Adolphe Bouguereau. Enchanted with Bouguereau's Madonna, Ellen would have liked the original, a purchase at that time quite beyond their means. (Woodrow, who thought Ellen's copy *better* than the original, saw that it was hung in every subsequent Wilson residence.)[17] She placed reproductions of two of her favorite sculptures, Winged Victory and a bust of the Apollo Belvedere, on the mantel in the family sitting room. At some time, perhaps in their recent move, "Victory" had had a wing broken, but Ellen found a handyman in Princeton who could mend it. When he came to pick up the statue, he said, "Give me the head, ma'am; I can put that back on, too, so you wouldn't hardly notice it." With a mien as serious as the repairman's, Ellen thanked him, and said that she wished she *did* have the head.[18]

In order to enjoy more thoroughly Woodrow's weekly letters about the places he was visiting in Great Britain, Ellen read voraciously in books about art and travel. She wrote frequently to keep her husband up-to-date on his professional correspondence, most of which she attended to herself. Once, when she was unsure of his exact address, she sent a letter to his London bank, the Cheque Bank, Ltd., but forgot to put Woodrow's name on the envelope. The English bank clerk who opened it was not a little startled to see a letter that began, "My own darling."[19] When Woodrow sailed from Glasgow for New York in late August, he resolved to return some day to the lake district with Ellen to share its beauty and serenity with her.[20]

Despite his "threatened writer's cramp," Woodrow began work on a major oration which the Princeton Board of Trustees had invited him to deliver at the college's sesquicentennial celebration to be held on October 20, 21, and 22. With Ellen's help as amanuensis, and sometimes pecking out words on his typewriter with his left hand, he slowly put together "Princeton in the Nation's Service." When he read the final draft to Ellen, she suggested that the ending needed wings, "something to lift it." To give him an idea, she cited John Milton's *Areopagitica*, the first great treatise on freedom of the press. The distinct change in style of the closing twenty-seven lines of the address as delivered supports Stockton's later assertion that his sister contributed the ideas for most of it.[21]

The sesquicentennial celebration was a "brilliant, *dazzling* success from first to last," Ellen wrote to Mary Hoyt. "And *such* an ovation as Woodrow received! I never imagined anything like it. And think of *so* delighting *such* an audience, the most distinguished, everyone says, that has ever been assembled in America; famous men from all parts of Europe. They declared there had been 'nothing to equal it since Burke.'" From her seat in Alexander Hall in the ladies' gallery, Ellen heard it all. She watched while some of Woodrow's classmates and colleagues "simply fell on his neck and wept for joy." It was all a sweet triumph, not a selfish success, and it all redounded to the honor of what was now "Princeton University."[22]

Ellen was pleased that Rosalie's husband, Mac DuBose, could be with them for the celebration. During the previous summer, Mac was in England, sent by his congregation for a rest and change, and the two wives had made an aborted attempt to have their husbands tour together.[23] Now in Asheville, with her growing family of three girls and a boy, Rosalie, too, was happy that Mac could be in Princeton and report directly to her about Ellen's "beautiful home, the children," and best of all, "your sweet self—just as fresh and lovely as ever." Rosalie had always believed that Ellen might marry a *great* man; now she was gratified to know that her friend had such a husband.[24]

As a consequence of the sesquicentennial celebration, Princeton had raised money to expand the campus and faculty, and with his eye on some of the unrestricted funds, Woodrow began to advocate a chair in history. The man he wanted was Frederick Jackson Turner, who had a Ph.D. from Johns Hopkins and was now a professor at the University of Wisconsin. Ellen prepared for the Turners an estimate of living expenses in Princeton based on the monthly budget of the Wilson family that "averaged ten persons." Two of these, Ellen explained to Turner, were servants, and two of them were "very large and hearty college boys" (i.e., Eddie Axson and George Howe). The monthly Wilson expenditures were: food and lights, $100; servants, $29; coal, $12; water, $4; and house rental for a new family, she approximated at $42. Items such as clothes, recreation, and charities were, of course, personal matters.[25] President Patton and the trustees rejected Woodrow's recommendation, however, because Turner, a Unitarian, might be offensive to the orthodox Presbyterians on the board of trustees. The decision left Woodrow "chagrined and mortified."[26]

Ellen shared his indignation over the inept handling of the Turner affair and over larger academic issues which increasingly indicated a lack of vision and leadership on Patton's part. "We can't hope," she said, "to be anything but a respectable, old-fashioned Presbyterian College; before [the sesquicentennial] we were that simply and without pretense; now we have merely made ourselves ridiculous before the whole academic world by making big promises that we have neither the will nor the power to carry out." Ellen confided to Annie Louise Perry and to the Hibbens that Woodrow might even leave Princeton.[27]

In the winter of 1897, not yet up to par physically, Woodrow began his tenth year of lectures at The Johns Hopkins University. He left sister Annie and her small daughter at Library Place, which, as usual, was more gratifying to him than to Ellen. Her first letter to Woodrow was late because Annie had occupied the library for her own writing, and, for Ellen, there seemed to be no other "convenient time or place."[28] Ellen's letters to Woodrow in January and February of 1897 lacked their usual enthusiasm and vitality, due in part, at least, to her own state of health. In December she had gone to a masseuse in Philadelphia,[29] and, in January, her physician had put her to bed for a week because of soreness in the vermiform appendix.[30] She was allowed to be up after several days, but the soreness persisted, and she did not go outdoors for three weeks.[31]

Concerned about his wife's health, Woodrow reminded her that if she wrecked herself, *his* career was over. He would be "absolutely *naught*" without her, he said. "Divorced from you, I should be nothing,—you would keep not only the children, but all my capital stock and character of every sort. I am not blue; this is one of my sane hours, when I can see without vanity or prepossession."[32] It was a strange note for him to inject in a letter to Ellen. The touchy situation with Patton's leadership at Princeton, the slow recovery of Woodrow's incapacitated right hand, and his general chafing at the restraints of academic life no doubt made him harder to live with in 1896 and 1897. Stockton Axson later asserted that his brother-in-law had returned from England in 1896 a different man, with a sharper sense of mission in the world.[33]

Woodrow's tenth year (1897) at Johns Hopkins was boring and unrewarding. His lectures, delivered to a popular audience, were spoiled, he thought, by dilution. "Nothing happens," he complained to Ellen. "I have nothing to do but think how lonely I am."[34] She urged him to try to escape loneliness by "ceasing to be *alone*." She suggested that he "go to see some of those bright women [who] . . . by their appreciation of you ought to reassure you as to your 'weight and significance.'"[35] This was a kind of therapy which Ellen would later advocate—and suffer from, because Woodrow followed her advice. But at this particular moment, he dashed up to Princeton for a short weekend with her. The results were salutary for both.[36]

In May 1897, the Wilsons made an important decision, postponed for more than six years, to unite with a Princeton church. They had alternately attended the First and Second Presbyterian churches, but were dissatisfied with both, partially because the two pulpits had a frequent change of ministers. With the arrival, in February 1897, of the Reverend John Hendrick De Vries at the Second Presbyterian Church, Woodrow's exacting standards for a preacher were finally met.[37] In March, he wrote to Dr. Hazen to ask for their letters of transfer from the Congregational church in Middletown, and on May 5, Ellen and Woodrow Wilson were received into the membership of the Second Presbyterian Church.[38] The First Presbyterian Church had its triumph that spring, however, when President and Mrs. Grover Cleveland, who had retired to Princeton from the White House, began to worship in that congregation.[39] The Clevelands' daughter, Ruth, became a playmate of Eleanor, and the two families, almost the only "prominent Democrats" in town, became friends as well as neighbors.

After Eddie Axson and George Howe's graduation from Princeton in June 1897, and the family entertaining that ensued, the Wilsons and Madge went south in July for a vacation in the Blue Ridge Mountains near Front Royal, Virginia, at "Mountain View," the antebellum mansion of Colonel and Mrs. Robert M. Stribling. An old family which had seen better days, the Striblings now took paying guests in their home.[40] The holiday in Virginia was important to the Wilsons, for here they met two women who at once became close and fiercely loyal friends. They were Mary Randolph and Lucy Marshall Smith, unmarried daughters of the Reverend Dr. Henry M. Smith, a former chaplain in the Confederate Army and later pastor of the Third Presbyterian Church of New Orleans. He had been an old friend and associate of Joseph Ruggles Wilson and of Ellen's cousin, the Reverend Dr. Benjamin M. Palmer, pastor of the First Presbyterian Church in New Orleans. Lucy, born in 1862, and Mary, in 1866, were, like Woodrow and Ellen, children of the manse who grew up in the South during Reconstruction. "Cousin Mary" and "Cousin Lucy" soon became as close to Ellen as her girlhood friends Rosalie and Beth. The Smiths were the only women other than those early companions with whom Ellen ever established a first-name intimacy. Cultivated, witty, and intelligent, the Smith sisters were favorites of both Wilsons. The two single women enjoyed having a compatible male friend like Woodrow, but it was Ellen whom they adored. Lucy told Ellen: "Frankly, you have truly bewitched me."[41]

Chapter 15

Extended Family Matters

The fall of 1897 marked a different grouping of the Wilsons' extended family.
Mary Hoyt, after two years in the Midwest, now taught at the Bryn
Mawr School in Baltimore. Stockton, who had joined the faculty
of Adelphi College, took Madge with him to study in the Adelphi
Academy division. Annie Howe now lived in New York near her son,
Wilson; she and Wilson rented a house in Brooklyn at 474 Waverly
Avenue, where Stockton and Madge took rooms. Through the help of
his Uncle Woodrow, George Howe had become tutor to the young son
of the James Waddel Alexanders who would be spending the year in
Europe. Eddie, tanned and handsome after a summer job on Lake
George, was back in the Wilson household while he worked on his
master's degree in chemistry at Princeton.[1] Ellen relied upon Eddie
while Woodrow was frequently away giving speeches—twenty-four of
them in the academic year 1897–1898.[2]

Unhappy about their separations during Woodrow's annual stint in
Baltimore—ten years altogether—Ellen wrote, in June 1897, to Woodrow's friend, John Bates Clark, professor of political economy at Columbia University, to suggest the possibility of a lectureship there instead of at Hopkins. Her tactful letter brought a favorable response
from Clark; but John W. Burgess, the chairman of the Department of
Political Science, was not a Wilson admirer, in part because of Woodrow's decidedly critical review a few years earlier of a book Burgess had
written. The Columbia idea died aborning.[3]

In 1897, a significant change took place in the lives of Margaret,
Jessie, and Eleanor Wilson: they acquired a German governess, Clara
Böhm. Since the fall of 1894, Ellen had held regular classes for her
daughters every weekday morning, from October through June. Whatever her methods, the results were stunning. A few months after her
fifth birthday, Nell, the youngest of the three pupils, could read "flu-
ently anything she could understand." Early in the children's schooling,
Ellen read aloud to them from Shakespeare's plays and the English
poets, from mythology and the Greek classics. Jessie and Nell, in par-

ticular, were drawn to Plato and talked about him at incredibly young ages.[4]

When Fräulein Böhm joined the Wilson household, she found three small, eager pupils. A shy young woman "with prominent teeth, hair in a pompadour and fringed bangs," Fräulein had wanted to leave her native Leipzig because, as an "old maid," she felt in the way. Her English was excellent, and she set about to teach first German, and then French, to the Wilson girls. (Ellen also worked with Fräulein to polish her skills in German.) Helped by constant conversation in the nursery, the children were competent enough after a year to quarrel in the new language. They gleefully discovered that their more colorful accusations were a mystery to their father who could laboriously read German but could not understand it when spoken.[5]

After one year as governess, Fräulein, who continued to live with the Wilsons and tutor the girls in languages, became a teacher at a private school opened by Mrs. William Dodge Scott.[6] When Margaret, Jessie, and Nell enrolled at Mrs. Scott's, Ellen learned that her daughters were "the most intelligent, the best-trained, and the most thorough" pupils that the headmistress had ever seen.[7]

With a governess in the household, Ellen accepted an invitation from Harry and Edith Reid to visit in Baltimore in late February, when Woodrow was scheduled to deliver the Caroline Donovan lectures at Hopkins. Edith Reid had been a great admirer of Woodrow since she first met him in February 1894 at a Hopkins gathering, and she was now eager to appraise his wife.

Ellen had very nearly cancelled the trip because of a midwinter slump in health. She tired easily, had a poor appetite, and her hand was "nervously jerky." A doctor in New York, who found her "nervous," with "stomach and liver misbehaving a little," prescribed calomel and salts for four nights and four mornings. The medicines made her nauseous; Woodrow feared that she was pregnant.[8] But Ellen went to Baltimore and Woodrow's friends there were not disappointed. One of them told Stockton: "I have just had one of the great treats of my life in meeting Mrs. Woodrow Wilson. To find a person who isn't busying herself to write books and all that sort of thing, and yet knows so much and appreciates so much, is . . . more a person of high education than so many of the people I meet who pass as intelligentsia."[9]

Before the Donovan lectures at Hopkins, Woodrow had gone to Washington for three weeks to do writing and research and to address the Washington Princeton Alumni Association. For the first time in his life, he visited the Congress. In the afternoons, as he watched the Senate and House in action, he felt again the youthful longing for public life. Yet he told Ellen: "Washington is nothing *but* the seat of the national government,—and of an idle society of rich people."[10]

On Valentine's Day, a week before Ellen was to meet Woodrow in Baltimore, he wrote to apologize for having pained her when he had abruptly declined to hear her read a passage to him from Arnold's *Sweetness and Light*, which "interpreted" Ellen's "loving judgment" of her husband.[11] Woodrow's letter made Ellen cry. "As far as there was any fault," she protested, "it was *altogether mine* for being so full of my thought that I could not wait to choose my occasion better. . . . Ah, if you were only here, and I were *close* in your arms and could close your mouth with kisses when you begin to talk so."[12]

The three Donovan lectures in February 1898 concluded Woodrow's appearances at The Johns Hopkins University. He also relinquished the lectureships at the New York Law School and the Brooklyn Institute of Arts and Sciences because a group of eight wealthy Princeton alumni contracted to supplement his salary by twenty-five hundred dollars per annum for the next five years.[13] The contributors were afraid of losing this distinguished young professor who was continually receiving recognition outside of Princeton.[14]

These honors were a source of pride to Ellen and a triumph to Woodrow's father, who, despite his son's urgings that he move to Princeton, clung stubbornly to his independence. After his retirement from teaching, Dr. Wilson had served several southern churches as interim pastor and he had continued as Stated Clerk of the Presbyterian Church in the United States, a post he had held since 1865. His increasingly poor health led him to resign the clerkship in May 1898, and thereafter he came to Princeton for what turned into a brief visit. He found his son absent and his son's home overflowing with guests, among whom were Annie Howe and Lucy and Mary Smith.[15]

In mid-July, the Wilson family, Fräulein Böhm, Stockton, and Lucy and Mary Smith, went to East Gloucester, Massachusetts, for a six-week vacation. They rented a cottage, "The Flying Jib," and took their meals at the nearby inn.[16] The choice of New England was made, in part, to please Stockton, whose erratic health, given various labels by physicians, was clearly more mental than physical. His bouts with "nervous depression" were becoming more intense, yet he always managed to bounce back to periods of high creativity. Now thirty-one years old, he was more leery than ever of marriage, something which Ellen felt might be his salvation. She fervently wished that Stockton would choose Mary Smith, a woman Ellen could "take to her heart." Stockton recognized his sister's concern about his welfare, and he agreed with her about the merits of marriage over bachelorhood. But he knew himself to be a person too introspective, of uncertain strength, and with an unpredictable future—qualifications which excluded marriage, at least for the time being. "Miss Smith" he regarded as the most satisfactory woman friend whom he had met for some time—and he hoped to keep her as such.[17]

Stockton's reluctance disappointed Ellen, but she could not quarrel with his reasoning. Her love and understanding always encouraged him during his bouts of depression, but her capacity to continue in this giving role had its limits. The needs of her own family, and Woodrow's in particular, made continual demands on her strength. She could not forget those final months of her father's life that almost crushed her, nor could she and Stockton fail to recognize the similarity of his symptoms to those of their father. Stockton hoped that when the time came for Ed to marry, he would find someone whom Ellen could readily "take to her heart." "I am looking to him to do *several* things that I have missed," Stockton said.[18]

With the air now cleared about his marital intentions, Stockton returned to his teaching post at Adelphi. Eddie, after finishing his M.A. degree from Princeton, had enrolled in the fall of 1898 for further graduate work at the Massachusetts Institute of Technology.[19] Following the one year at Adelphi in Stockton's brotherly care, Madge made a strike for independence by entering the Woman's College of Baltimore (now Goucher College). The transition from the provincial South to a more cosmopolitan North had gone so rapidly that Ellen was uneasy for fear that the seventeen-year-old Madge had gone "too far too fast."[20]

While she was still in Brooklyn, Madge had upset Stockton by announcing that her mind was "fully made up to go to Bryn Mawr College" in the fall of 1898. The news was unwelcome on two counts. Stockton dreaded going back to the "old manner of life with its barren loneliness," and he was worried about Madge's relationship to Aunt Louisa. Because of the entrance requirements at Bryn Mawr, Madge needed a foreign language, a deficiency which she planned to remove by studying German during the summer with Fräulein Böhm. This meant that Madge did not intend to visit Georgia, an omission which Stockton believed would cause "more pain and disappointment" to Aunt Louisa than "we have any right to inflict."[21] Stockton was reluctant to disrupt his younger sister's plans to prepare for Bryn Mawr, yet he felt that she *must* go to Georgia for at least part of the summer. He turned the whole sticky problem over to Ellen.

To begin with, Ellen persuaded Madge to change colleges. She disapproved of Bryn Mawr because the girls there were under "no more restraint or oversight than college men," and Woodrow, undoubtedly biased, thought the intellectual atmosphere bad. Once the choice of college was comfortably settled, Stockton brought up another problem: Madge and money. Stockton's budget for the summer was in trouble, and he suggested that Madge's visit to Georgia might now be postponed until the Christmas holidays. Stockton thought that Madge could perhaps manage in the summer with less than the "$4.00 per week" allowance which he, as her guardian, had given her throughout the school year. To turn Madge's inheritance over to her "in a lump sum next year in Baltimore" would not be advisable, Stockton believed, because he thought that Madge had not learned the value of money. "Boys are supposed to understand this," he said, "a good deal earlier than girls."[22] After a consultation with Woodrow, Ellen arranged to advance the money for Madge's summer travel and allowance, even though Ellen knew that her husband might have to borrow the amount that Madge needed.[23]

When Madge entered the Woman's College of Baltimore, Ellen could rely on the Hoyt cousins for periodic oversight of her young sister. Mary, an English teacher, and Florence, a graduate (1898) of Bryn Mawr in biology and chemistry, were both on the faculty of the Bryn Mawr School in Baltimore. The two sisters were now helping the younger Hoyts, Margaret and Will, with their education. An unexpected financial burden faced the Hoyts that fall when Florence, after a fall from her bicycle, developed tuberculosis of the bone in one leg and was unable to teach. Eventually, her leg had to be amputated.[24]

The news in 1898 from Ellen's old friends varied. Agnes and Arthur Tedcastle had moved to the Boston area. After the birth of her fifth child and second son, David St. Pierre,[25] Rosalie was unusually slow in regaining her strength. The arrival in March of Beth's eighth baby left her "more feeble" than she had ever been under similar circumstances.

"This long, long separation . . . is only brightened by the thoughts of your present happiness," Beth wrote.[26] Janie Porter Chandler wrote occasionally, but the sheer geographical distance between New Jersey and California impaired their relationship. Janie, now the mother of a five-year-old girl, had become stronger in the dry southwestern climate, but in 1898, after a long illness, she had undergone major surgery and was slowly recovering.[27] Concerned about the apparent deterioration in the health of these friends, Ellen could find some exceptions: sturdy "Old Anna," the unmarried schoolteacher, and the vigorous Smith sisters, from New Orleans.

In contrast to Rosalie, Beth, and Janie, Ellen seemed to be leading a charmed life as the end of the century approached. Her family and close relatives, Florence Hoyt excepted, were healthy, happy, and creatively occupied, a situation to which she and Woodrow had contributed significantly. The Wilsons' life in Princeton might now be said to fulfill the two touchstones of Wordsworth: "plain living and high thinking." They had established warm friendships with families that included Jenny and Jack Hibben, Annie Louise and Bliss Perry, Philena and Henry (Harry) Fine, and Eliza Ricketts and her daughter, Henrietta. During the college year, the Wilsons, the Perrys, and the Hibbens often took tea on Sunday afternoons with Eliza and Henrietta Ricketts at 80 Stockton Street. The conversation centered on "books and theories of life," occasionally touched on politics, and rarely descended to gossip.[28] In this group, congenial in mind and spirit, the closest friends were the Hibbens and Wilsons. The Wilsons were less intimate with such prominent Princeton families as the Allan Marquands, the Grover Clevelands, and the Junius Spencer Morgans, whose mansion, "Constitution Hill," built in 1897, was just west of Library Place. Ellen gave a considerable amount of time to the local benevolent societies and there were frequent teas and receptions at which she was asked to pour and to help receive.[29]

While friendships and family were always an important part of Ellen's life, its dominant focus was her husband. "You elevate, you stimulate, you satisfy, you delight me: every part of me enjoys you with an infinite ardour. . . . you satisfy and delight my *pride* as well as my love," she told him.[30] Now a distinguished teacher and literary scholar, Woodrow worked confidently on what would become a five-volume *History of the American People*.[31] The grueling lecture circuit and the writing to enhance his income were no longer necessary. He could decline unappealing requests that continued to come for literary contributions—such as the one from a southern publisher who, Ellen thought, was "a good sort of goose." She suggested that Woodrow write "an amiable little letter" and refrain from telling him what an "ass" he was.[32]

One commitment which Woodrow made unhesitatingly was to deliver, in late October 1898, five Thomas Museum Endowment Lectures at Richmond College (now the University of Richmond). This was apparently the first visit he had ever made to the capital city of his native state, and he relished a chance to enjoy its historic sights. He stayed with a fellow student from the University of Virginia Law School, Archibald W. Patterson.[33]

In January 1899, Ellen learned that on the twenty-third, Beth Erwin had died at age thirty-eight. Ellen unburdened her "great sorrow" to Anna Harris.

> [Beth] literally gave her life to her children, of whom she has left eight. They were terribly poor and she has all these years done *everything* for them and taught school besides, kept so cheerful through it all too, and retained her vivid interest in books and affairs. It was a truly *heroic* life, but the end was inevitable. She has been slowly dying for months from nervous prostration. . . . I cannot somehow shake off for a moment the weight it has laid upon my spirits.

Ellen said that she could not allow her grief to show because Woodrow "is almost terribly dependent on me to keep up his spirits and to 'rest' him." "If I am just a little sky-blue he immediately becomes blue-black!"[34] That she could not overtly grieve added to her pain, already overlaid with remorse because she had evaded opportunities when in the South to visit Beth. As a final token of love, Ellen and Woodrow later assumed responsibility for the education of their namesake, Ellen Woodrow Erwin, only twelve years old when her mother died.[35]

Woodrow's continuing need to be rested was not a whim. After his illness in 1896, Ellen watched him constantly to detect signs of exhaustion, and by the middle of the spring semester of 1899, she was convinced that he needed another rest and change. Enlisting Jenny Hibben's help, Ellen persuaded her husband to have another summer in Great Britain. He agreed, but only if she, too, went, a plan which, in late April, seemed feasible. However, in early June, Margaret, Jessie, and Nell came down with whooping cough, which Ellen then contracted from the children. Instead of Ellen's accompanying her husband, Stockton was now to join Woodrow on a bicycle tour of Britain.[36]

The main reason Ellen gave up the trip abroad was the children's whooping cough, which, if improperly cared for, could lead to serious complications. Margaret, still whooping vigorously well into July, also suffered a recurrence of "a nervous twitch" which had developed in early childhood, and she had frightened Ellen by suddenly walking in her sleep.[37] A second reason why Ellen decided against the trip was simply to encourage Stockton to go in celebration of his appointment, on June 12, as assistant professor of English at Princeton University, a position Stockton had won because of his growing reputation as a teacher.[38]

After Woodrow and Stockton sailed on June 17, Ellen immersed herself in books—novels, poetry, and the two volumes of *The Letters of Elizabeth Barrett Browning*, edited by Frederic G. Kenyon.[39]

While Ellen read to the children from Donald Grant Mitchell's *English Lands, Letters and Kings* and from Shakespeare's historical plays, she provided outline maps of England and Scotland so that Margaret, Jessie, and Nell could record historical locations as well as the places which their father described in his letters. To encourage the children to begin to take suitable outdoor exercise, Ellen bought a croquet set to replace their old one, reduced to "one mallet[,] three broken balls and no wickets . . . the careless wretches!"[40]

Frequent letters went from Library Place to England; so often, in fact, that Ellen apologized for the trivia. Woodrow learned that Puffin had given birth to five kittens in Ellen's closet; Princeton won over Yale 11 to 4 in baseball; "a most terrific thunderbolt" had frightened the three children and left Margaret "hysterical for some time"; Moses Taylor Pyne was kicked eight times in the legs by a horse in his own stables; a barn caught fire and the sounds from it were "simply unearthly"; George Allison Armour's house, at 83 Stockton Street, near the Wilsons', had been broken into and robbed of a quantity of valuable silver; a neighbor had made such an eyesore by enlarging his house that "our crying need is for someone to commit not burglary but arson." For most of July, the thieves were breaking into Princeton homes almost every night. When they were bold enough to venture into up-stairs bedrooms, Ellen began to sleep with a pistol by her bed. Only when Ed came home on July 21 did she turn over to him the responsi-bility of the family's protection.[41]

Eddie had found exams at M.I.T. much harder than at Princeton, yet his studies there had gone well. Instead of taking a second year of graduate work, as he wished, Eddie felt that he should now look for a job, preferably in research. One of his professors wrote that Eddie was a "clear thinker, an indefatigable worker" and had great skill in "devis-ing apparatus."[42] Turning down other opportunities, Eddie accepted a position as head chemist with the Buffalo Mining Company in Mannie, Tennessee, where there was "nothing but the furnace, a big store and a few straggling houses perched on the sides of the hills." There, he reasoned that he could live frugally and save money.[43]

Madge, who had been an interim houseguest of Edith Reid, and completely bored by a would-be beau, informed her older sister that *she* was never going to marry,[44] a pronouncement which Ellen recognized as an echo of her own views about men at age eighteen.

While Woodrow was away, Ellen had photographs made of herself at the Davis and Sanford studio in New York because she wanted *one* good likeness of herself for the children to have "when I am gone." She began to paint, but unwilling to start with a paid model, she worked again on an unfinished portrait of herself.[45]

In mid-August, Ellen took Margaret, Jessie, and Nell, with Eddie's help (*"such* a comfort to have him take and bring us back and take the children in bathing"), to Mrs. Topping's near Bridgehampton, Long Island, where the family had vacationed in 1890 and 1893.[46] They were back at Library Place in time to welcome Woodrow and Stockton home on September 4.

Monday, October 2, 1899, was a red-letter day for the three Wilson daughters and for generations of Princeton youngsters to come. Miss Fine's School (now Princeton Day School), established for the "educa-tion of girls and *young* boys," opened its doors in a residence at 42 Mercer Street. The school's founder, May Margaret Fine, a Wellesley graduate, was the sister of two eminent educators, Henry B. Fine, Dod Professor of Mathematics, and John B. Fine, headmaster of the Prince-ton Preparatory School for Boys. Within easy walking distance of 82 Library Place, Miss Fine's School was a welcome means for Margaret, Jessie, and Nell to complete their secondary education. Fräulein Böhm joined Miss Fine's staff as teacher of French and German, but continued to live with the Wilsons.[47]

In mid-November, with the three girls in school, Ellen went to Massachusetts for a week to visit her old friends, Agnes and Arthur Tedcastle, who had recently moved to Wellesley Hills. When Ed learned that Ellen would be near Boston, he asked her to do him "a special favor" (which she did), and call on Florence Choate Leach,[48] a young woman with whom Ed had become acquainted during his year at M.I.T. Unknown to Ellen at the time, Ed and Florence were engaged.

Nearly twenty-four years old, Ed had purposely avoided possible "entangling alliances" with women (his brother-in-law, Woodrow, labeled him "the reluctant Eddie") because he felt that his stammering would be a permanent impediment to marriage. Florence took her meals at the same house in Boston where Ed boarded, and their friendship had developed naturally without Ed's having to play the role of a suitor. He was able to talk freely with Florence about his stammering, a handicap which she regarded as "simply nothing," and one which she felt that Ed needlessly magnified. Florence had learned to live with a limp from having had infantile paralysis in childhood.[49]

Born in Portland, Maine, and orphaned at an early age, Florence was thrown on her own resources as a young girl. Her independence (she was a violin teacher) had not "had the effect on her which it has on one or two other girls I knew in Boston who are similarly situated," Eddie explained to Ellen. "I mean the effect of taking away an indefinable something and leaving them harder and less attractive." He felt compelled, however, to prove that he could provide adequately for Florence before he committed himself to marriage. While he worked in Tennessee for a year, Florence was to travel abroad with an elderly Boston couple who had made her their "daughter pro tem."[50]

Florence's cultural exposure during that period caused Ed to feel even more keenly his isolation in Mannie. He made a bargain with Jessie to send him, twice a week, packets of the *New York Times* which the Wilsons had finished reading.[51] No one understood Eddie's sentiments about cultural isolation and a postponed marriage better than Ellen, with whom his secret was safe until he and Florence made their official announcement the next year.

Ellen's trip to Boston preceded a more lengthy holiday in the South. Late in January 1900, the Wilsons went to Richmond as guests of the Archibald Pattersons while Woodrow lectured at the Academy of Music. On February 3, Ellen said goodbye to her husband and set off for New Orleans to visit Lucy and Mary Smith during Mardi Gras. Before returning to Princeton, she planned to spend a month with relatives in Georgia and to visit Rosalie in Asheville. Annie Howe, in charge of the household on Library Place, was looking after Margaret, Jessie, and Nell.[52]

The Belle of New Orleans

Ellen found the weather in New Orleans to be "perfectly glorious," *and she* felt as if she could "do anything" or walk any distance. The fragrance of the tea olive, of the crimson roses climbing over the south gallery outside her window, and a yellow jessamine, made her realize that she was in the "far South."[1]

She renewed her friendship with her cousin, Dr. Palmer, who, at eighty-two, was still pastor of the First Presbyterian Church. Ellen found him "lovely—so tender and affectionate," and in a mood to reminisce for hours about his and Grandfather Axson's younger days.[2] Also recalling Grandfather Axson's years in Liberty County was the Reverend Robert Q. Mallard, another New Orleans clergyman whose first wife, Mary Sharpe Jones (daughter of Charles Colcock Jones), and her family had been members of the Midway Church in Liberty County when the "Great Axson" was pastor there. The Mallards lent Ellen a recently published history of the Midway Church which she read with avid interest. Mrs. Mallard's sister-in-law, Susan Polk Jones, widow of Dr. Joseph Jones (a son of Charles C. Jones), honored Ellen with a reception at which sixty women were present.[3] Some were from families who had been patients of Ellen's late great-uncle, Dr. Forster Axson, only brother of I. S. K. Axson. Esteemed by rich and poor alike, Forster Axson had made calls "all over the city . . . without thought of reward." Axson and his wife, Laura Lewis Axson, had five sons and one daughter, all of whom died young, leaving no descendants to greet Ellen in 1900. Ellen met one "relation" about whom she wrote Woodrow with considerable amusement. The man in question was "old Uncle Mark Anthony," one of Forster's devoted servants, who called at the Smiths on hearing that an Axson was staying there. When Ellen assured him that she was a bona fide member of *the* Axson clan, he wept. "Den we's *close* related," he said.[4]

Ellen relished the whirl of social activities among the elite of New Orleans. She lunched with two women writers, Mary E. Moore Davis and Grace Elizabeth King, and with a "faded beauty," Phoebe Raymond—all friends of Lucy and Mary.[5] She went again and again to the French Quarter and observed with a critical and appreciative eye the art and architecture of New Orleans. On a visit to Sophie Newcomb College, well known for its excellent art department, Ellen stood enchanted before three "great Tiffany windows" in the chapel.[6]

She took New Orleans by storm. Lucy and Mary gave a lavish luncheon in her honor, and, on a Thursday, the Smiths' "At Home" day, more than twenty people called to see her, and "the callers were still calling when the dinner guests came." Some of the many dinners and receptions in her honor were staged because she was the wife of a distinguished Princeton scholar. "By the way," she wrote Woodrow, "will you please send me five pictures of yourself . . . with 'yours truly, Woodrow Wilson' written on them?"[7]

While the social whirl spun on in New Orleans, Ellen was oblivious of a crisis on Library Place. Stockton, for some time troubled by chronic appendicitis, had a violent attack which required surgery only a week after Ellen left. On February 8, the Wilson family physician summoned by telephone a surgeon from New York, Dr. Robert Fulton Weir. Princeton had no hospital, so Weir performed the operation at once in the Wilson home. Peritonitis had already set in, and in another twelve hours, Stockton would have gone the way of George Howe. Woodrow wrote candidly to Ellen, assuring her that there was absolutely *no* cause for alarm. "Not a thing went wrong," he told her. "The Dr. was perfectly satisfied with every step, and confidently expects a rapid recovery." A trained nurse was on night duty, Sister Annie was running the household by day, and Woodrow admonished Ellen not to be so foolish as to come home or they would never forgive her.[8]

Ellen realized that it would, indeed, be foolish to travel back to Princeton, for Stockton would be ambulant by the time she could get home. Since she planned to visit in Georgia, Woodrow suggested that Stockton meet her in Savannah for two weeks of rest in the mild climate. Ellen liked the idea and was willing to forego the side trip to Asheville to see Rosalie if Stockton's needs required her presence. Reluctant to give up Rome, she knew, however, that Stockton could never bear the thought of going there even when he was well. Stockton declined to come to Georgia, but chose instead to spend a few days in Atlantic City.[9]

Meanwhile, Ellen had yet to experience the Mardi Gras. Once the events began, despite her alleged dread of "this carnival business," Ellen found the spirit contagious. The opening ball was *"perfectly beautiful."* The illuminated processions and parades, "too fantastic, [too] barbaric," to be beautiful, were, nevertheless, "gorgeous."[10]

Her New Orleans career ended in a blaze of glory with an enormous reception in her honor given by a bank president's wife, Mrs. Robert M. Walmsley. Wearing her "pink dress," Ellen was "voted 'an incarnation of a Duchess de Brabant rose.'" She was "so petted and praised and made love to (by *women!*)" that she was almost bewildered. Forgetting her usual modesty, Ellen told Woodrow that one hostess had known scarcely *any* visitor who had made such a deep and delightful impression on New Orleans society, and that Ellen had *charmed everybody*. "But *you know* that I repeat it, *much* against my will, because it will please you to hear it, you dear, doting, foolish darling. . . . You *must* burn this!"[11]

When Ellen left New Orleans, the relationship with Lucy and Mary Smith was now as never before a firmly established part of her life. This bond was the closer for Ellen because of the mutual devotion between the Smith sisters and Woodrow. Ellen would never cease to love Rosalie and to admire Rosalie's husband, but the DuBoses had had a head start on Ellen's affections before Woodrow entered her life.

On Saturday, March 3, as the train crossed the swampy pinelands of Georgia en route to Savannah, Ellen's thoughts turned again to the scenes of her father's boyhood. The *History of the Midway Congregational Church*, still fresh in her mind, evoked some thoughts about Old Liberty County. "It is a Puritan idyl, a pathetic one on the whole, ending in the very abomination of desolation," she wrote Woodrow. In the entire book about Midway she found one passage that she thought was hilarious, an epitaph written by a clergyman for his wife's tombstone:

> She, who in Jesus sleeps beneath this tomb,
> Had Rachel's face, and Leah's fruitful womb,
> Abigail's wisdom, Lydia's faithful heart,
> And Martha's care, with Mary's better part.[12]

Eight years had passed since Ellen's last visit to Savannah, Atlanta, and Rome. The children were along then to occupy her mind and time; but, alone in March 1900, she had "too much time to think." The dear familiar faces, many of whom she saw at the Independent Presbyterian Church, were stamped irrevocably with the print of past tragedies.

Aunt Ella and Uncle Randolph in Savannah, Uncle Warren, Aunt Lou-isa, Cousin Ed and his lovely wife, Mary Celestine Mitchell Brown ("Meemee"), all now living in Atlanta, treated Ellen like a "princess for whom nothing was good enough." Aunt Louisa, the stoic of unshak-able faith, was still grieving over the death of her daughter, Loula (Mrs. Philip) Evans—ironically of childbirth complications. The baby sur-vived and was living with the Brown grandparents.[13]

When Ellen arrived on March 10 at the Rome depot, she found Uncle Will there to meet her in his buggy. A widower for three years, Uncle Will had, a few months before Ellen's arrival, married Annie Perkins, a woman in her mid-thirties from Cedar Bluffs, Alabama. The Hoyt sisters were outraged—and never went back to Rome—but Ellen found Annie attractive, with a sweet manner. Uncle Will was more comfortable than he had been since his boyhood days in Athens. His first wife, a Liberty County belle whom he had married in 1863 during a brief leave from the Confederate Army hospital staff, was apparently never drawn to the art of housekeeping. Uncle Will's home, the one Ellen had known all through her girlhood years, at last boasted "sweet, fresh, dainty room[s] . . . and the food perfectly cooked and well served."[14]

Ellen visited her parents' graves in Myrtle Hill Cemetery and ar-ranged for some maintenance work to be done,[15] which intensified her homesickness for Woodrow. "Oh, my darling," she wrote to him, "*you* are the breath of life to me; it seems to me that I literally *could* not live without you. . . . Just imagine . . . trying to construct a life for oneself out of such elements as have filled my days since I came here, and with love left out,—or even with most sorts of love left in! There is only *one* sort however that is soul-satisfying,—and that, thank God, is mine in good measure pressed down and running over."[16]

Ellen longed to return to Princeton, but she could not slight Rosalie. That Ellen did not see Beth in all those years was a "poignant and lasting regret," and she wanted to avoid the same heartache in regard to Rose.[17] She arrived at the DuBoses' on March 17 to find Rosalie "se-rene and sweet," and "almost always very grave." Now expecting her sixth—and last—baby, Rosalie had, the year before, lost her second daughter, Julia, to meningitis.[18]

Ellen left Asheville on March 20 en route to Atlantic City where Woodrow and Stockton awaited her. Stockton was recovering from the surgery, but his nerves were in such shambles that he could not bear to be alone. Until Ellen arrived to cheer him, he was willing to be tended by his brother-in-law as an acceptable second-best.[19] Both men were ecstatic to have her home again.

Woodrow now had a contract with Harper and Brothers to serialize in *Harper's Magazine* his evolving American history. For this he was to be paid one thousand dollars for each of twelve installments, the first to be delivered to the publisher on July 1, 1900.[20] Whether from pressure of facing deadlines, or from tension due to Ellen's long absence, or from a combination of reasons, Woodrow developed a tic in one side of his face. He began daily electrical treatments at home with a battery-powered apparatus prescribed by Dr. William B. Pritchard, a physician from New York. Woodrow reported to Pritchard in early July that the tic varied noticeably with his "general nervous condition." When he was overtired, or for any reason not at his best, the tic appeared with "provoking vigour." He looked forward to a vacation in early August, and he did not intend to take the apparatus with him.[21]

Ellen wanted Woodrow to have a complete rest in the summer of 1900, far away from professional demands. From early August to mid-September, they were at Judd Haven, in the Muskoka Lake district of Ontario, where they boarded in a rambling hotel with a grand view of the lake and countryside. Charmed with the area, the Wilsons bought approximately one hundred acres of land that included a small island in Lake Rosseau. They estimated that building a simple summer residence with the necessary dependencies and boats would cost about thirty-seven hundred dollars.[22]

The building project was postponed in lieu of Woodrow's more immediate plans to take the family abroad for fifteen months while he studied in Germany. The Princeton University Board of Trustees had responded unhesitatingly and affirmatively to his request for a leave of absence for the academic year 1901–1902 at full salary. The Wilsons intended to sail in June 1901 and return in September 1902, a plan that afforded two summers for travel.[23] Edward Graham Elliott, a Princeton graduate in the Class of 1897 and a protégé of Woodrow, and George Howe had gone to Germany for graduate work; Howe, in classics at the University of Halle, and Elliott, in jurisprudence and politics at the Universities of Berlin and Heidelberg. Annie Howe was in Germany to provide a home for her son.[24] To share some time in Germany with his sister was an additional lure for Woodrow.

Ellen still remembered the disappointment when his plan to study abroad had to be canceled in 1886, and she was eager for the family to go together. But once again the plans for Europe had to be given up when Woodrow's father, who was spending the winter with friends in Wilmington, North Carolina, suffered what was probably a heart attack, and was at the point of death. Leaving immediately for Wilmington, Woodrow arrived to find his father weak, though improved. Ellen urged that, if it was at all possible, "Dear Father" be brought to Princeton. Not until May 1901 was the elderly Wilson able to travel, and, escorted by his son, finally became a permanent resident in the Library Place house which he had helped to build.[25]

The Wilsons were gravely concerned about Woodrow's frail father, now in his eightieth year. Madge Axson remembered him as "a good-looking, irascible old man with a Paderewski-like shock of white hair, and eyes like shiny black diamonds," who awed the granddaughters into total silence.[26] Dr. Wilson's increasing infirmity in 1901 changed what had been a more gentle and affectionate grandparent. Less than two years before, he had written: "My darling granddaughter Jessie, I thank you for your little letter, received this morning, and send a quick reply to tell you that I love you dearly. I think of you and all the others in the dear house at Princeton, every day many times; and long to see you, your dear sisters and your dearer mother. . . . Please give my dearest love to all."[27]

Now, only his son, Woodrow, whom he adored, and on occasion, Stockton, who had exceptional conversational skills, could divert Dr. Wilson. Giving all the time he could spare, Woodrow read to his father and often soothed him at night by singing to him his favorite hymns.[28] Ellen had her own special way of sensing her father-in-law's whims and needs without being intimidated. At a much younger age, she had acquired the knack of coping with an unpredictable parent.

The postponement of Dr. Wilson's coming was fortunate. Early in April, Ellen had to take Jessie to the Philadelphia Orthopaedic Hospital for an operation to remove tubercular glands in the neck. Accompanying Jessie and Ellen, Stockton stayed on to see that they were comfortably situated in a "large cheerful room with two beds." Ellen did not leave Jessie's side until her fourteen-year-old daughter was ready to go home two weeks later. The timing of Jessie's surgery caused Ellen to miss the wedding of Eddie and Florence on April 9 in Cambridge. Stockton and Madge, housed with the Tedcastles, were there.[29]

On their way to Tennessee, Eddie and his bride stopped for a few hours in Philadelphia to see Ellen and Jessie. That another woman now had first place in Ed's affections was, in a sense, a graduation for both him and Ellen. For twenty years, she had been sister, mother, guardian, and confidante, while he had been son, brother, and protector. Their deep, symbiotic love was, and always would be, unfailing no matter what the future might bring.

Because of Joseph Ruggles Wilson's poor health, Ellen was doubtful that the family could take a vacation at all in the summer of 1901. Dr. Wilson solved the dilemma himself by arranging to spend his summer in the "Danville Sanatorium." By the time that Ellen wrote to engage rooms at Judd Haven, none was available, and the family went instead to a resort, "Heimera," at Rosseau Falls, Ontario.[30] Shortly before they left Princeton, Ellen received word that Aunt Ella Axson had died in Savannah, and less than a year later, Uncle Randolph followed.[31]

In the fall of 1901, life at Library Place began as serenely as possible with a frail Dr. Wilson now a part of the family. Madge was a junior at the Woman's College; Margaret and Jessie—both now "as tall as their mother"—and Nell were attending Miss Fine's School; Fräulein Böhm had left Library Place to live elsewhere in town.[32] As he worked on the final installments of his history for *Harper's Magazine*, Woodrow realized that he had reached a crucial point in his writing. For the next decade, he must devote himself to a task for which he had long been in training: writing his magnum opus, "Philosophy of Politics."[33] Barring unforeseen illness or natural catastrophes, the Wilsons' future for the years ahead seemed pleasantly predictable.

Part Five

1902–1906

Chapter 17

The Trustees Were Unanimous

On June 9, 1902, after accepting the resignation of Francis Landey Patton,
the Princeton Board of Trustees unanimously elected Professor Woodrow Wilson president of the university. The twenty-six trustees, reputed
never before to have agreed immediately on anything, were of one
mind from the first ballot. Another unusual circumstance was that
Woodrow would be the first president of Princeton University not to
be an ordained clergyman.[1]

By the time of the trustees' meeting in June, the outcome of their
deliberations was not entirely unanticipated. Ellen knew that her husband, and others on the faculty, had been unhappy with Patton's leadership since the sesquicentennial celebration, when expectations were
high for transforming the college into a great institution of higher
learning. Hopes had gradually changed, however, to "bitter discon-
tent."[2] Woodrow had even confided to the Hibbens that were it not for
them, he could easily leave Princeton.[3] While confidence in Patton diminished, the faculty and trustees were increasingly impressed with
Woodrow Wilson. By June 2, when Ellen was in Baltimore to attend
Madge's graduation from college, Woodrow wrote to her that Trustee
Cornelius C. Cuyler had said cryptically at a luncheon on that same day
that it looked as if he, Woodrow, was "going to have a great deal of
responsibility."[4] When the _Princeton Alumni Weekly_ of May 31 had
printed on its cover, in bold type, "Woodrow Wilson, '79, for President," Woodrow at first thought that "some fool" from the outside was
interfering in college politics. But, as he explained to Ellen, it turned
out to be a harmless joke: someone had written to an Indianapolis
newspaper suggesting that the Democrats nominate him for "the presidency of the United States,—that's all!"[5]

There was no doubt in Ellen's mind that her husband was the logical
person to lead the "strong power impelling the University forward";
yet her abundant faith in him did not take away the uneasiness which
she felt over the high expectations being laid upon this one man. Students, faculty, townspeople, and the press praised the trustees' choice.

Southerners took pride in his election as a symbol of the end of sectional antagonisms.[6]

Joseph Ruggles Wilson, sitting in his favorite barbershop on Nassau Street, swathed in sheets and towels, heard of his son's great honor when a little man tumbled in and gasped, "oh, Dr. Wilson, the Trustees have elected Woodrow president!"[7] Nell Wilson, playing outdoors on Library Place with friends, was puzzled when Frances Folsom (Mrs. Grover) Cleveland drove by in her carriage, stopped, and said, "Give my love to your father." Not until Nell got home and saw her mother's flushed, happy face, did she learn the true meaning of their neighbor's words.[8] Stockton, about to leave Princeton on a university errand, was summoned by messenger to come at once to Library Place to see his sister. With her "face glowing and eyes dancing," Ellen told Stockton of Woodrow's election.[9] Dr. Wilson, not at all surprised by his son's achievement, later summoned the three granddaughters to his room, lined them up, and commanded: "Never forget what I tell you. Your father is the greatest man I have ever known."[10] It was left to Aunt Louisa to put the climactic touch on the achievements of "Ellie Lou's" husband: "It's a pity he didn't enter the ministry."[11]

Ellen and Woodrow knew that his literary work would now suffer, and that for people of their temperaments, the change from teacher to administrator would involve sacrifices. Yet the election to the presidency, Woodrow said, had settled his future and given him a sense of "*position* and of definite, tangible tasks" which took the "*flutter* and restlessness" from his spirits.[12] Ellen wrote to Florence Hoyt that they must leave their "dear home and their sweet, almost ideal life" when Woodrow was a simple man of letters. They were both "rather heartbroken" about the responsibilities of officialdom but Ellen vowed that the duties which lay ahead would be fulfilled to the best of her ability, and there must be no more "weak-mindedness" with regard to them.[13]

For a brief time, Ellen struggled with feelings of inadequacy as she faced her new role as the wife of the president of Princeton University. Unburdening to the Hibbens, she was strengthened by the contents of a personal note from Jenny Hibben: "If *you* have a feeling of distrust about yourself, *we* have not, and we know that you will fill the place of the President's wife with the sweetness[,] distinction and grace which you already have—and we shall love you and be proud of you!"[14]

Annie Louise Perry, whose husband, Bliss, had resigned from the Princeton faculty in June 1900 to become editor of the *Atlantic*

Monthly, wrote Ellen that the event they had so often talked about and wished for had come to pass, and the Perrys, alas, were not there to enjoy it.[15]

Mamie Erwin, Beth's oldest daughter, sent a letter of congratulations, a poignant reminder to Ellen of her close girlhood relationship with the late Mrs. Hamilton Erwin. Answering promptly, Ellen wrote to Mamie: "Could you do me a little favor dear? I know that your mother kept my letters and I should be very glad to be *assured* that they had been destroyed. Or better still, if they have not yet been destroyed, will you send them all to me by express? Of course at my expense. . . . I should be exceedingly obliged to you."[16]

The Wilsons themselves had little opportunity to savor Woodrow's latest honor. They took separate vacations in the summer of 1902 so that one of them could be at home with "dear father." Ellen, accompanied by Madge, went first in early July, for a fortnight with the Tedcastles at their summer place on the Massachusetts North Shore.[17] The two sisters had a brief rendezvous with Florence and Eddie, who were in the North while he worked on a project at the Thomas A. Edison laboratory. In less than two weeks, Ed had solved a problem that some of Edison's staff had worked on for "two or three years," yet he declined further opportunities in New Jersey to return to Mannie, Tennessee. Uncomfortable with Ed's decision, but unwilling to interfere, Ellen thought that it was a pity he was not engaged in higher scientific work.[18]

When Woodrow's turn came in August for a New England holiday, he had finished *History of the American People*. When he began to write his inaugural speech, to be delivered on October 25, he told Ellen that he felt like "a prime minister getting ready to address his constituents."[19] Ellen fretted about the stacks of congratulatory letters which he had taken with him to answer, and begged him—just to please *her*—to have a stenographer in Massachusetts attend to them.[20]

Margaret, Jessie, and Eleanor were staying at Lavallette, New Jersey, with Mary Hoyt who, unknown to Ellen, was giving the girls lessons in housekeeping. With a full-time nurse to tend Woodrow's father, Ellen began to work vigorously on the renovation and redecoration of Prospect, the president's residence located on the campus.[21]

Designed in the Florentine style by John Notman, a Philadelphia architect, Prospect was built in 1849, and, in 1878, was given to the university for the use of its presidents. The house stood on the same land once owned by Ellen's great-great-great-uncle, Nathaniel FitzRandolph who, in 1753, had donated the ground on which the first building of the College of New Jersey, Nassau Hall, was erected.[22]

Ellen Axson Wilson, the fourth mistress of Prospect, wanted to rid the interior of its high Victorian decor imposed by former decorators.[23] The battle was not won overnight, but with the help of Edward J. Holmes, a Philadelphia decorator, Ellen prevailed. Nor did she allow Holmes to override her taste. "I know so exactly what I want," she told Woodrow, "that if Mr. Holmes doesn't agree with me,—so much the worse for Mr. Holmes! He will be dismissed with just so much less compunction!"[24] In the main rooms of Prospect she planned to use antiques for which she searched in Philadelphia, New York, and even Boston during her vacation. From James Fay, antiques, 438 Fourth Avenue in New York, she purchased dining room furniture, and from the Antique Furniture Company at 156 West 34th Street she ordered drawing room pieces to be done in rose brocade. Some Princetonians allegedly disapproved of Ellen's formal "rose and beige" colors, but she felt that a room designated for formal entertaining should *be* formal.[25]

While exploring in the basement of Prospect one day, Ellen discovered some fine old marble mantels, several carved cornices, and two early chandeliers which, in the high Victorian period, had been removed from the house. Ellen had these treasures cleaned, repaired, and installed.[26] She relished these activities, which sounded excessively strenuous to Woodrow; indeed, she reminded her husband of his own observation that "running about, going to the city, etc." agreed with her better than sitting at home sewing.[27] Working with the architect, Walter Cope of Philadelphia, and James MacNaughton Thompson, university curator of grounds and buildings, Ellen planned for another bathroom on the second floor and a lavatory on the first floor. A central heating system was installed for the first time, and she had pipes run into the third story of the square west tower where Woodrow could have an isolated retreat. After the Pattons moved out on August 11, the redecorating began in earnest. Two weeks later, Ellen reported that plumbing, heating, lighting, painting, papering, carpets, shades, bedding, hangings, upholstering, and refinishing were all settled in *detail* and contracted for.[28]

Under Ellen's direction, Prospect would again resemble the stately mansion which Notman had originally designed. The new home provided adequate space for official entertaining as well as for the ubiquitous stream of relatives. From the porte cochère, one entered a square vestibule which led into a rotundalike hallway. The dome over this hallway extended to the roof and was capped by a pale stained-glass skylight. An iron and brass balustrade encircled the opening on the upstairs level. In addition to the drawing and dining rooms, both with French doors leading to a back terrace, the first floor had a large shelf-lined study (for Woodrow), a small sitting room, a family library, and a servants' wing in which were located the butler's pantry, a conservatory, and storage and laundry rooms, with servants' sleeping quarters over-head. In the main section of the second story, there were eight bed-rooms, four with "dressing rooms," and one primitive bathroom. Ellen chose the southwest corner bedroom for herself and Woodrow; the larger northwest chamber, "the state room," was reserved for guests. Jessie and Eleanor shared the room over the library, while Margaret, a prim fourteen-year-old, preferred a room of her own. The servants' sleeping quarters were on the third floor, east, not to be confused with the four-story square tower on the west where the third-floor room, with windows on three sides, was Woodrow's sanctum. All of the main rooms, of course, had fireplaces.[29]

When the Wilsons moved into Prospect on October 18, they had sold their home on Library Place.[30] By the time that Ellen had the family settled, the inaugural ceremonies were imminent. Events were sched-uled to begin with the Board of Trustees' meeting on October 20 and continue through October 25.

Saturday, the twenty-fifth, was an unusually balmy October morn-ing. When it was time for Woodrow to leave Prospect to join the academic procession, Ellen, wearing "a new brown dress trimmed with fur, and a hat decorated with ostrich feathers," helped him to adjust his purple and orange hood, colors of The Johns Hopkins University. Woodrow then slipped into his father's room for a last-minute visit. Watching the procession from an outdoor spot, Ellen, Madge, and the three Wilson daughters did not take their reserved seats in Alexander Hall until the man whom they loved turned and smiled at them as he passed by.[31] It was a new experience for Ellen to see several promi-nent women educators, in academic attire, marching in the procession. Woodrow's former colleague, Carey Thomas, by then president of Bryn Mawr, was not among them; however, she sent a representative, Her-mann Collitz, professor of comparative philology and German. Other guests whom Ellen would receive at Prospect were Samuel L. Clemens

(Mark Twain), William Dean Howells, Booker T. Washington, J. Pierpont Morgan, and Henry C. Frick. Ellen had not forgotten to invite the DuBoses, Ed and Meemee Brown, the Smith sisters, and the Tedcastles, none of whom were able to come.[32]

Unable to have all the guests at luncheon, Ellen invited a group of fifteen to dine at Prospect after the ceremonies, while smaller luncheons were arranged in Princeton homes. After the Princeton-Columbia football game, the Wilsons gave a reception from 4:00 to 6:00 P.M. for everyone present. That Ellen received Booker T. Washington at Prospect scandalized Mrs. Thomas A. Hoyt, who said that, if she had *known* he was to be there, she would not have come. Ellen, radiant in her new ball gown of lace and white silk satin, was unperturbed by Sadie Hoyt's imprecations.[33]

Stockton Axson, who had marched in the academic procession but who had left the "crush and furor" of Princeton on Saturday without an opportunity to talk with his brother-in-law, wrote to Woodrow:

> I suppose few men have ever entered upon new and great
> phases of their careers with such universal approbation as you
> have won. There was but one opinion on all sides . . . that in a
> masterly address, most impressively delivered, you had struck ex-
> actly the proper note. . . . Princeton and its friends are certainly
> behind you in solid phalanx. . . . That life and health and joyous
> strength may be spared to you in order that you may embody
> your vision in realities, is, I am sure, the hope of all and the
> prayer of many.[34]

It was the unfailing hope and prayer of Ellen Wilson.

Shortly after Woodrow's installation as the thirteenth president of Princeton University, *History of the American People*, in five volumes, was published. The work was dedicated to: "E.A.W. in loving acknowledgment of gentle benefits which can neither be measured nor repaid." His professional success was now more visibly reflected in his annual income: an eight thousand dollar salary, plus two thousand dollars for entertaining and routine maintenance of Prospect; from royalties on his books, more than seven thousand dollars by the end of the academic year.[35]

Ellen realized that her husband's accomplishments were inevitably drawing him more and more into the public domain and away from the private hours which they both cherished. Woodrow needed those "delightful periods" in the day, when, he told her, he could go to her "as a tired boy would go to his mother, to be loved and petted."[36] There was a constant tension between Ellen's ambition for Woodrow and her concern for his health, between her own preference for privacy and the role of wife to a man increasingly in the public eye. Once, in the first month at Prospect, when Nell passed her parents' bedroom on her way to bed, she heard her mother crying. Her father, with great tenderness, said, "I should never have brought you here, darling. We were so happy in our own home."[37]

To restore her sagging spirits, Ellen provided her own special antidote: the creation of greater beauty and order around her. She told Mary Hoyt: "For myself, I have one ambition about all this; I think that life can be made beautiful without being expensive; I wish to have everything lovely without suggesting how much money I have spent. Even in formal entertainments, I hope I can emphasize the loveliness of life."[38]

With the interior of Prospect redecorated to her taste, Ellen now turned her attention to the grounds. From the stone terrace at the rear of the mansion, steps led to a large, formal French garden laid out in stiff, geometric patterns. This rigidity contradicted Ellen's belief that a garden should portray depth, mystery, and spontaneous color. She devised a less formal design by widening the small, narrow flower beds and joining them to form broad, triangular borders. She introduced quantities of white, pink, and yellow tulips; also daffodils, irises, peonies, and dahlias; and she had paths constructed between the beds. In the center of the design she placed a pool with a fountain. Groupings of cedar trees were planted at the rear for background and, in the corners, as accents. West of this central area, she created her rose garden. Beyond that, in an open space near Brown Hall, Ellen placed a long pergola covered with climbing roses. A sundial was centered in front of the pergola as an accent piece. Purple wisteria grew up the iron grillwork which ran from ground to roof on a small porch at the southwest back corner of the house.[39] Woodrow commented in the spring of 1904 that the garden, now "one of the most beautiful in Princeton," was a delightful display of Ellen's "inerrant taste."[40]

Planning the garden had been a salvation to Ellen. For, as the holiday season approached, she thought that there would be "no Christmas at all." Dr. Wilson, now unable to feed himself or to stand alone, had to be tended like a baby. During his frequent attacks and his unalleviated suffering, he moaned and screamed, an effect so harrowing that Ellen wished that her daughters did not have to see and hear so much of it. A full-time practical nurse was installed at Prospect and, of course, Annie Howe was there to be with her father. Ellen was glad that Woodrow, frequently out of town on university business, was not exposed to his father's agonies.[41] She had thought her own nerves could be depended upon, but, she wrote to Mary Hoyt: "I regret to say I have developed a habit of lying in bed awake half the night and holding myself!"[42]

On January 21, 1903, Dr. Wilson died at Prospect one month short of his eightieth birthday. After his body was placed in a coffin resting in the bay window in Woodrow's study, Ellen told her daughters to view their grandfather's now serene and "beautiful old face," so that they could remember him with dignity rather than as a helpless, sick, old man.[43] On Thursday, after a brief service at Prospect, Woodrow accompanied his father's body to Columbia, South Carolina, for the funeral and interment in the graveyard of the First Presbyterian Church.[44]

Ellen had not recovered from the burden of her father-in-law's final illness and death when Stockton had a nervous breakdown.[45] Frequently in and out of Prospect, and a favorite comforter of Dr. Wilson, Stockton's fragile emotions were highly sensitive to gloom. After his collapse, he needed Ellen with him "practically all the time," and for the next two weeks she tried to adjust her life to meet Stockton's whims.[46] Desperately tired, Ellen suggested that Madge might accompany him on a rest cure, but Stockton objected because he thought Madge "rather cold-hearted" and he did not love her as he did Ellen, Eddie, and Woodrow.[47] In due course, Stockton went to a private hospital in Bryn Mawr, where he spent most of the summer.[48] Stockton's illness was only a part of the cycle of life and death which revolved unremittingly in 1903: on June 2, at "Dr. Brigg's Infirmary" in Nashville, Tennessee, Eddie and Florence's son, Edward Stockton Axson, "a fine big boy,"[49] was born; not long afterward, Uncle Tom Hoyt died in Bryn Mawr.

Chapter 18

England and Italy

After this year of unusual personal pressures, Woodrow arranged to take Ellen abroad in the summer "on a second honeymoon" which would make up, he said, "for many, many things!"[1] Before they left, Ellen enrolled both Margaret and Jessie at the Woman's College of Baltimore where Madge had gone. When Margaret had taken the language entrance exams with "such a headache" that she was "in a state of *excessive* mortification" over possibly bad results, Ellen wrote to the dean of students, Dr. John Blackford Van Meter, who assured her that Margaret's grades were acceptable. Jessie had passed everything with "high marks."[2]

Leaving Margaret, Jessie, Nell, and Madge for the summer in Skyland, North Carolina, with Annie Howe, Ellen and Woodrow sailed on July 1 from New York on the R.M.S. *Oceanic* for Liverpool. Not only had Ellen's turn come to go abroad, but she would have nearly three months alone with Woodrow, uncluttered by relatives, a clamoring public, or even children.

The three daughters were to report in every letter *expressly* about their state of health,[3] but Ellen did not anticipate Annie Howe's ideas about upsets and sniffles. One unusually hot day, after a round of vigorous exercise, Jessie plunged her feet into a cold stream and sat with water up to her knees while she became lost in a book. The next morning, she awoke temporarily paralyzed from her waist down, a disability which would curtail her activities for several months.[4] Ellen was not told about Jessie's problem until they all returned to Princeton, when she learned that Madge had arranged to postpone Jessie's entrance to the Woman's College.[5]

The Wilsons docked in Liverpool on July 10, and headed for Grasmere, in the lake district, to spend several days savoring scenes from the life of William Wordsworth. (Under Ellen's tutelage, Wordsworth had become Woodrow's favorite poet.) From there, they went to Edinburgh, then worked their way from Scotland to London by way of

Durham, York, Lincoln, and Ely. In York, on Sunday, July 26, they worshiped in the great minster. On July 29, they arrived at the Buckingham Palace Hotel in London for eight days of sight-seeing. Ellen spent much of her time in London at the National Gallery, the National Portrait Gallery, the Royal Academy, and the Wallace Collection. Woodrow went with her to study the Elgin Marbles in the British Museum, and together they saw James M. Barrie's *The Admirable Crichton* and *Bishop's Move*, a comedy by Pearl M. Teresa Craigie, an American-born English dramatist.[6] From London, they went to Cambridge, where three days of perfect weather enabled them to row on the Cam and stroll about the backs in "glorious sunshine." At the Fitzwilliam Museum, Ellen saw the collection of fifty watercolors by J. M. W. Turner which John Ruskin had presented to the university in 1861. Painted by Turner during the period c. 1792–1840, the watercolors, "each an exquisite,—perfect little lyric," depicted subjects from both England and the Continent.[7]

After Cambridge, they toured Warwick and Kenilworth castles, the Shakespeare country, and then Oxford. By way of Wells and Salisbury, they returned on August 21 to Brown's Hotel in London for a two-day respite before crossing to Calais.[8]

In France the Wilsons visited Amiens, Notre Dame, Chartres, and Versailles, but the peak experience for Ellen, and one for which she had longed since her classes in art at the Rome Female College, was the Louvre. She arranged to go and come alone on the omnibus so that Woodrow was spared the fatigue of "taking her about" and those "long hours" in the galleries.[9]

After Paris, the Wilsons visited Basel, Lucerne, and Geneva, and crossed into Italy for two days at Como and Bellagio. On September 10, they were back in Paris for three days before they boarded the North German Lloyd liner *Bremen* at Cherbourg to return to New York. Woodrow kept a detailed record of their daily expenses which, in its way, provides an amusing account of their travels. He noted a newspaper purchase (0.02), rubber bands (0.02), a bus ride in London (0.02), and 0.12 in the collection plate at St. Mary The Virgin in Oxford. The entire trip, including first-class passage for two, cost $1,666.88.[10]

The Wilsons reached Princeton in time for the official opening exercises of the university on September 23. Ellen left Woodrow in Annie Howe's care to recuperate from "a congestion of the throat" while she hurried to Baltimore to visit Margaret, a freshman at the Woman's College of Baltimore.[11] The *Princeton Alumni Weekly* announced that President Wilson, in 1903–1904, did not intend to leave Princeton any more than was necessary in the line of his official duty in order to give his attention "more particularly to the pressing tasks of his office."[12]

Ellen knew that these "pressing tasks" extended far beyond the responsibilities of a single academic year. Woodrow was determined to develop a university with a prestigious faculty and high academic standards. To this end, he began to plan for added endowment, new buildings, revision of the curriculum, reform of the system of classroom instruction, and the addition of distinguished professors.[13] In October 1902, in his first report to the trustees, Woodrow had both stunned and challenged them by asking for more than twelve million dollars, about half of which was "to put existing work on a proper basis," the remainder to establish graduate, law, electrical, and science schools, and to erect a museum of natural history. High on his list of priorities was the addition of fifty young preceptors (or tutors), and in the fall of 1903 Woodrow began to work with a faculty committee to revise the course of study, a task which required most of that academic year.[14]

No college president ever began his duties with more enthusiastic support from faculty and alumni, but the continuing catalyst was Ellen. She was, he said, his "sweet guardian and inspirer," whose enthusiasm had been "like wine" to his mind. She was now "more indispensable" than ever to him—and "more dear."[15]

Ellen began to plan for the fall social season at Prospect by dividing the faculty into ten small groups for easy conversation at ten successive dinner parties. She carefully worked out the menus and decor, always enhanced with an abundance of fresh flowers and candlelight. To the three teenage daughters, peering down from prone positions in the upper hall, the house was festive, but the guests were only the parents of their playmates "all dressed up and being very polite."[16] Ellen also had open house for the 324 incoming freshmen, luncheon for the Board of Trustees at their quarterly meetings, and constant overnight visitors, many on college business. The clergymen who came to preach at the university chapel stayed at Prospect, and Ellen usually invited congenial friends to dinner on the preceding Saturday evenings.[17] Ellen wrote to Agnes Tedcastle that their busy life sometimes made Woodrow rebellious about the pause in his writing. She was "rather bored" at having to give and attend so many receptions and dinners, but it was "all in the day's work,—no use grumbling." Things had gone smoothly, and it had begun to be quite a matter of course.[18]

Since her son George's marriage, in October 1903, to Margaret Smyth Flinn of Columbia, South Carolina, Annie Howe was now a semipermanent resident in the Wilson home. Even with Annie in the house, Ellen did not feel free to leave Prospect that fall to attend the funeral of Uncle Will Hoyt who died on October 11. His death severed the last of the strong ties to Rome, Georgia.[19]

Another death which shocked Ellen—and the entire Princeton community—occurred on January 7 when Frances and Grover Cleveland lost their oldest child, Ruth, to diphtheria. The next day, in a fine drizzle of snow, the Wilsons attended the funeral at the First Presbyterian Church.[20] Not long afterward, Ellen was in bed for nearly three weeks with a "very stubborn and painful inflammation of the throat and ear passages,"—always her "weak points." She referred to the episode as her time of rest.[21]

With her three daughters apparently progressing nicely, Ellen could well have relaxed about their education. Margaret and Nell were sufficiently challenged, but Jessie posed a problem. She was almost free of the partial paralysis which had kept her activities restricted.[22] To have her attend Miss Fine's School as a postgraduate was one solution, but the Wilsons thought of a better plan. Mary Hoyt was already in Europe, and Woodrow urged Ellen, who had long wanted to tour Italy, to go abroad in the spring of 1904 and take Jessie with her. To make the proposed venture even more compelling, Lucy and Mary Smith were invited to join them. Once the travel plans were agreed upon, Ellen's preparation focused less on wardrobes for herself and Jessie than on a thorough study of Italian art and history.[23]

On March 19, 1904, Ellen, Jessie, Lucy, and Mary sailed from New York on the North German Lloyd liner *Hohenzollern* bound for Naples. Madge, Nell, and Woodrow went up to see the travelers off. Stockton, nursing symptoms of another decline, stayed in Princeton.[24]

Ellen and Jessie were excellent sailors without a single hour's seasickness even in rough weather. In ladylike fashion, Mary and Lucy Smith both capitulated to the perils of the sea. Lucy collapsed into bed fully clothed, shoes and hat included, and slept thus all one night. The perfect weather during the last days of the voyage enabled the Wilsons and the Smiths to take a steam tender ashore at Gibraltar for three hours of sight-seeing. When they got back to the ship, Ellen was enchanted with the color effects "beginning with deepest blue in the sea and bold, strong outlines and purple shadows in the mountains, fading softly until, just before sunset, sea & sky and mountains were all one glory and mystery of rose and violet, silver & gold,—opalescent tints blending and changing so subtly and wonderfully that it was almost more than one could bear."[25]

At Gibraltar, Ellen had sent Woodrow a cablegram with one word, "charcos," a code which she had devised to mean "all quite well, lodgings satisfactory, and everything goes smoothly and happily."[26] The voyage ended on March 31, when *Hohenzollern* docked at Naples. The four women checked into a convent, where they had reserved rooms, and began immediately to investigate Naples, "charming, in spite of the dirt."[27]

On the following Monday, they joined a five-day Cook's tour which took them to Pompeii, La Cava, Paestum, Salerno, Amalfi, Ravello and Sorrento, by boat to Capri, and thence by water back to Naples. In Sorrento, Ellen sat in a window overlooking the Bay of Naples, with Vesuvius looming in the distance, and wrote: "Yesterday [Amalfi to Ravello] was the most glorious day we have had. It was a perfect riot of colour,—a debauch of beauty from early morning until night. We went to bed feeling positively drunken." On the three-and-one-half-hour carriage ride from Salerno to Amalfi, Ellen provided herself and Jessie with a drink of brandy to help ward off possible ill effects from chills and dampness.[28]

Astonished to see the number of women who were traveling alone, Ellen wrote to Woodrow: "This is certainly the woman's century! They have taken possession of the *earth*! Everywhere one goes there are at least nine women to one man . . . women of *all* nationalities from Swedes & Russians down to the Indies,—all, all equally emancipated!"[29] Back in Naples on Friday evening, April 8, the Wilsons and the Smiths prepared to leave early Saturday for two weeks in Rome, where they were to meet Mary Hoyt.

On Sunday, they worshiped in Rome at "the Presbyterian Church," where Ellen heard a "*splendid* sermon" by Dr. Henry Cowan, professor of church history at the University of Aberdeen. It seemed good to her to hear such a "fine strong, bracing, intellectual address" after her ten days of "rioting in sensuous beauty."[30]

A great celebration was to take place on Monday at St. Peter's in honor of the thirteenth centenary of Pope Gregory the Great, an event for which spectators would have to stand for nearly five hours. When Ellen declined to go ("couldn't possibly stand the fatigue"), Madame Rinaldi, in whose pension they were boarding, obtained a seat-ticket for Ellen. She attended despite her dread of the crowds and objection to the required "black dress and veil."[31] Ellen was rewarded when Pius X was stopped for some time just beside her, and she could study his face. It was "beautiful & noble," a kind of countenance which she could not ascribe to the cardinals and bishops; the latter, she thought, looked like "imbeciles and *pigs!*"[32]

With the help of a Baedeker, Mary Hoyt and Ellen tried to plan an effective "Roman campaign," but they discovered all too quickly that the number of things which they wanted to see was overwhelming. No photograph could quite prepare Ellen for the paintings in the Sistine Chapel, or for Raphael's compositions, because the composition had "everything to do with it": "It is the largeness of the whole conception, the harmony of line and mass, the sense of air and space, the wonderful grouping of all those glorious, majestic, serenely god-like figures who are holding high converse together."[33]

Midway through their time in Rome, Woodrow wrote that Stockton, now in excellent shape, looked, spoke, and acted like a "normal, healthy citizen of a hopeful country." However, Nell had come down with the measles. Margaret, home from college for spring vacation, and precisely on schedule after exposure to Nell, also contracted the measles. Woodrow hired a nurse and canceled a projected trip to the South.[34] He also wrote that the university faculty had, with minor amendments, adopted the report from the Committee on the Course of Study.[35] Ellen was delighted to hear the good news not only for the sake of reform itself but because it proved so conclusively that Woodrow had a united and loyal faculty behind him.[36] She tried to be sensible about Margaret and Nell's illnesses, but she was sorry that Woodrow had the extra care and mental burden of it all. Something always seemed to happen when she left home (Stockton's appendectomy in 1900 and Jessie's paralysis in 1903), and she vowed never to go away again.[37]

Before leaving Rome, Ellen and her companions spent an afternoon at the Forum with Jessie as the competent guide whom May Margaret Fine had predicted her to be.[38]

Ellen went alone for one last morning at the Vatican.

It was . . . hard to turn my back on it forever! I could scarcely keep from crying,—it is the only place I have had any such feeling about. But I was so fortunate in one respect; one corner of the Sistine Chapel [had been] covered by scaffolding, hiding the Delphian Sibyl,—*much* the most beautiful of all,—so that I had given up all hope of seeing her. But yesterday, the scaffolding, which is on great rollers, had been moved along a little and she stood revealed!—and she is one of the two most beautiful creatures in the world!—the Venus of Milo of course being the other. . . . There is no other face so truly inspired. Beyond any doubt she sees in a vision "all the glory that shall be."[39]

Despite the frequent change of scenes and menus, the travelers stayed healthy, with splendid appetites which were adequately satisfied at Madame Rinaldi's table. Jessie, "positively ravenous," ate everything in sight "no matter how queer and foreign it was."[40] Concern about her young daughter's well-being led Ellen to be the very *soul* of prudence while the others were quite reckless—sleeping with their windows open, staying out at sunset and all the rest of it. As they left Rome on Tuesday, April 26, and headed for Florence by way of Assisi, everyone was "perfectly well" and Jessie "the very picture of health."[41]

The pronouncement itself almost seemed a curse: when they arrived in Assisi late that same evening, Jessie was stricken with diphtheria. The unspeakable intensity of Ellen's anxiety somehow gave her strength. She immediately called a local doctor who treated Jessie "through the night every hour." Early Wednesday morning, when the diagnosis was quite clear (the white patches had spread all over Jessie's throat), Ellen telegraphed Dr. William Bull, physician to the American embassy in Rome. Not the least reluctant to use any influence at her command, she wired: "The young daughter of Pres. Wilson of P. U. is seriously ill with diphththeria [*sic*] at [Hotel Leone in Assisi]. I implore you to come at once prepared to give antitoxine." Dr. Bull's first assistant, a Dr. Wild, left that evening for Assisi; meanwhile, a local physician sent to Perugia for serum and gave it to Jessie on Wednesday night. When Wild arrived Thursday morning, Jessie received yet another injection of a superior quality of serum. By Thursday afternoon, a nurse, sent by Dr. Bull, brought various necessities ("you can get *nothing* here—not even toilet paper"), and Dr. Bull himself appeared Friday. By this time, Jessie's throat was "wonderfully improved." On Sunday, May 1, the first day on which Ellen was able to write the details to Woodrow, Jessie was virtually out of danger. "You can imagine," she wrote, "what a blackness of desolation it was that first night and day. I am so inexpressibly grateful to God for so tempering the wind."[42] On May 3, Ellen sent a cable to let Woodrow know that their daughter had been ill and was recovering rapidly. By that date, Nell and Margaret were well, and Margaret was back at college.[43]

Ellen suffered agony during Jessie's week of illness. Memories of Ruth Cleveland's death in January haunted her. Inevitably, a dread lingered of the heart failure which had taken Ruth, but the doctor's daily examination of Jessie showed that all was normal.[44] Ellen would not allow Mary and Lucy to be exposed to Jessie, but Mary Hoyt, ignoring Ellen's pleas, helped with the daytime care when the nurse was off duty.[45] Dr. Bull, who stayed in touch with Ellen, told her that she had saved her child's life by acting "immediately in right time and . . . [in] the right way."[46] At the end of the first two weeks, he prescribed two more weeks in a convalescent convent home for Jessie to insure her complete recovery before taking ship at Genoa for New York. This meant that Ellen would miss Florence, to have been the pinnacle of her Italian tour, a treat which she was willing to forego to see Jessie well and home again. Jessie, on the other hand, determined that her mother *would* see Florence, wept, sobbed, and told Ellen that it would be "very, *very bad*" for her, Jessie's, health, if Ellen failed to go to Florence.[47] When the doctor insisted that his young patient should be humored or her recovery would be threatened, Ellen gave in and postponed their sailing until June 9. Out of quarantine by May 11 and able to be outdoors on the balcony, Jessie was now "as happy as a lark [and] everything," Ellen said, "is serene."

This was almost true. Ellen was distressed about the two additional weeks away from Woodrow and that he would be left in the lurch during commencement.[48] Her real worry, however, was the size of the medical bills which left her funds so depleted that she had to cable Woodrow for more money.[49] She need not have fretted. Woodrow commended her "courage, self-possession, resource . . . capacity," and the expense was not even to be thought of in this instance. The bout of measles with which he had to cope was "a trifling thing, an amusing incident" compared with the distressing disaster to "our precious Jessie."[50] As for the commencement functions, Madge was making preparations for them "with a great deal of good sense and quiet capacity," which reminded Woodrow a little of Ellen.[51]

By mid-May, Jessie was able to take daily outings in Assisi; she and Ellen were driven to San Domiano to see the "touchingly simple little church in which St. Francis' ministry began" and where, Ellen thought, one felt much closer to St. Francis than in the magnificent Church of San Francesco built in his memory.[52]

On May 20, after Ellen and Jessie arrived in Florence, she cabled "charcos" to Woodrow. Jessie had suffered no ill effects from the journey and was now so well that, with Mary Hoyt at hand, Ellen had sent the nurse back to Rome. Once settled, and alone with Mary Hoyt, Ellen broke down and wept bitterly over having to stay in Florence for those two extra weeks. Mary, who thought Ellen was crazy, and told her so, was thankful not to be married or in love if it made usually sensible people so ridiculous.[53]

Once Ellen lost herself in the riches of Florence, her regrets changed to exhilaration. After a first visit to San Marco, the Uffizi, the Pitti, and the Bella Arti, Ellen was left "gasping, overwhelmed," at the feast spread before her. Continually confronted by masterpieces which she had always longed to see, she rushed from one to another. Sometimes she sat and held her head in both hands "in a sort of despair." The Pitti had the best collection as a *whole*, but she found little in all of Florence that was not good. She wished that she had time to copy a great Giorgione (the three men with the "monk at the clavichord"). It might seem bold to speak of copying such a wonder but she knew she *could* do it; she *felt* the expression of the face down to the bottom of her soul.[54]

Jessie now went driving in the mornings to sightsee from the carriage, while, in the afternoons, she rested and read. At the end of the first week, when Jessie began to go about on foot, they spent a morning among sculptures at the Bargello: "Michel Angelos, Donatellos, Luca della Robbias, etc." Ellen allowed time at each place to sit quietly and study these works of art.[55]

Leaving Jessie with Mary Hoyt, Ellen spent two days in Venice with the Smiths. She saw "*perfectly* glorious Titians, Bellinis and Tintorettos," and at 2:00 A.M., too excited to sleep, she viewed the moon "riding high in the velvety *blue* Italian sky."[56] Some traveling companions told her that she was "the very image" of Titian's Flora, which Ellen thought that she resembled about as much as she did "Giotto's tower."[57]

Back in Florence on June 2, Ellen went to Masaccio's Chapel to stand alone on the same spot where "*all* the later great masters of Italian art had stood . . . day after day, week after week" to study those same paintings.[58] On their very last afternoon, Ellen and Jessie took a sheaf of white lilies to the small Protestant cemetery where Elizabeth Barrett Browning was buried and laid them on her grave.[59]

Chapter 19

Duties and Disruptions

On June 22, when the König Albert docked, Woodrow was in New York to accompany Ellen and Jessie to Princeton, and two weeks later, the Wilsons, Madge, and Stockton left for the summer in the Muskoka Lake region of Canada, their first time there since 1901. They stayed at their favorite spot, The Bluff, Judd Haven, on Lake Rosseau until September 10.[1]

While the family relaxed together in Canada, Ed Axson was the only one of the inner circle absent. Sometime in the summer of 1903, after Florence and their baby son were able to travel, Ed had moved from Mannie, Tennessee, to Creighton, Georgia, to become superintendent of the Franklin Gold Mining Company, situated nine miles northwest of Gainesville on the Chestatee River. For several months, they boarded in nearby Gainesville, where facilities were better for the mother and infant. By the summer of 1904, Ed and Florence were living at Creighton.[2] Ed had apparently not seen any of the Wilsons since July 1902. He had unsuccessfully urged Jessie and her sisters to come to Gainesville in the summer of 1903 (Madge had gone) when they were in North Carolina, and Stockton had spent a part of the following Christmas holidays with Ed and Florence.[3] Ellen, and undoubtedly Stockton, had reservations about Ed's stubborn determination to keep himself and his family in the southern hinterlands. It was Ed's decision, however, and there the matter rested.

When the Wilsons returned to Prospect in the fall, Ellen found a change in the landscaping that was not a part of her original design: Woodrow had ordered a spiked, wrought-iron fence built to enclose the house and five acres of ground. During the previous year, careless students on their way to and from eating clubs and ball games had trampled Ellen's garden—and consequently, Woodrow's sensibilities. Members of the incoming classes were considerably upset with the fence, and a few, on Friday night, September 30, tore a part of it down. An angry President Wilson had the fence rebuilt and, on days of ball games, used proctors to guard against further intrusions.[4] (The fence still stands.) Ellen ordered fresh stock for the garden and did "a good deal of superintending" of bulbs and plantings. In late November, she was getting all the flowers she wanted, including fine American Beauty roses.[5]

The usual mad rush of social functions began in October with the freshman reception, the trustee luncheon, and the influx of overnight visitors. Ellen had Katie Murray, a live-in seamstress, for a week to prepare an extensive wardrobe for Madge, who was to spend the year abroad. Adele Williams, an artist whose work Ellen had admired in the Pattersons' home in Richmond in 1900, was at Prospect to paint portraits of both Ellen and Woodrow "whenever posing was possible."[6]

"I think you would be greatly pleased at the comments upon Woodrow's picture," Ellen wrote later to Adele. "It is a *great* success." Opinions differed about Ellen's portrait. The artist had worked over the mouth—"the chief difficulty"—but the eyes, some thought, purveyed "tiredness." Ellen's portrait was hung in the drawing room over the piano, Woodrow's in the dining room over the buffet, both placements that Adele suggested.[7] Also in the dining room, over the mantel, was an oil portrait of Grandfather Axson, lent by Leila Axson for Ellen to copy. (She apparently never did so.)[8]

On October 15, the Wilsons entertained Mr. and Mrs. James Bryce from Sussex, England. Bryce, author of the classic work, *American Commonwealth*, and a visiting lecturer at The Johns Hopkins University in 1883, had written a favorable review of *Congressional Government*. Nell was upset by the Bryces' visit because Sunday, October 16, her fifteenth birthday, was given low priority. Ellen soothed Nell's bruised feelings by having four of her friends to dinner on Wednesday and inviting one to stay overnight.[9]

Five people, who were permanent, or semipermanent, members of the Wilson family were absent from Prospect that fall: Jessie and Margaret at the Woman's College of Baltimore; the Annie Howes, mother and daughter, now boarding at Chapel Hill, North Carolina, where George was on the faculty of the University of North Carolina; and Madge, in Europe. On the morning of November 2, Ellen and Woodrow went to New York to see Madge and a traveling companion, "a Miss [Emmeline] Thorpe," who had lived in Florence, board a small Italian vessel bound for Genoa. That afternoon, the Wilsons went to a matinee performance of *The College Widow* (Ellen did not know when she had laughed so hard before), and, in the evening, to see Mrs.

Patrick Campbell in *The Sorceress*. After the theater, they spent the night in the city.[10]

Before the Thanksgiving holidays, Ellen supervised a chore, usually done twice a year, but which had been neglected since their move into a redecorated Prospect—a thorough housecleaning. While "entertaining and being entertained," she spent a week of mornings overseeing the regular servants and day help from the village in putting the house in "the most apple-pie order from cellar to attic."[11]

With two daughters at college, Ellen tried to write weekly letters to each. At times she sent hurried notes, especially when allowances were overdue. Her financial counsel could be complicated. "I enclose check for $25.00 and another for $6.00, I having forgotten the fraternity dues when counting up what you needed. . . . Papa I find is engaged with callers so I can't get the second check now. Just take the $6.00 from that $20.00 you have of his. The other $14.00 will do for the next month's allowance . . . and so you need not trouble to send any of it back;—but be sure not to lose it in the meantime! This $25.00 is for lunch and sewing skirt. The rest for carfares and lunches."[12]

During that same fall, Ellen was disturbed by Stockton, "struggling desperately to keep out of the pit," who had another "nervous break-down." Suffering from exhaustion and melancholia, he entered a Philadelphia hospital in December, where he was a patient until the following summer. Highly esteemed as a teacher in his periods of good health, Stockton was chosen several times by the students as "the most popular professor." The trustees, equally fond of him, promoted him to full professor at their December 1904 meeting and voted to give him a year off at full salary.[13]

Ellen was also anxious about Woodrow's pending hernia operation to be done on December 15 at Presbyterian Hospital in New York. When Margaret and Jessie came home for the holidays, they and Nell spent "three miserable weeks" without their parents at Prospect. By the time the two older daughters returned to college, their father had developed phlebitis in one leg and had been ordered by his physician to a warm climate for four weeks of rest and recuperation. Ellen, of course, went along to look after him,[14] while Nell stayed with the Hoyts in Baltimore.[15] When the Wilsons returned from Palm Beach, Florida, in mid-February, Ellen, looking pale and thin, showed the effects of the long siege more than her husband.[16]

Shortly after his return to Princeton, Woodrow's plans for the tuto-

Edward William Axson, 1902.
Courtesy of the Very Reverend Francis B. Sayre.

rial system were announced in the press and in the *Alumni Weekly*. The system was designed to encourage more personal contact between teacher and pupil and to provide tutors to work as "guides, counselors and friends to small groups of students." Soon to be known as the "preceptorial system," the plan called for raising 2.5 million dollars to hire fifty "well-paid," promising young scholars for three years. With the help and leadership of a distinguished committee of alumni, Woodrow moved confidently to execute the plan.[17]

Uneasy about her irrepressible husband, Ellen was also watching Nell, who appeared to be developing the same kind of diseased neck glands which had led to Jessie's surgery four years earlier. Despite a visible swelling on one side of her neck, Nell was given permission by the family doctor, during the spring break from Miss Fine's School, to take part in a round of teenage parties.[18] Unfortunately for Nell's social schedule, she became gravely ill. For most of April, she was in bed with a high fever.[19]

With Nell in bed and Stockton still in the hospital, Ellen could only trust Providence to sustain Woodrow's strength. His "curtailed" spring schedule consisted of speaking engagements to alumni groups in Pittsburgh, Detroit, and Kansas City, as well as several addresses in the South.[20] Ellen knew that her husband thrived best when his creative ideas moved to fruition, as they certainly were doing with regard to reforms at Princeton. The health problems of other family members, although serious, were neither too strange nor abrupt for Ellen to meet them with anything other than composure.

On April 26, 1905, this composure was shattered when Ellen and Woodrow learned by telegram that Eddie, Florence, and their young son, Edward Stockton, had drowned that afternoon near Creighton in a bizarre accident. The three of them had set out for an afternoon holiday to a destination on the other side of the Etowah River, some reports said to a picnic, others, a baseball game. An excellent horseman, Ed was driving a two-seated carriage pulled by a team of horses unaccustomed to traveling together. To cross the rain-swollen river, they had to use a flat ferryboat moored at the bank at the foot of a winding road. Ed had almost reached the landing when the horses, suddenly frightened, dashed out on the flatboat and off the other end. As they fell, with the carriage almost reversing itself, they sank in the swift current, entangled where the horses plunged. With Florence on one arm and his son on the other, Ed made a brave fight for their lives. The only witnesses to the accident were two men on the opposite shore who were unable to swim. They crossed the river by a nearby footbridge and tried to get the ferryboat out into the stream. Before they could do this, Ed's strength gave out.[21]

The news of the tragedy, transmitted by telephone from Creighton to Atlanta, came to Ellen's cousin, Edward T. Brown, who then wired the Wilsons. Edward and his wife, Meemee, left at once by train to bring the bodies back to Atlanta. Writing to Ellen, Meemee groped for words which might offer some comfort: "Edward died a hero, holding Florence in one arm and the baby in the other. The men who stood helplessly on the bank saw him each time he sank—raise them to hold them above the water, until strength and consciousness were gone. No signs of distress or terror showed in their faces. Edward was magnificent—like the statue of courage—the baby like a heavenly being." Palmer Axson boarded the train in Atlanta to accompany the three bodies to Princeton, where, on the twenty-ninth, they were buried in Princeton Cemetery after a brief graveside service.[22]

Nell, still in bed, learned of Ed's death from her father, but Ellen took the responsibility of going to the Philadelphia hospital to try to protect Stockton from some of the shock.[23] Instead of sending a cablegram to Madge, then traveling in Switzerland, Ellen wrote to her. Without so much as a softening preamble, she plunged in, "It is useless to try to break it to you gently." For a time, it almost seemed that she had lost her capacity to be compassionate.[24] Nothing in Ellen's life had brought such intensity of grief, and nothing, other than losing Woodrow, would have been more painful. For several weeks she moved in a daze, seldom speaking. When Nell was well enough to travel, she and Ellen went to Atlantic City for a week in mid-May for Nell to have the sea air. Nell chattered away in a desperate attempt to interest and distract her mother, but Ellen responded only with a nod and a heartbroken look. At home again, she went about her household tasks with desperate concentration, as if her life depended on keeping her mind closed against memories.[25] On May 19, Ellen wrote a perfunctory note to Jessie, enclosing the May and June allowances for both daughters (who had been at Eddie's services) and money for Margaret's ticket home.[26]

To complicate matters, an unwell Stockton appeared unexpectedly in Princeton apparently to get advice as to whether or not to become engaged. Marriage, previously considered unwise because of his er-

ratic health, now loomed as a commitment which he should recon-
sider since Ed's death. The decision was deferred until his mind was
clearer.[27] During one of Stockton's earlier breakdowns, Ellen told Florence Hoyt: "I used to think that it didn't matter if you gave way if no
one knew. Now I know that every time you let yourself go weakens you.
I have not dared to give way a minute. Both Stock and Woodrow need
. . . me to be strong all the time. . . . I am sure that is the way to grow
strong—to act all the time as if you were strong."[28] In the face of Ed's
death, her theory on how to be strong was temporarily demolished.

It was a difficult time for Woodrow. He, too, had loved Ed like a
son. Ellen's resources, on which he had depended for twenty years,
were now drained, and he had neither Stockton, nor Madge, nor the
strength and stability of Jessie at hand. But he did have helpful colleagues and especially the Hibbens. Early in July, Professor Williamson
U. Vreeland told Woodrow about an artists' colony in Old Lyme, Connecticut, a place that would be diverting for Ellen and where the rest of
the family could spend the summer. Jack Hibben, on vacation with
his family in upper New York State, wrote to Woodrow that Lyme
sounded like a place where Mrs. Wilson, who had been "so brave" in
the midst of all her troubles, could not fail to get out of herself and
become absorbed in her art.[29]

By mid-July, Ellen, Woodrow, and the two younger daughters were
established in Lyme at Boxwood, a boarding house run in the summer
by a "Miss Thibets."[30] Woodrow's plan to surround Ellen with artists
proved wise. She began to enjoy painting landscapes in oil,[31] and, in
due course, this would supplant her former work in portraiture. Back
in Princeton in mid-September with her spirits vastly improved, Ellen
found Stockton in good health and ready to assume his normal teaching responsibilities—although not yet ready for marriage.[32]

One obligation still ahead, which Ellen dreaded, was to face Madge,
due home shortly after her year abroad. Ellen, by then, wanted to talk
about Ed; Madge could not bear to hear about it. Ellen wept, but
Madge was unable to weep with her. It fell to Woodrow, who perceived
Madge's locked-up emotions, to help her to untangle them. After a
long talk with her brother-in-law, Madge became more reconciled to
the loss of Ed, who Woodrow said, "had all the virtues I could have
wished for in a son of my own, even the virtue of not being too
good."[33]

By November, Ellen summoned the courage to write instructions to

Aunt Louisa for disposing of Ed and Florence's personal possessions, some of which were to be shipped to Prospect. "We have a very large attic," she wrote, "in which I will store these things until I see whether Madge or Stockton want them. They sometimes talk of going to housekeeping together." She regretted that she had no good pictures of Ed since he was a schoolboy,[34] but she thought of a better way to preserve his memory. At the Berry School, founded by Martha McChesney Berry near Rome, Georgia, to educate underprivileged and mountain children, Ellen endowed a scholarship in her brother's name.[35]

Ellen had never possessed Woodrow's unassailable religious faith, and she was plagued by doubts at this period in her life. Stockton later said that his sister had "what one might call a little streak of suppressed skepticism," and now she was unsure about many of the traditional beliefs she had once accepted. She began to read Hegel, Kant, and other philosophers in search of "the foundations of truth," or alternatively, to try to verify her doubts. She discussed Hegel with Jack Hibben who said of her that she knew more about this abstruse German writer than most professors of philosophy.[36] Ellen surely read Hibben's own treatise, *Hegel's Logic* (published in 1902), as well as *Hegel* and *The Philosophy of Kant* by the Scottish theologian Edward Caird; and John McLeod Campbell's *The Nature of Atonement*, all books in the Wilsons' library. From Hegel's philosophy of the relationships of opposites—that everything leads to its opposite, and opposites unite to form a complex whole—Ellen could form a kind of explanation for Eddie's death. This wanton tragedy had to lead to something *constructive*. The way was not yet clear, but she could still believe that Providence would guide her.

Her art, her reading, and the passage of time were effective healers; and the memory of her father's dissolution in the face of grief impelled her to conquer, rather than to give in to, her sorrow. Self-pity, she thought, a "contemptible vice."[37] She told Florence Hoyt that "the one clear duty of the hour is self-control, and that is a thing one can best achieve alone; too much sympathy weakens."[38]

More Illnesses

Stockton's needs, Nell's illness, Woodrow's surgery, and Ed's death did not end the seige of troubles. After an erratic semester in the spring of 1905, Margaret had dropped out of college in May because of a "nervous condition." As early as February 25, after a hurried trip to Baltimore because of Margaret, Ellen had written to Dr. Van Meter that her daughter was in the hands of *three* specialists who had recommended that Margaret should take no more examinations for the rest of the academic year, but that she should remain in college "on half work." "She has been a nervous child all her life," Ellen said, "and is evidently unfitted by temperament to take a full college course."[1] By May, Margaret's physician thought it best for her not to complete the spring term.[2]

The impact of Ed's death, her waning interest in academic subjects, and her desire not to disappoint her parents contributed to Margaret's depression. After studying voice at the Peabody Conservatory during her two years at the Woman's College, she now wanted to take lessons from a private teacher.[3] Before a decision was made about her future, however, Ellen and Woodrow elected to give her a trip abroad. On what date Margaret sailed, and with whom, is not revealed, but by early August 1905, she was in Heidelberg to begin a tour of Germany. The question of whether or not she would return to college was still unresolved, but Margaret wrote to Jessie: "I wish neither of us had to go back to college. I don't want to a bit."[4]

When Margaret returned in October, Ellen wrote to Dean Van Meter that the trip abroad had not restored Margaret's health as hoped, and after further consultation with doctors in Baltimore, the Wilsons had decided that their daughter should not return to the Woman's College in the fall of 1905. Instead, she would study vocal music at the Peabody Conservatory.[5]

The Goucher College records do not show Margaret as a student after May 1905, nor was she at the Peabody after that date. After Ellen's reference in October to her daughter's tenuous health, Margaret vanishes from the records until June 1906. Writing to Anna Harris a year later, Ellen, in a compilation of family ills during 1904–1905, mentioned Margaret's "nervous collapse."[6] In April 1906, Woodrow observed to Arthur Tedcastle that "the strain of last winter showed its effects upon Mrs. Wilson."[7] That fall he wrote to another friend: "[Margaret] looks and seems better than we have seen her look in several years and our hearts are light about her." At the same time, Ellen wrote to Jessie that Margaret looked remarkably well and was having "a nice time," she thought.[8] These comments suggest that Margaret had recovered from a period of poor health. Exactly where she was during those months is not clear. Had she been at home in December 1905, Margaret would not have been excluded, as the evidence indicates, from a spectacular social event that took place at Prospect.

While the Wilsons were in Lyme, an announcement was made from the White House that, in the fall, the President of the United States would attend a football game in Princeton. Woodrow immediately wrote to the President and Mrs. Theodore Roosevelt to invite them to lunch at Prospect on that day.[9] The occasion was the eleventh annual match between the army and navy teams to be played on the neutral ground of University Field. When the Roosevelts accepted Woodrow's invitation, Ellen went at once to Frances Cleveland to be tutored in the care and feeding of Presidents.[10]

On the day of the luncheon, Ellen laid places for eighteen—fifteen guests in the president's party, Madge, Woodrow, and herself. Except for the tie score of the football game recorded for posterity, the day on which the President of the United States dined at Prospect might have become a detail on the calendar had Madge Axson not been present. Her account survives:

> I was seated in proper obscurity half way down the long table next to a middle-aged man who introduced himself as the President's brother-in-law, Douglas Robinson. . . . In about two minutes we were talking away . . . and I was thinking what a very nice person he was to make a young girl feel so at ease. But suddenly I heard my name shouted from the end of the table—"Miss Axson," called . . . President [Roosevelt], "stop making eyes at that man on your left. He's a gray-headed old grandfather. Devote yourself to the chap on your right. He's a rich bachelor."

At intervals during the luncheon, Madge heard the president's "appall-ing roar" of "Miss Axson" and his fists would "slam-bang" on the table. She concluded that if this was the acceptable mode of "mild presidential banter," she never wanted to meet another head of state.[11]

In the spring of 1906, Woodrow continued with his schedule of public addresses, twenty-one between January 6 and May 19.[12] On the morning of May 28, in the midst of preparations for commencement activities, he awoke blind in his left eye. This was the trial that Ellen had feared most of all—Woodrow mysteriously, perhaps seriously, ill. Jack Hibben accompanied him that day to Philadelphia to be examined by the noted ophthalmologist, Dr. George Edmund de Schweinitz, who found that a blood vessel had burst in the eye. Dr. Schweinitz told Woodrow that this was a manifestation of a more general disease of the arteries, probably high blood pressure, and that the president of Princeton University must give up active work.[13] On June 12, Ellen wrote to Mary Hoyt, who was planning a visit to Princeton: "Two weeks ago yesterday Woodrow waked up perfectly blind in one eye!—it turned out to be from the bursting of a blood-vessel in it. Of course we had a dreadful week; all sorts of tests were made to determine the cause,—it is something wrong with the circulation due entirely to a general condition of overstrain. The doctors said he must stop *all* work at once, that it was impossible to exaggerate the critical nature of the situation. But now there is every cause for encouragement. The clot in the eye is being absorbed with extraordinary rapidity." Woodrow was highly nervous and easily irritated, even by the chattering of "seven women," one of whom was Annie Howe. "So if he feels thus about his own sister," Ellen told Mary, "I know you understand, dear, that I ought not to add to the number of the household;—even *you* and our dear Florence, whose sweet, quiet, gentle ways are so exactly to his taste."[14]

During the week of commencement, Woodrow slept at Professor John Howell Westcott's to be away from the confusion. Andrew F. West, who for six years had been dean of the small Graduate School, helped Ellen receive at the luncheon for the trustees, and Jack Hibben took over the presidential duties. After delivering the baccalaureate sermon on June 10, Professor Henry van Dyke read a message from Woodrow to the graduating class, the students whose four years at Princeton coincided with the four years when "some of the most significant things" Woodrow had planned and hoped for in the life of the university had taken shape and come to "a happy realization."[15] The tone of the message was elegiac. Woodrow's illness completely over-shadowed Nell's graduation in June from Miss Fine's School.

How Woodrow would spend the summer, a decision still pending when Ellen wrote Mary Hoyt, was resolved a week later in favor of the entire family going to England for several months. There, Woodrow had found rest and refreshment in 1896, 1899, and, briefly, with Ellen in 1903. To return in 1906 to the healing airs of the lake district was his wish as well as the prescription of Dr. Alfred Stengel, a Philadelphia internist.[16] Before the Wilsons sailed on the *Caledonia* on Saturday, June 30, Ellen dashed off a note to Florence Hoyt to say goodbye and to explain that what threatened Woodrow was "hardening of the ar-teries, due to prolonged high pressure on brain and nerves." "He has lived too tensely. . . . It is an awful thing—a dying by inches, and incur-able." From Dr. Stengel, Ellen learned that "50 year old arteries do not go back to an earlier condition," but a rest of three months should enable Woodrow to be in condition for a reasonable amount of work in the fall. Ellen thought Stengel's prognosis was somewhat contradictory, and instead of offering reassurance, left her "rather overwhelmed."[17]

During the six weeks at Rydal, Ambleside, where the Wilsons had rented Loughrigg Cottage, Woodrow unmistakably gained strength. Joined frequently by Ellen or the girls, he took long walks, some up to fourteen miles a day. It was on one of these rambles alone that Wood-row, in crossing Pelter Bridge over the Rothay River, met "a man with a rugged face and a mop of tousled gray hair," who turned out to be Frederic Yates, English painter of portraits and landscapes. The two men immediately struck up a warm friendship which would include Yates's wife, Emily, his daughter, Mary, and the entire Wilson family. Yates was soon helping fellow-artist Ellen Wilson with her painting.[18] He then began to do pastel drawings of Ellen, the daughters, and Woodrow; and, subsequently, executed a full-length oil portrait of Princeton's president in academic robes, commissioned by Moses Tay-lor Pyne as a gift to the university.[19] As Yates worked on Ellen's like-ness, he had difficulty catching an expression in her eyes which he had seen and wanted to portray. He waited. One day, as she posed and Woodrow read aloud Robert Browning's *Saul*, Yates shouted, "I've got it." The resulting portrait was "a perfect likeness."[20]

By early August, Woodrow was well enough to write to Annie Howe that he had never *felt* as if there were anything the matter with him.[21] Two weeks later, Ellen left Margaret to keep Woodrow company, while she, Jessie, and Nell visited Durham, Lincoln, York, and Cambridge, and, lastly, London, where they saw Ellen Terry in *The Winter's Tale* at His Majesty's Theatre. Woodrow sent intermittent instructions to the travelers ("You can tell the cabby in London that you wish to be driven to the Thackeray Hotel on Great Russell Street, opposite the Museum").[22]

While Ellen was in London, Woodrow went by appointment to Edinburgh to see two physicians, Drs. Francis D. Boyd, an internist, and George A. Berry, an ophthalmologist. Their reports were encouraging; in fact, Dr. Boyd was inclined to prescribe that Woodrow return to work in the fall. The doctors would give him their judgments in ten days, when Woodrow was to return to Edinburgh for the final medical report.[23] The family was together again in Rydal near the end of the first week in September, and a few days later, Woodrow was back in Scotland. The doctors concluded that he was able to return to work provided he took decent care of himself; and that "equable and reasonable work," rather than months of idleness, would be preferable—even good—for a man of his temperament. Woodrow promised to break the academic year with a midwinter vacation in a warm climate, to make as few outside engagements as possible, and to keep "within bounds" at home. These stipulations were not burdensome because he loved his work too much to be willing to run the risk of rendering himself unfit for it.[24] The long vacation, as restorative to Ellen as to Woodrow, was needful for both; the role of watchdog over his health fell inevitably to her.

As soon as the Wilsons were at home again, Ellen was involved in a rush of activities which included getting Jessie, a junior, and Nell, a freshman, off to college. Madge, who had spent the summer in Lyme with Princeton friends, had gone to the South for a round of weddings and house parties. Margaret was granted her wish to study voice privately and was to live at home.[25]

Nell, even less interested than Margaret in a full liberal arts course, was steered by her mother to St. Mary's School, an Episcopal boarding school and junior college for girls in Raleigh, North Carolina. The rector was none other than the Reverend McNeely DuBose, whose wife, Rosalie, was "school mother."[26] Enrolled as a junior, Nell planned to take two years at St. Mary's, as much for the experience of being away from home as for intellectual nurture. Both Jessie and Nell arrived late for the opening of their respective schools to face a staggering backlog of work.[27] The delinquent class work did not upset Nell, but the "horrible, silly, and abominable" rules outraged her. She was even ready to consider a transfer to the Woman's College of Baltimore.[28]

Nell's objections to St. Mary's were not unfounded. Ellen failed to realize that, irrespective of her family's southern roots, Nell had grown up in a considerably more cosmopolitan environment than most of her eighteen-year-old peers in Raleigh. Ellen chose the school because of Rosalie and Mac's presence there, and she knew full well about the restrictive rules. A little defensively, she pointed out to Jessie that Nell needed a regulated life just then, for "if she kept as late hours and disported herself" as she had the previous winter in Princeton, there would be little chance of a full recovery from the draining attack brought on by the tubercular glands.[29]

Ellen was a devoted mother, but Jessie was the daughter with whom she enjoyed the greatest rapport. Beautiful and brilliant, Jessie inherited some of the best qualities of both her parents. At the end of her sophomore year in college, she had received the highest marks of anyone in her class, achievements which she neglected to tell her family about in the midst of the distractions over her father's illness. Ellen and Woodrow found out about Jessie's scholastic honors through a preceptor, who had read the news in the *Baltimore Sun*. It was no trifling accomplishment considering her courses in 1905–1906: German, French, physics, geology, anatomy, and history.[30] After pledging Gamma Phi Beta in her freshman year, Jessie had been disturbed by the undemocratic methods used by the sororities to select members. She and her classmate Flora Lois Robinson now considered resigning from their sorority and agitating to abolish these organizations. It seemed to Ellen as if the whole business was managed "in the worst possible way at Baltimore." She was "intensely exasperated" about it all because she thought that it was "spoiling in large measure" Jessie's college course— years that ought to be among the happiest of her life.[31] The problem would become more acute before Jessie graduated.

The daughter closest to Woodrow was Nell. She could entertain and amuse him, and, like her Uncle Ed, had "the virtue of not being too good." Both father and daughter were latent ham actors, with a penchant for playfulness—rarely displayed on the father's part except in intimate family circles. Woodrow divided the family into what he called "the proper members" (Ellen and Jessie) and "the vulgar members" (himself and Nell); Margaret was "proper part of the time and vulgar all the rest."[32]

If Jessie had inherited from her parents a superior intellect, Margaret received the lion's share of her father's musical talent. Now at home, with time to practice on her Steinway piano and to pursue her voice training, she arranged to go to Baltimore for private lessons with Blanche Sylvana, a member of the faculty at the Peabody Conservatory. She spent nights either with the Hoyts or, on occasion, with Jessie.[33] Another activity which Margaret enjoyed was singing in a special choir recently organized at Princeton's First Presbyterian Church. George Dwight Kellog, a preceptor in classics who was also in the choir, was attentive to Margaret, and Dr. Herring Winship, a local physician, had been given permission by Margaret to call on her. Winship was doomed before he began, however, because Woodrow disliked him and asked Margaret to be cool with him when he came.[34]

Margaret's involvement in the choir of the First Presbyterian Church was an offshoot of a decision which Ellen and Woodrow had made the year before. In 1905, Jack Hibben, active in the First Presbyterian Church, and Woodrow, in the Second, had tried to bring about the union of the two congregations sitting diagonally across Nassau Street from each other. When their joint efforts failed, Woodrow, Ellen, Margaret, Jessie, and twenty-eight others had moved their membership in November 1905 to the First Church.[35]

For a while in the fall of 1906, Ellen relegated to her oldest daughter the task of writing to Jessie and Nell, because she, Ellen, was too busy. For one thing, she had lost her regular cook, and the search for a replacement consumed hours of her time. After exhausting the possibilities in Princeton and Philadelphia, she turned to employment agencies in New York. To her surprise, she discovered that absolutely no one would come to Princeton. One forthright applicant told Mrs. Wilson that *she* would not go to New Jersey even to cook for St. Peter. Ellen catered the luncheon for the trustees in October and a dinner on November 2 at the dedication of the remodeled faculty room in Nassau Hall.[36] She eventually found a cook, Elise Doeppel, a graduate of Mrs. Rorer's Philadelphia cooking school, where Ellen herself had gone.[37]

Miss Doeppel began her duties in time to prepare luncheon for Mr. and Mrs. Andrew Carnegie, in Princeton for the dedication of Carnegie's gift to the university of a lake. Named after its donor, the man-made facility would provide a place for undergraduate rowing, as well as recreational facilities for the Princeton community.[38] Margaret Wilson, present at the luncheon, observed that Mrs. Carnegie was "simply charming, so natural and sweet, and dear." But her husband was "most insignificant looking," "a vain little man," and "a flatterer."[39]

Ellen did not forget the doctors' admonition that Woodrow must have relaxation. She arranged for him, Margaret, and herself to go into the city on a Friday evening in November to see two Shakespearean plays, *King Lear*, at the Academy of Music, with Robert Mantell, and *Cymbeline*, at the Astor, a Saturday matinee starring Viola Allen. Woodrow and Ellen spent the night at a hotel, while Margaret stayed with Fräulein Böhm, now living with a family in Yonkers. Ellen reviewed both performances for Jessie:

> Mantell is really quite *wonderful* as Lear,—his support as a whole was very bad (Cordelia dreadful) but fortunately the clown and "Kent" were pretty good. The "Cymbeline" was altogether delightful. Viola Allen was *perfectly charming* as "Imogene"; and she was well supported, except, alas! in the case of "Posthumus." Such an unfortunate exception, and yet such a common one! It seems to me that as a rule the part of the "hero" is wretchedly acted when the "star" is a woman. And as the *lot* of [the heroes] are rather foolish weak creatures as represented by Shakespeare himself, it seems a pity to exaggerate those special qualities in the acting.[40]

Ellen undoubtedly projected her girlhood antipathies toward weak, indecisive men upon Shakespeare's gallery of males. She could see facets of her father's personality in Lear, Hamlet, Richard II, and Henry VI; and Uncle Will, who had given up medical studies abroad to return to the Confederacy, was something of an Antony whose love affair was with the South rather than an Egyptian queen.[41]

Ellen went into the city again on December 14 to hear Woodrow give the keynote address to six hundred men at the Southern Society banquet held at the Waldorf-Astoria. Seated, of course, in the box provided for women guests, Ellen was there not to "mingle" but to listen to the program.[42]

With the holiday season of 1906 near, Ellen looked forward to having Madge and her two younger daughters at home for Christmas. The whole family, Stockton included, appeared to be in good health, although Ellen was uneasy about Jessie's having had tonsillitis, due, she thought, to overexertion in catching up with classwork.[43] When the daughters arrived at Prospect, Ellen found that, instead of Jessie, it was Nell who had the serious health problem.

After one look at the ugly lump on Nell's neck, now considerably larger, Ellen rushed her to Dr. William W. Keen, the specialist who had treated Jessie. On the day after Christmas, Nell was admitted to the Philadelphia Hospital for surgery which was nearly fatal. One of the infected glands was found adhering to the jugular vein, and the surgeon had "to cut 1½ inches of the vein." Ellen, Woodrow, and Stockton stood by while Nell's life "hung by a thread"—and the skill of a surgeon's knife.[44] By the end of January, Nell was regaining color and strength, but Ellen could hardly bear to look at the awful scar. ("You would think a musket ball had ploughed into her neck.")[45] Woodrow, meanwhile, to fulfill the promise made to his doctors, left on January 12 for a month's vacation in Bermuda where he was "condemned" to go by himself.[46] Ellen could not leave Nell.

Part Six

1906–1910

Ellen Axson Wilson, 1910. Courtesy of William D. Hoyt.

Chapter 21

Calm before the Storm

By the end of January 1907, Ellen was sufficiently optimistic about Nell to renew plans to have a "coming out" dance in February for Margaret. Jessie's two sisters began a campaign to get her to Princeton for this, the first president's dance ever to be held at Prospect. Ellen, too, thought it would afford a rest which Jessie perhaps needed after her midterm examinations.[1] Whether or not Jessie joined her sisters is uncertain, but Woodrow was back from Bermuda to help Ellen receive the young guests. The only surviving eyewitness account comes from the diary of a preceptor in politics, William Starr Myers: "Bitter cold— thermometer 3 to 6° below zero. . . . In the evening, to a reception and dance at President Wilson's and a delightful time."[2]

Madge went to Georgia immediately after the dance to be with Aunt Louisa, who was terminally ill. On February 19, Aunt Louisa ("like a mother to all of us") died, leaving Uncle Henry as the last survivor among Nathan Hoyt's six children.

When Madge returned to Princeton, the young preceptors came to Prospect in a steady stream. Margaret, no match for the seductive Madge, retaliated by consistently addressing her as "Aunt."[3] Ellen arranged teas, small midweek dinners, and musicals to keep Margaret in the competition.[4] One of the preceptors, a classmate of Eddie Axson and a protégé of Woodrow, was especially interested in "Miss Axson." His name was Edward Graham Elliott, a southerner, who, after graduating from Princeton, had received a Ph.D. in political science and jurisprudence, summa cum laude, from Heidelberg University. When Madge was a teenager visiting the Wilsons on Library Place, Ed had met her and was fascinated. A mutual affection was beginning to grow.[5]

Another young instructor at Princeton, Charles Eugley Mathews, had caused a social problem by asking well ahead for more of Jessie's time during commencement week than she wanted him to have. When Jessie appealed to her mother for advice, Ellen generously complied: go with him to the dance, but tell him, *nicely*, of course, that the invitation to the glee club concert and the dance, in one evening, would be too taxing; refuse the invitation to the Triangle Club show by telling him that she had seen it; accept the Yale game. Or, if Jessie preferred the Triangle Club, go with him to that and refuse the game.[6] In the spring, Jessie had been asked to be president the following—her senior—year, of the Young Women's Christian Association, but her parents thought that it would be unwise for her to accept. Ellen thought that Jessie's constitution had received severe shocks (notably the one in North Carolina) at a critical age, and it was important not to overtax her strength until she reached "full maturity."[7] However, when the niece of the Wilsons' former neighbor, Harriete Foote (Mrs. George) Armour, wailed about how hard she thought college life was on girls—she knew a girl who was so broken down by college in two years that it had ruined her life in society—Ellen snapped, "Poor Martyr to . . . higher education!"[8]

Ellen continued to divide her time and energy between her own interests and the constant, official entertaining, between the activities of family members both at home and away, and between her need for periodic refreshment and Woodrow's dependence upon her. One Saturday afternoon, with less than an hour's notice, she went alone to Philadelphia to see Maude Adams in *Peter Pan* at the Broad Street Theater. Later, she and Margaret saw a matinee performance of *A Midsummer Night's Dream*, starring Annie Russell as Puck.[9] Following one of her husband's Blumenthal lectures at Columbia University, Ellen arranged for herself and Woodrow to see Nazimova in *Countesse Coquette*, a "little parlour comedy" which amused Woodrow. Ellen's preference would have been to see Nazimova in one of the Ibsen roles for which she was famous.[10]

When the paintings of the family, done in England by Fred Yates the summer before, and some of his landscapes, arrived at Prospect, Ellen began negotiations with the Macbeth Gallery in New York to arrange an exhibit of the collection. The portrait of Woodrow was the *most* impressive, she told William Macbeth. "It is in the full academic costume, black silk, purple velvet and gold [hood] . . . a full length portrait (7 ft.)."[11] The study of Jessie ("too good to be true") made Ellen homesick for her daughter, whom she could "hardly bear to have away for another whole year."[12]

In addition to Ellen's primary duties as hostess at Prospect, volunteer work consumed her time. During the years that Woodrow was president of Princeton University, she was a member of the Ladies Auxiliary, a group of faculty women initially organized in 1902 to raise money for ladies' rooms in the new gymnasium, and later she was head of the subcommittee on the college infirmary. The subcommittee began to improve services to students who were hospitalized on campus, and, by the fall of 1904, under Ellen's leadership, the women were paying for nurses and maids. Future plans called for raising funds to support "a young doctor at $1000 a year."[13]

From early May of 1907 through commencement week in mid-June, Ellen's schedule was relentless. There were unexpected visitors, "foreign and domestic," and a host of relatives, among whom were Palmer Axson and his bride, Margaret Calloway Axson, of Savannah.[14]

One of Ellen's less triumphant dinners, with the Allan Marquands present, took place late in May, when Gilbert Murray and his wife, Lady Mary, daughter of the ninth earl of Carlisle, were the guests of honor. Murray, a Fellow of New College, Oxford, had been at Harvard for a series of lectures and had come to Princeton to hear at firsthand about President Wilson's new educational methods. Ellen planned an elaborate meal, all of which the Murrays politely declined. When Woodrow blurted out, "But Lady Mary, you are eating nothing!" she explained that they were vegetarians—and a flustered Miss Doeppel prepared two servings of poached eggs. When Lady Mary had written to accept Woodrow's invitation to visit Prospect, she had revealed their eating habits in a postscript on an inner page which he had not found. Ellen, less upset than her husband, found the Murrays simple, natural people and thoroughly delightful houseguests.[15]

These and other visitors at Prospect in June 1907 were awed by a stained glass window recently installed in the east wall on the front stair landing. A gift of two of the trustees (one of whom was Cleveland H. Dodge), the window, designed by Ellen, was executed in Tiffany glass by two women artists, Julia P. Wickham and [Maria] Y. Stone, who worked in New York. The window portrays Aristotle, holding his *Ethics*, in a pose taken from the great Raphael fresco, *The School of Athens*. At the base of the window an inscription (in Greek) reads: "The human good is the activity of the soul in accordance with virtue." It was a timely message in view of Woodrow's plans for Princeton's reform.[16]

Chapter 22

Quadrangles

*During the first four years of his presidency, Woodrow had changed Prince-*ton from a gentleman's college to a place of serious learning by raising academic standards, reorganizing the curriculum, instituting the preceptorial system, and eliminating deadwood from the faculty. Had he stopped with these reforms, "his educational reputation would have been secured and it could have been said then that no man, in Princeton's one hundred and sixty years of existence, had made a greater contribution to the University's progress and greatness."[1] No one knew better than Ellen, however, that her husband was unlikely to rest on past achievements, and that he considered his contributions to Princeton unfinished.

Woodrow had returned from England in the fall of 1906 with intent to propose to the board of trustees a restructuring of Princeton's famous eating clubs. These were housed in elaborate student- and alumni-owned buildings situated on both sides of Prospect Avenue adjacent to the campus. Woodrow believed that they were socially undemocratic, were destructive to the "singularly fine and unselfish Princeton spirit," and did not provide an intellectually stimulating atmosphere.[2] Thus, at the trustees' quarterly meeting in December 1906, Woodrow had submitted a confidential preliminary report outlining his plan, a report which the board heard with apparent approval. They authorized the president to appoint a Committee of Seven, with him as chairman, to consider the proposal and report to a later meeting of the board.[3]

In June 1907, Woodrow presented the follow-up report. The committee proposed to group the undergraduates "in residential quadrangles, each with its common dining hall, its common room for intercourse and diversion, and its resident masters and preceptors; where members of all four classes shall be associated in a sort of family life, not merely as neighbors in the dormitories but also as comrades at meals and in many daily activities,—the upper classes ruling and . . . [helping to form] the lower, and all in constant association with members of the faculty."[4]

Before President Patton's resignation, the trustees had finally yielded to faculty agitation and established a small Graduate School, presided over by Andrew F. West.[5] Shortly before the board meeting in June, Dean West had completed a report about the construction of the proposed graduate college which recommended a location near, but not a part of, the undergraduate campus. In the fall of 1906, the dean had declined an offer to become president of the Massachusetts Institute of Technology on the understanding that he would be given by the trustees and the president full freedom to carry out his ideas about the graduate college. A bequest of $250,000 from Mrs. Josephine A. Thompson Swann was already in hand toward the construction of the buildings.[6]

But Woodrow believed strongly that the graduate college, which he wanted to be an academy of distinction, should be located in the heart of the campus where students and faculty could intermingle. This decision, he believed, was a necessary part of the overall plan to reorganize the university to maximize intellectual and social benefits.[7] Beginning with the publication of the quadrangle plan in the *Alumni Weekly* of June 12, 1907, and continuing through the next three years, the trustees, faculty, alumni, and, to a lesser extent, the students, sorted themselves into what eventually became pro-West and pro-Wilson factions. The controversies that arose from the quadrangle plan and the graduate college site would, in due course, overlap and be further inflamed by the clash of two strong personalities: Woodrow's and Dean West's.[8]

With tensions mounting, Ellen was determined to find a secluded place for the family's vacation during the summer of 1907. In April, Woodrow had been "so wretchedly ill and so depressed" that she could "hardly leave his side for a moment."[9] She had considered packing him off alone to England's lake district, a place which was always restorative.[10] The Wilsons settled, finally, on St. Hubert's, a village twenty-four miles from the railway near Keene Valley in the Adirondack Mountains.[11] Before the family left on July 9, Jack Hibben, disturbed by the hostility erupting toward Woodrow's quadrangle plan, and, in the role of compromiser and peacemaker, dropped in at Prospect. Finding only Ellen at home, Hibben heard unanticipated straight talk from Woodrow's wife. She told Hibben that he had merely disheartened Woodrow for the fight, robbed him of hope, and wounded him without avail, and that Woodrow now felt more than ever that the fight had to be waged to the finish. Hibben was dismayed that his "poor but well intended offices of friendship" had so miscarried; and he regretted that Ellen Wilson was so deeply distressed by his endeavors.[12] From St. Hubert's, Woodrow wrote Hibben an affectionate, conciliatory letter, which implicitly apologized for Ellen's frankness. At the same time, he urged that, in the struggle ahead, the two of them, Jack and Woodrow, despite their obvious differences of opinion, remain friends.[13]

The quiet of the Adirondacks was ideal for a family that loved and enjoyed one another as much as the Wilsons. A cluster of cottages stood in the woods near the St. Hubert's clubhouse, which had a large dining room for guests who chose not to cook. Ellen took two cottages, one with four bedrooms for Margaret, Jessie, Nell, and Madge, and, on occasion, the Hoyts; the other, much smaller and more secluded, was for herself and Woodrow. The summer settlement on the Au Sable River had a sprinkling of Princeton people—the Walter Lowries and the Allan Marquands in cottages, and Henrietta Ricketts, who preferred the more civilized clubhouse. Ellen hired a summer cook and maid to provide more privacy for her family and to give the Prospect staff a needed vacation. On Sundays, the Wilsons usually walked to a chapel in the woods to hear the Reverend Walter Lowrie give sermons which satisfied the taste of everyone from Woodrow to Madge, a very wide range indeed. Ellen spent many hours at her easel in a grove behind the cottage. She and Woodrow discussed the quadrangle plan, a subject which could hardly be avoided because of the flow of letters which indicated serious and growing opposition to the abolition of the eating clubs.[14]

The women amused themselves, and at times diverted Woodrow, with a Ouija board found in one of the closets. When Woodrow kept asking the Ouija to send up Dr. James McCosh (he had died in 1894), that wise old Scotsman did not appear, but Jack Hibben did—from his vacation spot in Vermont.[15] He had come again as a friend, to try to induce Woodrow to give up the quadrangle plan in the interest of harmony. Hibben was sure that Woodrow was going to split the college, and Woodrow was just as sure that Jack was timid.[16]

When the Wilsons returned to Princeton in mid-September, Ellen was not happy that much of her husband's vacation had been spent in revising the eight Blumenthal lectures for publication, and that university problems had invaded the Adirondacks. (The lectures, entitled *Constitutional Government in the United States*, were published as a book by the Columbia University Press the following March.)

The "quadrangling," as Ellen called it, was no longer solely a matter of university business. The entire Wilson family was now emotionally involved.[17] At a faculty meeting on September 26, Woodrow's friend, Jack Hibben, seconded Henry van Dyke's motion to ask the trustees to appoint a new "representative" committee (of trustees, faculty, alumni, and students) to investigate thoroughly the social conditions of the university and "to consider the best method" of solving the problems.[18] The motion lost, but Woodrow interpreted Hibben's action as a public stand with the opposition.

Ellen weakly defended Jack Hibben, whose actions were "hurting . . . [Woodrow] dreadfully." She thought that Hibben had been made a tool of and did not realize what he had done. "But since our brains were given us to use," Ellen said, "that is no excuse." She drew some comfort from believing that many of Woodrow's colleagues now considered Hibben's influence and prestige among the faculty gone forever.[19] Even so, the trustees, alarmed at the increase in opposition to the quad plan among the alumni and some of its own members, withdrew their approval at their meeting in October and voted to discharge the committee on social coordination. The trustees resolved, however, that they had no wish "to hinder" the president in his attempts to win board members and Princeton men to his cause.[20]

Woodrow, who reacted by planning to resign, was so tense that Ellen had to be with him constantly. Only the entreaties from friends and supporters on the faculty and the board of trustees persuaded him to remain at his post. Ellen felt that her husband, defeated only for the time being, was left "with all the honours of the field."[21] Woodrow did not share her optimism. He thought that he had got nothing out of it "except complete defeat and mortification."[22]

Stockton Axson, who had a deep sense of loyalty both to his colleagues and to his brother-in-law, found himself in a precarious position. To jump actively into the battle would require more emotional energy than Stockton had to spare, but he agreed with those on the faculty who thought that Woodrow was moving too far too fast. An alumnus from Pittsburgh, Lawrence C. Woods, asked Stockton to entreat the president to put a more conciliatory note in his talks, and Stockton passed the suggestion on to his brother-in-law. Woodrow was annoyed, and Ellen sniffed, "Mr. Woods ought not to try to instruct Woodrow." When she, too, was uncompromising on the club issue, Stockton knew that he was "wrestling with two warriors mightier than I."[23]

While Jessie's parents were immersed in the controversy at Prince-

Jessie Woodrow Wilson, 1906. From a drawing by Frederic B. Yates.
Courtesy of Marjorie Brown King.

ton, she continued to fight against social snobbery at the Woman's College of Baltimore. The attempts which she and Flora Robinson had made to reform the methods of selecting sorority members had been fruitless, and Jessie wanted to resign at once from Gamma Phi Beta. She was torn between two ethical choices: demonstration of her disapproval of the selection process by resigning, or the ignominy of leaving

Flora to fight alone. "I wish I could tell you, my precious one," Ellen wrote to her daughter, "just how deep my sympathy is with you in this time of strain and stress. One moment I am all pride in you, my brave, noble girl,—and the next my heart is just bleeding for my *poor little* one,—so young for such a trial!"[24] Woodrow, too, sent words of comfort to his "true and brave daughter."[25] (When Jessie did submit her resignation the following spring, she was called before a mass meeting of Gamma Phi Beta alumnae to state her reasons for withdrawing. It amounted to an inquest through which Jessie "stood calmly and with utmost dignity.")[26]

In the late fall, Ellen entertained Lucy and Mary Smith, Katie Murray was at Prospect for the usual week of seasonal sewing,[27] and, during several days of Indian summer, Ellen superintended new plantings in the garden. She set out several hundred new shrubs (hydrangea, snowball, etc.) "in masses for landscape effects."[28]

When Woodrow left on November 7 on a ten-day speaking tour in Tennessee and Ohio, Ellen was in bed with a heavy cold and inflamed throat. Stockton moved into Prospect to be with her and to help with her correspondence.[29] (Margaret was in Chapel Hill.) Stockton was such a devoted nurse that Ellen vowed she had not had such a "good time" being ill since her mother died.[30]

Not long after Woodrow returned from his tour, Ellen wrote to Agnes Tedcastle that he was having a serious time with "neuritis";[31] but she wrote to Jessie that he was better, though still far from comfortable. "The inflammation in the arm is sufficiently relieved now for him to be massaged and that is a great comfort to him. . . . Your father wants me and I must stop."[32]

Relaxation during the Christmas holidays did not cure Woodrow's neuritis, and Ellen persuaded him to have another winter rest in Bermuda. Before he sailed in mid-January, he faced a tense meeting with the board of trustees on the ninth. At that time, a resolution was passed asking the president to appoint a committee from among the trustees to confer with a group of alumni who recognized the "evils of the Upperclass Clubs" and who believed that the evils could be remedied through a less drastic approach than their abolition. The trustee committee members whom Woodrow appointed, all supporters of his, were to report back in April.[33]

Ellen asked Margaret to write to Jessie the details about the trustee meeting (Margaret's letter, if written, has not survived), because to go over it all again would make her ill. Even so, she tried to put matters in perspective. "It is all pretty bad, yet we must not exaggerate the troubles. . . . Your father is in the mood for a stern fight now, and has no idea of resigning under two years. . . . We will certainly win in the end."[34]

The day before Woodrow left for Bermuda, Ellen went into New York with him to spend the night and to see Alla Nazimova in *The Comet*.[35] Instead of accompanying Woodrow on his vacation, Ellen decided to go with Stockton ("very unwell") to Savannah, where he was scheduled to give a series of lectures on Shakespeare.[36] Nell, unhappy about the decision, wished that "sweetest, *dearest* mother" could go to Bermuda.[37] But the change of air and the success of his Shakespeare lectures made Stockton "well and bright again."[38] He returned to Princeton while Ellen remained in Atlanta with Edward and Meemee Brown.

Two years older than Ellen and one of her favorite cousins, Edward Brown had attended Davidson College and then studied law in Athens with Judge Howell Cobb. Meemee, an Ohio native and a graduate of the Cincinnati Conservatory of Music, had by her marriage to Edward in 1887, added to the family a woman whom Ellen found "satisfying in every respect." When Ellen stopped in Raleigh for two days with Nell, she "entirely lost her heart" to Edward and Meemee's fifteen-year-old daughter, Marjorie, "a little beauty and altogether charming." Marjorie, who overlapped one year at St. Mary's with Nell, was "a splendid student" and "immensely popular."[39] During her visit to Raleigh, Ellen did not see Rosalie because the DuBoses had left St. Mary's the preceding fall to take a pastorate in Morganton, North Carolina.

At home from her southern trip, Ellen immediately helped Madge and Margaret to pack for New Orleans where they would be guests of Lucy and Mary Smith during Mardi Gras. Except for Stockton, who came to "dine and sleep," Prospect was virtually empty.

Chapter 23

Triangles

While Ellen was in Georgia, Woodrow was the pet of a popular Bermuda hostess, Mrs. Mary Allen Hulbert Peck, and her entourage made up of her mother, Mrs. Charles Sterling Allen, her twenty-year-old son, Allen Schoolcraft Hulbert, and a stepdaughter, Harriet Peck, age twenty-two. Woodrow had met Mrs. Peck in 1907 two days before he left Bermuda. Both had been dinner guests at the home of Hamilton's mayor, William T. James.[1] Mrs. Peck had then invited the president of Princeton to dinner the next evening, his last in Bermuda.[2] In a note of thanks written to her before he had sailed for New York, Woodrow said that it was not often he had the privilege of meeting anyone he could "so entirely admire and enjoy."[3]

In January 1908, Mary Peck set about at once to soothe his frayed nerves with the help of her family and other island visitors, one of whom was Mark Twain. "Mrs. Peck . . . is very fine," Woodrow wrote to Ellen. "You must know her. She lives at Pittsfield, Massachusetts, and insists that when we go up to [Harry] Garfield's inauguration [at Williams College] we shall go down to visit her. I feel that we must manage it if possible, for I know that you would like her, despite her free western manner."[4]

The forty-five-year-old Mary Peck, a native of Grand Rapids, Michigan, was a vivacious, witty woman, skilled in music, sports, and social graces. In 1883, she had married Thomas Harbach Hulbert, an engineer, who died six years later as the result of a mining accident. The young widow, left with an infant son, Allen, had no means of support. A year later, she made an expedient marriage to Thomas Dowse Peck, an affluent widower with three children, and went to live at his home in Pittsfield, Massachusetts. For a number of years, Mary had spent the winters in Bermuda on the recommendation of her physician as therapy for melancholia. In truth, it was to escape from an oppressive marriage. This woman, with her "free western manner" who lived a daring life on her own in Bermuda, fascinated Woodrow. Mary saw in him something "fine and noble" that led to her own self-examination and a subsequent determination to end her artificial marriage.[5]

The relationship which was blossoming in Bermuda between Mary and Woodrow apparently did not alter his intense devotion to Ellen. "Give yourself up to enjoyment, my sweet pet. I do so long to think of you as free from care and in the midst of people [in Savannah] who love you," he wrote to her. "I love you, I love you! . . . If I had only not been fool enough to leave you behind!"[6] Ten days later he wrote Ellen that he was seeing "a great deal" of Mrs. Peck, who was "fine and dear." "But I am remembering your injunction. . . . It is a lively and engaging household, in which one can never be alone, and in the midst of which your husband is . . . young and gay . . . never, unless expressly challenged to it, saying a single serious word."[7] In early February, Woodrow began a note to Mary, in shorthand, which he never finished. "My precious one, my beloved Mary," he wrote.[8] None of Ellen's letters to Woodrow and only two of his to her (both sent to Savannah) written during this period of separation have survived. From Woodrow's comment, however, it is clear that Ellen issued some astute warnings.

When her husband was at home again, Ellen was pleased at how well he now looked.[9] He set out immediately to fulfill a formidable schedule of public addresses between mid-March and the semester's end at Princeton. In April, the trustee committee appointed in January to investigate the clubs and to talk with alumni reported that the system "contains much that is good," and that the obvious evils could be eradicated by evolutionary reform rather than by radical reorganization. This report, published in the *Princeton Alumni Weekly* of June 10, marked the effective end of Woodrow's plan for the quadrangles, but it was not the end of his unhappiness.[10]

At the same board meeting, a major subject came up for discussion that would lead to a battle surpassing in bitterness and duration that of eating-club reform: the location of the graduate college and, in due course, the administration of the Graduate School. In this early round, Dean West was offended when the university architect presented a plan, adopted by the trustees, for the location of the graduate college on a campus site which entailed moving Prospect. Woodrow was not averse to the idea, but his youngest daughter was outraged for the sake of her "own sweet mother" who had made Prospect "a beautiful place" with an exquisite garden. Ellen, too, was dismayed, but she tried to reassure Jessie and Nell. "I think one or two of the committee . . . are beginning to weaken about moving the house,—it is so excessively unpopular," she wrote. "So we won't worry anymore about it for the present. It may die a natural death."[11]

Before her graduation in June, Jessie was elected to Phi Beta Kappa. "How *perfectly splendid*," Ellen wrote to her daughter; "and it is . . . delightful that it should come to you just as it did, without your making any special effort to get it, or sacrificing other important interests to it. . . . We are very, very proud of you, my darling."[12]

During the spring semester at St. Mary's—Nell's last—she was selected by her literary society to uphold the affirmative side of the question, "Resolved that Lee did more for the Confederacy than Jefferson Davis." When Nell's team lost, despite help from her father, she wrote to her parents that she felt disgraced after Jessie had covered herself with such glory. But Nell wrote to Jessie: "I want to *see* you and tell you how *proud* I am of you and how much I love you."[13] Nell's antipathy toward scholarship and her loss of the debate did not alter Ellen's opinion that her youngest daughter was "unusually intelligent,"[14] nor were Nell's classmates deterred from choosing her, in 1908, as "most intellectual."[15]

The entire Wilson family met in Baltimore on June 3, when Woodrow delivered the commencement address to Jessie's graduating class. Undoubtedly thinking of both himself and his daughter, Princeton's president told the audience that the person who "declines to be a type is the noblest"; and he "who will not sell his independence is the man who will rule."[16] A few days later, speaking at an alumni luncheon in Princeton, he said that university men who lent themselves to hysterical movements should be "stricken from the rolls of their Alma Mater."[17] A tactless comment from the university's president, the words were indicative of Woodrow's own turbulent emotions.

Earlier in the spring of 1908, Ellen had made plans for the family to spend their summer vacation in Old Lyme, where she would take instruction in landscape painting. She wrote to Jessie on April 25: "I have just learned that Mr. [Frank] DuMond teaches the Lyme class this summer! Isn't that good!"[18] Two weeks later Ellen wrote to her daughters at college to tell them that Woodrow had decided to go abroad on June 20 and, "we will all go to Lyme the same day."[19] Nell thought "Father's going abroad" would "do him *so* much good." But, again, she wished that her "dearest mother" could go with him. "We could take care of ourselves or get Aunt Annie or somebody to take care of us,"

Nell wrote to her mother, "I *wish* you would."[20] The plans remained unchanged, however. While Ellen, her three daughters, and Madge, spent the summer in Connecticut, Woodrow went alone to the lake district of England, which he had found restorative on other occasions. The "neuritis" in his right arm that had troubled him in December still bothered him well into the summer.[21] The "troublesome Princeton problems" had made "the past year go very hard," he wrote to Cleveland H. Dodge in June. "It has been a struggle . . . to keep in any sorts of spirits."[22]

In addition to Woodrow's health, there may have been a more subtle reason for the separate vacations. A letter which he sent to Ellen from England in late July contains a passage both dissonant and penitent. At the end of a long travelogue, he wrote:

> I never in my life longed for *you*, my sweet sweet darling, as I do now or realized more entirely all that you mean to me,—everything that sustains and enriches life. You have only to believe and trust me, darling, and *all* will come right,—what you do not understand included. I know my heart now if I ever did, *and it belongs to you*. God give you the gracious strength to be patient with . . . me! "Emotional love,"—ah, dearest, that was a cutting and cruel judgment and utterly false; . . . but I never blamed you for it or wondered at it. I only understood—only saw the thing as you see it and as it is *not*,—and suffered,—am suffering still, ah, how deeply!—but with access of love. My darling! I have never been worthy of you,—but I love you with all my poor, mixed, inexplicable nature,—with everything fine and tender in me. Suffering and thinking over here by myself, *I know* it![23]

The editors of *The Papers of Woodrow Wilson* suggest that the "cutting and cruel judgment" probably refers to a remark which Ellen had made about Woodrow's feelings for Mary Peck; other writers state that Ellen had advocated her husband's seclusion in the lake district not only because of his health but perhaps to think carefully about his burgeoning interest in Mary Peck.[24] Woodrow, "suffering and thinking" by himself, affirmed—if there was any doubt—that his heart belonged to Ellen. (Even so, his interest in Mary Peck would be much more intense at a later time.)

There is no question that, Mary Peck notwithstanding, Woodrow had been difficult to live with during the past year. He, himself, realized the trouble which he had given Ellen, and "how much" and "how deeply" he had "occasionally distressed" her.[25] "There are times," he wrote to her in August, "when I am *with* you, as I am sure you know, when I grow faint and all life and hope seem to go out of me because you seem to grow a bit distant, to draw off a bit in feeling, and to look at me as I am,—not as the man whom you uncritically love and who loves you, . . . but as a fellow full of unlovable faults and grievous weaknesses whom you are yet bound by some blind compulsion of your heart to love and endure."[26]

The thirteen letters which Ellen wrote to Woodrow in the summer of 1908, and fifteen from the three daughters (he mentions each one), have not been found. In Woodrow's letters to Ellen, there is an undercurrent of pleading, as if her determination to mingle and work with professional artists was a declaration of independence. "My sweetheart, my sweetheart! Do you love me? Are you sure?" he asked her. "I don't care what happens to me if only you love me."[27] He was "fearful" that Ellen might find the Griswold boarding house in Old Lyme to be unsatisfactory. In truth, the house was unfamiliar to Woodrow, and his inability to picture Ellen's daily activities *"in detail"* was hurtful to him.[28] His reactions to her obviously glowing reports were ambivalent. "I am so glad you all went to Lyme. . . . You are having a better time . . . than you would have had with me."[29] Still later, he wrote: "You are better off and surer of refreshment and renewal doing what you are, and (perhaps, alas!) away from me."[30]

Whatever else Ellen may have said in her letters, she evidently did not hold back the assurance of her love for her husband. Woodrow wrote: "Your . . . letters, my incomparable darling, are too sweet and precious for words. . . . The eager, loving words with which you . . . close make me thrill every time I read them. . . . The exquisite little love passages [are] . . . life itself. . . . God bless you for your sweet letters and the cheer and comfort they have brought me."[31]

While Woodrow was "suffering and thinking," alone in the lake district, Ellen immersed herself in art. For the first time since her year at the Art Students League, she was able to work seriously with a professional instructor. Frank DuMond, her teacher, had studied in Paris at the Academie Julian, had won a gold medal at the Paris Salon in 1890, and several gold and silver medals in American exhibitions. In 1902, DuMond began the Lyme Summer School of Art, which soon became one of the foremost in the country. Impressed with Ellen's work, he encouraged her from the beginning; within a month's time, he noticed qualities in her painting which he had thought at first were lacking.[32] He arranged for her to have her own studio, a singular privilege for a summer student.

The surest measure of one's acceptance by the Lyme artists, however, was to secure occupancy in the Griswold house.[33] The artists had an informal understanding with "Miss Florence" that group approval was a prerequisite of staying in the "Holy House," as the students who were excluded labeled it. Near the end of the century, when Florence Griswold was the last surviving member of her genteel New England family, she had opened her Georgian mansion to summer boarders. She soon became the guardian angel to a growing number of artists. This mecca on the Lieutenant River was noted for its lovingly dilapidated interiors, its abundant meals, and its informality. The lack of elegance was compensated by the lively esprit de corps, with evenings "full of impromptu musical and theatrical entertainment" and days enlivened by practical jokes.[34] Ellen participated in the pranks, often with the enthusiastic cooperation of Florence Griswold. One victim of their combined creativity, a bachelor-artist who had hung his weekly laundry under the trees in the orchard, allegedly out of sight, later found four-inch flounces of lace sewn to the sleeves of his only nightshirt.[35]

Most of the artists whom Ellen came to know in 1908—Childe Hassam, Willard Leroy Metcalf, Walter Griffin, William Chadwick, Chauncey Foster Ryder, Robert Vonnoh, and others—formed the core of the first American Impressionists. With Hassam's arrival at Florence Griswold's house in 1903, the colony began its conversion to Impressionism, a school of painting which appealed to Ellen.[36] (She had first seen works by Hassam, Metcalf, and Vonnoh in 1893 at the Columbian Exposition, and she had met these three artists in 1905 in Old Lyme.)[37]

In September, the group's paintings, all for sale, were exhibited at the town library and in the Griswold mansion. The records do not verify Ellen as a participant,[38] but had she exhibited, this would have been the first public showing of any of her work and would have anticipated a later one-woman show. Whether she exhibited was unimportant compared with the exhilarating effect that the Old Lyme milieu had upon her. She "felt like a girl again knocking about the countryside with a lot of young . . . girls and young men in the chummiest sort of way."[39]

As the Wilsons' separate vacations came to an end, Woodrow vowed:

"I am coming back to you, my Eileen, singularly well, and I hope that, being more normal, I shall be less trying."[40] Ellen preceded him to Princeton to have Prospect "beautiful and in order."[41]

After Woodrow conducted the opening exercises for the one hundred and sixty-second year of the college, he began another season of traveling and speech-making.[42] Ellen went with him on two trips in October. One, completely to her liking, was a weekend at Haverford College, "a stout little Quaker institution of high repute," where Woodrow gave an address at the celebration of its seventy-fifth anniversary. Ellen was taken on a long motor ride that included a tour of Bryn Mawr, but Woodrow excused himself "to nurse a bad cold."[43]

The other trip was the long-promised visit to the Pecks in Pittsfield, Massachusetts. They arrived on Monday, October 5; on Tuesday, Woodrow and Ellen were guests of the "Wednesday Morning Club," a ladies' group which he addressed. The Wilsons then slipped up to Williamstown on Thursday, when Woodrow spoke at the inauguration of Princeton's former professor of politics, Harry A. Garfield, as president of Williams College. Ellen not only had the rare pleasure of hearing her husband speak but she also saw him receive an honorary degree, his eighth. Instead of returning to Princeton from Williamstown, the Wilsons went back to the Pecks on Friday. That evening Woodrow spoke to a group at the First Congregational Church of Pittsfield.[44]

At this first meeting of Ellen Wilson and Mary Peck, at least two common bonds were evident: their love of beautiful surroundings and their admiration for Woodrow Wilson. Whatever the extent of Mary's affection for Woodrow, she was sincerely fond of his wife; and without Ellen's tolerance and sustained poise, this triangle of developing friendship could have become very awkward indeed.

Unhappy during the academic year of 1908–1909, Woodrow had lost Jack Hibben as a confidant, and he continued to seethe inwardly over what he regarded as "the bounden duty" of the trustees to reform university life. The trustees were marking time on the graduate college while construction was under way for a science building, Palmer Physical Laboratory, and a new dormitory, Holder Hall. If Woodrow had to face yet another fight, he preferred the political arena to "the polite restraints of academic controversy."[45] The restraints were eased to some extent when he traveled as far as Denver, Colorado, to make speeches which had decidedly political overtones, and which made of him more and more a national figure.[46]

While her husband traveled and spoke, Ellen found companionship with Margaret, Jessie, and Nell, all of whom were now living at home. Ellen encouraged her daughters to develop their own interests, and she firmly believed that they should be able to earn a living. In February 1909, Ellen wrote to Emily Yates: "Jessie is the serious, humanitarian member of our little flock and is evidently destined for some sort of a 'career,' though I am glad to say that she is also enjoying very thoroughly the dancing and other merry-making of her first season 'out.' But with all of her exquisite sweetness and beauty she is a bit of a 'new woman,' and is I am told by her college mates 'very eloquent.'"[47]

After her graduation the summer before, Jessie had attended a Missionary Conference at Mountain Lake Park, Maryland, as a representative of her college's chapter of the Y.W.C.A. The experience led her to want to be a teacher-missionary, but her health was considered too fragile for international assignments. Frustrated for a short time in the fall, she wrote to her friend Alice Appenzeller, from Wellesley, that Baltimore had opened, Princeton had opened, everything had opened —and there she was studying nothing, doing nothing but "going to Trenton."[48] The "going to Trenton" was volunteer work in a settlement house for young girls, an activity which balanced Jessie's social life in Princeton, where she juggled the calls of admiring beaux.[49]

Nell had now decided to become an illustrator. She took a year off from the stresses of scholarship, however, before she enrolled as a day student at the Pennsylvania Academy of the Fine Arts. At first she had no thought other than to study at the Art Students League, but Ellen guided her to a school more qualified to teach the courses in which Nell was interested.[50]

More and more absorbed in her music, Margaret was taking voice lessons in New York. She, too, received invitations to dances at the Princeton eating clubs, the same clubs which her father abhorred, but the men came and went in her life. In 1906, she expected "to live and die an old irritable maid"; later, when her father's political star was rising, she wailed: "Why doesn't someone ask me to marry him, some fine man, so that I would be safe from the White House."[51]

After the summer of 1908 in Lyme with the four Wilson women, Madge left for a lengthy tour of California and Mexico.[52] While she was away, her patient admirer, Edward G. Elliott, at Woodrow's recommendation, was appointed dean of the college, a position created by the trustees in January, to be effective in September 1909.[53]

Ellen now began regular excursions into New York to visit the art galleries. She spent one afternoon in the studio of Willard Metcalf, whose work, she thought, "outranked every other American artist." Metcalf's moonlit view of the Griswold house, *May Night*, painted in May 1906, had won a prize from the Corcoran Gallery, and in due course became his best-known work.[54] Metcalf and Fred Yates, who were fellow students in Paris in the 1880s, had not seen each other's work, an omission which Ellen partially remedied by inviting Metcalf to luncheon in Princeton to see the portraits which Yates had done of the Wilson family.[55] She went into the city again to see a miniature sculpture which Bessie Potter Vonnoh had done of Jessie. Ellen observed that the sculpture had "a sort of large nobility about it in spite of its small size."[56] Vonnoh later sculpted a life-size bust of Jessie, now in the possession of Jessie's daughter, Eleanor Axson Sayre.

Ellen joined Woodrow in taking a special interest in an eating club founded by members of the Class of 1909 who had failed to be elected to any of the existing clubs. Calling themselves the Dial Lodge, the students refrained from using "club," because of President Wilson's dislike of the word. When the Dial Lodge gave a dance at which Ellen and her daughters were present, the "Wilson girls" taught one student "the barn dance" which was then coming into vogue. Dial Lodge members were later invited to a dance at Prospect.[57]

If Ellen could have compiled a preferred list from among the roster of Prospect guests, she would have chosen "interesting" over "noted." Sometimes she was fortunate, and her guests were both. One of these, Sir Henry Jones, held the chair of moral philosophy at the University of Glasgow. "It was a great experience for us all," Ellen said of his visit in the spring of 1909. "He is a mystic and a seer, and also a fiery, eloquent Welshman with a splendid prose style, which strangely enough for a mystic, is clear and luminous."[58] Ellen knew best Jones's book about one of her favorite poets, *Browning as a Religious and Philosophical Teacher*, published in 1891. A copy is in the Wilsons' library.[59]

Chapter 24

Controversy

"A week with the trustees," Woodrow said, *"wears my spirits out more than it* fatigues my body, and after it is over I sadly need sleep and silence."[1] The meeting in June 1909 was no different; in fact, a new element for dissension appeared on the agenda. William Cooper Procter, Class of 1883, president of Procter and Gamble, soap manufacturers of Cincinnati, had offered a gift of five hundred thousand dollars for the graduate college. Attached to Procter's gift were two provisos: the trustees had to raise an equal sum and a location other than the site of Prospect had to be chosen for the buildings. A third proviso was inherent— Procter was an old friend and ally of Dean West. Procter's offer, a shrewd achievement on the part of Dean West, required careful consideration. Woodrow wrote to one of the trustees that there was a "hopeful prospect of coming to some satisfactory conclusion."[2] The summer would presumably afford time to deliberate.

In mid-July, with Lucy and Mary Smith as chaperones, Jessie and Nell went abroad while Ellen, Woodrow, Madge, and Margaret were at Florence Griswold's boarding house in Old Lyme. Now an established member of the art colony, Ellen was told by her fellow artists that her work was "no longer that of an amateur" and, in fact, was better than "a good deal of that in the exhibitions."[3] After her previous summer at the Griswold house, Ellen knew that the amenities were bohemian, and she was pleased when the casual atmosphere, and the "irresponsible artists," appealed to Woodrow. He usually played golf in the afternoon, whereas in the mornings he worked and wrote letters, many of them to Mary Peck. Florence Griswold served meals out-of-doors on the piazza, women at one table, men at the other, so the artists could come dressed directly from their work. Within a week's time, Woodrow had discarded his coat at dinner, although he tried to wear "very pretty ties."[4]

The irresponsible lot of artists were pranksters who spared no one, not even the president of Princeton University. One morning when Woodrow sat down to breakfast, he was served what he thought was his usual shredded wheat. In truth, it was a fresh bunch of excelsior covered with heavy cream, a variation on cereal which went undetected until Woodrow tried to force it apart with his spoon.[5] Ellen enjoyed the artists, their playfulness, and Old Lyme so much that she and Woodrow began to search for property there. In 1909, they tried to buy a tract of land from David P. Huntley, but difficulties in clearing the title prevented final closing.[6]

Near the end of August, the art colony's summer exhibit was hung in the Phoebe Griffin Noyes Library on Old Lyme's main street.[7] Although Ellen had had "a blissful time sketching," she again appears to have exhibited nothing of her own.[8] Arthur Heming, one of DuMond's students, said that Ellen Wilson was more interested in helping the professional artists to sell their paintings because, for many of them, the summer's work was their only source of income.[9] Ellen wrote to Agnes Tedcastle that the summer made her feel as if it were a joy to be alive, and that she had become so recklessly absorbed in the "pursuit of art" as to become rather oblivious of all other obligations.[10] The relaxation would serve her well, because the next year— and Woodrow's last—at Princeton University would be far from restful. By Thanksgiving, Ellen had her family together again at Prospect.

The Princeton trustees had refrained from deciding about Procter's offer until Woodrow could have an opportunity to discuss the ramifications with Procter. After a conference between the two men on October 20, Woodrow learned that his arguments for a central campus location had had no impact. The prospective donor, with Dean West's guidance, still favored a location a mile from campus on the "Golf Links." At their October meeting, the board voted to rescind its choice of the Prospect site and to accept Procter's offer.[11]

Woodrow saw this action as an irrevocable step toward undercutting his overall plan and, more important, his leadership. On these two questions (the quadrangle plan and the graduate college), as important, he believed, as could arise in his administration, he thought that crucial decisions had been made "because money talked louder than I did."[12] He was disturbed by the idea that a donor could dictate policy to the university, but, on a more personal level, he now viewed the matter as a choice between his leadership and authority versus Dean West's. He wanted West "absolutely eliminated, administratively."[13]

Ellen summoned some comfort from the support that Woodrow was getting in newspaper editorials all over the country, yet she found the situation "very trying."[14] The enmity from academic circles was spilling over into the social life of Princeton and causing unpleasantness even among the wives and children.[15] Ellen tried to make her home a place where one "instinctively felt" that there was no hurry, no worry, and comfort was everywhere.[16] It was a formidable challenge to create this ambience at Prospect with Woodrow "low in mind, filled with scorn and disappointment," and fighting to hold his tongue "from words that might make all breaches irreparable."[17] Unfortunately for both Princeton and her husband, Ellen supported him every step of the way. Stockton said that his sister went to the bottom of all the controversies, and that she "really hated" some of Woodrow's opponents. To make the academic acrimony more tolerable, she devised uncomplimentary names for the main offenders. William Cooper Procter was "the soap fat man."[18] Although she alone might have swayed Woodrow to be more temperate in his approaches to reform, Ellen, too, was immersed in the bitterness.

In the fall of 1909, Woodrow found a willing source of levity and solace in Mary Peck. After Mary's move to an apartment in New York in November, he was constantly in touch with her by letter, by telephone, and in person. Mary reacted to the newspaper coverage of Princeton's controversies by sending Woodrow a note of encouragement. "God bless you! and whatever the outcome thank Him for making you what you are—so fine—so brave—so true. . . . I wish I could help in the tired moments."[19]

From the time of the Wilsons' first visit to Mary's home in Pittsfield in October 1908, Woodrow had written to her regularly. Her replies, spasmodic at first, were more frequent as the friendship deepened. Although Ellen was never a part of the correspondence, Woodrow rarely closed a letter in those first months without adding Ellen's "warm regards." Even after his second holiday in Bermuda in January and February 1908, until mid-April of 1909, his salutations in the surviving letters were perfunctory. Beginning with a letter written on April 13, the usual "My dear Mrs. Peck" changed to "Dearest Friend," and the tone of the letters grew more intimate.[20]

In March 1909, Mary and Woodrow had met in New York when she was summoned from Bermuda to Pittsfield by the illness of her recently married stepdaughter, Harriet. After Mary received word to come to Massachusetts, she had cabled the president of Princeton University to meet her at the pier in New York.[21] Woodrow did so, and he surely went up again to see her there when she was en route back to Bermuda in early April. He had learned from her at some time during her quick trip to Pittsfield that she had decided to separate legally from Thomas Peck and establish herself in New York. The letter Woodrow sent to his "Dearest Friend" in April had not only changed in tone—it was also full of solicitude and advice: "I dare not in such circumstances use my heart in counselling you; I *must* use my head," he told her.[22] (Her divorce would not be final until July 1912, when she assumed her former name, Mary Allen Hulbert.) In the fall of 1909 and the spring of 1910, when Woodrow moved inevitably toward dissolving his ties with Princeton University, Mary Peck became his confidante, a veritable replacement for Hibben's lost friendship.[23]

The Christmas holidays of 1909 were celebrated at Prospect with an undercurrent of tension. Earlier in December, Woodrow had suggested to Moses Taylor Pyne that the graduate college controversy could be resolved by building two graduate dormitories, one on the campus and the other a mile away on the Golf Links. Pyne was so astonished that he followed their discussion with a letter in which, after carefully repeating Woodrow's suggestion, he asked, "Will you kindly let me know if I have correctly grasped your idea?"[24]

Sometime before this, after sharing his academic troubles with Mary Peck, Woodrow had asked her, "What do *you* think?"[25] To divide the graduate college was a proposition that strongly suggests Mary's method of coping with perplexing problems. An obvious example, of course, was the dichotomy in her own life (Bermuda and Pittsfield). If, indeed, the idea came from her, Woodrow picked it up. So did Pyne, who presented it, tongue in cheek, at the board of trustees' meeting on January 13, 1910, as a plan acceptable to Procter. Thrown completely off balance, Woodrow became confused, embarrassed, and self-contradictory.[26] The meeting ended in bitterness and the next few days were very tense indeed. Once again, it appeared that the president of Princeton would resign, but, on February 6, when Procter withdrew his offer, Woodrow held fast with "an unspeakable sense of relief."[27]

Ellen was glad to have her husband leave the turmoil of Princeton the next week to take another midwinter vacation in Bermuda. For a third time, she did not go with him to his island haven. Her daughters, all at home, commuted to places of individual interest. Margaret continued to study voice in New York; Jessie was involved in work at the Lighthouse Settlement House, a social center for women mill-workers at Kensington, Pennsylvania, a Philadelphia suburb; and Nell was at the Pennsylvania Academy of the Fine Arts, where she had enrolled on February 4.[28]

Woodrow, alone in Bermuda, had neither Ellen nor Mary (who probably for financial and legal reasons remained in New York) to console him. He had seen Mary before he sailed, a visit that left him "sad, lonely, homesick, friendsick."[29] Woodrow missed both his wife and Mary Peck. "How I wish you were beside me this morning," he wrote to Ellen. "How sweet it would be to sit by you and hold your hand and talk! There is so much to talk about, with the clouds thickening and lowering more and more at Princeton. . . . It makes me feel deeply selfish to think of having left you there in all that horrid weather so trying for you, and in the midst of all the talk that must be distressing you, or the silence that may be puzzling you . . . but the bliss of being together would be compensation enough!"[30]

Each time Woodrow wrote endearing letters to Ellen, in Princeton, he wrote letters of equal length to Mary, in New York. The letters to Mary, although not as specific in their expressions of affection as those to Ellen, suggested an intimacy. As he reminisced with Mary about Bermuda, the words carried romantic overtones: when he entered "the little cottage with the bouganvillia" his "pulses throbbed"; when he thought that Mary *might* come to the islands after all, but that their stays would overlap by "only twenty-four hours," it would make him "wild." Shortly before he was to return to New York, he wrote to Mary that he had been "waiting, waiting, waiting for the happy moment" when he could have one of the hours with her that meant "so much" to him. He closed "with infinite tenderness."[31]

While Woodrow was in Bermuda, Mary missed *him* "*horribly*—wofully." To have him so far away was even worse than she had feared; in fact, she could hardly *bear* not being there with him. "I can never learn . . . restraint," she reminded him. "I give so much of myself to people who love me." "Why, *why* can I not be there—to fling *myself* where I would!"[32]

In Ellen's first letter to Woodrow after he had arrived in Bermuda, she apologized for not having written immediately. However, she thought it just as well for him to have a week's rest from Princeton, with not a word to break the calm. He had a pile of "nice letters" from alumni, but she decided not to send even those. "We miss you more than we can say," Ellen told her husband. "As for me, you know, dearest, that it is quite impossible to express my love. It is greater than ever,—and I thought that too was impossible."[33]

Ellen was undoubtedly aware of Woodrow's continuing fascination with Mary Peck. What else she knew, or what else there *was* to know in 1909 and 1910, is a matter of conjecture. There is no unambiguous evidence to prove how intimate the relationship became between Woodrow and Mary. Several years later, he referred to the Peck affair as "a contemptible error," a "madness of a few months," an episode in his life that left him "stained and unworthy."[34] At some point, Ellen had a forthright discussion with her husband, possibly in the summer of 1910 when he made the decision to enter politics. In any event, he must have asked Ellen's forgiveness as is indicated in an "admission," left undated among his papers, and composed in a shorthand shaky with agitation. The transcription reads:

> Even while it lasted I knew and made explicit what it *did not* mean. It did not last, but friendship and genuine admiration ensued.
>
> These letters [to Mary] disclose a passage of folly and gross impertinence in my life. I am deeply ashamed and repentant. Neither in act nor even in thought was the purity or honor of the lady concerned touched or sullied, and my offense she has generously forgiven. Neither was my utter allegiance to my incomparable wife in anyway by the least jot abated. She, too, knew and understood and has forgiven, little as I deserved the generous indulgence.[35]

Ellen later confided to the family physician, Dr. Cary Travers Grayson, that the Peck affair was the only unhappiness which her husband had caused her during their entire married life. Not that Ellen thought there was anything wrong or improper about it, but just that a brilliant mind and an attractive woman had temporarily fascinated her husband's mind. She, Ellen, did not want to share his confidence or his inner mind with anyone.[36]

Ellen had sanctioned Woodrow's friendship with sparkling companions such as Jenny Hibben, Lucy and Mary Smith, Henrietta Ricketts, Edith Reid, and Nancy Toy, the wife of a professor at Harvard, all women whom Ellen loved and admired. Woodrow had told her once that if a jealous woman had married him, she would have found "the catholicity of his admiration for women a source of exquisite torture."[37] Despite appearances to the contrary, Ellen neither liked nor admired Mary Peck.[38] Stockton commented that, as Woodrow's interest in Mary "became pronounced," it was scarcely "beer and skittles" for his sister.[39]

More important to Ellen than the transitory Peck affair was her emphatic belief in the principles for which she believed her husband was working. She was determined not to abet his enemies by providing them with grounds for a scandal. Since most of Mary's letters to Woodrow have not been found, the finger points to Ellen as a likely person who destroyed them. Helen Bones once walked in on Ellen in the White House to find her in "the act of burning some letters." Ellen was manifestly annoyed, an unusual reaction in circumstances which were ostensibly innocent.[40]

Outwardly countenancing the Peck relationship, Ellen encouraged her daughters, and Madge, to regard Mary as a family friend.[41] On at least some of the occasions when Mary was a houseguest of the Wilsons, Ellen joined in, or herself issued, the invitations.[42] To be caught between Woodrow's professional battles and his private peccadillos was not an enviable position, but Ellen persevered. In protecting her husband, she was, inadvertently or not, protecting her own ambitions for him.[43]

Ellen could taunt Woodrow when the right occasion arose. While he was still in Bermuda, she and Nell went into New York to see the Ben Greet players in *She Stoops to Conquer*, at a theater opposite Mary Peck's apartment, and Ellen could not resist a chance to "look in." She described the visit to Woodrow:

> As we reached the Theatre at one sharp we decided to run and "say howdy" to her. But unfortunately she was not dressed and took all of fifteen minutes to "do" her hair. When it was already time for the curtain to rise we had to apologize to Mrs. Allen and fly. But Mrs. Peck ran out in her wrapper as we were taking the elevator and begged us to come in for tea after the play. We did so and had a delightful little visit with her,—were there almost an hour.[44]

When Ellen wrote to Woodrow again, she told him that his supporters from among the faculty and trustees had decided it would be unwise to press just then, as Woodrow wanted them to do, for the retirement of West as dean of the Graduate School. Ellen was incensed. "They actually think, after last year's experience, that they *can* ignore him." There was one advantage in this plan which had its appeal, she said; it would set Woodrow free again to leave, if he wished, to go into politics. "If I were you I should accept their proposition cooly, rather indifferently, . . . then keep my counsel, stay in for the present and next year run for governor. This thing has strengthened you *immensely* throughout the whole country. . . . Your position is so commanding that we can really afford to laugh at the howling of the Alumni, 'mongrel, puppy, whelp and hound, and curs of low degree!' "[45]

In March, when Woodrow was back in Princeton, he began to seek support for his views on the graduate college. On April 16, in an address to an alumni group in Pittsburgh, he let go his pent-up fury at all the decisions which had frustrated his plans for Princeton University.[46] The speech antagonized not a few people, but it signaled the emergence of the president of Princeton as a man full of fight and courage and a leader of the forces of democracy and righteousness. The signals did not escape the attention of politicians, and in particular those Democrats in New Jersey who were looking for a winning gubernatorial candidate to run the following November.[47]

The "thickening clouds at Princeton" oppressed Ellen—so much so that the whole air about her seemed "poisoned." She sent a copy of an editorial about Princeton's controversies to Florence Hoyt—not important "but it will make you laugh as it did me,—and that is a very good thing," Ellen wrote.[48] While Woodrow's speaking tour continued, Ellen declined an invitation from Agnes Tedcastle to come to Massachusetts because, she told Agnes, "engagements and duties and obligations too numerous to mention" held her fast at home.[49] One of the university guest preachers who was at Prospect while Woodrow was away told Ellen that he could but marvel at her kindness and interest in his comfort when he knew how burdened and anxious she was at that time.[50]

Ellen's daughters arranged their activities so that the "poisoned" air was less offensive. In April, Jessie was off for a month's tour of Georgia to visit her mother's girlhood haunts in Savannah, Atlanta, and Rome. With various relatives and friends vying for the opportunity to entertain Jessie, Ellen charged her daughter: "Do exactly as you please . . . dear! Don't feel that you have to do [things] . . . to satisfy me!" Margaret was making progress with her voice, described by her teacher as "truly beautiful . . . with an exquisite quality."[51] Nell invited her cousin, Marjorie Brown, to Princeton for the Charter Club dance (one of the clubs Woodrow wanted to abolish) and the Triangle Club show in mid-May. Marjorie, now a student at the Edgeworth School in Baltimore, and a polished young woman of eighteen, fairly bewitched the entire household "from Woodrow down" on this first visit to Prospect. Ellen had "never seen such a perfect blend" in so young a girl of "charm, intelligence, poise, wit and beauty."[52]

Shortly before commencement week, Isaac Chauncey Wyman, Class of 1848, died at his home in Salem, Massachusetts, leaving the university a bequest of approximately "two million dollars." Normally this would have been welcome news for the president of Princeton University, but in this instance, Dean West was named a coexecutor and trustee of the Wyman estate. The dean had once again been successful in wooing an affluent alumnus to his cause.[53] The Wilson family was stunned. Woodrow observed: "We've beaten the living but we can't fight the dead."[54] Woodrow again considered resigning as president of Princeton, but once more friends persuaded him to remain at his post, lest resigning look like sour grapes over Dean West's victory.[55]

At the meeting of the board of trustees in June 1910, Procter's offer was renewed and accepted. The graduate college, using the Swann, Procter, and Wyman bequests, would be built on the Golf Links, the site a mile from the heart of the campus.[56] Without enthusiasm, Ellen engaged waiters and supervised the luncheon for the trustees. She was, of course, the only woman at the dining room table filled with more than thirty men. The senior trustee, usually an old gentleman dull and burdensome to talk to, took her in to lunch. The other slow, elderly members of the board gathered at her end of the table, while the younger and livelier ones migrated toward Woodrow's chair. After dessert, Ellen excused herself while the men enjoyed a round of smoking.[57] This luncheon for the board of trustees was the last such that she would ever give.

Before leaving for another summer at Florence Griswold's house, Ellen and Woodrow celebrated their twenty-fifth wedding anniversary with the purchase of a painting by one of the Old Lyme artists, Chauncey Foster Ryder. On exhibit at the Macbeth Gallery, the painting, entitled *Valley of Assisi*, made Ellen "positively drunk with the glorious colours of it, and the noble composition."[58] She told Macbeth that it was "rather crazy" of her to buy "$600.00 pictures"—but she *must* have it. Mr. Ryder should feel flattered, she said, "that a woman is willing to give up new evening gowns, etc. etc. for two years in order to possess a picture of his!" Although it would be "rather heart-breaking," Ellen confided that she might have to return Ryder's work to the gallery for resale in about a year.[59] There is no doubt that she was anticipating Woodrow's departure from Princeton University, and his entry into politics.

Instead of going to Connecticut immediately, Jessie stayed in Philadelphia to help at the settlement house until July 15, and Margaret spent some time with George and Margaret Howe. Ellen found it hard to be "quite amiable" about her daughters' independence and especially about Jessie in the July heat.[60] Nell, in Old Lyme, gave her sisters a summary of all they were missing: "If I hurry up and tell you how thrilling Lyme is this year you'll take the next train immediately. Well there are about three artists here, one of them German looking and rather harmlessly pleasant, the other a stick and married (wife not here), and the third a stick." Nell waited a week "for luck" and then joined DuMond's class, a group that frequently worked out in the "wilds." After two days of fighting mosquitoes and heat, she took her easel back to the cool interior of Florence Griswold's house. Ellen was working hard and, in her daughter's opinion, was "doing some ever so nice rock studies."[61]

Lucy and Mary Smith, who came up to try Old Lyme as a vacation spot, decided after a few days that they would stay on for six weeks. (They were probably guests at the Old Lyme Inn.) With the Smiths there to share the news, the Wilson family was in a state of suppressed excitement over Madge's secret: her pending marriage to Ed Elliott. When she had become engaged in May, Madge, "the most secretive and elusive of mortals," had told only Ellen. The Wilsons were highly pleased with Ed Elliott, "one of the finest men in Princeton," who, Ellen said, had "served like Jacob for seven years!"[62] The groom-to-be confessed to his former mentor and present superior, soon to be his brother-in-law, "I have loved Margaret a long time and I pray that my life and love may be worthy of her."[63]

Madge went to Boston to stay with Agnes Tedcastle who would help to shop for a trousseau. Ellen was relieved to have Agnes take over this chore, because Madge, nerves on edge, was hostile toward the whole family, her fiancé included. Ellen was afraid that it was about to be a case of "marrying at leisure and repenting in haste."[64]

Neither Ed nor Madge wanted a huge wedding nor did they relish the idea of facing the strained social atmosphere in Princeton. As dean of the college, Elliott's colleagues were the entire faculty, irrespective of factions. To circumvent what Ellen called "the insoluble problem," the marriage took place on September 8 in the Old Lyme Congregational Church, with only the immediate families present.[65] After a brief honeymoon, Dean and Mrs. Elliott would be "at home" on campus in the historic Joseph Henry House, designated the year before as the dean's residence. By late October, Ellen reported with relief that Madge seemed perfectly happy and settled in her new home.[66]

Part Seven

1910–1912

Ellen Axson Wilson, 1912. Photograph by Marceau.
Courtesy of William D. Hoyt.

Chapter 25

Politics

While her art and the preparations for Madge's wedding in Old Lyme occupied Ellen in the summer of 1910, she and Woodrow faced a dramatic decision about his professional life. In February, when Ellen had advised her husband to stay as Princeton's president "for the present" and then to run "next year" for governor, the idea of Woodrow's entering politics was neither new nor startling. As early as February 1906, Colonel George B. M. Harvey, editor of *The North American Review*, had suggested at a dinner given in Woodrow's honor at the Lotos Club of New York that Woodrow Wilson "of Virginia and New Jersey" be the Democratic party's nominee in 1908 for president of the United States.[1] Within his family circle, Woodrow had laughed at Harvey's suggestion, even when Ellen asked cautiously, "Was Mr. Harvey joking?"[2] Never losing sight of his dream to put Woodrow in the White House, Harvey believed that an interim office was a necessary stepping-stone. He tried unsuccessfully in 1908 to promote Woodrow's candidacy as Democratic senator from New Jersey; at the Democratic national convention held in Denver that same summer, rumors were circulating that Woodrow might be nominated for vice-president, a move to which Woodrow was firmly opposed.[3] Link states that although Princeton's president had ostensibly rejected Harvey's earliest political overtures, he later boosted his own cause through the "increased tempo of his political addresses" in which he spoke out in favor of reform at both the state and national levels.[4]

By the spring of 1910, with his quadrangle plan defeated and his ideas for the graduate college repudiated, Woodrow was increasingly susceptible to the lure of politics. That same spring, in an overnight visit to Prospect, Colonel Harvey had discussed at length the gubernatorial situation in New Jersey with Woodrow (and probably Ellen). At that time, Harvey found Woodrow willing, but not eager, to become a gubernatorial candidate.[5] The Democrats, who had not elected a governor in New Jersey since 1892, were, at Harvey's relentless prodding, more and more interested in the outspoken president of Princeton

University. By the summer of 1910, with the gubernatorial nominating conventions imminent, the Democrats were running out of time. Woodrow, secluded at Old Lyme with his family, still had made no firm commitment. Finally, in late June, in response to an urgent plea from Harvey, Woodrow went to Deal, New Jersey, to meet with state political leaders.[6] When he returned to Connecticut, he told Ellen, his daughters, and the Smith sisters that he had promised to become a nominee only after he had discussed the matter with several Princeton trustees who were still his staunch supporters. These men reacted favorably, and, in mid-July, Woodrow agreed to be a nominee for the governorship.[7]

The family was still in Old Lyme when he went to Princeton on September 14, the day before the Democratic state convention was to meet in Trenton. On the evening of September 15, after the Democrats had nominated Woodrow Wilson as their party's candidate for governor of New Jersey, he made an electrifying acceptance speech, which by its sincerity and simple eloquence helped to win over the factions of a somewhat divided Democratic party.[8] Ellen wired from Connecticut: "Congratulations from all the household love from the family."[9]

The Wilsons were back in Princeton for the opening exercises of the university and the beginning of Ellen's ninth year as mistress of Prospect. Because the gubernatorial election would not be held until November 8, Woodrow hoped that he might remain as Princeton's president until that date. Several of the trustees, however, pressed him to present his resignation at the next meeting of the board. On the morning of October 20, Woodrow read a brief letter of resignation and requested its acceptance at once. The trustees stood in silence while he left the room and forever "passed . . . from his connection with the University."[10] Ellen and Woodrow later learned that the trustees had voted to accept his resignation "with deep regret" and to continue his salary until the end of the fall semester. The trustees also moved that he be awarded the degree of Doctor of Laws, *honoris causa*, and that "he be invited to continue to occupy the premises at Prospect."[11] The Wilsons remained at Prospect until early January, but Woodrow accepted his salary only through October 20.[12]

Instead of entertaining distinguished scholars and clergymen, Ellen was now experiencing her first purely political guests.[13] Long ago she had told Woodrow that she thought the wear and tear on an office-seeker must be so terrible that he would need "the hide of a rhinocerous."[14] She was beginning to discover that the office-seeker's wife was not immune to the pressures. To provide information for the press about the Wilson family, she gave her first interview to Cloe Arnold for *Delineator* magazine. "One of the most interesting things about Woodrow Wilson is his wife," Arnold began. Arnold was impressed with the achievements of the three Wilson daughters, each of whom was following her own interests and was prepared to earn a living. After describing Ellen's capabilities as governor's wife, Arnold wrote: "She [has] high talent as a landscape painter. Not the kind of thing that goes with a few well-decorated china plates and a plaque to fill wallspace; nor . . . the quality that does placecards and an entertaining sketch book. But real, big artistic talent."[15]

Ellen was outraged when Mrs. James Wilson Woodrow, wife of Woodrow's first cousin, published articles in popular magazines under the pen name of "Mrs. Wilson Woodrow," an authorship which readers attributed to Ellen. Aside from the unpleasantness of being held responsible for this "trash," Ellen feared that Woodrow would be demeaned in the eyes of a public that supposed that the candidate's wife was "that sort of person." Robert Bridges, now an editor at Charles Scribner's Sons, counseled Ellen to ignore the matter because any action would only call attention to it.[16]

Shortly after Woodrow's resignation, Ellen learned that Andrew C. Imbrie, the financial secretary of Princeton University, had, for economic reasons, ceased to provide a gardener for Prospect. Hurt and angry, she wrote an indignant letter to Henry B. Thompson, chairman of the Trustees' Committee on Grounds and Buildings. Thompson agreed with Ellen about the "necessity of maintaining the garden up to its present standards," and he was sorry that Imbrie had not consulted with him first. However, it would now be difficult, Thompson said, to go over Imbrie's head.[17] A peeved Thompson chastised Imbrie,[18] but the order stood. During the time between Woodrow's resignation and his successor's move to Prospect, the garden became overgrown, and eventually Ellen's pergola rotted and collapsed.[19]

The gubernatorial campaign involved Woodrow full-time only from October 20 to November 8, the day on which he won a decisive victory at the polls.[20] After his defeats in the academic world, his political success was sweet, indeed, to Ellen. She wrote to George Harvey: "We are a very happy and excited family! Excited chiefly over the size of the majority, of course. Yet . . . great as . . . [is] the result, it is not so great or wonderful as the *campaign*! I am more proud of that than of any-thing else."[21] And to Meemee Brown she wrote, "Certainly it is 'a famous victory.' The size of it almost takes ones breath away."[22]

The last family gathering at Prospect took place on December 31, when Woodrow's niece, Annie Howe, now twenty years old, was mar-ried to Perrin C. Cothran of Greenwood, South Carolina. The cere-mony, performed at the First Presbyterian Church, was followed by a reception at Prospect.[23]

The Howe-Cothran nuptials were celebrated without Stockton, who had had a severe nervous breakdown. Ed Elliott (called "Egie") helped to relieve Ellen of some of the burden by going with her to New York to confer with Stockton's attending physician, Dr. William B. Prit-chard, who had placed Stockton in a sanitarium in Hartford, Connecti-cut. After the consultation, Ellen returned to Princeton, "frightfully tired and distressed" by both Pritchard and his prognosis. Also dis-pleased with Pritchard, Egie nevertheless went to Hartford to try to convince Stockton that his stay at the sanitarium would be kept "an absolute secret." Egie decided eventually that it would be wise for him to bring his brother-in-law to Philadelphia where Dr. Francis Xavier Dercum had treated Stockton successfully in 1905.[24]

For four years, Stockton had dodged the cross fire between his col-leagues and the president of Princeton; now, the events which were catapulting Woodrow into high-level politics had their unnerving as-pects. Stockton questioned Woodrow's physical capacity to meet the strain and feared it would "kill him quickly." And if Woodrow died, Stockton, regarded by his nieces as "our other father," would have to assume responsibility for them and for Ellen. These worries were unal-leviated by Ellen's attitude. She told her brother that they must not think about the physical strain on Woodrow; he was "greatly fitted for political leadership," it was what he wanted, and they must do all that they could to help him.[25] She had written to Meemee Brown near the end of the gubernatorial campaign that Woodrow's heavy schedule did not "hurt him at all" and his reserve of strength was "most re-assuring."[26]

Stockton had tried to cope with his own increasing tensions through self-medication, apparently by the use of drugs. Dr. Pritchard made the suggestive statement that the only hope for recovery lay in Stockton's staying at Hartford and "getting over this habit."[27] When Ellen tried to persuade her brother to resume his college teaching in a school less demanding than Princeton, he lamented that his "moral collapse had been so complete it would be a farce . . . to talk to boys about literature and life." For a time he considered going into a monastery.[28] Under Dr. Dercum's skilled supervision and with Ellen's constant support, Stockton began slowly to mend. After one of Ellen's visits to him, he sent her a brief note instead of "another letter," because he did not want to worry her. "Oh dearest sister," he wrote, "I do love you so much."[29] By the fall of 1911, he had resumed his normal teaching duties at Princeton where he would remain until May 1913. Although Ellen tried to be optimistic about Stockton, she despaired of his ever being really well.[30] During his breakdown in 1910, she had a distressing but necessary talk about him with her daughters. Nell thought afterward that there never was a more "absolutely *wonderful* person" than her mother—"so sweet and cheerful and adorable."[31]

In January, the Wilsons moved from Prospect to the Princeton Inn. As Ellen and her daughters sorted, discarded, and packed twenty years of accumulated possessions, she vowed never again to save anything. Woodrow's book-lined study, a sometime conference room for awed New Jersey politicians, was not emptied until the last day.[32] On the weekend before Woodrow's inauguration on January 17, Ellen, Woodrow, Jessie, and Nell, with only their personal possessions around them, were settled in three bedrooms and a sitting room at the Princeton Inn where they would also take their meals. Margaret was established in New York City in an apartment house on West End Avenue. She took her meals around the corner at the "Three Arts Club," and studied voice with Ross David. Jessie spent Monday through Thursdays in Philadelphia, working at the settlement house; and Nell, a daily commuter to the Pennsylvania Academy of the Fine Arts, was usually in Princeton for dinner.[33]

Because New Jersey did not provide a year-round governor's mansion, Ellen had few social obligations. For the first time in her twenty-six years of marriage, there were no housekeeping chores—a change which she found "pleasant and restful." She accepted the chairmanship of "the Department of Art and Music" of the Present Day Club,[34] a women's group which she had helped to organize in Princeton in 1898 "to stimulate an interest in science, literature, art and social and ethical culture."[35] With more free time in her new role than she had anticipated, she was able to spend hours reading newspapers and analyzing the political issues. Assisted by two secretaries, she and Woodrow coped with "a mountain" of correspondence. She talked at length with her husband's supporters and colleagues, one of whom, Joseph Patrick Tumulty, a young Irish American, was the governor's newly appointed private secretary. Tumulty, in due course, discussed problems and tactics with Ellen, whom he considered a better politician than the governor.[36]

George Harvey, with the support of a "provisional" preconvention committee, was now well on the way toward his goal to place the Princeton scholar in the White House. Woodrow continued, however, to protest publicly that he was not a presidential candidate, prompting Ellen to caution him: "*Please* don't say again that you 'are not thinking about the presidency.' All who know you well know that it is *fundamentally* true, but *superficially* it can't be true; and it gives the cynics an opening which they seize with glee." She illustrated her point with an editorial which she had clipped from the *New York Sun*, entitled "Really!"[37]

In March, when the new governor went to Atlanta to speak to the Southern Commercial Congress, Ellen declined invitations from Georgia cousins and friends. She wrote to Anna Harris that it was such "a flying trip" that it would not have been worth "the fatigue and expense." "[Woodrow] is living under *such* high pressure now-a-days. It is very important that I should 'stand by' ready to help when he needs me. He says nobody else can 'rest him.' "[38] Irrespective of what Ellen had told Stockton, she was "sadly anxious" about Woodrow. In fact, after the gubernatorial election in November she had thought that he ought to have a vacation in Bermuda.[39]

While Ellen stood by at home, William Jennings Bryan, a major figure in the Democratic party, came to address the students and faculty of the Princeton Theological Seminary. Three times nominated as the Democratic candidate for the presidency, and three times defeated, Bryan was nevertheless still the brilliant orator who could sway audiences. When Ellen learned that he was scheduled to speak in Princeton on Sunday afternoon, March 12, she sent a telegram to Woodrow to urge his immediate return from Atlanta for a possible meeting with Bryan. She then invited Bryan and his New Jersey host, Thomas H. Birch, to have dinner that evening at the inn with Jessie, Nell, Woodrow, and herself. This informal meeting erased most of the reluctance on the part of both Wilson and Bryan to become political friends.

Tumulty said of this political coup, "[Mrs. Wilson,] you have nominated your husband [for the presidency]."[40]

Not long afterward, Ellen received some heartbreaking news from
Rosalie. On April 15, when Mac was hunting ducks near Morganton
with his two younger sons, David and St. John, he went into the water
to get a duck that he had shot. He never returned, and his body was
not found for several days. Mac was an excellent swimmer, and the
mystery of his death was haunting to Ellen, who recalled the tragedy of
Ed and Florence.[41] As close as she had been to Rosalie, Ellen did not
go to her friend; she thought that she must stay near Woodrow to
soothe him after the grinding days in politics.

By the time that the New Jersey legislature adjourned in the late
spring, Woodrow had achieved unprecedented successes—the four major reform bills which he had advocated were adopted.[42] Elated, he
turned to plans for an extended speech-making tour of the Far West—
in effect, the public launching of a preconvention campaign. "It has all
been so *dramatic*," Ellen wrote to Meemee Brown. "As for Woodrow,
his physical strength is not the least wonderful thing about his new
development. He keeps us all gasping."[43] Woodrow was riding the
crest of a wave of popularity which could clearly take him to the presidency. Nothing, not even her concern over her husband's health, Ellen
thought, should thwart his brilliant career.[44] He left Princeton on May
3 on a rail journey that crisscrossed the nation, and, en route home, he
made a swing southward to deliver the commencement address at the
University of North Carolina in Chapel Hill.[45]

Chapter 26

Sea Girt and Cleveland Lane

On the Saturday after Woodrow left Princeton, Ellen, Jessie, and Nell went to Sea Girt, New Jersey, to inspect the gubernatorial summer home on the Jersey shore. The large, white frame house, erected at the Chicago World's Fair in 1893, was later moved in sections to Sea Girt where it was renovated for the governors and their families. Ellen arranged at once to have pictures, rugs, cushions, and art objects taken from storage in Princeton and sent to Sea Girt.[1]

While the summer mansion was being readied, Ellen went alone to Old Lyme. Margaret, Nell, Jessie, and Lucy and Mary Smith joined her a fortnight later. From telegrams which Woodrow sent en route, and from news reports, Ellen followed his western progress. In Denver, he was the supper guest on May 7 of a group of Bryn Mawr alumnae from whom came the question: "Governor Wilson, have you been taught most by your wife? Or by your three daughters?" He answered: "From Mrs. Wilson, not only have I learned much but have gained something of a literary reputation. Whenever I need a poetic quotation she supplies it, and in this way I acquire the fame of possessing a complete anthology of poetry. From my daughters, however, I have learned what every parent knows of himself—that I do not know how to raise children."[2]

Sifting through the major eastern papers, Ellen clipped editorials and extracted helpful comments to send on to her husband. As she read snatches about his "wonderful triumph," she was made happy by everything he, this "man of destiny," said and did.[3] But she scolded him nevertheless over a matter related to Princeton University.

As the trustees deliberated about Woodrow's successor, one member of the faculty, Edward Capps, a pro-Wilson man, favored the choice of James Rowland Angell, dean of the faculties at the University of Chicago. Ellen was disturbed that Angell's name had been dropped simply because Woodrow had "thrown cold water" on the idea. Angell, Ellen wrote, was a man who had grown a great deal in the last few years, "a man of splendid courage and the highest ideals." She urged Woodrow to write to Trustee Melancthon Williams Jacobus to modify what he had said about Angell because "we are so mortally afraid of this growing movement to stampede the alumni for Hibben."[4] Woodrow apparently ignored her suggestion.

At Lyme, Ellen set to work at her easel more slowly than usual. She finished a painting of rocks which one of the professionals thought "rather stunning," and she joined a group that tried to paint "apple-blossom subjects," an endeavor that left "everybody swearing over them and declaring them impossible."[5] By June 9, Woodrow was able to meet her in Old Lyme for the weekend; he was up again from Trenton for two days on June 23, and, in mid-July, the family, including Lucy and Mary Smith, congregated at Sea Girt for the rest of the summer.[6]

Sea Girt was a veritable goldfish bowl. Trains thundered by at the rail junction "a stone's throw away," and the New Jersey National Guard Parade Grounds, directly in front of the house, attracted hordes of tourists. Visitors popped in from all along the Jersey coast, many of whom expected to see the interior of the governor's residence.[7] Lucy Smith assumed the role of tour guide. There were comical moments, such as the time when Ellen gave a piece of cake to a small boy who had wandered in, and sent him on his way. As the Wilsons later learned, he told his family that he had been to see the governor, who had given him some cake, but the governor's husband was not at home.[8] Sundays were often usurped by Woodrow's fellow Democrats who came to discuss presidential politics. He began to refer to himself as the "Possibility."[9]

The family had brief reunions with Stockton, Madge, Egie, and the Hoyts, whose cottage at Lavalette was not far away. Toward the end of the summer, Ellen and Woodrow invited Mary Peck, summering with friends in Pittsfield, to Sea Girt.[10] Charmed with this houseguest, Nell watched with envy and interest while Mary puffed "at one cigarette after another."[11]

In her new role as honorary director of the New Jersey State Charities Aid Society, Ellen accompanied Woodrow on an inspection trip of state institutions. With their hostess, Mrs. Caroline Bayard Stevens Alexander, a member of the executive committee of the society, they visited the Soldier's Home and the Homes for Feeble Minded Women and Children in Vineland; from there they went to the State Home for Delinquent Boys in Jamesburg; then to the Tuberculosis Sanitarium at

Glen Gardner, the State Village for Epileptics at Skillman, the State Hospital for the Insane at Morris Plains, and finally the State Reformatory at Rahway. Although New Jersey now provided the governor's family with an automobile, the tour of inspection was Ellen's first experience in extensive travel by car.[12]

On October 3, the Wilsons were back in Princeton, in a half-timbered Tudor house at 25 Cleveland Lane. Rented from Parker Mann, an artist, the house was smaller than both Prospect and their home on Library Place, but it was comfortably and tastefully furnished.[13] At the back of the house, on a lower level reached by eight stair steps from the parlor, Ellen was charmed with the large, well-lit studio room which looked out on a garden.[14] Expecting to be alone much of the time, Ellen invited Lucy and Mary Smith to live with the Wilsons and to share expenses for the next year.[15] Nell now had an apartment near the Pennsylvania Academy of the Fine Arts, and, along with Jessie, also in Philadelphia, would be at home only on the weekends.

By the end of 1911, there was no doubt in the mind of any member of the Wilson family that Woodrow was a candidate, and a highly promising one, for the Democratic party's nominee in 1912 for president of the United States. Wilson clubs were springing up across the country, and the nucleus of a national campaign office was functioning at 42 Broadway in New York. Two leaders of the Wilson movement were William Frank McCombs, a lawyer practicing in New York and a former student of Woodrow's at Princeton, and William Gibbs McAdoo, a Georgia-born lawyer who was then president of the Hudson and Manhattan Railroad Company. At about this time, Colonel Edward Mandell House of Texas joined the Wilson movement.[16] Indeed, Ellen and Woodrow received a telegram at Christmas from McAdoo who predicted that by the next Christmas "the Governor will find the White House in his stocking."[17]

Earlier in December, Nell had left with her friends, Mary and Schuyler Lawrence, to spend six weeks in Mexico. With the inner circle broken at Christmas for the first time, Ellen planned an unusual ceremony for the family (the Smiths and Stockton included) on Cleveland Lane. In the studio room, she pinned their "stockings" to the sides of the cloth on a round table and piled the gifts in the center. They all then held hands and danced "about it," as they tried to think of "what a good time" Nell was having.[18]

While in Mexico, Nell fell in love with, and became secretly engaged to, Benjamin Mandeville King, a self-made engineer who was in the lumbering business. Nell was so attracted to King that she extended her holiday for another month.[19] In mid-February, guerrilla warfare broke out among the Mexican *insurrectos*, and Nell was abruptly cut off from the outside world. The Wilsons, hopelessly far away, were frantic. Dazed by romance and the adventure, Nell arrived in early March at the Texas border accompanied by Ben King, his friends, and a courageous party of newspapermen who dared to go into a rail terminus where a bridge was demolished and bring Nell out by auto.[20]

Thankful to have their daughter returned safely, Ellen and Woodrow were nevertheless upset by Nell's engagement to a man of whom they knew nothing. Ellen, who wrote cordially but forthrightly to "Mr. King," asked him for three letters of recommendation, and she requested that Stockton, when his classes were over at the university, visit and appraise King.[21] Meanwhile, Ben had gone to the Mayo Clinic in Rochester, Minnesota, to be treated for an injury to his hip sustained in a logging accident. Stockton met him there and found him to be "one of the dearest and best people in the whole world."[22] Any remaining apprehensions were allayed when Ellen received both a letter and a visit from Charles Robinson Smith, of Menasha, Wisconsin, Princeton 1876, now a prominent businessman who knew Ben.[23] When the engagement was approved by Nell's parents, Ellen requested that it be kept secret "for the present *only* because of the inordinate curiosity about our affairs shown by the public."[24] Later, when "dear Ben" was recuperating, Ellen invited him "to come and spend your convalescence with us."[25] (He could not.)

Ellen continued to experience the old tension between her concern for Woodrow's health and her aspirations for his career. She responded to warnings from a New Jersey political ally, Judge John Wesley Wescott, who would later nominate Woodrow for the presidency:

> My dear Judge Westcott,
>
> Your kind, though necessarily disturbing letter, is at hand, and I thank you deeply for writing it, and for all your interest in Mr. Wilson's health and work. He has frequently spoken to me of your watchful friendship in respect to his health. I am the more grateful to you because it is my own special grievance that few of his friends seem to realize that he is even *mortal*. They are pitiless in their demands upon his time and strength.

Of course my own anxiety, though concealed from him, is constant and intense. He is, as you say, "very willful," but he assures me that after this month he will do much better. In the meantime I can only "keep guard" & save him from friends, cares and anxieties,—in short make of his home, when he *is* in it, a place of peace.

I must add one reassuring circumstance. He went some ten days or so ago to Dr. Stengal, the great Phila. diagnostician, and was exhaustively examined—as to blood-pressure and everything else—and the doctor was able to give him a perfectly clean bill of health! He said he was actually in *finer* condition than he was when he last examined him, some fifteen months ago. So we have reason to trust that the symptoms you observed were due to nothing more than fatigue and a rather heavy cold. But as you say, he absolutely *must* have more rest! With kindest regards, I am,

Yours most cordially, Ellen A. Wilson.[26]

Woodrow's rising popularity as a Democratic presidential nominee elicited the inevitable backlash from conservatives in his own party. The Princeton scholar, presumed to be the man for the conservatives, had emerged from academe as a political progressive.[27] Among his disenchanted supporters was, ironically, George Harvey, who began a subtle campaign to undermine Woodrow's candidacy. He coaxed the aged editor of the *Louisville Courier-Journal*, Henry Watterson, to help spread damaging and false rumors in the South about Woodrow. Ellen took on Watterson through an influential middleman, Judge Robert Ewing of Nashville, Watterson's brother-in-law and also the husband of Ellen's first cousin, Harriet Hoyt. In a letter to Ewing, Ellen gave a clear and detailed account which refuted the Harvey-Watterson rumors of alleged insults and derogatory statements attributed to Woodrow. Ewing, of course, sent a copy of Ellen's letter to Watterson, an old-time southern gentleman, who was severely jolted by this canny defense from the pen of a lady. From this time on, Watterson's role as an effective political enemy deteriorated to little more than a "good burlesque."[28]

Ellen helped to thwart still another attempt to damage her husband's candidacy. The conservative editor of the *New York Sun* had disclosed in a front-page story that Woodrow had applied to the Carnegie Foundation for the Advancement of Teaching for a retirement allowance, or pension, after his resignation from Princeton University and before his election as governor. Ellen explained to a friend: "We were utterly without income for three months,—and people were declaring his election impossible!" Editors labeled Woodrow's application "dishonorable," because, as one jibed, "The Carnegie Foundation was created for indigent teachers and not for indigent politicians." Woodrow's friend, Richard Heath Dabney, dean of the Graduate School of the University of Virginia, requested clarification about the Carnegie pension affair so that he could answer Virginia conservatives who were asking questions about Woodrow's integrity. Because Woodrow had not found time to write to Dabney, Ellen answered his queries so as to give, what seemed to be, "the right point of view about it." There were, in effect, *two* sorts of Carnegie pensions—"one an *old age* pension given to all who were sixty-five years old and otherwise eligible, and the other a *distinguished service* pension, given after twenty-five years of teaching in specially selected cases." Even though Woodrow might have qualified under the second category, he had not been awarded a grant. Ellen told Dabney about the embarrassing state of their finances, and, although she began her letter by saying that she was writing at Woodrow's suggestion, she confided in closing, "I don't know what he would do to me if he knew I was writing all this, but I am sure I can trust your discretion."[29] The Carnegie affair was a serious embarrassment to the Wilson supporters, and Ellen made her contribution by helping Wilson spokespersons who were trying to counteract the unfavorable impressions which it had made.[30]

These attacks upon Woodrow Wilson were, according to Arthur S. Link, "ominous enough, but they were mere sputtering criticisms . . . when compared to the aggregation of whispering campaigns, organized misrepresentations, and outright conspiracies to defeat Wilson's nomination. Few candidates for the presidency have been the object of an attack so overwhelming, so well-concerted, so effective."[31] Woodrow took the attacks philosophically,[32] but Ellen could not. Worried about her mother, Jessie wrote to Margaret: "She walks around in a dream. Nothing but an article about father can galvanize her into attention. . . . Everything against him makes her *sick*. It is dreadful!" Jessie believed that the "silence and the attitudes of Princeton friends" were also wearing on her mother.[33]

Ellen's distress was not alleviated when she learned that the Princeton Board of Trustees had chosen John Grier Hibben to be the fourteenth president of the university. A month later, she sent to Hibben a letter seething with ill-concealed resentment:

> Dear Mr. Hibben,
>
> I beg to acknowledge your note with regard to seats in the college Chapel; and at the same time to offer my congratulations on your recent success.
>
> All who know you will feel that you have fully earned it, and that you are ideally fitted for what is expected of you; since conditions which to others would be a burden too grievous to be borne will be to one of your temperament a source of unalloyed pleasure. Still in an imperfect and ungrateful world it does not always follow that even such useful, unwearying and conspicuous service as yours is so promptly and fully rewarded. Your friends are therefore the more to be admired in their unhesitating recognition of your very unusual loyalty and availability.
>
> It is unfortunate, of course, that in the hour of your triumph you should have cause for anxiety, because the circumstances of your "election" will not bear the light. But since for the credit of Princeton all parties are equally determined to bury those facts in oblivion, you need have no serious concern on that score.
>
> In the full confidence that you will continue as prudent and successful in the future as you have been in the past, and that you will enjoy, as always, the satisfaction of a conscience void of all offense toward God and man, I remain
>
> Very sincerely, Ellen A. Wilson.[34]

She had once told Florence Hoyt that her "besetting sin" was her resentful nature. She found it hard to forgive injuries—not to herself— but to those whom she loved.[35] She had felt more bitter even than Woodrow over Jack Hibben's disloyalty to her husband and had attributed Woodrow's ill health in 1908 to the loss of Hibben's friendship.[36] After Hibben's inauguration (which Woodrow carefully avoided), Ellen believed that Princeton would now be "the most charming Country Club in America."[37]

In the spring of 1912, both Wilsons went on a campaign trip through Georgia. In Gainesville, Ellen was besieged by ladies who sent bouquets of flowers to the special train "on behalf of Georgia women." That evening, shortly before Woodrow appeared on the platform at the Atlanta city auditorium, Ellen was escorted to a ladies' box near the

Ellen Axson Wilson with her husband in the 1912 campaign in Georgia.
Courtesy of Marjorie Brown King.

front. As she came in, the audience, seven thousand strong, gave her a standing ovation while the band played "Dixie." Woodrow's reception a few minutes later was "unparalleled in Georgia."[38] From Atlanta they went to Albany, in southern Georgia, then eastward to Waycross, and briefly to Jacksonville, Florida, before turning north to Savannah. When they arrived there on April 19, they were escorted from the station to the DeSoto Hotel on East Liberty Street. Ellen barely had time to freshen before she was taken to the Axson home on Hall Street where Palmer's wife held a reception for 150 guests. In the evening, Woodrow spoke to an enthusiastic overflow audience in the Savannah Theater. The next morning, on their way back to the depot, the Wilsons were driven by the old manse on South Broad Street, but there was no time to stop. The two of them, sitting side by side on the back seat of the automobile, held hands as they went slowly by and recalled the events of June 24, 1885. Both were visibly affected as the car moved on. They were due in Macon at one o'clock.[39]

In Macon, they visited the campuses of Mercer University and Wesleyan College. Ellen heard her husband say in a brief informal talk to the "young ladies" at Wesleyan: "The most significant thing in modern life is the larger and larger role woman is playing in it. She is taking up now as she never took up before the things which concern the welfare of society. I have come to a rather unusual conclusion. I have always heard men say women are illogical, but my observation is just exactly the opposite. I think women are the most logical people in the world." He added that history had ignored the influence of women, an omission which should be rectified in the classroom.[40]

Woodrow had progressed in his views about women since he had taught them at Bryn Mawr, but he was not ready to support woman suffrage. On this issue, his two older daughters considered him behind the times. Jessie, who now publicly supported suffrage after her experience with the oppressed women in settlement houses, argued with her father. She pointed out that he, only one person, had the vote, while she, her mother, and two sisters—four persons—were unrepresented. Jessie had less difficulty in convincing her mother of women's need to have the right to vote, but Ellen would not embarrass her husband by speaking out on the matter.[41] (He would finally support woman suffrage on a state level late in 1915 and on the national level in 1916.)[42]

On Saturday, June 15, 1912, the Wilson family was at Sea Girt to await the outcome of the Democratic National Convention scheduled to meet in Baltimore on June 25. Ellen had no ambition to be first lady; but her role was now inseparable from that of her husband, who was, she believed, supremely qualified to be president of the United States.[43]

Chapter 27

First Lady Elect

When the family arrived at Sea Girt, Ellen found the governor's summer home sparkling. It had been completely redecorated with soft colors and fresh wallpaper which she had selected.[1] As they sat around the breakfast table on Sunday, Woodrow said: "Two weeks from today we shall either have this sweet Sunday calm again or an army of reporters camped on the lawn and an all-day reception." Nell asked her father which he would rather have. "Need you ask?" he responded.[2]

Ellen, too, had her ambivalent moments. After seeing a performance of *Macbeth* in New York, she told Stockton on her return home:

> It makes one pause and think; Lady Macbeth wanted Macbeth to have the crown because *he* wanted it, not because she wanted to become Queen of Scotland. Maybe these husbands ought not always to be encouraged to get the things to which their ambitions lead them, but how can wives who love them do anything except help them? Of course, I don't mean when the object of the ambition is something wrong as it was in Macbeth's case, but even when it is right, it may wear out their strength and health and spirits; yet they will never be happy unless they get it.[3]

Ellen was beginning to show the effects of the strain of public life. The confusion and clutter in the house on Cleveland Lane were a trial to her, who had "a passion for order." Nell was shocked one afternoon in Princeton when she realized that the small figure "walking slowly and wearily" ahead of her was her mother, a woman of usually quick and eager movements. After a conference with Lucy and Mary Smith, Nell and Jessie decided that they should drop their professional activities and stay at home to help, but Ellen vigorously opposed any disruption to her daughters' careers.[4]

The peaceful interlude at Sea Girt was short-lived. When the convention opened in Baltimore, the Wilson forces, led by McCombs and McAdoo, faced a group of delegates divided among eight candidates. The three serious contenders, in addition to Woodrow, were James

Beauchamp ("Champ") Clark of Missouri, Speaker of the House of Representatives; Judson Harmon, governor of Ohio; and Oscar W. Underwood, a congressman from Alabama. The Wilson family kept in constant touch with Woodrow's headquarters in Baltimore through a private telephone wire. Ellen, Margaret, Jessie, and Nell, joined by Mary Hoyt, followed each development as it came by telegraph or telephone. (Stockton was lecturing in California; Madge and Egie were on a ranch in Buffalo, Wyoming.)[5]

On June 28 Clark had moved into the lead, and his nomination seemed inevitable. Woodrow composed a letter to McCombs releasing the Wilson delegates, and he and Ellen began to plan a trip to England when his gubernatorial term would expire.[6] The next morning, before receiving the letter from Sea Girt, McCombs called on the telephone. He was discouraged and suggested that the governor authorize him to withdraw Woodrow's name from the balloting. Woodrow then sent a telegram to that effect. Later in the morning, an outraged McAdoo called Woodrow and urged him not to withdraw. When Ellen came into the room and found a wilted Tumulty and a wavering husband, she asked them what would be gained by withdrawing. "You must not do it," she urged Woodrow. He then countermanded the earlier order to McCombs.[7]

Sunday, June 30, was a day of rest for everyone. The family motored to Spring Lake to attend worship services conducted by the Reverend James Meeker Ludlow, pastor of the East Orange Presbyterian Church. On Monday, Woodrow "was busily engaged in reciting limerick verses" to Ellen and the daughters "on the veranda of the . . . summer home." It was an unusual but apparently effective way to cope with the almost unbearable undercurrent of excitement as reports now showed the "slow upward movement of the Wilson Column." At the close of Monday's deliberations, with forty-two ballots cast, Woodrow was now leading Clark, but by only five votes.[8]

That night, in the privacy of Jessie and Nell's bedroom, the three daughters shared their thoughts with one another. Jessie confessed that she could "never imagine us in the White House." Nell agreed. Margaret retorted: "That's not the way to think of it. Can you imagine father failing in anything?" They all admitted that they could not—and slept fitfully.[9]

On the next day, July 2, at 2:48 P.M., Woodrow, in the library at Sea Girt, learned through a telephone call that his nomination on the forty-sixth ballot was imminent. He walked out into the reception hall to look for Ellen, who, with the daughters, had gone to their rooms for a brief rest. When Ellen heard his footsteps on the stairs, she knew instinctively why he was coming. Instead of telling her that he was nominated, Woodrow said, "Well, dear, I guess we won't go to Mount Rydal this summer after all." They went down, a smiling Ellen on Woodrow's arm, to greet reporters gathered below. The press corps stood, heads bared, in sober silence. Ellen broke the strain for all and, for the first time in her life, began to chat freely with the reporters. "Isn't it fine?" she said. "I didn't think the hard, pounding battle could win. It is a hopeful thing, a beautiful thing, to see what the people can do when they take the case in their own hands. . . . I never had a moment's fear about the outcome if Woodrow could only get the nomination, but I did fear he'd be defeated in the convention." She confided that they had almost given up on Friday and were planning a summer trip.

Only an hour before, the reporters had unsuccessfully begged the governor to ask the women in his family to appear. Now, as Ellen talked, the journalists wrote furiously. Two hours later, Sea Girt was bedlam. A brass band from Manasquan rendered "Old Nassau"; buggies and automobiles lined the side of the beach road a mile deep. When the band stopped playing, and shouts rose from a thousand throats, Woodrow came out on the long porch to acknowledge the cheering crowd. The demonstration that began at 4:30 finally ended at 5:10 in the afternoon. That night, the family, Woodrow included, slept like the dead.[10]

The next morning, Margaret, Jessie, and Nell took Ellen's breakfast to her room and sat with her while she ate. It was one of the few private moments that they would experience for many weeks.[11] On July 3, the Wilsons had as dinner guests William E. Gonzales, editor of the Columbia *State*, and Dean and Mrs. Henry B. Fine, who were leaving the next day for a year abroad. Thirty-five members of the Democratic National Committee called on July 4; and later, Ellen had for luncheon the "people's lawyer" from Boston, Louis D. Brandeis. Except for one brief interlude, Woodrow was constantly in conference with party leaders from the time of his nomination until his acceptance speech in August. A few of these meetings took place in Trenton, but most were held at Sea Girt.[12]

The brief interlude took place on a yacht, *Corona*, which belonged to Cleveland H. Dodge. On July 22, Ellen, Woodrow, and Margaret slipped away from Sea Girt for a week of cruising in Long Island Sound to escape the crowds and to allow Woodrow to prepare his acceptance speech. On August 7, from the porch of the governor's house at Sea Girt, with Ellen, Margaret, Jessie, and Nell seated behind him, he spoke to a throng gathered on the grounds.[13]

On the day before, Republicans who had bolted to form a separate Progressive party, had, at their meeting in Chicago, chosen Theodore Roosevelt as their candidate. Woodrow faced a contest not only with Roosevelt, but also with the official Republican party candidate President William Howard Taft, who had been nominated in June. By late August, the Wilson family circle knew that the race was primarily between Woodrow and Roosevelt.[14] Woodrow announced to the press in August that, pending the outcome of the election, he intended to remain as governor of New Jersey.[15]

The three Wilson daughters were, of course, now the subject of national publicity. They were asked about every detail of their lives, and if the answers were not forthcoming, the reporters invented their own.[16] One morning, Ellen opened the paper to read that the wife of the Democratic presidential candidate, on a shopping tour in Philadelphia, had just purchased some seven gowns at from $200 to $300 apiece. She sent the paper a terse note, including a precise list of that day's outlay: "Two ready-made gowns, one hat, one chiffon waist, material to repair two old gowns and two pairs of gloves: total cost $140.84."[17] Ellen was offended by another widely published statement to the effect that she approved of women's smoking. She handed her own press release to the reporters at Sea Girt in which she indignantly denied that she approved of women smoking. In fact, she said that she so intensely disliked the smoking habit that the real danger lay in her being unjust and unkind to those whose opinions differed.[18]

In the appalling accumulation of mail that arrived daily at Sea Girt, Ellen gladly fulfilled one request which came from the editor (a college mate of Woodrow's) of the *St. Louis Post-Dispatch*, who wanted an "accurate personal description" of the Democratic candidate. Ellen wrote:

> Gov. Wilson is 5 feet 10 1/2 inches in height, chest measurement 39, collar 16, size of hat 7 3/8, weight 170 pounds. His weight has been practically the same for 10 or 15 years. He has good shoul-

ders, the neck round, strong and very young-looking. He has no accumulation of flesh about the waist. He has an excellent constitution—very elastic—steel rather than iron. He is a splendid sleeper—can go to sleep at any moment that he makes up his mind to do so. He decides beforehand just when he will wake up, and always does it to the moment, with his mind perfectly clear. He is in much better physical condition than when he was a young man. Then, owing to bad food at colleges, etc., he suffered from chronic indigestion, but, living since under more wholesome conditions, he has entirely outgrown all tendency to trouble of that sort. He had once an attack of writer's cramp (in his author days), which makes his friends a little anxious as to the handshaking ordeals. He has dark brown hair, now turning iron-gray, a rather dark and somewhat ruddy complexion and very large, dark gray eyes, with dark eyebrows and very long, dark lashes. People are apt to say after meeting him that, strange as his face is, they were even more impressed with the sympathy and kindliness of expression of his eyes and his smile.[19]

Still unfamiliar with the art of dictating letters, Ellen answered much of the incoming personal correspondence by hand. Friends whose good wishes poured in received cordial replies. The inevitable crackpot letters needed attention, such as one from an insurance agent in Pueblo, Colorado, who wanted "no office or appointment," but only to do good for the "President elect and his family." The good which he coveted was to write a large life-insurance policy on Woodrow, a matter which "Mrs. Wilson" would of course take up with the governor "at the opertune time."[20] Invitations came from Mary Hulbert to have a rest on Nantucket at Mary's summer home; from Nancy Toy to visit Cambridge; from Anna Harris to Jessie to come to Georgia.[21] Three people, including Mary Hulbert, offered places to the family for a postelection holiday. The Wilsons chose Mary's house, Glencove, Padget West, in Bermuda where they planned to spend four weeks.[22]

Ellen and the daughters returned to Cleveland Lane on October 1, and, on the next day, Woodrow left for a ten-day tour which took him as far as Denver. He was hardly back in Princeton when, on October 14, Theodore Roosevelt, in Milwaukee, was shot in the chest by a fanatic. Ellen at once wired her solicitude and sympathy to Roosevelt's wife, Edith.[23] The next week, Colonel House assigned a tall, lean former Texas Ranger, William J. McDonald, who carried a pair of pistols in hip holsters, as Woodrow's bodyguard.[24]

As election day approached, Ellen was exhausted and tense, but she remained eager and interested. The climax of the campaign came with Woodrow's speech on the evening of October 31 at Madison Square Garden. The four Wilson women, who had joined him for dinner in New York, were there in their ladies' box. When Woodrow entered the auditorium, the enormous crowd went wild. Ellen's eyes met her husband's again and again during the hour-long demonstration.[25]

On election day, November 5, the Wilsons were at home in the Cleveland Lane house. Stockton, Joseph R. Wilson, Jr., and two cousins, James and Fitzwilliam Woodrow, joined the family group. Madge and Egie were now in California on sabbatical leave. Late in the afternoon, McAdoo arrived from New York with Josephus Daniels, an old Wilson campaigner and editor of the Raleigh *News and Observer*. Accompanied by McDonald, Woodrow went in midmorning to the firehouse on Chambers Street to vote a straight Democratic ticket. As Jessie might well have reminded him, four women waited at home, unable to cast their ballots.

Ellen and Woodrow spent the rest of the day quietly, both of them sensing that the door had closed forever on their lives as private citizens. After dinner, Woodrow read Browning aloud to the family. Shortly before ten o'clock, the bell in Nassau Hall began to ring in muffled tones and was soon tolling like "a thing possessed." Ellen ran to the front door to hear Tumulty's voice calling from the middle of a group of newsmen, "He's elected, Mrs. Wilson." Turning around, she walked across the parlor to the large studio room where Woodrow stood in front of the fireplace. As the grandfather clock struck ten, Ellen placed her hands on his shoulders and kissed him, saying, "My dear, I want to be the first to congratulate you." Woodrow then embraced his three daughters.[26]

From the vicinity of the campus, the sounds of "Old Nassau" became clearer and clearer. The students, gathered around Prospect, were told by President Hibben that the next day, November 6, would be a university holiday. Hibben had then ordered the bell in Nassau to be rung. Armed with flags and torches, the students marched to Cleveland Lane, singing and cheering. Woodrow, bareheaded, went out on the small porch to greet the crowd. Someone dragged a broken rocking chair out for him to stand on, a hazard Nell tried unsuccessfully to point out in the confusion. People were coming from all directions to join the throng of students. The crowd, suddenly quiet, looked up at the president-elect, waiting for him to speak. Gravely and slowly, Woodrow told them, "I have no feeling of triumph tonight, but a feeling of solemn responsibility. I know the great task ahead of me and . . . I look almost with pleading to you . . . to stand behind me. . . . I believe that a great cause has triumphed for the American people. I know what we want, and we will not get it through a single man or a single session of Congress, but through the long process extending through the next generation."[27]

After Woodrow had finished speaking, he and Ellen stood inside the front door to greet neighbors who came from the nearby streets. The Allan Marquands, with their fifteen-year-old daughter, Eleanor, all of whom had been avid Taft supporters, came nevertheless to tender their best wishes. Eleanor, embarrassed that her homemade Taft label still dangled from her coat, hoped that no one would notice a young girl's political faux pas. When the Marquands entered the house, Ellen Wilson, brown eyes lit with excitement, shook Eleanor's hand and said, "So this is our little Taft girl!"[28] President Hibben did not appear, but he sent a congratulatory telegram. Woodrow responded, also by telegram: "I need not tell you how gratifying it was to me to receive through you the congratulations of my alma mater. I hope sincerely that she may never have the occasion to be ashamed of her son."[29]

On November 16, Ellen, Woodrow, Jessie, and Nell sailed from New York on S.S. *Bermudian* for a vacation in Mary Hulbert's cottage. Ellen loved the island with its lush, floral beauty; yet even in this tropical paradise they were made aware of their new status by the ubiquitous Secret Service agents. Except for a few unavoidable teas and an occasional dinner dance, the family was for the most part left alone to swim, sail, and picnic. After the long campaign, it was "almost too good to be true" for the Wilson women to have Woodrow all to themselves.[30] During the last week in Bermuda, Ellen and Nell managed to paint "some of the exquisite scenery."[31]

They returned to New York on December 16, and, in Jessie's words, "back into the whirl and confusion . . . learning to take each day as it comes" and trying not to "lose our sense of proportion."[32] The three daughters had now given up their individual pursuits to live in the White House, at least for the first year.

On the Saturday before Christmas, the Women's Democratic Club of New York City gave a victory luncheon at the Waldorf-Astoria to honor Ellen and her three daughters. Instead of the estimated five hundred guests, fifteen hundred women packed the reception room "to suffocation." The headline in the *New York Times* described the affair as "Crush at Waldorf to See Mrs. Wilson."[33]

On Christmas Day at Cleveland Lane Ellen wondered, "What will next year bring?" Florence Hoyt sent a piece of exquisite handworked linen, a gift that made Ellen feel in touch with old times; but as she wrote to her cousin, "I must not let myself think of all that now, much less speak of it. I must make believe very hard now that I am a different kind of woman,—in *some* respects,—not *all*, thank Heaven."[34]

On December 28, Woodrow and Ellen went to Staunton, Virginia, to take part in ceremonies celebrating the fifty-sixth anniversary of his birth. After Woodrow addressed the guests assembled in front of the Mary Baldwin Seminary, he and Ellen spent the night in the room in the Presbyterian manse where he was born.[35]

The weeks between the return from Bermuda in December and the inauguration in March were, without question, the most harassed period in Ellen's life. The family lived from day to day with Ellen's usual sense of order temporarily abandoned. As the president-elect's wife, she, too, was a public figure. There were some private hours when she was closeted with Woodrow to listen and counsel as he worked on the selection of his cabinet.[36] He was ambivalent about the appointment of William Jennings Bryan as secretary of state, but Ellen thought there was no alternative. She also urged him to retain Tumulty as press secretary in the face of "numerous protests" because Tumulty was a Roman Catholic.[37] Woodrow followed both of her suggestions, and, as president, he would continue to discuss political issues and governmental problems with Ellen because he wanted her reaction to them.[38]

Ellen had her own list of chores to be done before the inauguration: a suitable First Lady's wardrobe had to be selected and purchased; arrangements must be made for a smooth transition to the Executive Mansion; women journalists clamored for her time; and the ubiquitous stack of mail must be read and answered.

With Henrietta Ricketts acting as go-between, Ellen sought help on her wardrobe from one of Princeton's most tastefully dressed women, Josephine Perry (Mrs. Junius Spencer) Morgan. In January, Henrietta wrote to Josie Morgan: "Mrs. Woodrow Wilson has just been here to ask me if I would ask from you the address of the Miss Hanley to whom you once sent her long ago—the dressmaker. She also wishes to know if you still like [Miss Hanley]. . . . Other people have recommended dressmakers to her but she says that Woodrow thinks you are always so beautifully and perfectly dressed without being extreme in any fashion. . . . I really do want her to be well-dressed and she seems to be uneasy about it. She really dreads Washington, I think."

Josephine Morgan was more than happy to oblige. A week later, the dressmaker from K. E. Hanley Co., 71 West Forty-Sixth Street, New York, wrote to her: "I am happy to say that Mrs. Wilson has been in to see me and we are to make her important gowns, and also the Misses Wilsons'. You may be sure I shall give myself over entirely to this order—and will attend to the designing as well as all the details."[39]

On one of her shopping trips to New York, Ellen came home with an "inauguration present" for each daughter; for Margaret and Jessie, necklaces of seed pearls, and for Nell, a bar pin set with small diamonds. When Woodrow realized that Ellen had nothing for herself, he went out and bought her a diamond pendant, affectionately called by the family "the crown jewel." To pay for what Ellen called their "Washington trousseaux" and other expenses incurred in the move, Woodrow had borrowed five thousand dollars from the Princeton Bank (now the Princeton Bank and Trust Company), a sum which he had repaid in full by September 1913.[40]

One of Ellen's first chores after her return from Bermuda was to interview the Tafts' housekeeper, Elizabeth Jaffray. After satisfactory recommendations from the White House, Ellen hired Jaffray.[41] President Taft wrote about another matter which Ellen would pursue after the move to Washington. Enclosing a plan of the second floor of the White House, Taft explained that he was "always anxious, and Congress would have been willing, to spend four or five thousand dollars to fit up a number of bed-rooms in the third story . . . and if you agree with me on that subject and would like to have the matter attended to at once, I will have Colonel [Spencer] Cosby make an estimate for that improvement so that it may be done conveniently during the summer of your first year."[42]

The Wilsons were grateful for Taft's kindness and suggestions.[43] Neither Woodrow nor Ellen had ever been in the White House, although at the time of Joseph Ruggles Wilson's death, Woodrow had canceled plans to stay overnight with the Theodore Roosevelts. In fact,

Ellen had seen the outside of the Executive Mansion only once, when she was en route to New York in September 1884. At Helen Taft's invitation, Ellen would make a preinaugural inspection tour of the White House on Monday, March 3.[44]

Ellen now gave interviews to members of the press who clamored for some of her time. Two articles appeared in the *Ladies Home Journal*, one a double-page spread with photographs of "personally selected American-designed fashions" worn by Ellen and the three daughters; the other reproduced, in color, two of Ellen's landscape paintings, *The Lane* and *The River*, which she regarded as "among the best" she had ever done.[45] *Harper's Weekly* ran a centerfold layout of family photographs and later printed a reproduction of Arthur Garfield Learned's etching of Ellen.[46] The *Review of Reviews*, *Literary Digest*, and *Independent* published photographs of her—the *Digest*'s, a study done by Harris and Ewing, was captioned "The Happiest Lady in Washington."[47] Frances McGregor Gordon, who entitled her *Collier's* profile, "The Tact of Mrs. Woodrow Wilson," retold the story of Ellen's role in arranging the dinner meeting between her husband and Bryan.[48] *Current Opinion* pointed out that she was the first "typical Southern woman" to hold the position of first lady in more than sixty years.[49] The most extensive profiles of Ellen were written by Mabel Potter Daggett for *Good Housekeeping* and Hester E. Hosford for the *Independent*. Hosford, who wrote two stories a few months apart, was a friend of the Wilson family as well as a professional journalist.[50] Two Washington women, Susie Root Rhodes and Grace Porter Hopkins, began to compile and edit recipes from "prominent wives of the cabinet and Congress" to be published in 1913 as *The Economy Administration Cook Book* and dedicated to Helen [*sic*] Axson Wilson.[51]

The mail which had staggered Ellen after Woodrow's nomination was only a preview of what now deluged the Wilsons. Temporary stenographers moved into the Cleveland Lane house, and Helen Bones, then living in Chicago, came to Princeton in January to be Ellen's personal secretary. While Helen made her way through the stacks of letters, Ellen moved through the rooms and, for the first time in her life, pretended that she did not see the disorder.[52]

Part Eight

1913–1914

Ellen Axson Wilson, official First Lady portrait, 1913.
Courtesy of the Very Reverend Francis B. Sayre.

_____*Chapter 28*_____

Inauguration

As inaugural day approached, the Wilsons found their "hearts very heavy" at the thought of leaving the little town where they had spent most of their married life.[1] On Saturday evening, March 1, more than fifteen hundred students and townspeople marched to Cleveland Lane to present a silver loving cup to Woodrow and, once more, to sing "Old Nassau" on the spot where the election-day serenade had taken place. Although Woodrow had told the members of his family not to appear, Ellen was unable to resist peeking through the partially open front door. When she saw the silver cup, she came out of the house and took it in her hands to see and feel its beauty.[2] Later, in the privacy of the studio room, with only the family gathered around, Woodrow read aloud his inaugural address.[3]

On Sunday morning, the family attended worship services at the First Presbyterian Church, where they sat together for the last time in "pew 57." Instead of hearing their own pastor, the Reverend Dr. Sylvester W. Beach, they heard a sermon from the Reverend Dr. John De Witt, retired professor of church history at Princeton Theological Seminary. When the Wilsons came out of the sanctuary, friends and neighbors surrounded them to offer best wishes and to say goodbye. Although Woodrow soon arranged for a seating at the Central Presbyterian Church in Washington, he and Ellen kept their memberships at the Princeton church, and Dr. Beach would later participate in events important in the lives of the first family.[4]

Monday was a crisp, sunny spring day. By ten o'clock in the morning, a line of motorcars, with a contingent of Secret Service men, waited to take the president-elect and his family from Cleveland Lane to the Princeton station, off the main tracks which were located three miles to the southeast at Princeton Junction. Ellen and Woodrow came out of the house, paused, looked at each other, and set out alone to walk the few blocks to the station. They walked up Library Place, past the home they had built and loved, past the McGill house they had first rented, past old friends who were standing along the way to wave or, now and then, to shake hands. Waiting at the station at the foot of Blair Arch were two parlor cars for the Wilson family and seven coaches loaded with Princeton students. The undergraduates, as part of a tribute to this distinguished alumnus, provided a baggage car to move the Wilsons' luggage and personal effects from Cleveland Lane to the White House. Woodrow, Ellen, and the three daughters, standing on the back platform of the train, smiled and waved to cover their sadness as the Gothic towers of Princeton faded from sight. Ellen would come back only once more, and that briefly.

When the presidential party arrived in Washington, the students, forming a lane from the train to the President's Room in Union Station, stood silent, with heads bare, as the first family passed between the lines. En route to the Shoreham Hotel, the students, now joined by alumni, escorted the Wilsons in automobiles decorated with the orange and black of Old Nassau.[5]

At the hotel, the president-elect's suite was full of flowers, friends, relatives, reporters, and Secret Service men, all of whom created a babble and confusion in which the family tried vainly to compose themselves. Nell was disturbed at how pale and fragile Ellen looked; she took her mother to her bedroom, locked the door, and gave orders to Helen Bones that no one should be allowed to enter. When it was nearly time for Ellen and Woodrow to go to the White House to meet the Tafts, Nell helped her mother to dress. Ellen, who had said almost nothing, broke down and wept when Nell kissed her. Her composure restored after Nell brought spirits of ammonia, Ellen smilingly assured her daughter that she was "all right," that the noise and confusion had temporarily upset her, and, above everything, Nell was not to tell anyone about the episode.[6]

Ellen found the Tafts so friendly and helpful that she came away undismayed at the prospect of managing an establishment as large as the White House. She had earlier learned from the Tafts that Congress was "very generous" to the president. All transportation and the salaries of all the servants (except for personal servants) were paid for. Flowers for entertainments and general use were furnished by the conservatory, and, if they did not suffice, a flower fund was available. The Marine Band, or some other group, would provide music for all social events. In the summer, when the Wilsons left for cooler climates, any needed household staff could, at government expense, accompany the president's family. Altogether, the Wilsons' costs of living would be only those of feeding their family and the servants, plus their own personal expenses, out of an annual salary of seventy-five thousand dollars (and an allowance of twenty-five thousand dollars for traveling).[7]

On Tuesday—inauguration day—the weather cleared into a beautiful sunny afternoon, the warmest March 4 since 1873. For her inaugural costume, Ellen chose a suit of "smoke brown cloth with black velvet trimming," and a large black hat decorated with ostrich plumes in various shades of brown. At noon, with his hand on Ellen's small Bible, Woodrow took the oath of office. He then turned to the podium and began his inaugural address.[8] Unable to see her husband's face from her reserved seat on the portico of the Capitol, Ellen stepped from her chair and moved over until she stood directly beneath him. There, "utterly oblivious of the thousands watching her, she gazed up at him, . . . a look of rapture on her face."[9]

There was time only to serve a quick, stand-up luncheon for 189 people at the White House before Ellen and Woodrow entered the reviewing stand on the south side to see the inaugural parade. Fred Yates stood with them, "the dear President . . . raising his hat as the colours passed . . . [and] Mrs. Wilson . . . looking like an angel[—]how beautiful she looked now and again in her old enthusiasm waving a little lace handkerchief and smiling her radiant smile."[10]

That evening, for their first dinner in the Executive Mansion, Ellen planned a family affair with Yates, of course, included. They ate in the State Dining Room where the table, decorated with masses of roses, was softly lit by the "great silver candelabra." Proud family faces turned admiringly toward "their great man" who sat quietly and not a little tired at the head of the table. At the other end was the woman whose unwavering love and support had, indeed, enabled him to stop short of nothing noble of which his powers were capable.[11] After dinner, the group watched from the White House as an enormous display of fireworks ended the day's festivities—for everyone except the president. With Margaret as his guest, he slipped out at nine o'clock to attend a dinner given in his honor at the Shoreham Hotel by the Princeton class of 1879.

Ellen began her official entertaining on Wednesday, March 5, with a reception in the East Room for more than one thousand guests. On Thursday, another for 920; and on Friday, for 295 persons, followed later in the afternoon by a small tea for about 50 guests, among whom were Theodore Roosevelt's daughter, Alice, and her husband, Congressman Nicholas Longworth. On March 13, Ellen and Woodrow, with the Secretary of State and Mrs. Bryan, received the diplomatic corps and their wives. Margaret, Jessie, Nell, Helen, Annie Howe, and Annie Cothran assisted as hostesses. During the same week, Ellen gave a tea for the cabinet wives and then for the wives of the justices of the Supreme Court. Later, she replaced these teas with regular luncheons for the cabinet wives, so that she could become better acquainted with the women, most of whom, like herself, had been uprooted from established homes. Between March 5 and June 11, there were forty-one White House receptions, with an average attendance of more than 600 persons. These events usually required the initial presence of both the president and the first lady, but more than once Ike Hoover, the head usher, noted in his White House diary that Mrs. Wilson continued to receive up to the hour of closing. In addition to these affairs, Ellen had small groups, such as the women journalists, to tea.[12]

Probably with Margaret's help, Ellen arranged a series of musicals which began on March 11 with a piano recital by Herbert Sachs Hirsch. At the April dinner for cabinet members and their wives, there was a program of Scandinavian music; at the May dinner, three Englishwomen, the "Misses Fuller," sang old English and Scots ballads. The East Room provided the setting for concerts by the Russian cathedral choir of New York, by Manalito Funes at the piano, and for both instrumental and vocal trios.[13]

In April, May, and June, Ellen invited many friends and relatives for overnight or the weekend. Among these were the Cleveland H. Dodges, the George M. Harpers, the William U. Vreelands and their daughter, May, the Tedcastles, and Edith and Harry Reid; relatives who came were Stockton, George Howe, the Hoyts, Ed Brown, and Woodrow's brother, Joseph, soon to move to Baltimore to take a position with the United States Fidelity and Guaranty Company. On Friday, May 9, at Ellen's invitation, Mary Hulbert arrived for the weekend.

The young people, too, had their share of guests. Among them were Meemee and Ed Brown's daughter, the "little Miss Marjorie," now a young lady of twenty-one; Rosalie's daughter, Rainsford DuBose, who was to be married in September; Beth's daughter, Ellen Woodrow Erwin; and from Princeton, Mary Blanchard Scott and Sarah Elizabeth Duffield. Ben King, Nell's fiancé, and Francis Bowes Sayre, a friend of Jessie's, were frequent dinner guests.[14]

On March 14, when Ellen posed for her official photograph as first lady, she broke precedent by going to the studio of Harris and Ewing rather than have their representatives come to the White House. The *Washington Post* published this photograph on March 16 with the caption: "It shows the 'first lady of the land' in one of her most characteristic poses, and wearing that happy and cheerful expression which all Washingtonians, who have had the opportunity to meet or see her, will recognize."[15] The pose, full-length and seated, shows her in a gown which, according to Margaret Wilson, her mother had had made for the inaugural ball[16] that was canceled by Woodrow because of the "unnecessary expense upon the government."[17]

Ellen inherited a well-trained White House staff, and she knew how to delegate responsibility. In addition to Helen Bones, Ellen now had a social secretary, Isabelle ("Belle") Hagner, who, after serving both Edith Roosevelt and Helen Taft, was well acquainted with Washington protocol. Belle's office, set up in the west sitting room of the family quarters, was a center of activity at the start of each day when calendars were checked and appointments scheduled. Margaret, Jessie, and Nell, thrown immediately into "a mad social whirl," found their preferences and invitations regulated by Miss Hagner, who insisted that they should try not to go to the same parties. White House favors must be equitably distributed![18]

These tightly scheduled days of receptions, luncheons, teas, and dinners gave few opportunities for Ellen and Woodrow to be together alone. Whenever he was able to take a break from the Executive Office, usually in the late afternoon, he and Ellen would slip out for a drive through the nearby Virginia countryside. They began to use this way of escape as early as March 5; thereafter, it became a habitual weekday recreation which sometimes gave them as much as two hours together.[19]

On a Saturday morning in early June, Woodrow, Ellen, Margaret, and Helen decided on the spur of the moment to take an "all-day ride in the country." Not unlike other husbands, the president was faced with a minor crisis over a satisfactory place for lunch. Ellen refused to eat in a run-down looking country hotel in Maryland. Margaret suggested a quaint tea room on the outskirts of Baltimore to which the chauffeur was directed. When Margaret slipped in to see whether a table was available and found there would be a short wait, Woodrow balked at the possible inconvenience to other customers who would be asked to leave so that the proprietors could accommodate a presidential party. Famished, they finally ate at a large hotel in downtown Baltimore.[20]

Another favorite family recreation, the theater, offered abundant choices in Washington. The Wilsons went almost weekly to the Belasco, Keith's, the National, or the Colonial; they also indulged occasionally in a new form of entertainment, the "moving pictures." Sometimes Ellen sent weekend guests off to a play, or "movie," while she read or simply went to bed.[21] Her experience as the wife of a university president and of the governor of New Jersey, ten years altogether, had helped to prepare her for the role of first lady, but there was no way that she could foresee the frustration of having her life chopped into a hundred small, often unrelated, segments of time each day.

One project that she undertook brought visible results within a matter of weeks and afforded her pleasure even in the planning stages: renovation of the White House living quarters. In 1902, Edith and Theodore Roosevelt rendered a long-overdue service to the nation by planning and enduring a major renovation of, and an addition to, the Executive Mansion. A new one-story west wing, which removed the executive offices from the family quarters for the first time, now provided ample space for the president and his staff. Refurbishing the main floor in 1902 had changed Louis Tiffany's art nouveau decor, executed for Chester A. Arthur, to more nearly the simplicity of the federal period. The Roosevelts created new bedrooms on the second floor over the East Room, to make a total of seven on the same level as the president's study and the oval parlor.[22]

When the Wilsons moved in, they found that each of these family rooms opened onto a long, wide corridor, "the Great Passage," that ran from east to west and ended in two open sitting rooms, each lit by a large Palladian window that supplied the only natural light in the hallway. Deep green burlap on the walls, a maroon carpet, and ornate tables placed against the walls of the corridor gave a feeling of gloom that Ellen could not abide. Working with Colonel Spencer Cosby from the Corps of Engineers, she arranged to have the walls stripped and redone in a natural grass cloth shot with gold. Ellen replaced the red carpet with one of "mahogany velvet" which she extended into the sitting rooms. Some of the Wilsons' furniture, books, and art objects, including Ellen's copy of Bouguereau's Madonna, were sent down from Princeton; and bright flowered chintz was hung at the east and west windows. From the Corcoran Gallery, Ellen reclaimed an oil painting by George Watts, "Love and Life," depicting two curvaceous nudes, which Edith Roosevelt had hung in the family corridor and which Helen Taft had banished.

On the south side of the Great Passage were located Ellen and Woodrow's bedrooms, the president's study, the oval parlor, and, at the east end, Margaret's quarters, spacious enough to accommodate her Steinway grand piano. Jessie and Nell, still preferring to share, had a room on the north side. Finally, there were the housekeeper's apartments, two small guest rooms, and, to the east of the staircase, the Rose Room.[23]

Ellen set in motion the plans suggested by President Taft to renovate the third floor during the summer months while the family would be away. But before that time, she redid one of the north bedrooms ("Number 13") for Jessie and Nell and Woodrow's room ("Number 23"). She changed Number 13 from a dark, unattractive space to one filled with brightness and light by the use of soft yellow, two-toned wallpaper that blended with yellow draperies and cream woodwork. She also ordered white enameled furniture, with twin beds, and a walnut colored "velvet" rug.

She took special pleasure in refurbishing Number 23. For the walls, she selected a colonial-design paper in off-white and delft blue; then, using fabrics and floor-coverings handwoven by women from the mountains of North Carolina and Tennessee, she redecorated the entire room in blue and white. For Lincoln's carved rosewood bed (eight feet long by nearly six feet wide), she ordered a custom spread in natural tones with four stripes in varying shades of blue to outline the edges.[24]

Use of the mountain crafts in the White House created an interest in the work of these women and developed a fashionable market for patchwork quilts, counterpanes, and homemade rugs. Ellen became honorary president of the Southern Industrial Association and attended various events which the association sponsored in Washington to benefit the Pine Mountain School in Kentucky.[25]

While the family was on vacation, renovation of the White House continued with the addition of five bedrooms and three baths on the third floor and the purchase of furniture for the new accommodations. The rest of the living space on the second floor was thoroughly cleaned and redecorated to Ellen's taste in soft colors and lighter, daintier fabrics. Her own room was filled with flowered chintz and pastels (her "indoor garden"); and one small third-floor room, with a skylight, was converted to a studio. She hoped to find the time someday to use it.[26]

For her White House china, Ellen was indebted to the good taste of Edith Roosevelt; and for the crystal and the silver flatware, to none other than her old friend and neighbor, Frances Cleveland. Embarrassed in 1902 by an insufficiency of matching china, Mrs. Roosevelt had ordered 120 place settings of a creamy white English Wedgwood in a simple pattern called "Ulunda," with the great seal of the United States added on a border decorated in red, yellow, and brown enamels. The lead crystal was cut in the "Russian" pattern, by the T. G. Hawkes Company of Corning, New York, on blanks manufactured by the Dorflinger glassworks of White Mills, Pennsylvania. The White House silver of the Chrysanthemum pattern had a simple beaded border and rounded handles on which the Great Seal of the United States was engraved.[27]

Ellen sorely missed the friends and freedom of Princeton, but with her own pictures and books about her she began to feel more at home.[28] Only a few weeks later, Ellen reported to Emily Yates: "Everything is going wonderfully well with us and we, in health, are all very well,—considering the heavy strain. Woodrow had a hard time with neuritis in his arm for several weeks, but it yielded promptly to treatment. He is playing golf again now and is much brighter and fresher than he was a month ago." Margaret was "rather nervous and overwrought" and needed a change. Woodrow, Ellen thought, had been "extraordinarily successful," and everybody was "in love with the girls," but what astonished Ellen was that she, too, had been "equally successful."[29]

She was uninterested in setting trends in fashion; in fact, a reporter quoted her as saying that she spent "less than $1,000 per year on clothes."[30] "A person would be a fool who let his head be turned by externals," Ellen told Florence Hoyt; "they simply go with the position."[31] She soon recognized that a first lady had influence, which she began to use in matters important to her. Early in her husband's term, she became involved in an activity unlikely to attract Washington's elite unless the first lady led the way. It began on Saturday morning, March 22, when Ellen received Charlotte Everett Wise (Mrs. Archibald) Hopkins at the White House.[32]

Hopkins, chairman of the District of Columbia section of the woman's department of the National Civic Federation and a social activist, was an intelligent, enthusiastic woman with original ideas. She came to tell the new first lady about the deplorable living conditions of most of Washington's blacks, who were crowded into disgraceful shacks in alleys, some of them within sight of the Capitol. Hopkins explained to Ellen that the crying need was for improved housing, a condition made more difficult by the unwritten law which excluded blacks from buying homes in the better parts of Washington. Most of the slumlords barely kept within the housing codes, which often meant "no water and no plumbing." The resulting conditions, conducive to crime and immorality, degraded all who lived there. Ellen, who understood at once the import of this woman's message, set a date to make her own tour of the alleys.[33]

On March 25, she first visited the Home for Incurables, going into every room, shaking hands with each patient, and saying a few comforting words. This was the first time in the history of the home that the wife of a president had entered its doors. After leaving there, with Charlotte Hopkins as her guide, Ellen was driven through the alleys—Logan's Court, Neil Place, and Goat and Willow Tree alleys, the last a shocking slum within three blocks of the Capitol. On another morning, Ellen toured 109 two-family dwellings built as model "sanitary" houses of from two to four rooms, with supervision by a social worker employed by the National Civic Federation. Ellen talked with the black occupants without letting them know who she was. After these tours, she became a stockholder in the newly organized Sanitary Housing Company.

Soon afterward, Ellen became honorary chairman, with a special interest in the housing committee, of the woman's department of the National Civic Federation. The Washington gossips soon purred that no one could move in polite society who could not talk about alley slums. When members of the federation took congressmen through the alleys, often with Ellen along, they always ended at the model houses to show how the problem could be solved. Blacks soon realized that it was, indeed, the president's wife who made these visits to their neighborhoods.

A Committee of Fifty, made up of leading men and women from charitable and civic organizations, was formed to draft a comprehensive alley bill to be introduced in Congress. In May, Ellen gave a tea for the committee and invited senators and representatives and their wives to hear about the alley slums. In June, she attended a meeting of the

Committee of Fifty held in a large private home at which many other prominent people were present. Secretary of State Bryan, who addressed the group, said of Ellen:

> The most eloquent speech here tonight is the one that has not been made at all, for actions speak louder than words. The fact that the wife of the President is with her presence here . . . lending support to the movement is enough. As crowded as my life is, I feel that if she can find time out of her busy days to be here and to work for this cause, I can too.[34]

The alley bill, carefully worked over during the next several months, was introduced in February 1914.[35]

On October 30, 1913, at a White House luncheon, Ellen sat beside Colonel House, a man whom she respected as her husband's chief adviser and confidant. She laid before him the need to improve conditions under which government employees, particularly women, worked. In late October, after visiting the Post Office Department, she told Colonel House that she had found that building especially objectionable because of its "unsanitary conditions," a matter which she had called to the attention of Postmaster General Albert S. Burleson with no effect. Appalled by the lack of rest room facilities, Ellen was determined to have this situation rectified. The conversation between Ellen and the Colonel, not an exchange of pleasantries, caught the attention of the "entire table," and House hastily promised her "to take it up and see that something was done along the lines of her suggestion."[36]

On October 31, Ellen went, unannounced, to the Government Printing Office to inspect the conditions of "light, space and air, and other things essential to . . . [the] health and comfort of Government employees."[37] But her work on the Washington slums and her efforts to improve the environment of women employees in government buildings did not appease persons active in racial justice.[38] Blacks and whites who had looked to President Wilson to eliminate the Jim Crow sections in government offices, were, instead, bitterly disappointed at the spread of segregation in the summer of 1913 in government departments. Aggrieved blacks presented the president with a protest in the form of a petition signed by twenty thousand persons from thirty-six states.[39] Black newspapers, the *Washington Bee* in particular, angrily denounced Woodrow; later, however, the *Bee* commented, when Margaret Wilson became involved in social settlement work and desegregation, that Ellen Wilson, one of the "noble" women who had done work among the blacks, had established a precedent for American white women, among whom was her "fine" daughter.[40] While Woodrow was denounced, Ellen played down her role in slum clearance. She laughingly told Woodrow that one woman had said that she, Ellen, had "done more good in Washington in four months than any other President's wife had *ever* done in four years—had completely changed the conditions of life for 12,000 people,—or was it 12,000 alleys?" The woman, Ellen said, took "the will for the deed."[41]

Despite the worry of Helen Bones and her three daughters over her strenuous pace, Ellen still managed to find time to help Woodrow. According to Nell (and to Stockton and to Wilson's authorized biographer, Ray Stannard Baker), her father discussed with her mother his "every important move" and they went carefully over his prepared speeches.[42] When Woodrow asked a reluctant Dean Henry B. Fine to become ambassador to Germany, Ellen solicited the support of Fine's sister. Cleveland Dodge would help with the ambassador's expenses "up to $25,000 a year," Ellen wrote to May Margaret Fine. And if the dean accepted, Ellen thought it would be a "splendid 'vindication,'" like the presidency for Woodrow—and just think how *furious* it will make West and the others! He need not keep it longer than he likes, and the prestige of it would give him later almost any academic position he wished."[43] Henry Fine declined the post.

Special requests for favors from the president continued to come to Ellen from both relatives and strangers. She took care of what appeared to be legitimate needs, such as an appeal from Egie Elliott's mother, a widow from Murfreesboro, Tennessee, for the position of postmistress, an appointment which Ellen asked Woodrow to make.[44] In two other such instances, the president considered Ellen's personal wishes over political judgment, by naming Hamilton Erwin postmaster at Morganton, North Carolina, and J. Park Bowie, a friend of the Axson family, postmaster at Rome, Georgia. Ellen also asked that "Miss Elizabeth C. Williams, elderly postmistress in Lexington, Kentucky," because of "desperate need," be retained.[45] A woman from the Midwest wrote to Ellen to ask whether her nine-year-old son, who had an "incurable heart condition," might be allowed "to shake the President's hand and have this memory." The meeting was duly arranged, and a small, sickly boy named Allan Davis, on March 23, from "9:30 to 9:35 A.M." met with the president of the United States.[46]

These specific instances of Ellen's helpfulness to her husband were less important, however, than her extraordinary understanding of political issues and of human nature. Among Woodrow's advisers she was, according to William G. McAdoo, *"the soundest and most influential* of them all."[47] McAdoo commented that she "did not abuse her power" by thrusting herself into situations, and the president trusted the wise counsel of this woman who was "the only human being who knew him perfectly."[48]

Ellen followed with eager interest her husband's legislative program. Woodrow came to the presidency with specific plans for tariff, currency and banking, and antitrust legislation. In a precedent-shattering move, he went to the Capitol on April 8 to address a joint session of Congress on tariff reform, the first of his legislative goals. Ellen and Helen Bones were in the visitor's gallery to hear him. When he spoke again to the Congress on June 23 about banking and currency reform, Ellen, Jessie, Nell, and Helen were present.[49]

Two days before the president's second address to a joint session of Congress, the following announcement appeared in the newspapers: "Upon the advice of her physician, Mrs. Wilson has decided to abandon active participation in the philanthropic movements which have commanded much of her attention since she came to Washington. Mrs. Wilson is not seriously ill, but will remain quietly in the White House until she goes to Cornish [New Hampshire]."[50]

The family physician, Dr. Cary Travers Grayson, assigned to the Naval Dispensary during the Roosevelt and Taft administrations, won the Wilsons' admiration in the first few hours after Woodrow's inauguration. When Annie Howe had fallen on the stairs of the Executive Mansion and cut her forehead, the young naval aide attended to her so efficiently and graciously that Woodrow requested his assignment to the White House. Grayson would be physician and friend to Ellen and Woodrow as long as they both lived.[51]

That Grayson advised Ellen to curtail her activities was hardly a surprise considering her killing pace since March. When the Wilson women left for the mountains of New Hampshire on June 27, Grayson, a bachelor, moved into the White House to look after the president.

Cornish

The place selected by the Wilsons for summer 1913 was Harlakenden, a Georgian mansion situated on two hundred acres overlooking the Connecticut River in Cornish, New Hampshire. From information supplied in the spring by Arthur Tedcastle, Ellen had reviewed several possibilities in New England for the family's vacation. After seeing photographs and reading a description of Harlakenden, Ellen wrote to Tedcastle in March that she would settle the matter immediately if prudence permitted, but that she was a little dubious about the expense. Two thousand dollars for rent was about the limit which the Wilsons had set for themselves, and a more modest place had come to her attention. "I would be extremely grateful," she wrote to Tedcastle, "if you or Agnes would send me an estimate of the expense for the two places for four months." She explained that "poor Woodrow has such very heavy family burdens, $2500. this year for his nephew [Wilson Howe] and his family, and $2000. every year for his sister [Annie Howe]."[1]

In early April, Woodrow signed the lease for Harlakenden after tactfully writing to Mary Hulbert on March 16 that he wished that they *could* have rented her house on Nantucket, but that they were already committed to engage one in New Hampshire.[2] Ellen thanked Tedcastle for doing what the Wilsons could not possibly have done for themselves. "Never having had any great *business* men in our family on either side, I observe your methods with a great admiration."[3]

A suitor of Jessie's, manifestly boring to the family, had made a desperation call on the Tedcastles, for which Ellen apologized. "He is mad about Jessie—has been told at least fifty times that it is no use, but he is one of the bull-dog sort. . . . A very fine fellow, too, but a bore."[4]

Her feeling about "bores" remained unchanged since her early twenties when she had written: "Alas, Alas, with what blank eyes do some of our fellow-mortals look out on life, and what a totally unmeaning affair they find, or make it! Shakespeare didn't include, among his seven ages, the 'automatic stage,' yet not less surely do multitudes travel that way. . . . It is melancholy to see how large a proportion of the middle-aged there are who appear to have reached that condition. . . . If I thought it a necessary consequence of growing old I would humbly beg leave to go out and hang myself while I had enough enthusiasm left to accomplish so much."[5]

Ellen had no reason to worry about Jessie, who, like her mother, knew when she had found the right partner. He was Francis Bowes Sayre, to whom Jessie had been secretly engaged since the previous October. The official announcement, made from Cornish on July 2, thrilled the entire country at the prospect of a White House wedding.

Sayre was born in South Bethlehem, Pennsylvania, the second son of Martha Finley Nevin and Robert Haysham Sayre. After graduation from Williams College, with membership in Phi Beta Kappa, Frank entered Harvard Law School where he earned the LL.B. degree *cum laude* in 1912. He had worked for two summers during college with Dr. Wilfred T. Grenfell, a medical missionary in Labrador, and, after law school, became an assistant in the New York district attorney's office.[6]

Frank met Jessie Wilson during his last year at Harvard. The meeting came about through the matchmaking efforts of Auntie Blanche Nevin, who invited Jessie and Eleanor for a weekend at her country house, Windsor Forges, near Lancaster, Pennsylvania. When the Wilson women arrived, they found Blanche's nephew there on spring break from law school. Blanche Nevin, an artist and sculptor, had met Woodrow in Bermuda in 1910 and had modeled a bust of him.[7] Through subsequent letters between Blanche and the Wilsons, she had found out about Jessie, "the angel of the family," and decided that here, at last, was the perfect match for her adored Francis.[8] Blanche's conspiracy worked well. Jessie and Frank continued their courtship through his senior year at law school and her last year of settlement work in Philadelphia; in the fall of 1912, when he was in New York, Frank often came to Princeton.

Heavily involved in politics and frequently away from home, Woodrow was unaware of this serious romance going on under his nose. In fact, Jessie told only her mother until after the presidential election. Under constant surveillance by the press, the Wilsons passed Frank off as a family cousin, a deception that enabled the engaged couple to keep their romance hidden from the public until July 1913.[9]

The summer at Harlakenden, with its seclusion and beauty, was one of the happiest periods in Ellen's life. After one "gorgeous violet and green and gold day, with splendid clouds," she found the world "a beautiful place in spite of all drawbacks." Jessie and Frank, often together in Cornish for long weekends, radiated a joy that reminded Ellen of a Miss Axson and a Mr. Wilson of nearly thirty years ago. Margaret and Nell and their friends ("much superior to the Lyme set of young people") were in and out.[10] Mrs. Jaffray and needed staff from Washington took care of the housekeeping, so that Ellen had the leisure to paint almost every morning. She found a sympathetic, interesting group of artists near Cornish who took her in as one of them.

The only blemish on the entire vacation was Woodrow's inability to join her except for brief, scattered visits. On July 5, he came up for a week, and he was there again for the weekends of August 30 and September 12.[11] Nearly one hundred letters passed between them during this period of separation, letters that show a vivid freshness in their love reminiscent of the period before their marriage. Jessie and Frank no doubt stimulated some of this tenderness, but the emotional intensity in Ellen and Woodrow's correspondence reverberated from a depth that could never be truly sounded.

Woodrow liked to read in the newspapers about Ellen's activities in Cornish and to see an occasional photograph of her. "Bless you, how everybody up there will love and admire you before the summer is over," he wrote to her. "The glimpses you give me of what you are doing enable me to see just how charming and natural and genuine a friend and neighbour you are making of yourself. . . . No President but myself had *exactly* the right sort of wife! I am certainly the most fortunate man alive!"[12]

In Cornish, Ellen participated in two clubs, one composed solely of artists, some of whom had been fellow students at the Art Students League; the other was a "discussion group" made up of summer residents. She met "piles of New England spinsters" whom she liked—"Mary Hulbert notwithstanding."[13]

When it was Ellen's turn to have the Artists' Club at Harlakenden, the subject which she chose for discussion was "How can we best promote a fuller and more general appreciation of *American* art?" When the group concluded that Americans, like the French, should have a governmental bureau of art to purchase works of art, award prizes, and encourage artists in every way, Ellen commented that "the Congressmen who would take that view . . . [are] not yet born."[14]

Among this congenial company of artists were Kenyon Cox; Maxfield Parrish and his father, Stephen; the sculptor Annetta Johnson

Saint-Gaudens, sister-in-law of Augustus Saint-Gaudens; the architect and etcher Charles Adams Platt; Adeline Valentine Pond Adams and her sculptor husband, Herbert; and Robert William Vonnoh and his wife, Bessie, who had done the bust of Jessie. Robert Vonnoh began painting a group portrait of the four Wilson women "posed in his studio window with the grape vines and columns outside." "I am pouring tea at a tiny table. It bids fair to be a nice thing of the sunny, impressionistic sort," Ellen wrote to her husband. "Fortunately, we do not all have to pose at once."[15] One evening, when she had dinner at the home of an artist, another guest was George De Forest Brush, her teacher at the Art Students League, whom she had not seen since 1885. She "broke it to him gently" that she was an old pupil.[16]

In August, Lucy and Mary Smith came, "just as dear and funny as ever." Their arrival set off a round of teas among the summer colony. On a brilliant, cool Thursday morning, Ellen and the daughters were driven "in the great splendid" White House limousine to Franconia Notch, where she had visited in the summer of 1882. At Bridgewater, New Hampshire, they saw the old Hoyt graveyard, and then they went to Hebron, a small village on Newfound Lake where the Hoyts were born. Tracking the past made her long for Woodrow. "*Could* you not come up for a few days next week?" she asked him early in August. "I know I must be a soldier's wife—but I was just wondering." She wrote more often than he, but once he surprised her. His "dear, *dear*, *dearest* letter" that she was not expecting for several days reached her on a Wednesday. "Oh, how ineffably lovable and splendid you are. Words fail me entirely; only the greatest of poets could do justice to you."[17] "I love you, *love* you, *love* you!—you adorable one! I *idolize* you,—I love you till it *hurts*."[18]

Woodrow's visit in July left her feeling so close to him that she could hardly sense that they were really separated. One of the neighbors told Ellen that it was a great pleasure to watch Woodrow pass on his daily walks, because he had such an unusually *happy* expression—"like a boy out of school."[19] The eight days that he spent at Cornish were, Woodrow said, like a new honeymoon. All were days "of contentment, renewal, and delight."[20]

Ellen worried about her husband in hot, humid Washington, and she was deeply concerned about "the way in which anxieties and 'crises' of all sorts" seemed to be "heaping up" about him.[21] In one of the

Ellen Axson Wilson (serving tea) and her three daughters.
Left to right: Margaret, Eleanor, and Jessie, 1913.
From an oil portrait by Robert Vonnoh.
Woodrow Wilson House, Washington, D.C.

most troubling of these, revolution and counterrevolution had placed in power in Mexico City a wily military dictator, General Victoriano Huerta. When Woodrow took office in March, Huerta's regime, unsteady and still unrecognized by the United States government, was a sore problem to the new president.[22] Ellen was anxious about the Mexican situation, "merely as it affects *you* I am afraid!" As the Mexican situation worsened, she flung some ideas at the president. "Perhaps it would save us trouble in the long run to give them arms and let them exterminate each other if they so prefer."[23] "A plague on the Monroe Doctrine! Lets throw it overboard! All the European nations have interests and citizens there as well as we, and if we could all *unite* in bringing pressure upon Huerta we could bring even that mad brute to hear reason."[24]

Another source of worry was Nicaragua, where unrest and revolution over a period of several years were pushing a ravished country toward disaster. The United States government, involved since 1909, when President Taft sent marines to Nicaragua, wavered between the "good intentions of Secretary of State Bryan" and the expediency of "dollar diplomacy," matters which would not be settled until near the end of Woodrow's first term.[25]

The battle for tariff reform, the first thorough-going downward revision of the tariff laws since 1846, moved slowly through the hot summer in Washington. When the Senate approved legislation on September 9, Ellen was "so glad,—so very, very happy over the passing of the tariff bill." "I had just come up to bed last night when the telegram came and the girls rushed up wildly with it," she told Woodrow. "You may imagine the rejoicing and excitement in the house."[26]

Triumphant but lonely, the president wrote to his wife: "I seem to love my darling more every day of my life, and to realize more clearly what she means to me, what part her love plays and has always played, even when I was least conscious of it, in all that I have ever done or been. Without it the best things in me would never have come out. It has kept my soul awake. . . . Love alone keeps my pulses going and makes the world of anxious business endurable."[27]

In early August, when she had not seen Woodrow for a month, Ellen weakened. "Oh *please* let me go to Washington for a few days. Indeed, dear, I must go! I want you! I love you unspeakably."[28] He begged her not to come because his steadiness there depended upon seeing his program through to the end. There was even a dramatic effect upon the imagination of the members of the House, Woodrow told her, that came from his "sticking it out alone." If Ellen would be a Spartan wife, it would be easier for him to be a Spartan statesman.[29]

His plea held her back temporarily. On August 20, she wrote: "At 6:30 [tomorrow] I take the train for *Washington*! Haha! What is my Lord going to do about it? Nothing!—except perhaps meet me at the train. When he gets this it will be too late to say me Nay." She telegraphed to Grayson that she and Nell would arrive on Friday, but he was not to tell Woodrow.[30] She wanted to be with her husband during this particular week because on August 27 he planned to go before a joint session of Congress to speak about his proposed policies in regard to Mexico. Ellen and Nell were there to share this, the president's third address to a joint session. Other than this event, the week went quickly, with one evening at the theater and daily drives in the big touring car. One morning Ellen slipped away for an hour, alone and unrecognized (except by a startled congressman, Allan Bartholomew Walsh of New Jersey) to see the artwork in the Library of Congress. The murals, mosaics, and sculpture, all done by American artists, were accomplishments which she applauded.[31]

When Ellen and Nell returned to Cornish on August 29, Woodrow went with them for three days. Something unpleasant happened during the weekend, perhaps a brief spat set off by a misunderstanding. The president wrote from the White House to apologize for causing "grief and consternation to . . . the one person in all the world to whom I try to show myself completely and truly!"[32] Ellen replied, "Oh how I love you, my darling. It is *I* who ought to ask *your* pardon,—and I do ask it, for being so sensitive and, so to say, taking you too literally. Of course I know how well you love me, dearest,—how *much* more than I deserve,—and I should not let a mere word hurt me and so, by reaction, hurt you."[33]

Ellen and Woodrow returned to their respective routines during her last month at Harlakenden; he mainly to struggle with foreign affairs and to monitor the finishing touches on the tariff bill and the legislation on the Federal Reserve bill; Ellen to her painting, a quiet social life, and attention to financial matters. She invested more than twelve thousand dollars in bonds at 5 percent and twenty-five hundred dollars in a 6 percent mortgage; in addition to repaying their debt (of five thousand dollars) at the Princeton Bank, she had sent twenty-four hundred dollars to Annie and her son, Wilson, temporarily out of work. She sent a statement of their finances to Woodrow, urging him to deposit his next salary check promptly, because she had "saved out less than usual this month."[34]

She continued to pose for Vonnoh and to work with Jessie and Frank on their wedding plans. She was now quite satisfied that Frank, "a perfect dear," loved Jessie as much as he should.[35] Nell, still engaged to

Ben King, was ostensibly "unavailable," but Margaret was entertaining men. One of them, Boyd Archer Fisher, a Harvard graduate, writer, and social worker from New York City, was, Ellen thought, a very attractive fellow. "He has such an interesting mind,—so quick to take, not only an idea but a point of view or an impression. . . . I am afraid I think him more interesting to be with than either Frank or Ben!" The crux of the matter was, however, that Jessie and Nell were in love and Margaret vowed, "with evident truth," that she was not.[36]

After a final pose for Vonnoh on September 8, Ellen concluded that her head, "very dainty now," was sufficiently like her. Vonnoh startled her when he came to Harlakenden one morning to criticize her own painting. He found that she was "a real artist," and he said that, if she continued with her work, it would be "*very* distinguished." She had "any amount of individuality" with variety, and did several things "equally well—and with equal feeling."[37] While in Cornish, Ellen sold four of her paintings to a "Mrs. Barnett" and her son, a sale that brought $350 of the $1,000 which she planned to raise for the Martha Berry School.[38]

This burst of creative energy, which sustained Ellen through the months of painting in Cornish, came to some extent from a successful testing of herself begun before her husband had been elected president of the United States. Aware that his increasing prominence as a politician placed her own name in the public eye, she had, in November 1911, entered one of her canvasses under an assumed name, to be judged for a New York exhibition. Sent by Adams Express to the Macbeth Gallery at 450 Fifth Avenue from a "W. Wilson" of Metuchen, New Jersey, the painting was insured for $2,000 in the name of the estate of "Edward Wilson." (Ellen usually signed her work "E. A. Wilson.")[39]

Even after this entry won a place on its own merits, Ellen was reluctant to compete in prestigious shows. In the spring of 1912, she wrote to Macbeth, who was still apparently unaware of the true identity of "Edward Wilson": "My friends have been urging me for sometime to send my pictures for exhibition to the Penna. Academy, etc., etc., but I am excessively shy about them. . . . As I am sending a few into New York anyhow to be framed, I am going to ask you to do me the great favour of looking at them and telling me what you think of them."[40]

Macbeth reacted favorably. He told Ellen that he thought her paintings would hold their own very well in any public exhibition.[41] She needed his encouragement, Ellen said, because, working as she did alone, she was "sadly lacking in self-confidence." "*Your* good opinion means more to me than anyone else I know. . . . I should have probably gone on forever endeavoring to conceal the fact that I painted at all, had not the newspapers mysteriously 'got hold of it!'" Such statements as Cloe Arnold's in the *Delineator* about "real, big artistic talent" made Ellen feel that she must "make good a little" and exhibit, or else appear "perfectly ridiculous."[42]

Amused at her diffidence, Macbeth wrote to her that once journalists became interested in an artist, "it is impossible to escape their attention, and I have never known of an artist who is anxious to escape it!"[43] Now her agent and advocate, Macbeth helped her to choose paintings in the fall of 1912 for consideration in several forthcoming juried shows. A single canvas, *Autumn*, won a place in the twenty-fifth annual exhibition of the Art Institute of Chicago, which had opened on November 5. From the Art Institute of Chicago, *Autumn* moved in December to an exhibit at the John Herron Art Institute of Indianapolis.[44] In February and March 1913, two landscapes, *The Old Lane* and *Autumn Day*, had hung in the 108th annual exhibit of the Pennsylvania Academy of the Fine Arts.[45] Ellen became a member of Pen and Brush, Inc., an organization founded in 1893 in New York for professional women writers and artists; and in the spring of 1913, by invitation, she joined the Association of Women Painters and Sculptors (now the National Association of Women Artists, Inc.).[46]

Shortly before the inaugural ceremonies in March, Ellen's first one-woman show—fifty landscapes—had opened at the Arts and Crafts Guild at 237 South Eleventh Street in Philadelphia. The show was successful: twenty-four paintings were sold, the proceeds to go to the Berry School.[47] In a review of her Philadelphia show, a *New York Times* critic wrote:

> Mrs. Wilson's paintings show her to be a real lover of nature and the possessor of a fine faculty for interpreting it. In her landscapes . . . she has striven for substance rather than symbol. It is nature in repose that attracts her art. The peace and quiet of her scenes are marked by subdued colors and a sacrifice of detail. In two charming sketches of old-fashioned flower gardens, on the other hand, there is a wealth of color and detail. In several smaller

sketches, Mrs. Wilson sought her effects with a combination of both methods. Sky and clouds stand out in startling relief above the blurred and indistinct foreground of water or field.[48]

News of the Philadelphia show prompted James L. Smith, a philanthropist of Ashtabula, Ohio, to purchase one of her landscapes and to exhibit it in a store on Main Street so that "all Ashtabula people who are interested in Mrs. Wilson and her art may . . . see it at first hand."[49]

One newspaper reporter angered Ellen and embarrassed Macbeth by implying that Macbeth was the source of a statement which she had allegedly made about her career as an artist. According to the *Trenton Evening Times*, Ellen said: "I had always had the greatest desire to be a painter, . . . but the bringing up of three daughters and the cares of a housewife have taken up most of my life since my marriage, and just when my girls are quite able to care for themselves and my domestic problems seemed over with on that account[,] I am confronted with the prospect of the White House and the duties of the Nation's hostess." "But," she was quoted as saying, "whatever the result of the election, I intend never entirely to desert my art."[50]

Ellen directed Helen Bones to write immediately to Macbeth: "Mrs. Wilson understands perfectly your troubles with the reporters and begs that you will not let the false accounts that have appeared in the papers worry you. She has been so utterly misrepresented herself that she has begun to think the papers prefer to publish anything rather than the truth."[51] Ellen never intended to desert her art, but not with the petulance implied by the Trenton newspaper. She now believed that no one could "rest on the laurels of another person [and] must grow to the limits of . . . [her] own spirit, mind and ability."[52] As her husband had grown, so had she.

Macbeth continued to work on Ellen's behalf. He failed to place any of her paintings in the Carnegie International annual exhibit, sponsored by the Carnegie Institute in Pittsburgh. This and the show at the National Academy of Design were the leading national artistic events.[53] Ellen did win a place in the Academy show which was to open in New York in December 1913. The choice of "Mrs. Woodrow Wilson's" work annoyed some artists, however, who regarded this as "an act of blatant favoritism."[54]

Frederic Allen Whiting, director of the Cleveland Museum of Art, wrote directly to Ellen to ask that one of her paintings be sent for the

Cleveland Art Loan Exposition (to be held in November), a request that Ellen asked Macbeth to fulfill.[55]

Five of Ellen's New Hampshire landscapes were selected to be hung in New York in the fall exhibit of the Association of Women Painters and Sculptors. Of the five oils, entitled *Ascutney, Autumn Fields, Light and Shade, Terrace*, and *Cornish*, three were sold: *Ascutney* to a "well known western collector," *Autumn Fields* to a Princeton man, Alexander M. Hudnut, and *Light and Shade* to the wife of a "prominent New York physician." The sales added $350 to her Berry School fund.[56]

These continuing successes, which brought her work as an artist to fruition in parallel with her husband's career in politics, were virtually anticlimactic. As first lady elect, and then as mistress of the White House, she had had little, if any, time to savor her artistic triumphs. With her own studio ready at the White House, and her social activities now curtailed by Dr. Grayson, Ellen hoped to be able to give more time to her painting when she returned to Washington. Meanwhile, she continued to work at her easel in Cornish until the last hour.

On an unseasonably warm day in early October, Ellen sat out-of-doors sketching all morning in a shirtwaist and bareheaded. She was sure that heaven itself could not be more perfect than the whole day had been for beauty and "for the delicious fresh yet soft *feel* of it!" "And then the profound peace of this dear spot."[57] Ellen loved the Cornish hills so intensely that to leave them was "a sort of torture." Yet, as the vacation drew to a close, she wanted her husband so much that she could "hardly bear to talk about it."[58]

She read the newspapers thoroughly and followed his every move. On October 3, when he signed the tariff bill, she experienced "a soul-satisfying quality" of happiness. "Now at last everybody in the civilized world knows that you are a great man and a great leader of men. Also a great constitutional Statesman," she wrote to Woodrow. "The sort of honour that is yours by right and that you 'covet' *is* yours beyond a peradventure,—and you *have* won it for your friends and party as well as for yourself. How profoundly I thank God for giving you the chance to win such victories,—to help the world so greatly;—for letting you work for him on a large *stage*;—one worthy of the splendid combination of qualities with which He endowed you. . . . It has been the most remarkable life history I ever even *read* about,—and to think I have *lived* it with you. I wonder if I am dreaming, and will wake up and find myself married to—a bank clerk,—say!"[59]

With the "dear Smiths" gone, and Mrs. Jaffray to close Harlakenden, Ellen and the daughters left for Washington on Wednesday, October 15. They stopped overnight in New York to celebrate Nell's twenty-fourth birthday and Ellen warned Woodrow that she would probably get to him "a wreck."[60]

Woodrow was "a grateful husband and father" when the family arrived on Friday at the old mansion where, during "about half of the time" he had been in office, he had been there alone. Several months of consorting with "mere men" was a bitter medicine which Woodrow rolled upon his palate because, he told Ellen, "I want by so much the more to enhance the sweetness of what I am to have at the end of the week. . . . I think when I get you in my arms again I cannot let you go till I have kissed you out of breath and consciousness, at any rate out of all co[n]sciousness of anything but that you are in my arms."[61]

_____ *Chapter 30* _____

An East Room Wedding

With Jessie's wedding only six weeks away, a considerable amount of plan-
ning had taken place in Cornish. Frank, who had accepted a position,
to begin in January 1914, as assistant to President Harry A. Garfield of
Williams College, was able to come to Cornish frequently from New
York. He, Jessie, and Ellen had made two visits to Williamstown, Massachusetts, to look for a house, a search that ended successfully in late
July with the lease of "a *charming* house" from a professor going on
sabbatical leave.[1]

Ellen's experience in arranging the weddings of Madge and Annie
Howe Cothran was child's play compared to the magnitude of a wedding in the White House. Political considerations had to be taken into
account, and their family and old friends all had to be invited because
neither Ellen nor Woodrow wanted to offend anybody. Jessie and her
mother spent several evenings in Cornish going over the endless list of
names.[2]

Before they left Cornish, Jessie and Frank had prepared a list of
about five hundred names of people who were to receive invitations
and several hundred more who would receive announcements. The
family regretted the glaring publicity that inevitably focused on the
marriage of the daughter of a president, and they knew that the bride
and groom could never enjoy complete privacy even on their honeymoon. A compelling invitation came from the president's friend, the
ambassador to the Court of St. James's, Walter Hines Page, for Jessie
and Frank to visit London.[3] Jessie asked her father not to commit them
to Page's suggestion until she and Frank could discuss it. When their
decision was reached, Jessie wrote to Mrs. Page and accepted the invitation to spend most of December and January in London.[4]

The wedding date was set for Tuesday afternoon, November 25, after
which the newlyweds planned to slip away for two nights in Baltimore.
They would return to the White House for Thanksgiving before they
sailed to Liverpool. For the brief time in Baltimore, Jessie and Frank
would have the use of a private home belonging to Alice (Mrs. Thomas

Harrison) Garrett, whose three sons had attended Princeton in the 1890s.[5]

When Ellen returned to Washington on October 17, White House activities focused on both official entertaining and wedding preparations. Her physical strength, so depleted in June, was somewhat restored by the summer in Cornish, although, while there, she made frequent references to being tired, or of taking needed rests.[6] At the first large reception in late October, she and Woodrow received 535 delegates to the executive meeting of the Women's Home Missions of the Methodist Episcopal Church. She gave a tea for the wives of the Supreme Court justices, and, in November, resumed her luncheons for the cabinet wives. On November 14, assisted by the Secretary of State and Mrs. Bryan, the Wilsons held a "glittering" reception for the diplomatic corps. Margaret, Jessie, Nell, and the Smiths, again at the White House, helped to receive the 104 guests.[7]

With a smoothly functioning staff, and Lucy and Mary Smith to help, Ellen enjoyed the last-minute preparations for her daughter's wedding without feeling rushed or strained. "And with such an angel of a bride the atmosphere remains perfectly clear,—very different from the racking time we had when poor Madge was about to be married,"[8] Ellen wrote to Stockton. In the hospital in Philadelphia, and threatened with another nervous breakdown, Stockton would not be able to attend Jessie's wedding. In addition to Stockton's absence, four other "regrets" disappointed Ellen—Palmer, Margaret, and Leila Axson, and Rosalie.

Soon after her engagement was announced, Jessie had begun to record her approximately five hundred gifts.[9] From her father, she received a check for five thousand dollars, to have as her own, "to do with as she wished, even if her husband might not approve"—this, surely, Ellen's idea.[10]

On November 25, the wedding day, Ellen, Nell, Jessie, and Margaret retired after luncheon to the family quarters for a private hour together. When it was time for Jessie to dress, Ellen and her three daughters "barred the door" while the bride slipped into her long, soft ivory satin and lace-trimmed gown. Ellen then pinned on the full-length veil.[11] This day of supreme happiness carried as well an unspoken sadness; Jessie's marriage was a rite of passage that marked the first break in the family circle.

Ellen, exquisitely dressed in a gown of ecru brocaded chiffon velvet, entered the East Room on the arm of an aide. The first pair of brides-maids, Nell and Mary George White (a college classmate), dressed in deep rose and carrying bouquets of roses, were followed by Marjorie Brown and Adeline Mitchell Scott (a long-time Princeton friend), in a paler shade of pink, and then Margaret, in shell pink.[12]

On the arm of her father, Jessie entered "as fair and white as a bride could be—with a luminous whiteness that was not pallor." When the responses began, she "flushed, slowly but completely into the sweetest pink blush" until she, who began "by looking like an angel," ended "by looking like a pink rose." Woodrow gave the bride away and then stepped back by his wife's side. With his right hand behind him, he felt with his left for Ellen's hand, which he held through the rest of the ceremony,[13] conducted by Dr. Beach and Frank's brother, the Reverend John Nevin Sayre.

Later, when Jessie and Frank Sayre had driven away for their brief honeymoon in Maryland, Woodrow put his arm around Ellen and drew her close to him as they walked back to the White House elevator. Meemee Brown observed that it made her throat ache to see the presi-dent and Ellen, who looked like her daughter's older sister (instead of her mother), saying goodbye.[14]

With her thoughts constantly on her married daughter, Ellen sorted the wedding presents and supervised the packing and storing. All of Jessie's silver, furniture, pictures, and books which were to go to Williamstown were sent to the White House attic; the rest went to the vaults of a storage company in Washington.[15] Ellen halted the packing long enough to invite Charlotte Hopkins in to tell her about progress on the alley bill.[16]

On November 31, Ellen resumed her regular social schedule with a luncheon for the cabinet wives. Woodrow, in bed most of the week with a severe cold, left to her the reception of the Spanish ambassador, the Dutch minister, and their wives. On Thursday, assisted by Secre-tary Bryan, she received 100 boys, champion corn growers from Ohio, whose reward was a visit to Washington. On Friday, with an aide to make the presentations, she received 312 guests for refreshments and a musicale, "a sort of 'consolation' party for senators and 'society people' who could not be invited to the wedding."[17]

Ellen surprised the British ambassador, Sir Cecil Spring Rice, who had been unable to come to the wedding because of illness, with a huge arrangement of flowers. The ambassador had, on November 25, conveyed to the president and Mrs. Wilson "the hearty congratulations" of His Majesty, George V, on the marriage of Miss Wilson, and His Majesty's offer of "good wishes for her future happiness."[18]

Almost back to back, Ellen received two Baltimore women, the one, "a shining light in the anti-suffrage association," the other, Mrs. William Ellicott, "a prominent suffragist." Both groups were holding conventions at the same time in Washington, and feeling was "very high." On December 3, the suffragists voted unanimously that the president lost his "one and only chance of being forever remembered" because he had not recommended a suffrage amendment in his first annual message to Congress. Ellen, who simply reported all of this in a letter to Jessie, did not take sides. The suffragists were "fairly besieging" Woodrow, she wrote, and were "to come here tomorrow, en masse, if he is well enough." (He was not.)[19]

After several more days on a curtailed schedule, Woodrow joined Ellen for a state dinner largely for the cabinet members and their wives, but at which a number of friends were present, including Robert Bridges, Philena and Henry Fine, President and Mrs. Harry A. Garfield, and the Princeton trustees, Henry B. Thompson and David B. Jones and their wives. After dinner, Margaret Wilson joined other vocalists to sing in the East Room.[20]

On the following Tuesday, the family went to the Oval Office to watch the president sign the Federal Reserve bill. Later the same day, Woodrow, Ellen, Margaret, Eleanor, and Helen Bones, with Dr. Grayson and two maids, left for a three-week vacation at Pass Christian, Mississippi, where they arrived on Christmas morning. They had rented a "little house [with] six bedrooms from a friend of the Smiths, a lady who would keep house" for the Wilsons. Ellen thought that Woodrow was far from well, and that they "must have the three weeks holiday on his account."[21] His severe cold had turned into "grippe," and work brought on "severe headaches, showing a generally depressed condition."[22] Ellen wrote to Meemee Brown from Pass Christian: "The pressure *has* been very great in a score of different ways—tho all of them would not have delayed my writing had Woodrow been well. He wants me almost constantly beside him when he is ill and everything else *must* give way. Today he seems well again, tho still sorely in need of rest."[23]

This was the first holiday season without Jessie, and, for many years, without Stockton. Woodrow wrote to his daughter that the family's thoughts of her were happy thoughts because she was happy. "Your dear mother is wonderful. She has spoken no word since you left but of happiness and content. I can see in the depths of yearning that she cannot always hide in her eyes what lack her mother's heart feels, but she loves you more than she loves herself and wishes for nothing but your happiness."[24] Before Jessie's first letters came from abroad, the Wilsons read about her activities in the newspapers. For once, Ellen was in a "very good humour" with the reporters.[25]

Stockton, the other absentee at Christmas, wrote to his sister that all the real happiness in his life had come from being a part of Ellen and Woodrow's family. "Neither . . . world-important things, nor . . . separations" could ever alter "the sweetness and serenity" of the love among them, he said.[26]

While the Wilsons were at Pass Christian, Nell was reunited with Ben King, who, for the past six months had been prospecting for lumber tracts in Honduras. Reporters, following Nell like "a pack of hungry wolves," described Ben as a young "Mississippian" who was "very attentive to Margaret."[27] Nell's engagement remained a closely guarded family secret.

Chapter 31

Interim and Another Wedding

*The Wilsons returned to Washington on January 13. That evening, begin-*ning at nine o'clock, Ellen and Woodrow held a diplomatic reception for more than two thousand guests, to which every member of the various embassies and legations was invited. The following Tuesday, January 20, Ellen gave a more intimate diplomatic dinner for seventy-nine guests.[1]

She had dreaded the foreigners, yet they had proved easy to get along with after all. Jules Jean Jusserand, the Frenchman, on whose arm she went to dinner, was "charming," and Johann-Heinrich von Bernstorff, on her other side, was "not at all bad." The most difficult task came after dinner, when she had to move around and talk to all the women, some of whom spoke little or no English.[2] After these affairs Ellen believed that everything else would be plain sailing.

On the day after the diplomatic dinner, she went to Princeton on a two-fold mission: to remove some family valuables from the Princeton Bank and to take the White House's head gardener, Charles Henlock, to see some of her earlier landscaping. In Princeton, she stayed with the Fines, who gave a reception in the afternoon "to all our friends and a few of our enemies," and a dinner that evening. Accompanied by a Secret Service man, Ellen came away from the bank the next morning with "all our worldly goods" in a suitcase.[3]

On January 26, the Wilson family welcomed Frank and Jessie home. The young couple had a week in Washington before leaving for Wil-liamstown and "the final wrench."[4] After they were gone Ellen had a good hard cry in the "big silent house." She was glad to get it over with when she was alone, for Woodrow, who came in, very blue, declared that this leave-taking was much worse than the wedding because it seemed so final. Both Woodrow and Ellen were comforted to think of "dear Frank," and of the sort of care he would take of Jessie. "Dear, *dear* little daughter, how I wish I could tell you what a *perfect joy* you have been to me all your life long, and how tenderly I love you," Ellen wrote to the new Mrs. Sayre.[5]

Officialdom pervaded the social schedule again. After the reception for the diplomatic corps, there followed the judicial reception for 2,162 guests; dinner for the Supreme Court justices and their wives; the congressional reception for 1,765; the Speaker's dinner; the army and navy reception for more than 2,000; and a reception for the governor and several hundred residents of New Jersey. The Wilsons were guests of honor at dinners given in turn by each cabinet member; and, although Woodrow declined, Ellen, Margaret, and Nell thought it imperative that they should be present at the Southern Relief Ball at the New Willard Hotel. A few days later, Ellen attended a meeting of the Southern Industrial Education Association, of which she was honorary president.[6]

She appeared to keep abreast of the pace, but, in February, Woodrow came down with another "heavy, feverish cold," followed by "a rather sharp attack of indigestion," an indisposition that required "a good deal" of her time.[7] During the week of February 14, she sat for her portrait by a "Mr. Forster."[8] At about the same time, the artist, S. Seymour Thomas, finished a portrait of Woodrow, commissioned by Cleveland H. Dodge and Cyrus H. McCormick. Before the portrait would be hung in the White House, it was to be shown in England. Ellen wrote to Dodge that Thomas, "a real enthusiast" about Woodrow, had created a likeness which would "serve as a corrective to the innumerable caricatures of him,—(some 'so intended'—others *not*) with which the press is flooded. The interest in him in England and Scotland is very great, and they ought to know how he looks."[9]

While the White House grounds lay in winter dormancy, Ellen completed plans for redoing the gardens from the south portico to the presidential offices on the west and on the east to the end of the arcade. She thought that designs submitted by a landscape architect from New York were too expensive and decided that she and Charles Henlock could draw the new layout. In the east garden, she planned to install a pool for water lilies and goldfish; in the west, a rose garden with narcissi planted in between the rose bushes. A statue of Pan would be at the westernmost end; at the other, a curved marble bench on a small terrace. Ellen wanted the president to be able to enjoy a "rose walk" from the White House to his office.[10]

Even before the official entertaining was over in February, the flow of overnight guests began. Among them were Princeton University trustees Edward W. Sheldon, Melancthon W. Jacobus and his wife,

Clara C. Jacobus; Henrietta Ricketts, Ed Elliott, Nancy Toy, Margaret DuBose (now Mrs. Isaac Thomas Avery), and friends of Margaret and Nell.[11] In fact, Margaret wrote to Jessie on March 1 to apologize for a two-month silence because her time was consumed in entertaining callers or houseguests "every minute." The social demands in the White House left Margaret "so distressingly weary" that she believed herself to be "inadequate" in the role of oldest daughter of the president.[12]

Margaret's feelings of inadequacy were aggravated by reporters who were determined to invent serious romances for her where none existed. Rumors of her engagement that appeared in newspapers were quickly denied by the White House press secretary.[13] Boyd Fisher, still a good friend, took her out when she went to New York for voice lessons; but her major interest continued to be music. To be able to continue her voice lessons during vacation, Margaret persuaded her teacher, Ross David, whom she called "father," to plan to come to Cornish for the following August.[14]

Margaret had performed for groups in New York and at the White House, and she had given a concert at the Bellevue-Stratford Hotel to benefit the Kensington home for working girls in the mill district of Philadelphia.[15] In the summer of 1913, when prominent artists in the summer colony at Cornish gave a masque in which Margaret and Nell participated, Ellen was angry with the newspapers that "paid . . . [Margaret] no compliments."[16] At times, Margaret had lent her influence and high station to support her mother's interest in welfare work.[17] In spite of the pressures of being the president's oldest daughter, Margaret thought that she was living in "wonderful times and a wonderful country," and she would not willingly give up the experiences and opportunities of life in Washington "in spite of all its horrors."[18]

The Washington whirl imposed a crushing burden of publicity on the Wilsons, except for Nell, whose willing participation in capital society had brought her to an unexpected crisis in her life. She had fallen head-over-heels in love with Secretary of the Treasury William G. McAdoo, a man twenty-six years older than she. McAdoo, who had been close to the family since the beginning of the Wilson presidential campaign, had lost his wife, an invalid for eight years, shortly before he had first met Nell at Sea Girt. An unusually youthful looking man for his fifty years, McAdoo was the father of three sons and three daughters; the youngest, Sallie, was twelve.

Ellen did not need to listen to Washington gossip to know that her

Margaret Woodrow Wilson in the 1920s.
Woodrow Wilson Birthplace, Staunton, Va.

youngest daughter and McAdoo were seeing far more of each other than officialdom could tolerate with equanimity. Nell was deceiving both Ben King and herself, circumstances intolerable to Ellen, who urged her daughter to break her engagement at once. Nell did so in a turbulent letter written to Ben in February.[19] McAdoo left Washington at about the same time to be gone for five weeks, and Ellen stipulated that he and Nell must not communicate during his absence.[20] When McAdoo returned to Washington, he went directly to the White House, and Ellen wrote to Jessie: "It's *all* settled. Nell said she could not, to save her life, have helped telling him that she cared. . . . Of course he came to see me the next day and has also seen your father."[21] Before Nell planned to make an official announcement of her engagement, Washington papers printed it, on the front page, on March 13. The engagement was confirmed, with Ellen and Woodrow's approval, from the White House press office later the same evening.[22]

The family was not overjoyed. Disturbed that McAdoo was twice their daughter's age, Ellen and Woodrow were still deeply fond of Ben King.[23] Tumulty caused further agitation when he told Nell that her marriage to McAdoo would put both the president and the secretary of the treasury "in an awkward position." Ellen thought that this was absurd because Woodrow had appointed Mac to the second highest position in the cabinet well before Nell's romance began.[24] All other concerns dimmed in the light of the fact that Mac and Nell were "simply *mad* over each other."[25]

In an affectionate letter written to Ben King on March 22, Woodrow commented that Ellen had had "an ugly fall," and that she was "recovering very slowly from the shock and general shaking up it gave her. But at last she is really coming out of the pain and prostration, and we are assured."[26]

The "ugly fall" had occurred on the first of March, when Ellen slipped on the polished floor of her bedroom. She was in her bed for all of the following week. On March 10, Dr. Grayson summoned to the White House Dr. Edward Parker Davis, a Princeton classmate of Woodrow's, then professor of obstetrics at the Jefferson Medical College. Dr. Davis was at the White House again early on the morning of March 12[27] and performed minor surgery (probably on that day) necessary presumably as a result of Ellen's fall. Nell wrote to Jessie on the twentieth: "Mother is getting along beautifully—the doctor hopes to have her up and around her room by the first of next week. It's always a long tiresome siege after the sort of operation she had, but she'll be a 'new person soon' the doctor says."[28] Yet on April 2, Woodrow canceled a conference in New York with Colonel House because Ellen was still distressingly weak and he was too concerned to leave her. The doctor hoped that she would be well enough in a week or so to be taken to one of the Virginia springs for rest and recuperation.[29]

Not until April 6 could Ellen take a short automobile drive, and then she was accompanied by Nell and Dr. Grayson. For the next four days, she took similar outings, always with Grayson along. The weekend of April 10, Woodrow, Nell, and Grayson took her to White Sulphur Springs, where Ellen remained with a nurse until the following weekend. The president went again to the springs to bring her back to Washington.[30]

Ellen's health improved for the rest of April. On the twentieth, she went to the Capitol to hear Woodrow's message to Congress about the Mexican situation, again in a state of crisis. Two days later, she attended the marriage of Brigadier General William L. Marshall's daughter, Maitland, for whom Nell was a bridesmaid. The National Park System honored the first lady in late April by naming a lake in Glacier National Park "Lake Ellen Wilson."[31] Ellen requested through Arthur Tedcastle that some improvements be made at Harlakenden before June in view of Woodrow's plan to be there with the family for much of the summer.[32] She also promised the people of Rome, Georgia, that she and one of the daughters would visit them in late October for a homecoming week to honor former Romans.[33]

Most of Ellen's ebbing strength went into plans for Nell's wedding, set for the evening of May 7. Due in part to Ellen's health, Nell would have a simple wedding. She vowed that hers was to be a *marriage*, not a wedding, because it was simply a choice between having the whole world or no one except families and she would *not* have "tout le monde."[34]

The guest list, pared to fewer than a hundred people, was made up of cabinet members, close family, and a few friends. Nell was attended by Margaret and Jessie, with Sallie McAdoo and her friend, Nancy Lane, the young daughter of Secretary of the Interior Franklin K. and Ann Wall Lane, as flower girls. Cary Grayson was the best man. Stockton, Mary and Florence Hoyt, George and Margaret Howe, Ed Brown and his daughter, Marjorie, the Cleveland Dodges, and several of Mac's children were present.[35] Ellen wept openly while Dr. Beach read the ceremony shortly after 6 P.M. in the Blue Room. After the benediction, the bride turned immediately to clasp her mother in a long embrace.

Eleanor Wilson McAdoo in the 1920s.
Special Collections, University of California at Santa Barbara.

Woodrow, sad at losing this daughter, was even more distressed at Ellen's grief.[36] The bride and groom slipped into an inconspicuous automobile and were driven to College Park, Maryland, where a private Pullman car awaited them for their trip to Cornish and a honeymoon at Harlakenden. The Secretary of the Treasury and Mrs. McAdoo were at home in June at 1709 Massachusetts Avenue.[37]

Chapter 32

"It would not be a sacrifice to die for you"

Ellen tried to believe what the doctors told her about her own health. "They say it is because I was utterly exhausted nervously so that the fall was sort of an all around crash," she wrote to a relative in mid-May. "It really was pretty serious & I am still far from well. . . . Nobody who has not tried can have the least idea of the exactions of life here and of the constant nervous strain of it all,—the _life_, combined with the constant anxiety about Woodrow, his health, the success of his legislative plans etc. etc. If I could _only_ sleep as he does I could stand twice as much!"[1]

The rally which enabled her to get through a second White House wedding was short-lived. Acute indigestion began to plague her constantly so that she could scarcely choke down any food.[2] Helen Bones thought that the strength Ellen summoned for Nell's wedding came from sheer willpower, "that wonderful will that has carried her through so much." Grayson wanted to get her to Cornish where she could enjoy the serenity and the cool, fresh air, but she would not consider leaving Woodrow. To lighten the gloom that her illness inevitably brought to the family, Ellen invited Lucy and Mary Smith to come to the White House. They arrived in Washington on June 18.[3]

Meanwhile, Woodrow asked Jessie and Frank to open Harlakenden on July 8 and to keep it running as well as possible until the rest of the family could get there. Helen reported to Jessie on June 28 that Ellen was holding her own, but the heat was beginning to be bad for her. Helen wanted Jessie to write such an enthusiastic letter from Harlakenden that Ellen might want to go.[4] A week later, Helen wrote: "Your dear little mother is _so_ much better! She goes out into the garden early every morning now before it begins to be hot, and then does exercises and takes rubs and baths and things afterwards. We don't go in to see her before afternoon, and then don't stay long. . . . She is easily tired and very easily worried, but Dr. Grayson says we must expect her to be that way for some time to come."[5]

When attendants helped Ellen out into the rose garden, she sat and watched Charles Henlock as he worked on the design which she and he had planned together. One morning she gestured to him to come to her, and, in a feeble voice said, "It will be so lovely, Charlie, but I'll never live to see it finished."[6] Keeping her thoughts from the family, Ellen helped Grayson to maintain the pretense that she would get better. Woodrow worried about her staying on in the awful Washington heat, but he continued to think that she gained "slowly (ah, how slowly!)."[7]

Nell, who wanted to believe that her mother was getting better, wrote to Jessie on July 6: "She walks in the garden on the nurse's arm and seems to enjoy it very much. She will be quite well again . . . before very long."[8] Two days later, Margaret left, unwillingly, for a three-weeks respite in Pennsylvania, prescribed apparently for her own well-being.[9] While the family struggled to be hopeful about Ellen, Mary Smith came down with appendicitis and was taken to the hospital on July 9 to undergo surgery. The appendectomy went well, but Lucy devoted much of her time for the next two weeks to her sister.[10]

Shortly before Jessie and Frank left Williamstown for Cornish, Ellen's spirits were lifted by thrilling news from the Sayres: Jessie was pregnant! Not entirely sure about her condition, Jessie told her mother as early as she dared, but asked her to keep the secret. On July 6, in a shaky script, Ellen composed a letter in pencil to her daughter, the last she would ever write to anyone:

> My darling:
>
> I hope you will excuse pencil. I have not even yet been able to sit at a desk and write since my last relapse. The doctor says that considering how *very* ill I was, the progress is very rapid, but it seems snail-like indeed to me. It is delightful to think of you and Frank at Cornish, darling. I am so glad it could be arranged. I hope you and Frank will have a beautiful month there alone together. The house is lucky to be the retreat of two pairs of lovers in one season.
>
> My real reason for trying to send a little scrawl myself today is anxiety about that walking-tour! I am so afraid it means that you were disappointed after all, and that it was not as we had hoped. But still I [am] trying not to borrow trouble,—and of course

walking *is* the best form of exercise! So I am hoping it was a very little trip carefully adapted to the circumstances. But, *please*, darling, send me a letter by the next mail to relieve my mind and tell me *exactly* how you are. It has been a real trial that it has been a secret from others in view of my illness because of all it has kept me in ignorance of about you that I would have learned for myself if I had been well.

You remember, dear, that Nevin was supposed to pay $100.00 for your dining-room furniture and I for the rest? I am going to ask that I may change that, late as it is, and let it be my gift entirely! I think it would be nice for Nevin to give the *desk* for the new living-room, don't you?

Ellen enclosed a check for five hundred dollars, four hundred of which would be "for the little layette" unless Jessie and Frank had "a special sentiment" about doing that themselves. "I hope you can read this," she continued. "It is the first letter . . . I have written since I last wrote you, and I can do nothing with my poor hand! But the doctor says I am making a splendid fight for health, and that I am sure to win in time. . . . With a heart full of love for dearest Frank and love inexpressibly tender and devoted for my darling, I am dear heart, Your Mother." Helen Bones addressed the envelope.[11]

By July 10, Jessie, now certain about her pregnancy, shared the news with the rest of the family.[12] The knowledge that Jessie expected her first child helped Ellen to face the discouraging days which were now more frequent. Grayson continued to tell her that she would have ups and downs for some time. When he suggested that she would be better off in Cornish, she refused even to talk about it. Her one wish, now, was to stay with Woodrow. During the week of July 19, Ellen had some painfully uncomfortable days which were attributed to the heat and to an upset caused by medication. (Even after this setback, Helen thought Ellen "beautiful to look at," with lovely color and bright eyes and no lines in her face.)[13]

On July 23, Dr. Grayson moved into the White House to be available around the clock. He knew that Ellen's illness was due to Bright's disease, now in its last stages, yet he could not bring himself to tell the president that her condition was hopeless. Burdened by foreign affairs which pointed toward a European war, Woodrow watched Ellen with lead at his heart.[14] Much of the time, day and night, he spent in her room. On August 3, he canceled another conference in New York with Colonel House because Ellen was so weak and in great pain.[15]

That same day, Grayson informed the president that it was now necessary to summon the daughters. Margaret arrived late on August 3, Jessie and Frank, two days later. Nell, of course, was in Washington with her husband.[16] On August 5, Woodrow sent a telegram to Stockton, who was teaching in summer school at the University of Oregon: "Ellen is ser[i]ously ill. If you are free to leave hope you will come directly to Washington."[17] Now that the president knew the truth, he allowed the first press release that revealed the gravity of her condition. When the Elliotts received a telegram, Egie wired back, "All our love. . . . Margaret's physician forbids her to leave."[18] On Thursday morning, August 6, Dr. Edward P. Davis came from Philadelphia. After examining Ellen, it fell to him to take the president downstairs to the Red Room, away from the family, to tell him that Ellen could live only a few hours longer. Woodrow then told Margaret, Jessie, and Nell.[19]

That same morning, Ellen had said to Woodrow that she would "go away more cheerfully" if the alley bill were passed by Congress. Tumulty took her request at once to the Capitol; the Senate adopted the bill, and the House agreed to pass it the next day. Tumulty brought the news back in the early afternoon, while Ellen was still able to understand that the alley legislation would be enacted. From about two o'clock on, she began to lapse in and out of consciousness. When her eyes went to each daughter and to Woodrow, she smiled in recognition. Just before she became unconscious for the last time, she whispered to Grayson, standing at her bedside, "Doctor, if I go away, promise me that you will take good care of my husband."[20] She never spoke again. Woodrow was holding her hand when she died at five o'clock, "with a divine smile playing over her face."[21] He looked up and asked, "Is it all over?" Grayson nodded. The president rose quickly and went to the window facing the south grounds. Sobbing like a child, he cried out, "Oh my God, what am I to do?"[22]

Stockton had left Oregon at once when he received Woodrow's telegram, but he did not arrive at the White House until Monday, August 10. Mary and Florence Hoyt and Meemee and Marjorie Brown were already there. The family gathered in Ellen's room where she lay on a sofa, "serene and beautiful in the final sleep."[23]

At two o'clock on August 10, there was a brief funeral service in the East Room with only the family, members of the cabinet and their wives, and a delegation from Congress present. After the invited guests had assembled in chairs facing the casket in the south end of the room, the family entered and took their seats. Dr. Beach, assisted by the Reverend Dr. James H. Taylor, pastor of the Central Presbyterian Church in Washington, conducted the service. There was no music, only Scripture readings from John 14 and the fifteenth chapter of First Corinthians, followed by a prayer by Beach: "We magnify Thy name for the gift of this precious life, for Thine image graciously reflected in her spirit and character; for her love so tender, her loyalty so unflinching, her devotion to duty, her Christly unselfishness, her self-forgetfulness, her service for others, her charity." The flowers, a tribute from the whole world, extended for forty feet along the east and west walls on either side of the casket.[24]

Immediately after the benediction, the family retired to the second floor. Ahead of them lay a long train journey to Georgia. After conferring with Margaret, Jessie, and Nell, Woodrow had decided to take Ellen to her girlhood home in Rome for burial. The casket, followed by Woodrow, Stockton, George Howe, and Joseph R. Wilson, Jr., was removed at three-thirty from the East Room to Union Station. A short time later, the rest of the family left the White House for the departure of the special train.[25]

As they moved through the Virginia piedmont and across the Carolinas, church bells tolled and crowds stood silently along the way. For most of the journey, Woodrow sat beside the casket and was deaf to Grayson's admonition that he should take some rest. He was oblivious of everything except the gray casket on which rested a single wreath of flowers, his last gift to Ellen.[26]

The train stopped in Spartanburg, South Carolina, to pick up James Woodrow, and again in Atlanta to take on Leila and Carrie Belle Axson. At two-thirty on Tuesday afternoon, August 11, when the train arrived at the Southern Railway Station in Rome, Edward T. Brown and the Reverend Giles Granville Sydnor, pastor of the First Presbyterian Church, were there to greet Woodrow as he stepped off the train. The casket was removed to a horse-drawn hearse by eight pallbearers, six of whom were Ellen's first cousins: Edward T. Brown, Palmer and Randolph Axson, and three of Uncle Bob's sons—Nathan, Robert, and Wade C. Hoyt. The other two pallbearers were Edward T. Brown, Jr., and Frank C. Gilreath, married to Uncle Bob's daughter, Birdie Hoyt.

Tomb of Ellen Axson Wilson, Myrtle Hill Cemetery, Rome, Ga.
Princeton University Library.

The family entered carriages for the procession to the little church where Woodrow had first seen Ellen thirty-one years before. Rome friends, who had been admitted by ticket, were waiting in silence in the sanctuary when the Wilson family arrived. Seven of Ellen's class-mates from the Rome Female College were seated together. The casket, placed at the front of the church on a catafalque, was banked high with flowers, tributes to her from all over Georgia. The service began with a quartet singing two of Ellen's favorite hymns, "For All the Saints Who from Their Labors Rest" and "Art Thou Weary, Art Thou Languid?" Dr. Sydnor read from the Scriptures, and spoke briefly of the beauty and charity of Ellen Axson Wilson.

The cortege then moved to Myrtle Hill Cemetery along streets lined with schoolgirls dressed in white and holding laurel branches. Every store, office, school, and factory was closed. Crowds stood in front of buildings draped in black. On a grassy slope in East Rome, women of the garden club had, in early summer, planted flowers in the shape of "Welcome Home" to honor Ellen on her anticipated visit in October.

As the procession reached the cemetery, a thunderstorm broke and became a torrential downpour. The immediate family was protected by a canopy suspended over the grave site. Woodrow stood with bowed head while Dr. Sydnor read words of the final rites. When Ellen's body was lowered into the grave, the president's iron control gave way and the tears flowed unchecked.[27] When the services were over, Stockton sent a telegram to Madge, "We have buried sister beside father and mother."[28]

Woodrow had said to her once long ago, "Nothing so fills me with exalted sensations as the thought,—so wonderful, and yet so assured,—that you love me. The sweet proofs I have of that love cling about me like a perpetual blessing."[29] With this blessing to keep near him, the president of the United States turned his face toward Washington.[30]

Notes

Abbreviations in the Notes

EAE	Elizabeth Adams Erwin
EAS	Eleanor Axson Sayre
EAW	Ellen Axson Wilson
ELA	Ellen Louise Axson
ELAd	Elizabeth Leith Adams
ERW	Eleanor Randolph Wilson
EWM	Eleanor Wilson McAdoo
FBS	Francis Bowes Sayre, Jr.
HFNC	Historical Foundation of the Presbyterian and Reformed Churches
JAH	*Journal of American History*
JWS	Jessie Wilson Sayre
JWW	Jessie Woodrow Wilson
L and L	*Woodrow Wilson: Life and Letters*
MAH	Mary Allen Hulbert
MAHP	Mary Allen Hulbert Peck
MJH	Margaret Jane Hoyt
MJHA	Margaret Jane Hoyt Axson
MWW	Margaret Woodrow Wilson
PWW	*The Papers of Woodrow Wilson*
RSB	Ray Stannard Baker
SEA	Samuel Edward Axson
WW	Woodrow Wilson
WWS	Woodrow Wilson Sayre

Chapter 1

1. WW to ELA, Oct. 11, 1883, Link et al., eds., *The Papers of Woodrow Wilson*, 2:468 (hereafter cited as *PWW*); Editorial Note, ibid., p. 333; ELA to WW, Apr. 7, 1884, ibid., 3:115. During a visit between the Wilsons and the Axsons, WW is alleged to have played with EAW when he was "seven or eight" and she a toddler. This could have occurred in Athens or Madison, but not in Rome, Ga., as Cary T. Grayson asserts (interview with Cary Grayson, the Ray Stannard Baker Collection of Wilsoniana, R. S. Baker Papers, Library of Congress, Washington, D.C.; hereafter cited as RSB Coll.). The incident is also repeated in Baker, *Woodrow Wilson: Life and Letters*, 1:161 (hereafter cited as Baker, *L and L*).

2. WW to ELA, Oct. 11, 1883, *PWW*, 2:468.

3. ELA to WW, Aug. 9 and Sept. 8, 1884, ibid., 3:279, 323; June 9, 1885, ibid., 4:697; WW to ELA, Sept. 29, 1883, ibid., 2:446; Apr. 22, 1885, ibid., 4:515; ELAd to ELA, Nov. 18, 1880, the Papers of Woodrow Wilson, Library of Congress, Washington, D.C. (hereafter cited as Wilson Papers); Mary Eloise Hoyt memorandum for R. S. Baker, Oct. 1926, RSB Coll. A lock of ELA's hair is tucked in the pocket of the back cover of WW's diary for 1884. He wrote her later that, even though his friends asked what she was like, he would not show them "what I have tucked in my pocket-book in order that they may see the colour of your hair" (WW to ELA, Apr. 22, 1885, *PWW*, 4:515).

4. WW to ELA, Oct. 11, 1883, *PWW*, 2:468.

5. WW to ELA, Dec. 19, 1883, and Jan. 4, 1884, ibid., pp. 592–93, 646; ibid., 8:493; ELA to WW, May 12, 1885, ibid., 4:586; Editorial Notes, ibid., 2:333–34, 361–63.

6. ELA to WW, May 12, 1885, ibid., 4:586; *New York World*, Dec. 18, 1910, quoted in Link, *Wilson: The Road to the White House*, p. 93; Stockton Axson, "Memoir of Woodrow Wilson," unpublished MS in possession of Arthur S. Link (hereafter cited as Axson Memoir).

7. ELA to MJHA, Apr. 8, 1878, and Dec. 18, 1879, Wilson Papers; ELAd to ELA, c. Sept. 1879, Apr. 2 and Sept. 4, 1881, and Feb. 21, 1883, ibid.; ELA to WW, Oct. 11, 1883, Nov. 12, 1883, and Jan. 7, 1884, *PWW*, 2:469, 471 n. 1, 526, 651; May 9 and 12, 1884, *PWW*, 3:170, 175.

8. ELAd to ELA, Sept. 4, 1881, Wilson Papers.

9. Agnes Tedcastle told RSB that, presumably before the Sunday when WW saw ELA in church, ELA was on the porch of the Tedcastle home in Rome, Ga., saw WW walking past in the street, and asked who he was. Agnes had said: "I don't know whether to tell you or not, you manhater. That is Tommy Wilson." (Agnes Tedcastle to RSB, May 21, 1925, RSB Coll.; also related in Baker, *L and L*, 1:161.) ELA said that "the first *meeting* of any consequence" took place at the home of Agnes Tedcastle (ELA to WW, Oct. 11, 1883, *PWW*, 2:469, emphasis added).

10. Rosalie Anderson to ELA, July 5, 1877, Wilson Papers.

11. Woodrow Wilson gave his own birth date as Dec. 28; however, Joseph Ruggles Wilson recorded his son's birth in the family bible as "12¾ o'clock" on

Dec. 28. Jessie Woodrow Wilson wrote her son on his twenty-first birthday that he was born so near midnight that she was unsure of the exact date (*PWW*, 1:3, 332–33). Known as "Tommy," WW dropped this name in 1881, after he left the U. of Va. (Baker, *L and L*, 1:137).

12. Link, *Road to the White House*, pp. 1–11; Baker, *L and L*, 1:1–167; Mulder, *Woodrow Wilson: The Years of Preparation*, pp. 29–33, 37–43, 60, 68, 71–72; WW to Richard Heath Dabney, May 11, 1883, *PWW*, 2:350–51.

13. WW to ELA, May 28, 1883, *PWW*, 2:363.

14. ELA to WW, May 28, 1883, ibid.

15. Editorial Note, ibid., pp. 362–63; ELA to WW, Oct. 11, 1883, ibid., p. 469; WW to ELA, Oct. 14, 1883, ibid., p. 473; Battey, *A History of Rome and Floyd County*, pp. 290–91; Edith Lester Harbin, "Oft-told Tales," unpublished MS in possession of Jane Griffin Dix; Mary E. Hoyt, memorandum for RSB, Oct. 1926, RSB Coll.

16. Rosalie Anderson to ELA, July 2, 1883, Wilson Papers.

17. Editorial Note, *PWW*, 2:426.

18. Ibid.

19. WW to ELA, Sept. 18, 27, 29, and Dec. 18, 1883, ibid., pp. 427, 444, 446, 592; May 19, 1885, ibid., 4:607; ELA to WW, Sept. 21 and 25, 1883, ibid., 2:434, 440.

20. Axson, "Mr. Wilson as Seen by One of His Family Circle," *New York Times*, Oct. 8, 1916, Sec. 5, p. 6.

21. ELA to WW, Oct. 2, 1883, *PWW*, 2:451.

Chapter 2

1. Hoyt family genealogy, Family Collection of William Dana Hoyt.

2. Ibid.; Hoyt, *A Genealogical History of the Hoyt, Haight, Hight Families*; Washington and Washington, *Carleton's Raid*.

3. Hoyt family genealogy.

4. Ibid.

5. Rice and Williams, *History of Greene County Georgia 1786–1886*, pp. 214–17; the quotation from Psalm 144 was on the first diplomas issued by the institution.

6. Axson, "Traditions and Early History of the Axson Family."

7. Christian and FitzRandolph, *The Descendants of Edward FitzRandolph and Elizabeth Blossom, 1630–1950*; Mary Tyndall May, "Isaac Randolph: A Brief Sketch of His Life," and Mary Tyndall May to Henry W. Savage, June 10, 1947, Princeton University Library. Hennig, ed., *Columbia 1786–1936, A Mid-Century Supplement, 1936–1966*, pp. 263–64. Rebecca Axson's Paris gold-banded china chocolate set from which Lafayette is alleged to have drunk is now in the possession of Ben Palmer Axson, Jr.

8. Stacy, *History of the Midway Congregational Church*; Axson, "Traditions and Early History of the Axson Family"; Rebecca Randolph Axson to MJHA, Apr. 12, 1864(?), Wilson-McAdoo Collection, University of California at Santa Barbara (hereafter cited as Wilson-McAdoo Coll.).

9. Axson, "Traditions and Early History of the Axson Family."

10. *Minutes of the Synod of Georgia, October 28th–November 2nd, 1885,* "Memorial of Rev. Samuel Edward Axson," pp. 11–13, Historical Foundation of the Presbyterian and Reformed Churches, Montreat, N.C. (hereafter cited as HFNC).

11. SEA to MJH, Feb. 6, 1857, Wilson Papers.

12. Elliott, *My Aunt Louisa and Woodrow Wilson,* p. 8.

13. MJHA to SEA, Sept. 29, 1860, Wilson Papers.

14. W. D. Hoyt to MJH, Aug. 16, 1856, ibid.

15. W. D. Hoyt to MJH, May 12, 1855, and Feb. 29, 1856; SEA to MJH, Dec. 1, 1856, ibid.

16. Axley, *Holding Aloft the Torch,* pp. 76–77; SEA to MJH, Nov. 28, 1857, and Apr. 1, 1858; MJH to SEA, Jan. 12, 1858, Wilson Papers.

17. ELA to WW, Apr. 15, 1884, *PWW,* 3:129.

18. SEA to MJH, Nov. 16, 1858, Wilson Papers.

19. "Records of the Charleston Presbytery," Apr. 7 and May 22, 1859, HFNC.

20. MJHA to SEA, Apr. 28, 1860; W. D. Hoyt to MJHA, May 23, 1860, Wilson Papers; ELA to WW, Dec. 10, 1883, *PWW,* 2:576; Aug. 25, 1884, *PWW,* 3:306; Axley, *Holding Aloft the Torch,* p. 95. ELA was born in Savannah rather than at the home of her Hoyt grandparents because of Nathan Hoyt's poor health (Margaret Bliss Hoyt to MJHA and SEA, Apr. 23, 1860, Wilson-McAdoo Coll.).

21. "Records of the Charleston Presbytery," Feb. 9, 1861, HFNC; Thomas, *An Historical Account of the Protestant Episcopal Church in South Carolina,* p. 502; *The State,* Columbia, S.C., Apr. 14, 1957, p. 2–C; "Minutes of the session of the Stoney Creek Independent Presbyterian Church," Jan. and Feb. 1861, HFNC.

22. MJH to SEA, Dec. 19, 1856; MJHA to SEA, Nov. 12, 1861, Wilson Papers; MJHA to SEA, Dec. 24 and 28, 1860, Wilson Collection, Princeton University Library (hereafter cited as Wilson Coll.).

23. MJHA to SEA, Aug. 25, 1860, Wilson Papers; Dec. 24 and 28, 1860, Wilson Coll.

24. ELA to WW, July 3, 1884, *PWW,* 3:227.

25. Charley Hutson to MJHA, c. May 29, 1863, and Dec. 22, 1863, Wilson Papers; Myers, *The Children of Pride,* pp. 1456–57; *Minutes of the General Assembly of the Presbyterian Church in the Confederate States of America,* 1863.

26. *Minutes of the General Assembly of the Presbyterian Church in the Confederate States of America,* 1864; "Minutes of the Charleston Presbytery," Nov. 10, 1865; Hicky, *Rambles through Morgan County,* p. 17; interview with Mrs. Caroline C. Hunt, July 14, 1980.

27. Aycock, *All Roads to Rome*; Battey, *A History of Rome and Floyd County,* p. 111. The 1860 census reported for Floyd County: 9,200 whites, 5,927 slaves, and 16 free blacks.

28. Florida Bayard (Mrs. John J.) Seay to Sara Jonas (Mrs. Thomas) Fahy, Oct. 9, 1914, Woodrow Wilson File, Carnegie Library, Rome, Ga. (hereafter cited as WW File).

29. Leyburn, *Historical Sketch of the First Presbyterian Church, Rome, Georgia*

(1845–1921); Cothran, "A History of the First Presbyterian Church of Rome, Georgia."

30. Florida B. Seay to Sarah J. Fahy, Oct. 9, 1914, WW File; records of the Presbytery of Cherokee, 1866, 1867, HFNC.

31. MJHA to Thomas A. Hoyt, Dec. 18, 1872, Wilson Papers; *Southern Presbyterian*, Jan. 30, 1873, HFNC.

32. Books of Deeds, O, P, R, T, pp. 406, 61, 610, 94, Floyd County, Superior Court Records, Rome, Ga.; minutes of the session, First Presbyterian Church, Rome, Ga., Book 1, HFNC; Harris, "Proposed Parsonages," library, First Presbyterian Church, Rome, Ga.; Florida B. Seay to Sara J. Fahy, Oct. 9, 1914, WW File. The Axsons' last home, at 402 East Third Avenue, was torn down in 1970; a modern house occupies the site.

33. Minutes of the session, First Presbyterian Church, Rome, Ga., Book 1, 1848–1895, HFNC; *Minutes of the General Assembly of the Presbyterian Church in the United States*, 1871.

34. Minutes of the session, First Presbyterian Church, Rome, Ga., Book 1, HFNC.

35. Wilkerson, *Rome's Remarkable History*, p. 8; Elizabeth Caldwell was educated at the Troy Female Seminary established in 1821 by Emma Willard, a pioneer in education for women.

36. Wilkerson, ibid., p. 16.

37. Maria [?] to ELA, Feb. 8, 1874, Wilson Papers; Rosalie Anderson to ELA, Oct. 6, 1877, ibid.; EAW to WW, May 27, 1886, *PWW*, 5:265.

38. Undated clipping from the *Nashville Banner*, c. Jan. 1913, Wilson Coll.

Chapter 3

1. Rosalie Anderson's letters to EAW are in the Wilson Papers.

2. Curatorial Records, National Academy of Design, New York.

3. Agnes Vaughn to ELA, Apr. 12, 1878, Wilson Papers; ELAd to ELA, Dec. 16, 1878, ibid.; Wilkerson, *Rome's Remarkable History*, p. 10.

4. ELA to WW, Apr. 28, 1885, *PWW*, 4:539.

5. Rosalie Anderson to ELA, June 13 and 29, and July 12, 1877, Wilson Papers.

6. ELA to WW, Dec. 17, 1883, *PWW*, 2:588; Battey, *A History of Rome and Floyd County*, p. 419; Stockton Axson memorandum to RSB, undated, RSB Coll.; Agnes V. Tedcastle to RSB, May 21, 1925, RSB Coll.

7. WW to Richard H. Dabney, Feb. 17, 1884, *PWW*, 3:27.

8. Rosalie Anderson to ELA, Apr. 19, 1879, and July 10, 1881, Wilson Papers.

9. SEA to Joseph R. Wilson, July 14, 1875, ibid.

10. MJHA to Louisa Hoyt Brown, Apr. 3, 1880, Wilson Coll.; SEA to Louisa H. Brown, Aug. 25, 1880, ibid.

11. *Minutes of the General Assembly of the Presbyterian Church in the United States*, 1881.

12. ELA to WW, Dec. 20, 1884, *PWW*, 3:562.

13. ELA to MJHA, Feb. 2, 1878, Wilson Papers.

14. Ibid.

15. ELA to WW, Oct. 2, 1883, *PWW*, 2:451.
16. Emma Hoyt to ELA, Jan. 30, 1878, Wilson Papers.
17. ELA to MJHA, Apr. 8, 1878, ibid.
18. ELAd to ELA, Sept. 2, 1878, ibid.
19. Elizabeth had an older brother, Samuel Caldwell, and a younger sister, Mary Millican ("Mamie"). In 1883, Lawrence Adams married Rebecca Branch Bond (Erwin and Adams family records, courtesy of Elizabeth Erwin Hutchins and Rebecca Bond Jeffress Barney); see also the Parish Register of St. Paul's Episcopal Church, Augusta, Ga.
20. ELAd to ELA, Apr. 24, 1879, Wilson Papers.
21. ELAd to ELA, June 23, 1880, ibid.
22. ELAd to ELA, July 18, 1880, ibid.
23. ELAd to ELA, Oct. 11, 1880, ibid.
24. ELAd to ELA, Sept. 17, 1880, and July 31, 1881, ibid.
25. ELAd to ELA, Nov. 18, 1880, and Feb. 18, 1881, ibid.
26. ELAd to ELA, c. Sept. 1879, ibid.
27. ELAd to ELA, July 18 and Dec. 25, 1880, ibid. As provocative as Beth's words sound, these lavish expressions of affection were no different from many other known instances of friendship between women in the nineteenth century. Such expressions of devotion served an emotional function in a Victorian society which placed severe social restrictions on intimacy between young men and women. These bonds between women friends, frequently physical as well as emotional, were often marked by a romantic and even sensual note that was simply a part of a young girl's developing sexuality. Friendships were known to revolve around intense scholarly interests. (Smith-Rosenberg, "The Female World of Love and Ritual," *Signs*, 1:1–29.)
28. ELAd to ELA, Sept. 2, 1878, Nov. 25, 1879, Oct. 11 and Dec. 25, 1880, and May 1, 1881, Wilson Papers.
29. ELAd to ELA, July 18, 1880, and Feb. 22, 1881, ibid.
30. ELAd to ELA, Feb. 22 and Sept. 4, 1881, ibid.
31. ELAd to ELA, Apr. 27, 1881, ibid.
32. *Rome Courier*, c. June 9, 1881.
33. Battey, *A History of Rome and Floyd County*, p. 419.
34. *Rome Courier*, c. June 9, 1881; Ellen Axson's entry, "A Study of Antinous," was a crayon drawing of one of Emperor Hadrian's favorite pages known for his beauty.
35. ELAd to ELA, Aug. 17, 1881, Jan. 9 and 14, 1882, Wilson Papers.

Chapter 4

1. ELA to MJHA, Sept. 17, 1881, Wilson Papers.
2. ELA to MJHA, Sept. 30, 1881, ibid.
3. SEA to Louisa Hoyt Brown, Oct. 10 and 24, 1881, Wilson Coll.; ELAd to ELA, Nov. 21, 1881, Wilson Papers.
4. ELA to WW, Nov. 17, 1883, *PWW*, 2:532.
5. ELA to MJHA, Dec. 18, 1879, Wilson Papers.

6. ELA to MJHA, July 10, 1880, ibid.

7. Mary E. Hoyt to WW, Nov. 22, 1914, ibid.

8. Janie Porter to ELA, Dec. 8, 1881, ibid.

9. WW to ELA, Apr. 13, 1884, *PWW*, 3:126.

10. ELAd to ELA, Jan. 1, 1882, Wilson Papers; SEA to Louisa H. Brown, July 18 and Aug. 29, 1882, Wilson Coll.

11. Lucy Bowie to ELA, June 13, 1882, Wilson Papers.

12. SEA to Louisa H. Brown, Dec. 26, 1881, and July 18, 1882, Wilson Coll.

13. SEA to Louisa H. Brown, July 18, Aug. 22, Sept. 8 and 30, and Oct. 4, 1882, Wilson Coll.; *PWW*, 3:331 n. 2; ELA to WW, June 9, 1884, *PWW*, 3:211.

14. Janie Porter to ELA, Oct. 18, 1882, Wilson Papers.

15. ELAd to ELA, Dec. 25, 1880, ibid.; EAE to ELA, May 13, 1885, ibid.

16. Rosalie Anderson to ELA, Nov. 10, 1883, ibid.

17. ELA to WW, Nov. 13 and 28, 1883, *PWW*, 2:527, 554–55.

18. ELA to WW, Nov. 28 and Dec. 10, 1883, ibid., pp. 555, 575.

19. ELA to WW, Nov. 28, 1883, ibid., p. 555.

20. WW to ELA, Sept. 18, 1883, ibid., p. 428.

21. Jessie W. Wilson to WW, June 7 and 21, 1883, ibid., pp. 365, 370–71.

22. Jessie W. Wilson to ELA, Dec. 1, 1883, ibid., p. 559.

23. WW to SEA, Sept. 19, 1883, ibid., pp. 430–31; ELA to WW, Sept. 21, 1883, ibid., p. 434; SEA to WW, Sept. 24, 1883, ibid., p. 436.

Chapter 5

1. WW to ELA, Sept. 18, 1883, *PWW*, 2:428.

2. ELA to WW, Sept. 21, 1883, ibid., p. 435.

3. ELA to WW, Mar. 28, 1885, ibid., 4:430.

4. WW to ELA, Sept. 27, 1883, ibid., 2:444.

5. WW to ELA, Feb. 18, 1894, ibid., 8:493.

6. ELA to WW, Nov. 5, 1883, ibid., 2:517.

7. WW to ELA, Oct. 30, 1883, ibid., p. 499.

8. WW to ELA, Oct. 18, 1883, ibid., pp. 481–82.

9. WW to ELA, Apr. 15, 1884, ibid., 3:133.

10. WW to ELA, Dec. 18, 1883, ibid., pp. 554–55.

11. ELA to WW, Mar. 30 and May 12, 1885, ibid., 4:434, 586.

12. ELA to WW, Sept. 7, 1883, ibid., 2:420.

13. ELA to WW, Sept. 25 and Oct. 6, 1883, ibid., pp. 440–41, 460.

14. ELA to WW, Oct. 23, 1883, ibid., p. 489.

15. Minutes of the session, First Presbyterian Church, Rome, Ga., Book 1, HFNC.

16. ELA to WW, Oct. 30 and Nov. 6, 12, 18, 22, and 28, 1883, *PWW*, 2:505–6, 519, 525, 533, 545, 553.

17. ELA to WW, Nov. 28, 1883, ibid., p. 554; Axson family genealogy. Leila's name in the family records is "Alethea," but she was always known by the shortened version.

18. Charles Shinn to WW, Jan. 21, 1884, *PWW*, 2:661, 662 n. 3; Frederick

Jackson Turner to Caroline Mae Sherwood, Jan. 21, 1889, ibid., 6:58.

19. ELA to WW, Jan. 28, 1884, ibid., p. 665.

20. ELA to WW, Jan. 28, 1884, ibid.; WW to ELA, Jan. 31, 1884, ibid., pp. 667–68.

21. ELA to WW, Feb. 4, 1884, ibid., 3:7.

22. ELA to WW, Feb. 18, 1884, ibid., p. 31; Rosalie Anderson to ELA, July 2, 1883, Wilson Papers.

23. ELA to WW, Feb. 25, 1884, *PWW*, 3:47.

24. ELA to WW, Feb. 25, 1884, ibid., p. 46.

25. ELA to WW, May 6 and 9, 1884, ibid., pp. 162, 171.

26. WW to ELA, Apr. 24, May 1 and 8, 1884, ibid., pp. 145, 155–56, 167.

27. ELA to WW, Apr. 29, 1884, ibid., p. 150; WW to ELA, May 1 and 4, 1884, ibid., pp. 155–56, 160.

28. ELA to WW, May 6, 1884, ibid., p. 162; WW to ELA, Feb. 19 and Mar. 11, 1884, ibid., pp. 36, 80.

29. WW to ELA, May 8, 1884, ibid., p. 166.

30. ELA to WW, May 12 and 19, 1884, ibid., pp. 175, 187; WW to ELA, May 15, 1884, ibid., p. 180.

31. Joseph R. Wilson to WW, May 17, 1884, ibid., pp. 183–84.

32. WW to ELA, May 29, 1884, ibid., p. 197.

33. ELA to WW, June 2, 1884, ibid., p. 202.

Chapter 6

1. SEA to ELA, Feb. 12, 16, and 19, and Mar. 6, 1884, Wilson Papers.

2. SEA to Joseph R. Wilson, July 14, 1875, ibid.

3. ELA to WW, Dec. 3, 1884, *PWW*, 2:563.

4. Sermons of the Rev. Samuel Edward Axson, Wilson Papers. About 350 items are in the collection.

5. Annie Wilson Howe to WW, Jan. 29, 1884, *PWW*, 2:666; records of the Milledgeville State Hospital, Milledgeville, Ga., Jan. 13, 1884.

6. SEA, "Cogitations," The Sermons of SEA, Wilson Papers.

7. ELA to WW, July 31, 1883, *PWW*, 2:401.

8. ELA to WW, Dec. 17, 1883, ibid., pp. 588–89.

9. ELA, "Somebody's Child," "The Old Maid," and "The Raindrop's Story," Wilson Papers.

10. ELA to MJHA, Aug. 22, 1876, ibid.

11. ELA to WW, Dec. 26, 1883, *PWW*, 2:605.

12. ELA to WW, Feb. 4, 1884, ibid., 3:7.

13. ELA to WW, Mar. 7, 1884, ibid., p. 64.

14. ELA to WW, Jan. 25, 1885, ibid., 4:184.

15. WW to ELA, May 10, 1885, ibid., p. 578; ELA to WW, May 12, 1885, ibid., p. 586.

16. SEA to ELA, Mar. 6, 1884, Wilson Papers.

17. Mary E. Hoyt to WW, May 29, 1884, ibid.

18. *Rome Courier*, May 31, 1884; ELA to WW, June 5, 1884, *PWW*, 3:207;

Professor Emeritus George Williams, Rice University, Houston, Texas, to author, July 11, 1980.

19. Benjamin Morgan Palmer to ELA, June 12, 1884, Wilson Papers, emphasis added. Palmer was the son of the Rev. Edward Palmer and a first cousin to I. S. K. Axson.

20. The author is indebted to Dr. Edwin A. Weinstein for a copy of SEA's medical records from the state hospital, Milledgeville, Ga. Death certificates for Baldwin Co., Ga., exist only after 1923 (Clerk of Probate Court, Baldwin Co., Ga., to author, Jan. 12, 1979).

21. Minutes of the session, First Presbyterian Church, Rome, Ga., HFNC; Myers, *Children of Pride*, p. 1482.

22. Joseph R. Wilson to ELA, June 9, 1884, Wilson Papers.

23. ELA to WW, June 2 and 5, 1884, *PWW*, 3:201, 207.

24. ELA to WW, June 5, 1884, ibid., p. 208.

25. Stockton Axson memorandum to RSB, Sept. 6, 1931, RSB Coll.

26. ELA to WW, June 28, 1884, *PWW*, 3:220.

Chapter 7

1. "Estate of S. E. Axson," account book of Randolph Axson, Aug. 1, 1884–Dec. 1, 1901, Georgia Historical Society, Savannah.

2. Stockton Axson memorandum to RSB, undated MS, RSB Coll. The allegations that ELA studied in 1882 at the National Academy of Design (*PWW*, 3:464 n. 2) or at the Art Students League (Weinstein, *WW: A Medical and Psychological Biography*, p. 75) are not supported by existing evidence (Barbara Krulik, Nat. Acad. of Design to author, Aug. 18, 1982; SEA to Louisa H. Brown, July 18, Aug. 22, Sept. 8 and 30, and Oct. 4, 1882, Wilson Coll.; Stockton Axson memo to RSB, undated, RSB Coll.).

3. ELA to WW, July 14 and 19, 1884, *PWW*, 3:244, 251–52; Rosalie Anderson to ELA, July 20, 1884; Jessie Woodrow Wilson to Rebecca Randolph Axson, July 11, 1884; Rebecca R. Axson to Jessie W. Wilson, July 12, 1884; Rebecca R. Axson to ELA, July 12, 1884, Wilson Papers.

4. EAE to ELA, June 5, Aug. 10, and Sept. 6, 1884, Wilson Papers.

5. ELA to WW, July 28, 1884, *PWW*, 3:265–66.

6. ELA to WW, Aug. 11, 1884, ibid., pp. 284–85.

7. ELA to WW, Aug. 15, 1884, ibid., pp. 290–91; WW to ELA, Aug. 23, 1884, ibid., pp. 300–301.

8. WW to ELA, Sept. 16, 1884, ibid., p. 329.

9. WW to ELA, Oct. 5, 1884, ibid., p.332; ELA to WW, Oct. 6, 1884, ibid., p. 336; Editorial Note, ibid., pp. 329–30.

10. ELA to WW, Oct. 4, 5, 7, 11, and 16, 1884, ibid., pp. 330, 333, 337, 347, 356–58.

11. ELA to WW, Nov. 19, 1884, ibid., p. 463.

12. Campbell, *The Art Students League of New York*, pp. 15–20; Landgren, *Years of Art*, pp. 17–47.

13. ELA to WW, Oct. 6, 1884, *PWW*, 3:336.

14. ELA to WW, Oct. 31, Nov. 11 and 17, 1884, ibid., pp. 391, 425, 451; Landgren, *Years of Art*, p. 41.

15. ELA to WW, Nov. 1, 11, 15, and Dec. 4, 1884, *PWW*, 3:395, 425, 439, 510–11.

16. ELA to WW, Nov. 19, 1884, ibid., pp. 462–63.

17. ELA to WW, Dec. 6, 1884, ibid., pp. 519–20.

18. ELA to WW, Dec. 12, 1884, ibid., p. 537.

19. ELA to WW, Dec. 13, 1884, ibid., p. 539.

20. ELA to WW, Nov. 3 and Dec. 3, 1884, ibid., pp. 400, 509.

21. ELA to WW, Oct. 17 and 22, Nov. 13 and 15, 1884, ibid., pp. 361, 366–67, 434, 439; Mar. 22, 1885, ibid., 4:397.

22. ELA to WW, Nov. 18 and Dec. 3, 1884, ibid., 3:454, 509.

23. ELA to WW, Nov. 16, 22, and 26, 1884; Jan. 22, 1885, ibid., pp. 443, 470–71, 486, 632; Jan. 25 and 27, 1885, ibid., 4:184, 188.

24. WW to ELA, Nov. 1, 1884, ibid., 3:392–93; ELA to WW, Nov. 3, 1884, ibid., p. 400.

25. ELA to WW, Mar. 3 and Nov. 16, 1884, ibid., pp. 58, 443.

26. ELA to WW, Oct. 5, Nov. 7, 25, and 26, Dec. 12, 1884, ibid., pp. 334, 374, 412, 487, 535; Robert Bridges to WW, Dec. 15, 1884, ibid., p. 541.

27. Charles H. Shinn to ELA, Oct. 27, 1884, Wilson Papers; ELA to WW, Nov. 9, Dec. 12 and 20, 1884, *PWW*, 3:416, 536, 562–63.

28. ELA to WW, Nov. 11, Dec. 17, 1884, and Jan. 11, 1885, *PWW*, 3:425, 551, 600–601; Feb. 1, 1885, ibid., 4:210–12.

29. WW to ELA, Jan. 13 and 24, 1885, ibid., 3:603–4, 4:4–5.

30. ELA to WW, Jan. 14, 1885, ibid., 3:609; Feb. 1, 6, 11, and May 17, 1885, ibid., 4:210, 219–20, 234, 602.

31. ELA to WW, Oct. 26 and Nov. 15, 1884, ibid., 3:376, 436.

32. ELA to WW, Nov. 9 and 16, 1884, ibid., pp. 419, 441.

33. ELA to WW, Jan. 11, 1885, ibid., p. 600; Feb. 8 and 10, 1885, ibid., 4:224–25, 233–34; WW to ELA, Feb. 9, 1885, ibid., p. 227.

34. ELA to WW, Nov. 29, 1884, ibid., 3:498.

35. W. D. Hoyt to ELA, Oct. 30, 1884, Wilson Papers.

36. ELA to WW, Dec. 21, 1884, *PWW*, 3:568; Rosalie Anderson to ELA, Dec. 16, 1884, Wilson Papers.

37. EAE to ELA, Nov. 16, 1884, Wilson Papers.

38. Mary E. Hoyt to ELA, Nov. 22, 1884, and Feb. 28, 1885, ibid.; Mary E. Hoyt to EAW, Nov. 7, 1885, ibid.

39. Thomas A. Hoyt to ELA, Dec. 20, 1884, ibid.

40. ELA to WW, Dec. 8 and 19, 1884, and Jan. 2, 1885, *PWW*, 3:525–26, 559, 575, 576 n. 1.

41. WW to Robert Bridges, Dec. 20, 1884, ibid., p. 563.

42. WW to ELA, Jan. 2, 1885, ibid., p. 577; Feb. 8, 1885, ibid., 4:222–23.

43. ELA to WW, Jan. 4, 1885, ibid., 3:581–82.

Chapter 8

1. WW to ELA, Oct. 7 and Nov. 28, 1884, *PWW*, 3:337, 493; Link, *Road to the White House*, pp. 14–15.

2. WW to ELA, Jan. 24, 1885, *PWW*, 4:3, emphasis added.

3. WW to ELA, Feb. 15, 1885, ibid., p. 255.

4. ELA to WW, Feb. 22 and 25, 1885, ibid., pp. 280, 297–98.

5. WW to ELA, Feb. 24, 1885, ibid., pp. 287–88.

6. WW to ELA, Oct. 25 and 30, Nov. 1 and 25, 1883, ibid., 2:490, 499, 511, 549.

7. ELA to WW, Mar. 6, Apr. 6 and 16, 1885, ibid., 4:337, 461, 493; WW to ELA, Jan. 4, 1884, ibid., 2:647; Dec. 18, 1884, and Jan. 4, 1885, ibid., 3:554, 581; Feb. 17, 19, and 21, 1885, ibid., 4:263, 269, 271–72.

8. WW to ELA, Feb. 19, 1884, ibid., 3:36; Feb. 19 and 26, 1885, ibid., 4:269, 300; Editorial Note, ibid., p. 12.

9. WW to ELA, Jan. 29, Mar. 5, and June 20, 1885, ibid., pp. 199, 335, 728.

10. ELA to WW, June 17, 1885, ibid., p. 723.

11. WW to ELA, Feb. 2, 1884, ibid., 3:3.

12. ELA to WW, Apr. 3, 1885, ibid., 4:448–49.

13. ELA to WW, June 7, 1885, ibid., p. 690.

14. ELA to WW, Feb. 27, 1885, ibid., p. 307.

15. ELA to WW, Nov. 13, 1884, ibid., 3:433–34; Feb. 8, Mar. 4 and 14, 1885, ibid., 4:225, 332, 366.

16. Stockton Axson memorandum to RSB, Aug. 27, 1928, RSB Coll. Mulder writes that Ellen's love for Woodrow "included a near-worship of his abilities and a subordination of herself to his plans and ambitions." (Mulder, *WW: The Years of Preparation*, p. 87.) Both Axson and Mulder have overlooked what EAW, herself, stated about her ambitions.

17. ELA to WW, Apr. 11, 1885, *PWW*, 4:475.

18. ELA to WW, Mar. 10, Apr. 3 and 30, 1885, ibid., pp. 350, 444–45, 546.

19. ELA to WW, Apr. 11, 13, and 27, 1885, ibid., pp. 475, 480–81, 533; Antoinette Farnsworth to EAW, Nov. 30, 1885, Wilson Papers.

20. WW to ELA, Mar. 27, 1885, *PWW*, 4:420–21.

21. ELA to WW, Mar. 28, 1885, ibid., pp. 428–31.

22. WW to ELA, Mar. 30, 1885, ibid., p. 435.

23. Agreement between the trustees of Bryn Mawr College and Woodrow Wilson, M.A., ibid., 3:597.

24. Finch, *Carey Thomas of Bryn Mawr*, p. 155; Dobkin, *The Making of a Feminist*, pp. 260–66.

25. WW to ELA, Nov. 30, 1884, *PWW*, 3:499.

26. ELA to WW, Nov. 28, 1884, ibid., pp. 494–95.

27. ELA to WW, Jan. 20, 1885, ibid., p. 625.

28. WW to ELA, Jan. 22, 1885, ibid., pp. 629–30.

29. ELA to WW, Jan. 14 and 20, 1885, ibid., pp. 610, 625; Jan. 28 and 30, Feb. 12 and 16, 1885, ibid., 4:193, 201–2, 244, 260–61; WW to ELA, Jan. 13, 14, and 16, 1885, ibid., 3:605–6, 607, 614; Feb. 8, 11, 14, 15, 18, and 19, 1885, ibid., 4:223, 235, 251–52, 256, 265–66, 269.

30. ELA to WW, Apr. 13, 1885, ibid., 4:484–85.

31. WW to ELA, Apr. 15, 1885, ibid., p. 488.

32. ELA to WW, Apr. 16, 1885, ibid., p. 494.

33. ELA to WW, Mar. 11, 15, and 17, 1885, ibid., pp. 354, 369, 381.

34. ELA to WW, May 26 and 29, 1885, ibid., pp. 664–65, 673.

35. ELA to WW, Apr. 19, May 25, and June 1, 1885, ibid., pp. 502, 627, 677–78.

36. WW to ELA, June 3, 1885, ibid., p. 681. The Howe house at 1531 Blanding Street, now restored and occupied by the Jarvis Corp., is open to the public.

37. WW to ELA, June 10 and 20, 1885, ibid., pp. 703, 727.

38. ELA to WW, June 12, 1885, ibid., pp. 705–6.

39. WW to ELA, June 13, 1885, ibid., p. 710; ELA to WW, June 16, 1885, ibid., p. 718; McAdoo, *The Priceless Gift*, p. 147; Axson, *Mr. Wilson As Seen by One of His Family Circle*.

40. A News Item, *PWW*, 4:735.

41. ELA to WW, June 18, 1885, ibid., p. 725; W. D. Hoyt to ELA, June 18, 1885, Wilson Papers.

42. Rosalie Anderson to ELA, May 10, 1885, Wilson Papers.

43. Godley, "Savannah's Most Famous June Wedding," *Savannah Life Magazine* (June 1947), p. 4.

44. WW to Thomas Woodrow, June 8, 1885, *PWW*, 4:692.

45. A News Report, *PWW*, 23:554.

46. Jessie W. Wilson to WW, July 17, 1885, ibid., 5:5; Robert Bridges to WW, July 19, 1885, ibid., p. 6.

47. *Charlotte Observer*, July 8, 1928, p. 4. The *Observer* cited an incorrect date for the Wilsons' visit to Morganton (see EAE to EAW, Aug. 8, 1885, Wilson Papers). "Maplewood," partially renovated, is now privately owned.

48. *PWW*, 5:15 n. 1; Jessie W. Wilson to WW, Jan. 26, 1885, ibid., 4:198.

Chapter 9

1. Addie C. Wildgoss to WW, July 24 and 30, 1885, *PWW*, 5:8, 9, 10 n. 1; Finch, *Carey Thomas of Bryn Mawr*, pp. 164–65; McAdoo, *The Priceless Gift*, p. 147.

2. Mary E. Hoyt to EAW, Nov. 7, 1885, Wilson Papers.

3. Ibid.

4. Louisa H. Brown to EAW, Nov. 20, 1885, ibid.

5. Rosalie Anderson (hereafter cited as Rosalie A. DuBose) to EAW, Nov. 10, 1885, ibid.

6. EAE to EAW, Nov. 15, 1885, ibid.

7. EAE to EAW, Feb. 14, 1886, ibid.

8. Antoinette Farnsworth to EAW, Nov. 30, 1885, ibid.

9. Mary E. Hoyt to WW, Jan. 6, 1886, ibid.; W. D. Hoyt to EAW, Jan. 6, 1886, ibid.

10. Louisa H. Brown to EAW, Mar. 4, 1886, ibid.

11. Jessie W. Wilson to WW, Jan. 4, 1886, *PWW*, 5:98.

12. McAdoo, *The Priceless Gift*, p. 148.

13. Louisa H. Brown to WW, Apr. 16, 1886, *PWW*, 5:158–59.

14. EAW to WW, Apr. 24, 1886, ibid., p. 170.

15. EAW to WW, May 2, 1886, ibid., p. 191.

16. WW to EAW, May 6, 1886, ibid., p. 200.

17. WW to EAW, May 12, 1886, ibid., p. 216.

18. WW to EAW, May 13, 1886, ibid., p. 221.

19. WW to EAW, May 21, 1886, ibid., p. 246.

20. WW to EAW, May 29, 1886, ibid., p. 267.

21. WW to EAW, May 30, 1886, ibid., p. 269.

22. EAW to WW, June 2, 1886, ibid., p. 279.

23. EAW to WW, May 3, 6, and 14, and June 4, 1886, ibid., pp. 194, 200, 225, 284.

24. EAW to WW, May 4, 10, and 11, 1886, ibid., pp. 196, 212, 215.

25. WW to EAW, May 14, 1886, ibid., p. 224; Marion W. Kennedy to WW, Sept. 8, 1886, ibid., pp. 348–49.

26. Editorial Note, ibid., p. 57.

27. Axson Memoir; RSB memorandum of interviews with Stockton Axson, Feb. 8, 10, and 11, 1925, RSB Coll.; Mary Hoyt to EAW, Nov. 21, 1886, Wilson Papers.

28. Randolph Axson to EAW, Nov. 19, 1886, Wilson Papers; Stockton Axson to EAW, Dec. 11, 1886, ibid.

29. Joseph R. Wilson to WW, Nov. 15, 1886, *PWW*, 5:390–91, 391 n. 1.

30. Ibid., p. 615 n. 1.

31. Ibid., p. 429 n. 2; EAE to WW, Jan. 11, 1887, ibid., p. 429; Mary E. Hoyt to EAW, Feb. 23, 1887, Wilson Papers; Hannah R. Garrett to EAW, Jan. 18, 1887, Wilson Papers.

32. Louisa H. Brown to EAW, Mar. 1, 1887, Wilson Papers.

33. Randolph Axson to EAW, May 9, 1887, *PWW*, 5:503–4; WW to Robert Bridges, May 29, 1887, ibid., p. 509.

34. Jessie W. Wilson to WW, Apr. 30, 1887, ibid., pp. 500, 501 n. 1.

35. Stockton Axson to EAW, Mar. 26, 1887, Wilson Papers.

36. Mary E. Hoyt to EAW, June 28, 1890, ibid.; May 4, 1887, *PWW*, 5:502.

37. Louisa H. Brown to EAW, Mar. 1 and May 19, 1887, Wilson Papers; Gainesville History, typed MS, Chestatee Regional Library, Gainesville, Ga.; EAW to Anna Harris, July 25, 1887, Wilson Coll.

38. Randolph Axson to EAW, Oct. 1, 1887, *PWW*, 5:597; Louisa H. Brown to EAW, May 19, 1887, Wilson Papers; Edward W. Axson to EAW, Feb. 15, 1887, Wilson Papers.

39. Stockton Axson to EAW, Feb. 12, Oct. 23, and Dec. 22, 1886, Jan. 14, Mar. 26, and Apr. 20, 1887, Wilson Papers; Randolph Axson to EAW, May 9, 1887, ibid.; interview with Ben P. Axson, Jr., Mar. 29, 1979.

40. Stockton Axson to EAW, Apr. 7 and 20, 1887, Wilson Papers; Axley, *Holding Aloft the Torch*, p. 96.

41. EAW to WW, July 13, 18, 20, and 24, 1887, *PWW*, 5:522, 523 n. 1, 527 n. 1, 528, 532, 538.

42. EAW to WW, July 27 and 29, 1887, ibid., pp. 541, 545.

43. Joseph R. Wilson to WW, Sept. 6 and 22, 1887, ibid., pp. 584, 592.

44. I. S. K. Axson to Warren A. Brown, Sept. 22, 1887, Wilson Papers; EAW to WW, Sept. 29 and Oct. 3, 1887, *PWW*, 5:593, 599.

45. EAW to WW, July 27, 1887, *PWW*, 5:541; Stockton Axson to EAW, Apr. 20, May 17, Oct. 17, 1887, and June 13, 1888, Wilson Papers.

46. Stockton Axson to EAW, Mar. 26, 1887, Wilson Papers; Randolph Axson to EAW, Oct. 1, 1887, *PWW*, 5:597; EAW to WW, Oct. 6, 1887, *PWW*, 5:609–10.

47. WW to Robert Bridges, Nov. 30, 1887, *PWW*, 5:632; Robert Bridges to WW, Nov. 28 and Dec. 7, 1887, ibid., pp. 631, 634.

48. WW to EAW, Oct. 4, 1887, ibid., p. 605.

49. WW to EAW, Oct. 7, 1887, ibid., p. 611.

50. EAW to WW, Oct. 5, 1887, ibid., p. 607.

51. McAdoo, *The Priceless Gift*, pp. 159–60, 163.

52. WW to EAW, Apr. 22, 1888, *PWW*, 5:723.

53. Agreement Between the Trustees of Bryn Mawr College and WW, Ph.D., Mar. 14, 1887, ibid., pp. 468–69; Edson W. Burr to WW, June 30, 1888, ibid., p. 748; Mulder, *WW: The Years of Preparation*, p. 101.

54. WW to the President and Trustees of Bryn Mawr College, June 29, 1888, *PWW*, 5:743; From WW's Confidential Journal, Oct. 20, 1887, ibid., p. 619.

55. Stockton Axson to EAW, Sept. 27, 1888, Wilson Papers; I. S. K. Axson to EAW, July 12, 1888, ibid.; Joseph R. Wilson to WW, Sept. 8, 1888, ibid.; WW to Robert Bridges, Aug. 26, 1888, *PWW*, 5:763, 765 n. 2.

56. Louisa H. Brown to EAW, June 19, 1888, Wilson Papers.

57. Edith Finch, biographer of Carey Thomas, said that during the Wilsons' Bryn Mawr years, Woodrow's "pretty wife" with her "southern manner" misled his colleagues into thinking her "frivolous." Finch, in retrospect, acknowledged that Ellen, although distracted by illness and "domestic tasks," was, "of course, serious minded and a very positive help" to her husband (Finch, *Carey Thomas of Bryn Mawr*, p. 330 n. 3).

Chapter 10

1. *PWW*, 6:16 n. 2.

2. WW to Robert Bridges, Nov. 27, 1888, ibid., p. 25.

3. EAW to WW, Feb. 14, 1889, ibid., p. 94; John F. Jameson to WW, Nov. 20, 1888, ibid., pp. 23–24.

4. EAE to EAW, Aug. 21 and Oct. 11, 1888, Wilson Papers; Mary M. ("Mamie") Adams to EAW, May 10, 1887, ibid.

5. EAE to EAW, Feb. 19, 1889, ibid.

6. Rosalie A. DuBose to EAW, May 15, 1887, and Nov. 10, 1888, ibid.

7. Janie P. Chandler to EAW, May 28, 1888, ibid.

8. Thomas A. Hoyt to EAW, Dec. 4, 1888, ibid.

9. Stockton Axson to EAW, Dec. 21, 1888, ibid.

10. WW to EAW, Feb. 12, 1889, *PWW*, 6:85.

11. EAW to WW, Feb. 17, 1889, ibid., p. 102.

12. WW to EAW, Feb. 19, 1889, ibid., p. 106; EAW to WW, Feb. 25, 1889, ibid., p. 111.

13. EAW to WW, Feb. 19, 1889, ibid., pp. 106–7.

14. WW to EAW, Feb. 24 and Sept. 1, 1889, ibid., pp. 110, 111 n. 1, 386. The Wilsons apparently used condoms as a contraceptive (WW to EAW, Feb. 12, 1898, ibid., 10:389).

15. EAW to WW, Feb. 27 and 28, Mar. 3, 8, and 19, 1889, ibid., 6:115, 121, 126, 135, 161; WW to EAW, Mar. 5, 1889, ibid., p. 129.

16. WW to EAW, Mar. 11, 1889, ibid., p. 143; EAW to WW, Mar. 12, 1889, ibid., p. 144.

17. WW to EAW, Mar. 9, 1889, ibid., p. 139.

18. WW to EAW, June 23, 1892, ibid., 8:17–18.

19. EAW to WW, Mar. 15, 1889, ibid., 6:155.

20. Stockton Axson to WW, May 10, 1889, ibid., pp. 219–20; Stockton Axson to EAW, May 27, 1889, ibid., p. 242; Stockton Axson to WW, June 11, 1889, Wilson Papers.

21. WW to Robert Bridges, Jan. 27, 1890, *PWW*, 6:481.

22. EAW to WW, Aug. 29 and 30, 1889, ibid., pp. 377, 379; WW to EAW, Sept. 2, 1889, ibid., p. 387; George Howe, Jr., to WW, Sept. 2, 1889, ibid., p. 389.

23. George Howe, Jr., to WW, Aug. 23, 1889, ibid., p. 371.

24. McAdoo, *The Priceless Gift*, p. 171; Joseph R. Wilson to WW, Oct. 30, 1889, *PWW*, 6:408; Thomas A. Hoyt to WW, Nov. 14, 1889, Wilson Papers; EAE to EAW, Oct. 20, 1889, Wilson Papers; Randolph Axson to WW, Oct. 26, 1889, Wilson Papers; Louisa H. Brown to WW, Oct. 26, 1889, Wilson Papers.

25. Elijah R. Craven to WW, Feb. 17, 1890, *PWW*, 6:526.

26. Albert Bushnell Hart to WW, Dec. 14, 1889, ibid., p. 452.

27. Albert B. Hart to WW, Apr. 23, 1889, ibid., pp. 174–75, 326 n. 1.

28. William H. Pace to WW, June 20, 1887, ibid., 5:520; WW to Horace E. Scudder, Dec. 23, 1889, ibid., 6:456–57.

29. WW to EAW, Mar. 10, 1889, ibid., p. 142.

30. WW to Robert Bridges, Jan. 6, 1890, ibid., pp. 472–73; George Howe, Jr., to WW, Apr. 2, 1890, ibid., pp. 611–12.

31. Edward W. Axson to EAW, May 21, 1890, Wilson Papers.

32. Edward W. Axson to EAW, June 4, 1890, ibid.; Thomas A. Hoyt to EAW, June 9, 1890, ibid.

33. Marsh and Wright to WW, June 9, 1890, *PWW*, 6:641 and n. 2; EAW to WW, June 17, 1890, ibid., p. 672. Steadman Street was changed to Library Place by borough ordinance, June 4, 1895.

34. Stockton Axson to EAW, Oct. 3, 1890, Wilson Papers; *PWW*, 7:181 n. 3.

Chapter 11

1. Myers, *Woodrow Wilson: Some Princeton Memoirs*, pp. 1–2.

2. Marion W. Kennedy to WW, May 20, 1890, *PWW*, 6:629; Joseph R. Wilson to WW, Aug. 16, 1890, ibid., p. 690.

3. George Howe, Jr., to WW, Nov. 5 and 24, 1890, ibid., 7:70–71, 80.

4. Joseph R. Wilson to WW, Feb. 26, 1891, ibid., p. 168.

5. Joseph R. Wilson to WW, Mar. 27, 1890, ibid., 6:561.

6. WW to Robert Bridges, Sept. 22, 1891, ibid., 7:290; George Howe, Jr., to WW, July 30, 1891, ibid., p. 249.

7. Stockton Axson to WW, Aug. 29, 1891, ibid., p. 278; Randolph Axson to Louisa H. Brown, Oct. 16, 1891, Wilson Coll.; EAW to WW, Mar. 31, 1892, *PWW*, 7:534.

8. WW to Albert Shaw, Mar. 29, 1891, *PWW*, 7:183; Caleb T. Winchester to WW, Oct. 24, 1891, ibid., pp. 316–17.

9. Francis L. Patton to James W. Alexander, Apr. 20, 1891, ibid., p. 192.

10. WW to EAW, Mar. 5 and Apr. 3, 1892, ibid., pp. 445, 446 n. 1, 540.

11. EAW to WW, Mar. 13, 1892, ibid., p. 481. The Independent Church, destroyed by fire in April 1889, had been rebuilt in perfect replica, with the interior painted in "softer and more harmonious colors" (EAW to WW, Mar. 6, 1892, ibid., p. 449).

12. EAW to WW, Mar. 5 and 6, 1892, ibid., pp. 446, 449.

13. WW to EAW, Mar. 6, 24, and 27, 1892, ibid., pp. 447–48, 510, 525.

14. WW to EAW, Mar. 17, 1892, ibid., pp. 492–93.

15. WW to EAW, Mar. 20 and Apr. 10, 1892, ibid., pp. 500, 557–58.

16. Aug. 23, 1884, ibid., 3:302.

17. WW to EAW, Mar. 15, 1892, ibid., 7:487.

18. Translation of a Boudoir Scene, c. Mar. 9, 1892, ibid., pp. 462–66.

19. EAW to WW, Mar. 8 and 15, 1892, ibid., pp. 459, 488; WW to EAW, Mar. 19, 1892, ibid., p. 496.

20. WW to EAW, Mar. 24, 1892, ibid., pp. 509–10.

21. EAW to WW, Mar. 15, 1892, ibid., p. 488; WW to EAW, Mar. 19, 1892, ibid., p. 496 and n. 2; Stockton Axson to EAW, Mar. 23, 1892, Wilson Papers; Epitaph, *PWW*, 7:544–45 and n. 1.

22. Mary E. Hoyt to EAW, Jan. 29, 1887, Wilson Papers.

23. EAW to WW, Mar. 24, 1892, *PWW*, 7:511.

24. EAW to WW, Mar. 23 and Apr. 2, 1892, ibid., pp. 508, 539.

25. EAW to WW, Mar. 27 and Apr. 3, 1892, ibid., pp. 522, 541.

26. EAW to WW, Apr. 3, 1892, ibid., pp. 541–42.

27. WW to EAW, Feb. 20, 1890, ibid., 6:531.

28. EAW to WW, Apr. 13 and 15, 1892, ibid., 7:564, 568.

29. EAW to WW, Mar. 23 and Apr. 15, 1892, ibid., pp. 508, 569; WW to EAW, Mar. 24, 1892, ibid., pp. 509–10.

30. EAW to WW, Apr. 26, 1892, ibid., p. 592.

31. EAW to WW, May 6, 1892, ibid., p. 623.

32. WW to EAW, Apr. 24, 1892, ibid., p. 590.

33. EAW to WW, Apr. 27, 1892, ibid., p. 596; WW to James C. MacKensie, Jan. 4, 1893, ibid., 8:77–78.

34. WW to EAW, Apr. 27 and 28, 1892, ibid., 7:598, 600.

35. EAW to WW, Apr. 30 and May 1, 1892, ibid., pp. 604, 607.

36. EAW to WW, Apr. 28, May 1 and 3, 1892, ibid., pp. 600, 607–8, 609.

37. WW to EAW, May 4, 1892, ibid., p. 616.

38. EAW to WW, May 8 and June 22, 1892, ibid., pp. 625–26; ibid., 8:16.

39. Elijah R. Craven to WW, June 30, 1892, ibid., 8:19, 7:635 n. 1.

40. EAW to WW, June 16, 17, 19, and 21, 1892, ibid., 8:3 n. 1 and n. 2, 4, 8–9, 13–14.

41. Editorial Note, ibid., p. 147.

42. Stockton Axson to WW, July 18, 1892, ibid., pp. 19–20.

43. EAW to Anna Harris, Nov. 22, 1892, ibid., p. 48; Editorial Note, ibid., p. 147.

44. Stockton Axson memorandum to RSB, Sept. 6, 1931, RSB Coll.

45. Arthur S. Link to Frederic Fox, Feb. 15, 1979, University Archives, Princeton University Library.

46. Leitch, *A Princeton Companion*, pp. 260–61; *Princeton Alumni Weekly*, 44:4 (June 16, 1944); Minutes of the Faculty of Princeton University, Wed., Jan. 18, 1893, Princeton University Library.

47. WW to Caleb T. Winchester, May 29, 1893, *PWW*, 8:219; WW to Horace Scudder, Mar. 19, 1893, ibid., pp. 179–80; WW to Charles W. Kent, Apr. 18, 1893, ibid., p. 193; WW to Richard McIlwaine, Apr. 23, 1893, ibid., pp. 197–98; WW to William E. Boggs, May 17 and 29, 1893, ibid., pp. 213–15, 220–21, 225 n. 4.

48. WW to Charles Scribner's Sons, July 3, 1893, ibid., p. 275 and n. 1.

49. An Address, ibid., p. 285 and n. 1.

50. WW to Albert Shaw, Aug. 7, 1893, ibid., p. 308; Mary E. Hoyt to EAW, July 31, 1893, Wilson Papers.

51. Mary E. Hoyt memorandum for RSB, Oct. 1926, RSB Coll.

52. Bancroft, *The Book of the Fair*, p. 257; EAW to WW, Sept. 7, 1893, *PWW*, 8:358.

53. Bancroft, *The Book of the Fair*, pp. 257–303.

54. When Ellen was in Gainesville in 1886, she asked Woodrow to send "*charcoal* for sketching" (EAW to WW, June 3, 1886, *PWW*, 5:282). Some of the French Impressionists exhibited at the Columbian Exposition were Manet, Monet, Degas, Pissarro, Renoir, and Sisley whose works were borrowed from private holdings in the United States (Connecticut and American Impressionism, Catalogue, The William Benton Museum of Art, University of Connecticut at Storrs, 1980, p. 43).

55. EAW to WW, Sept. 7, 8, and 10, 1893, *PWW*, 8:358, 360, 364–65.

56. WW to EAW, Sept. 7 and 11, 1893, ibid., pp. 359, 367.

57. EAW to WW, Jan. 26, 1894, ibid., p. 434 and n. 1. Helen W. Bones had been living with her older sister, Jessie B. Brower, then a resident of Chicago.

58. Franklin W. Hooper to WW, Aug. 17, 1893, ibid., p. 313 and n. 3; Editorial Note, ibid., 7:470–71; see listing, WW, Public Addresses and Lectures, ibid., 8:696–97.

59. WW to EAW, Mar. 20, 1892, ibid., 7:500.

60. Stockton Axson memorandum to RSB, undated, RSB Coll.; Reid, *WW:*

The Caricature, the Myth and the Man, p. 41.

61. Diary of Edward W. Axson, Sept. 20, 1893–Aug. 4, 1894, passim, Wilson Papers.

62. WW to EAW, Jan. 26, 1894, *PWW*, 8:433.

63. WW to EAW, Jan. 27, 29, 30, and Feb. 8, 1894, ibid., pp. 435–36, 442, 464; EAW to WW, Jan. 28, 1894, ibid., p. 436.

64. WW to EAW, Jan. 30, 1894, ibid., pp. 442–43.

65. EAW to WW, Feb. 1, 1894, ibid., p. 447.

Chapter 12

1. EAW to WW, Jan. 31, 1894, *PWW*, 8:446.

2. McAdoo, *The Woodrow Wilsons*, p. 9.

3. EAW to WW, Apr. 17, 1904, *PWW*, 15:266.

4. McAdoo, *The Woodrow Wilsons*, pp. 12, 15.

5. Ibid., p. 8.

6. Ibid., p. 11.

7. EAW to WW, Jan. 31, 1894, *PWW*, 8:446.

8. McAdoo, *The Woodrow Wilsons*, pp. 10, 30–31.

9. Ibid., p. 6.

10. Ibid., p. 45; Elliott, *My Aunt Louisa and WW*, pp. 120–21; Diary of Edward W. Axson, Wilson Papers.

11. Diary of Edward W. Axson, Wilson papers.

12. Ibid.

13. EAW to WW, Feb. 12, 1894, *PWW*, 8:479.

14. Diary of Edward W. Axson, Wilson Papers. Bliss Perry was professor of Oratory and Aesthetic Criticism at Princeton, 1893–99.

15. EAW to WW, Jan. 31 and Feb. 12, 1894, *PWW*, 8:446, 479; WW to EAW, Feb. 4, 1894, ibid., p. 453; Lyman P. Powell to WW, Feb. 18, 1894, ibid., pp. 495, 496 n. 2; Diary of Edward W. Axson, May 18, 1894, Wilson Papers.

16. WW to EAW, Feb. 4, 1894, *PWW*, 8:453; EAW to WW, Feb. 5, 1894, ibid., pp. 458–59.

17. Diary of Edward W. Axson, June 18, 1894, Wilson Papers.

18. Elliott, *My Aunt Louisa and WW*, pp. 97–103; Diary of Edward W. Axson, June 19–Aug. 3, 1894, Wilson Papers; Axson Memoir.

19. *PWW*, 8:597 n. 1, 623 n. 1.

20. EAW to WW, July 20, 24, and 25, 1894, ibid., pp. 618, 624, 625; Diary of Edward W. Axson, July 21–Aug. 2, 1894, Wilson Papers; EAW to WW, July 27, 1894, *PWW*, 8:629.

21. EAW to WW, Aug. 2, 1894, *PWW*, 8:640.

22. Ibid., p. 623 n. 1.

23. WW to EAW, July 23, 1894, ibid., pp. 620 n. 3, 623.

24. WW to EAW, July 24 and Aug. 1, 1894, ibid., pp. 624, 637.

25. WW to EAW, July 27, 1894, ibid., p. 628; EAW to WW, July 31 and Aug. 3, 1894, ibid., pp. 634, 642.

26. WW to EAW, Aug. 23, 1894, ibid., pp. 645–46.

27. EAW to WW, Aug. 22 and 23, 1894, ibid., pp. 645, 657.

Chapter 13

1. Edward S. Child to WW, Jan. 14, 1895, *PWW*, 9:121, 122 and n. 2.

2. WW to EAW, Jan. 25, 1895, ibid., pp. 126, 127 and n. 2.

3. WW to Child and de Goll, Architects, Jan. 19, 1895, ibid., p. 123.

4. WW to EAW, Jan. 27 and Feb. 2, 1895, ibid., pp. 133, 163; Cornelius C. Cuyler to WW, Jan. 26, 1895, ibid., pp. 134–35; EAW to WW, Jan. 28, 1895, ibid., p. 139.

5. WW to EAW, Jan. 28, 1895, ibid., p. 137.

6. EAW to WW, Jan. 28, 1895, ibid., pp. 138–39.

7. WW to EAW, Jan. 28, 1895, ibid., p. 137.

8. EAW to WW, Feb. 9, 1895, ibid., p. 183.

9. Cornelius C. Cuyler to WW, Jan. 31, 1895, ibid., pp. 164–65; WW to EAW, Feb. 2, 1895, ibid., p. 163.

10. John W. Fielder, Jr., to WW, Mar. 18, 1895, ibid., pp. 238–39 and n. 1; Frederick G. Burnham to WW, July 5, 1895, ibid., p. 313.

11. EAW to WW, Feb. 6, 1895, ibid., pp. 175–76.

12. EAW to Anna Harris, June 1, 1895, ibid., pp. 281 and n. 4, 291 n. 1.

13. Editorial Note, ibid., pp. 326–27; Henry M. Alden to WW, June 28, 1895, ibid., p. 311 and n. 2.

14. Stockton Axson memorandum to RSB, undated MS, RSB Coll.

15. WW to EAW, Feb. 18, 1895, *PWW*, 9:205–6.

16. EAW, Reading, ibid., p. 603.

17. McAdoo, *The Woodrow Wilsons*, p. 15.

18. WW to Howard Pyle, Oct. 7, 1895, *PWW*, 9:324; Editorial Note, ibid., p. 326; WW to H. M. Alden, Nov. 30, 1895, ibid., p. 353.

19. WW to Howard Pyle, Dec. 30, 1895, ibid., p. 370; EAW to WW, Feb. 16, 1896, ibid., p. 429.

20. EAW to WW, Jan. 24 and 30, 1896, ibid., pp. 388, 398.

21. EAW to WW, Feb. 12, 1896, ibid., pp. 420–21.

22. EAW to WW, Feb. 13, 1896, ibid., p. 423.

23. EAW to WW, Feb. 14, 1896, ibid., pp. 424–25.

24. EAW to WW, Feb. 15, 1896, ibid., p. 426.

25. EAW to WW, Feb. 19, 1896, ibid., pp. 434–35.

26. EAW to WW, Feb. 21, 1896, ibid., p. 439.

27. EAW to WW, Feb. 24, 1896, ibid., p. 446.

28. WW to EAW, Feb. 20, 23 and Mar. 2, 1896, ibid., pp. 435, 443, 475.

29. WW to EAW, Jan. 23, 1896, ibid., pp. 385, 386 n. 2; EAW to Arthur W. Tedcastle, Mar. 16, 1913, Wilson Papers.

30. EAW to WW, Feb. 27, 1896, *PWW*, 9:458.

31. McAdoo, *The Woodrow Wilsons*, p. 18.

32. There are several rough sketches of furniture placement in rooms that

appear to fit the house on 82 Library Place, Wilson Papers.

33. McAdoo, *The Priceless Gift*, p. 201.

Chapter 14

1. WW to EAW, Feb. 28, 1896, *PWW*, 9:466; EAW to WW, Feb. 16 and Mar. 1, 1896, ibid., pp. 430, 475.

2. WW to Howard Pyle, Mar. 24, 1896, ibid., p. 490.

3. Harper and Brothers to WW, May 5, 1896, ibid., p. 500; H. M. Alden to WW, May 14, 1896, ibid., p. 502.

4. Horace E. Scudder to WW, Apr. 25, 1896, ibid., p. 498 and n. 1; WW to EAW, June 19, 1896, ibid., p. 522 and n. 2.

5. WW to Henry Mills Alden, ibid., p. 503.

6. McAdoo, *The Priceless Gift*, p. 201.

7. WW to EAW, June 17 and 23, July 3, and Aug. 18, 1896, *PWW*, 9:519, 527, 532, 573. For other reports on WW's arm and hand, see WW to EAW, June 11, 13, 21, and 26; July 5, 9, and 23; Aug. 3 and 6, 1896, ibid., pp. 513, 514, 523, 528, 533, 538, 547, 556, 561. Later, when EAW was copying lengthy Hoyt genealogical records, she wrote WW: "I should have writer's cramp in a month if I made a business of it [writing]." (Ibid., Feb. 25, 1897, p. 173.) Stockton Axson referred to WW's problem as "neuritis" (Axson Memoir). For more about this, see Chapter 20, n. 13.

8. EAW to WW, June 1, 1896, *PWW*, 9:508–9.

9. EAW to WW, June 29, 1896, ibid., p. 530.

10. EAW to WW, June 22, 1896, ibid., pp. 524, 525 n. 1.

11. EAW to WW, June 18, 1896, ibid., pp. 520–21.

12. EAW to WW, July 16 and 21, 1896, ibid., pp. 541, 543.

13. Elliott, *My Aunt Louisa and WW*, p. 119; Stockton Axson, "Mr. Wilson As Seen by One of His Family Circle," typed MS, p. 4, RSB Coll.; Baker, *L and L*, 1:317.

14. WW to ELA, Jan. 6, 1885, *PWW*, 3:384; Elliott, *My Aunt Louisa and WW*, p. 127.

15. *Daily Princetonian*, Jan. 15, 1892, Feb. 11 and Mar. 27, 1898.

16. EAW to WW, July 30, 1896, *PWW*, 9:552; see illustrations, ibid., 30: between pp. 298–99.

17. Stockton Axson memorandum to RSB, Sept. 6, 1931, RSB Coll. Ellen's copy of Bouguereau's Madonna was left by Eleanor W. McAdoo to her daughter, Mary Faith McAdoo Bush, who sold it privately after Eleanor's death.

18. McAdoo, *The Woodrow Wilsons*, p. 19.

19. WW to EAW, Aug. 3, 1896, *PWW*, 9:555.

20. WW to EAW, June 29, 1896, ibid., p. 529.

21. WW to Frederick Jackson Turner, Nov. 5, 1896, ibid., 10:41; WW to Waterman Thomas Hewett, Nov. 11, 1896, ibid., p. 49; *A Commemorative Address*, ibid., pp. 11–31, 11–12 n. 1; Axson Memoir; RSB memorandum of interviews with Stockton Axson, Feb. 8, 10, and 11, 1925, RSB Coll.

22. EAW to Mary E. Hoyt, Oct. 27, 1896, *PWW*, 10:37–38.

23. EAW to WW, July 16 and 27, Aug. 6, 1896, ibid., 9:540, 549, 559.

24. Rosalie A. DuBose to EAW, Nov. 8, 1896, Wilson Papers.

25. EAW to Frederick J. Turner, *PWW*, 10:79–80.

26. WW to EAW, Feb. 16, 1897, ibid., p. 164; WW to Frederick J. Turner, Mar. 31, 1897, ibid., p. 201.

27. EAW to WW, Jan. 31, 1897, ibid., pp. 134–35.

28. EAW to WW, Jan. 28, 1897, ibid., p. 122.

29. Ibid., p. 151 n. 2.

30. Wilson's Diary, Jan. 15, 1897, ibid., p. 102.

31. EAW to WW, Feb. 8 and 9, 1897, ibid., pp. 144–45.

32. WW to EAW, Feb. 4 and 5, 1897, ibid., pp. 144, 149.

33. Mulder, *WW: The Years of Preparation*, pp. 132, 148; RSB memorandum of interviews with Stockton Axson, Feb. 8, 10, 11, and 24, 1925, RSB Coll.

34. WW to EAW, Feb. 4, 1897, *PWW*, 10:144.

35. EAW to WW, Feb. 5, 1897, ibid., p. 150.

36. EAW to WW, Feb. 7, 1897, ibid., p. 151; WW to EAW, Feb. 9, 1897, ibid., p. 152.

37. Mulder, *WW: The Years of Preparation*, pp. 112–13.

38. Azel W. Hazen to WW, Apr. 1, 1897, *PWW*, 10:210–11 and n. 1.

39. Frances Folsom (Mrs. Grover) Cleveland moved her letter to the First Presbyterian Church on December 2, 1899, but Grover Cleveland never became a member (First Presbyterian Church, Princeton, N.J., 1909–1924: Accessions by Examination and Letter, Dismissions, Ordinations, Deaths, Suspended, etc., Speer Library, Princeton Theological Seminary.)

40. WW to Edith G. Reid, June 18, 1897, *PWW*, 10:273, 274 n. 4; McAdoo, *The Woodrow Wilsons*, pp. 31–32.

41. *PWW*, 10:310 n. 1; McAdoo, *The Woodrow Wilsons*, pp. 32–33; Lucy Smith to EAW, Jan. 22, 1898, Wilson Papers.

Chapter 15

1. EAW to WW, Aug. 3, 1897, *PWW*, 10:284, 285 n. 9; George Howe III to WW, Aug. 29, 1897, ibid., pp. 313–14, 402 n. 1; Edward W. Axson to JWW, Aug. 22, 1897, family letters in possession of the Very Reverend Francis Bowes Sayre (hereafter cited as FBS Papers).

2. WW, Public Addresses and Lectures, *PWW*, 10:605–6.

3. EAW to John B. Clark, June 8, 1897, ibid., pp. 262–63.

4. EAW to Anna Harris, June 1, 1895, ibid., 9:280; Jan. 31, 1899, ibid., 11:101; WW to EAW, Mar. 2, 1897, ibid., 10:181, 182 n. 1; McAdoo, *The Woodrow Wilsons*, p. 26.

5. McAdoo, *The Woodrow Wilsons*, p. 33–35; Axson, "Woodrow Wilson As Man of Letters," *The Rice Institute Pamphlet*, 22:251.

6. EAW to Anna Harris, Jan. 31, 1899, *PWW*, 11:101, 55–56 n. 2.

7. EAW to Anna Harris, Jan. 31, 1899, ibid., p. 101.

8. EAW to WW, Feb. 3, 4, 8, and 20, 1898, ibid., 10:374, 375, 376, 379–80, 404–5; WW to EAW, Feb. 8, 1898, ibid., p. 380.

9. EAW to WW, Feb. 8, 1898, ibid., p. 382; RSB memorandum of interviews with Stockton Axson, Sept. 4, 5, and 6, 1931, RSB Coll.

10. WW to EAW, Feb. 4 and 6, 1898, *PWW*, 10:374–75, 377.

11. WW to EAW, Feb. 14, 1898, ibid., pp. 392–93.

12. EAW to WW, Feb. 15, 1898, ibid., p. 396.

13. Cornelius C. Cuyler to WW, Apr. 18 and May 16, 1898 (with enclosure), ibid., pp. 520–21, 529–30.

14. Among the honors received by WW between June 1895 and Feb. 1902 were: election to the American Philosophical Society, the Doctor of Laws degree from Johns Hopkins and Tulane, and the Doctor of Literature degree from Yale; offers to become chancellor of the University of Nebraska, and president of the universities of Alabama, Texas, Virginia, and Washington and Lee; *PWW*, 9:285, 499, 500 n. 1, 503; 10:324, 481–83, 522–24, 557; 12:69–70, 71 n. 1, 106–7, 194, 282.

15. Joseph R. Wilson to WW, May 29, 1898, ibid., 10:538.

16. RSB memorandum of inteviews with Lucy and Mary Smith, Mar. 12 and 13, 1927, RSB Coll.; RSB memorandum of interview with Jessie Wilson Sayre, Dec. 1, 1925, ibid.

17. Stockton Axson to EAW, Nov. 29, 1897, Wilson Papers.

18. Ibid.

19. Edward W. Axson to JWW, July 21, 1898, FBS Papers; Edward W. Axson to EAW, Sept. 27, 1898, Wilson Papers.

20. Elliott, *My Aunt Louisa and WW*, p. 175.

21. Stockton Axson to EAW, Jan. 10, 1898, Wilson Papers.

22. Stockton Axson to EAW, Jan. 14 and June 15, 1898, ibid.

23. EAW to WW, June 17, 1898, *PWW*, 10:560.

24. EAW to WW, July 10, 1899, ibid., 11:160, 162 n. 1; Apr. 12, 1901, ibid., 12:131.

25. Rosalie A. DuBose to EAW, May 25, 1898, Wilson Papers.

26. EAE to EAW, Feb. 21 and Mar. 1, 1898; Jan. 18, 1897, ibid.

27. Janie P. Chandler to EAW, Jan. 31, 1898, ibid.

28. Perry, *And Gladly Teach*, pp. 153–55.

29. EAW to Anna Harris, June 1, 1895, *PWW*, 9:280.

30. EAW to WW, Aug. 14, 1899, ibid., 11:229–30.

31. Editorial Note, ibid., pp. 360–64.

32. EAW to WW, July 27, 1899, ibid., p. 193.

33. Ibid., p. 42 n. 2; Patterson, *Personal Recollections of WW*, pp. 26–28.

34. EAW to Anna Harris, Jan. 31, 1899, *PWW*, 11:102 and n. 4.

35. EAW to WW, Mar. 12, 1900, ibid., p. 503; WW to EAW, Aug. 30, 1902, ibid., 14:118 and n. 2.

36. Ibid., 11:117 n. 2; WW to EAW, Aug. 9, 1899, ibid., p. 214; EAW to Louisa H. Brown, June 15, 1899, Wilson Papers.

37. EAW to WW, July 6 and 10, 1899, *PWW*, 11:154, 160.

38. Ibid., p. 141 n. 2.

39. EAW to WW, June 19 and 22, Aug. 14, 1899, ibid., pp. 129, 131, 228.

40. EAW to WW, July 10, 1899, ibid., p. 161.

41. EAW to WW, June 26, July 6, 13, 17, 20, and 24, 1899, ibid., pp. 135, 154, 167, 174, 182, 187–88.

42. EAW to WW, June 26 and July 27, 1899, ibid., pp. 134, 193; Edward W. Axson to EAW, May 31, 1899, Wilson Papers.

43. Edward W. Axson to JWW, Dec. 17, 1899, FBS Papers; Edward W. Axson to EAW, Oct. 27, 1900, Wilson Papers.

44. EAW to WW, July 13, 1899, *PWW*, 11:168.

45. EAW to WW, July 17 and Aug. 7, 1899, ibid., pp. 174, 212.

46. EAW to WW, Aug. 3, 1899, ibid., p. 202.

47. *Miss Fine's School: The Past and the Present*, Princeton Day School Archives.

48. EAW to WW, Nov. 20, 1899, *PWW*, 11:281 and n. 3; Agnes Tedcastle to RSB, Mar. 28, 1925, RSB Coll.

49. Edward W. Axson to EAW, Aug. 12, 1900, Wilson Papers.

50. Ibid.

51. Edward W. Axson to JWW, Dec. 17, 1899, FBS Papers.

52. Patterson, *Personal Recollections of WW*, p. 29; WW to EAW, Feb. 4, 1900, *PWW*, 11:384, 385 nn. 1, 2.

Chapter 16

1. EAW to WW, Feb. 5 and 14, 1900, *PWW*, 11:385, 409.

2. EAW to WW, Feb. 6, 1900, ibid., pp. 389–90.

3. EAW to WW, Feb. 11, 18, and 24, 1900, ibid., pp. 402, 422, 438.

4. EAW to WW, Feb. 16 and 21, 1900, ibid., pp. 414, 429; Axson Family Genealogy, Ben Palmer Axson Papers.

5. EAW to WW, Feb. 6, 10, and 16, 1900, *PWW*, 11:390, 399–400, 414.

6. EAW to WW, Feb. 9, 13, and 16, 1900, ibid., pp. 397, 407, 414.

7. EAW to WW, Feb. 14, 15, and 20, 1900, ibid., pp. 409, 412, 427.

8. WW to EAW, Feb. 8 and 15, 1900, ibid., pp. 395–96, 397 nn. 1, 2, 413.

9. EAW to WW, Feb. 12, 19, and 22, Mar. 4, 1900, ibid., pp. 405–6, 424, 433, 482; WW to EAW, Feb. 8, 18, and 26, 1900, ibid., pp. 396, 423, 447.

10. EAW to WW, Feb. 21, 22, and 27, 1900, ibid., pp. 429, 432, 449.

11. EAW to WW, Mar. 2, 1900, ibid., p. 457.

12. EAW to WW, Mar. 3, 1900, ibid., pp. 480–81.

13. EAW to WW, Mar. 5, 7, 9, and 15, 1900, ibid., pp. 486, 490, 494, 495 n. 3, 514.

14. EAW to WW, Mar. 11, 1900, ibid., pp. 499–500; EAW to WW, Aug. 7, 1900, ibid., p. 213 and n. 3; interview with William D. Hoyt, Aug. 2, 1980.

15. EAW to WW, Mar. 12, 13, and 16, 1900, *PWW*, 11:504, 508, 517.

16. EAW to WW, Feb. 25, 1900, ibid., p. 442.

17. EAW to WW, Mar. 12, 1900, ibid., pp. 503–4.

18. EAW to WW, Mar. 18, 1900, ibid., p. 521, 522 nn. 1, 2.

19. WW to EAW, Mar. 17 and 25, 1900, ibid., pp. 519, 526.

20. Harper and Brothers to WW, Feb. 16, 1900, ibid., pp. 416–20.

21. William B. Pritchard to WW, Apr. 30 and June 29, 1900, ibid., pp. 539, 553;

WW to William B. Pritchard, July 5, 1900, ibid., pp. 553–54.

22. WW to Edward G. Elliott, Aug. 3, 1900, ibid., p. 565; McAdoo, *The Woodrow Wilsons*, p. 83 (Mrs. McAdoo was confused about the dates); A Memorandum, Aug. 29, 1900, *PWW*, 11:572; Thomas L. Snow to WW, Dec. 14, 1900, *PWW*, 12:49–50 and nn. 1, 2.

23. WW to the President and Board of Trustees of Princeton University, Oct. 19, 1900, *PWW*, 12:27–28; *Daily Princetonian*, Dec. 17, 1900.

24. WW to Edward G. Elliott, Sept. 17, 1900, *PWW*, 12:3 and nn. 2, 3; Annie W. Howe to WW, June 2, 1901, ibid., p. 148.

25. James Sprunt to WW, Jan. 12, 1901, ibid., p. 72 and n. 2; WW to EAW, Jan. 18, 1901, ibid., p. 74; EAW to WW, Jan. 18, 1901, ibid., p. 76; WW to Robert R. Henderson, May 20, 1901, ibid., p. 144.

26. Elliott, *My Aunt Louisa and WW*, p. 122.

27. Joseph R. Wilson to JWW, Aug. 9, 1899, FBS Papers.

28. McAdoo, *The Woodrow Wilsons*, p. 68.

29. Stockton Axson to WW, Apr. 2, 1901, *PWW*, 12:117–18 and n. 1; EAW to WW, Apr. 9, 1901, ibid., p. 126.

30. EAW to Thomas L. Snow, May 27, 1901, ibid., pp. 146–47 and n. 2.

31. Ella Law Axson died July 18, 1901, and Randolph Axson on May 9, 1902, both in Savannah.

32. WW to John F. Jameson, Feb. 21, 1900, ibid., 11:431; Princeton City Directory, 1901, Princeton University Library.

33. WW to Albert B. Hart, *PWW*, 12:232 and n. 1.

Chapter 17

1. From the Minutes of the Board of Trustees of Princeton University, June 9, 1902, *PWW*, 12:401.

2. Editorial Note, The Crisis in Presidential Leadership at Princeton, ibid., pp. 289–93.

3. WW to Jenny Davidson Hibben, June 26, 1899, ibid., 11:136.

4. WW to EAW, June 1, 1902, ibid., 12:390, 391 n. 1.

5. *Princeton Alumni Weekly*, 2 (May 31, 1902); WW to EAW, June 1, 1902, *PWW*, 12:390–91.

6. EAW to Florence S. Hoyt, June 28, 1902, *PWW*, 12:464; Link, *The Road to the White House*, p. 37.

7. Elliott, *My Aunt Louisa and WW*, p. 166.

8. McAdoo, *The Woodrow Wilsons*, p. 59.

9. Stockton Axson memorandum to RSB, Sept. 6, 1931, RSB Coll.

10. McAdoo, *The Woodrow Wilsons*, p. 59.

11. Elliott, *My Aunt Louisa and WW*, p. 155.

12. WW to EAW, Aug. 10, 1902, *PWW*, 14:70.

13. EAW to Florence S. Hoyt, June 28, 1902, ibid., 12:463–64.

14. Jenny D. Hibben to EAW, c. June 10, 1902, ibid., p. 407.

15. Annie L. Perry to EAW, June 10, 1902, ibid., pp. 405–6.

16. EAW to Mary ("Mamie") Adams Erwin, Aug. 7, 1902, Margaret Brady

Lovejoy Family Papers. (This letter is now in the Wilson Coll.)

17. EAW to WW, July 12, 1902, *PWW*, 14:4, 5 n. 1.

18. Ibid., p. 4.

19. WW to EAW, July 19, 1902, ibid., p. 27.

20. EAW to WW, ibid., p. 53.

21. Mary E. Hoyt, "Jessie Wilson Sayre," p. 14, FBS Papers; WW to EAW, July 13, 1902, *PWW*, 14:6, 7 n. 4; EAW to WW, Aug. 3, 1902, ibid., p. 50 and n. 1.

22. Hageman, *History of Princeton and Its Institutions*, 2:245; Leitch, *A Princeton Companion*, pp. 187, 393–94.

23. Elliott, *My Aunt Louisa and WW*, pp. 177–78; Potter family genealogy, in possession of Verna (Mrs. John P. C.) Matthews.

24. EAW to WW, July 17, 1902, *PWW*, 14:23.

25. WW to EAW, July 14, 1902, ibid., pp. 7 n. 7, 9; Elliott, *My Aunt Louisa and WW*, p. 179.

26. McAdoo, *The Woodrow Wilsons*, p. 62.

27. EAW to WW, Aug. 25, 1902, *PWW*, 14:107.

28. EAW to WW, Aug. 3, 5, and 25, 1902, ibid., pp. 49, 50 nn. 2, 3, 55–56, 107; see also Report to the President and Board of Trustees, Oct. 20, 1902, ibid., p. 150. This was the last major renovation of Prospect until 1957 (Records, MacMillan Building, Princeton University).

29. From a copy of John Notman's floor plans, Princeton University Archives and Records, MacMillan Building, Princeton University; McAdoo, *The Woodrow Wilsons*, pp. 62–65; Elliott, *My Aunt Louisa and WW*, p. 180. Prospect was converted to a faculty-staff facility in 1969, but its basic floor plan was unaltered except for a glass-enclosed dining ell extending from the rear at the southeast corner.

30. The Wilsons' house on Library Place sold on Sept. 5, 1902, to Robert Garrett, Class of 1897, who with his mother, Mrs. T. Harrison Garrett, and his brother, John, all of Baltimore, planned to use it as a Princeton home. The Garretts sold in Jan. 1908 to Mrs. Alexander Maitland, a widowed daughter of James McCosh. With the exception of Woodrow's study, Mrs. Maitland extended the first floor for six feet at the back. On December 27, 1919, Henrietta G. Ricketts became the next owner who, at her death in May 1950, willed the property to the trustees of Princeton University. A rental property for the next six years, the house was then purchased successively by John W. and Lucia H. Ballantine (Aug. 30, 1956), John A. and Margaret B. Stephenson (Apr. 5, 1972), Sherwood and Garnette Ross (Oct. 9, 1975), and Patricia J. Kassling (Jan. 30, 1981). See *PWW*, 14:123, 147; EAW to JWW, FBS Papers; records, Borough Hall, Princeton, and Mercer Co. Court House, Trenton, N.J.

31. McAdoo, *The Woodrow Wilsons*, pp. 67–68.

32. Inauguration of President Woodrow Wilson, order of Academic Procession, Oct. 25, 1902. Correspondence in regard to WW's inauguration and, in particular, letters from Edith F. S. Westcott, Rosalie A. DuBose, Agnes V. Tedcastle, and Lucy and Mary Smith to Charles W. McAlpin (Princeton University Archives); Minutes of the Faculty of Bryn Mawr College, Oct. 13, 1902

(Bryn Mawr College Library); Bryn Mawr Catalog, 1902; News Report of Wilson's Inaugural, Nov. 1, 1902, *PWW*, 14:191–93. The women educators were Dean Laura Drake Gill, Barnard; Dean Agnes Irwin, Radcliffe; President Mary E. Woolley, Mount Holyoke; and Professor Alice V. Brown, Wellesley.

33. News Report, *PWW*, 14:194–95; RSB memorandum of a conversation with Jessie Wilson Sayre, Dec. 1, 1925, RSB Coll. The gown Ellen wore at the inaugural reception at Prospect, now on display at the Woodrow Wilson birthplace, Staunton, Virginia, is one that she designed and made, according to the birthplace records.

34. Stockton Axson to WW, Oct. 27, 1902, *PWW*, 14:187–88.

35. The Finance Committee's Report to the Board of Trustees of Princeton University, Oct. 14, 1902, ibid., pp. 144, 439 n. 3.

36. WW to EAW, July 18, 1902, ibid., p. 24.

37. McAdoo, *The Woodrow Wilsons*, p. 65.

38. Mary E. Hoyt, "Jessie Wilson Sayre," p. 41, FBS Papers.

39. Rich, "Prospect: The Search for a Garden," *The Princeton University Library Chronicle*, 42:9–15; McAdoo, *The Woodrow Wilsons*, pp. 65–66; Elliott, *My Aunt Louisa and WW*, p. 220; Mabel Potter Daggett, "Woodrow Wilson's Wife," *Good Housekeeping*, 56:321; Sherwin Hawley, "The Wilson Garden at Princeton, N.J.," *Country Life in America*, 24:44–45.

40. WW to EAW, May 9, 1904, *PWW*, 15:317.

41. EAW to Mary E. Hoyt, Dec. 15, 1902, ibid., 14:293–94.

42. Ibid., p. 294.

43. McAdoo, *The Woodrow Wilsons*, p. 68.

44. A News Item, Jan. 24, 1903, *PWW*, 14:330; A News Report, Jan. 24, 1903, ibid., p. 331.

45. WW to Robert Bridges, Mar. 30, 1903, ibid., p. 403.

46. EAW to WW, Apr. 22, 1903, ibid., p. 422.

47. EAW to WW, Apr. 23 and 30, 1903, ibid., pp. 424, 438.

48. EAW to WW, Apr. 23, 1903, ibid., pp. 423–24; WW to Stockton Axson, June 28, 1903, ibid., pp. 498–99 and n. 1.

49. Edward W. Axson to JWW, June 6, 1903, FBS Papers.

Chapter 18

1. WW to EAW, Apr. 22, 1903, *PWW*, 14:422.

2. EAW to John B. Van Meter, July 3, 23, and Nov. 5, 1902, Mar. 30 and Apr. 8, 1903, Goucher College alumnae records.

3. EAW to JWW, July 6, 1903, FBS Papers.

4. Mary E. Hoyt, "Jessie Wilson Sayre," p. 10, ibid.

5. Margaret R. Axson to John B. Van Meter, July 21, 1903, Goucher College alumnae records.

6. Record of a European Trip, July 10–Sept. 22, 1903, *PWW*, 14:521–30.

7. EAW to JWW, Aug. 9, 1903, FBS Papers; Malcolm Cormack, *A Catalogue of Drawings and Watercolours in the Fitzwilliam Museum*, p. vii.

8. Record of a European Trip, *PWW*, 14:530–34.

9. EAW to JWW, Aug. 30, 1903, FBS Papers.

10. Record of a European Trip, *PWW*, 14:535–43.

11. A News Item, ibid., 15:4; EAW to WW, Sept. 29, 1903, ibid., pp. 7–8.

12. *Princeton Alumni Weekly*, 4:6–7.

13. Link, *The Road to the White House*, p. 39.

14. Ibid., pp. 39, 41; WW to the Board of Trustees, Oct. 21, 1902, *PWW*, 14:150–61. Wilson made an error of five hundred dollars in adding the total sum in his report to the trustees, ibid., pp. 156, 160.

15. WW to EAW, Mar. 20, 1892, *PWW*, 7:500; Sept. 30, 1903, ibid., 15:9.

16. McAdoo, *The Woodrow Wilsons*, p. 71.

17. Ibid., pp. 69–70, 75–76; *PWW*, 15:112 n. 1; Elliott, *My Aunt Louisa and WW*, p. 187.

18. EAW to Agnes Tedcastle, Feb. 16, 1904, Wilson Papers.

19. Family Collection, W. D. Hoyt.

20. Wilson's Diary, Jan. 7 and 8, 1904, *PWW*, 15:119–20.

21. EAW to Agnes Tedcastle, Feb. 16, 1904, Wilson Papers.

22. WW to EAW, Sept. 30, 1903, *PWW*, 15:9.

23. Mary E. Hoyt, "Jessie Wilson Sayre," p. 16, FBS Papers; Elliott, *My Aunt Louisa and WW*, pp. 204–5.

24. WW to EAW, Mar. 21, 1904, *PWW*, 15:201, 202 n. 1; WW to EAW, Apr. 17, 1904, ibid., p. 264.

25. EAW to WW, Mar. 26, 1904, ibid., pp. 208–12.

26. Ibid., p. 211.

27. EAW to WW, Apr. 3, 1904, ibid., p. 229.

28. EAW to WW, Apr. 7, 1904, ibid., pp. 235–36.

29. EAW to WW, Apr. 24, 1904, ibid., p. 275.

30. EAW to WW, Apr. 10, 1904, ibid., p. 241.

31. Ibid.

32. EAW to WW, Apr. 15, 1904, ibid., pp. 250–51.

33. EAW to WW, Apr. 10 and 15, 1904, ibid., pp. 241, 250.

34. WW to EAW, Apr. 4, 12, and 17, 1904, ibid., pp. 231, 243, 264.

35. WW to EAW, Apr. 26, 1904, ibid., p. 296.

36. EAW to WW, May 11, 1904, ibid., p. 323.

37. EAW to WW, Apr. 17, 1904, ibid., pp. 266–67.

38. EAW to WW, Apr. 20, 1904, ibid., p. 269; May Margaret Fine to JWW, Mar. 18, 1904, FBS Papers.

39. EAW to WW, Apr. 26, 1904, *PWW*, 15:298.

40. EAW to WW, Apr. 10 and 15, 1904, ibid., pp. 241, 250.

41. EAW to WW, Apr. 26, 1904, ibid., p. 298.

42. EAW to WW, May 1, 1904, ibid., pp. 302–4.

43. EAW to WW, May 4, 1904, ibid., p. 308; WW to EAW, May 3, 1904, ibid., p. 306.

44. EAW to WW, May 4, 1904, ibid., p. 308.

45. EAW to WW, May 1, 1904, ibid., p. 304.

46. William Bull to EAW, May 5, 1904, ibid., p. 316.

47. EAW to WW, May 7, 1904, ibid., p. 313.

48. EAW to WW, May 11, 1904, ibid., p. 320.

49. EAW to WW, May 4, 1904, ibid., p. 310.

50. WW to EAW, May 16, 1904, ibid., pp. 335–36.

51. WW to EAW, May 29, 1904, ibid., p. 341.

52. EAW to WW, May 15 and 18, 1904, ibid., pp. 334, 338.

53. WW to EAW, May 23, 1904, ibid., p. 344; EAW to WW, May 23, 1904, ibid., pp. 346–47.

54. EAW to WW, May 25, 1904, ibid., pp. 348–49.

55. EAW to WW, May 29, 1904, ibid., pp. 353, 354.

56. EAW to WW, June 5, 1904, ibid., pp. 358–59.

57. EAW to WW, May 29, 1904, ibid., p. 354.

58. EAW to WW, June 5, 1904, ibid., pp. 357–58.

59. Ibid., p. 358.

Chapter 19

1. WW to Robert Bridges, June 16, 1904, *PWW*, 15:383; A News Item, June 18, 1904, ibid., p. 391; WW to Frank Thilly, Aug. 12, 1904, ibid., p. 440.

2. Edward W. Axson to JWW, June 6 and Aug. 9, 1903, FBS Papers.

3. Edward W. Axson to JWW, Aug. 9 and 28, 1903, ibid.; EAW to Agnes Tedcastle, Feb. 16, 1904, Wilson Papers.

4. McAdoo, *The Woodrow Wilsons*, p. 78; Leitch, *A Princeton Companion*, p. 394; *Daily Princetonian*, Oct. 3, 1904.

5. EAW to JWW, Nov. 4, 1904, FBS Papers.

6. Patterson, *Personal Recollections of Woodrow Wilson*, pp. 30, 31; EAW to JWW, Nov. 4, 1904, FBS Papers.

7. EAW to Adele Williams, c. Dec. 16, 1905, Adele Williams Papers, in possession of Catherine Williams Bayliss, Richmond, Va.

8. EAW to Leila Axson, Mar. 15, 1904, Archives, Independent Presbyterian Church, Savannah; McAdoo, *The Woodrow Wilsons*, p. 63. The portrait of I. S. K. Axson now hangs in the home of Ben Palmer Axson, Jr., to whom it was sent in 1948 by Margaret Axson Elliott.

9. ERW to MWW and JWW, Oct. 23, 1904, FBS Papers.

10. EAW to JWW, Nov. 4, 1904, ibid.

11. EAW to JWW, Nov. 19, 1904, ibid.

12. EAW to JWW, Oct. 17, 1904, ibid.

13. EAW to Anna Harris, Mar. 11, 1905, *PWW*, 16:28, 29 n. 3.

14. McAdoo, *The Woodrow Wilsons*, p. 84; *Princeton Alumni Weekly*, 5:317; EAW to Anna Harris, Mar. 11, 1905, *PWW*, 16:29.

15. ERW to MWW and JWW, Dec. 7, 1904, FBS Papers.

16. EAW to Anna Harris, Mar. 11, 1905, *PWW*, 16:29; McAdoo, *The Woodrow Wilsons*, p. 84.

17. *Princeton Alumni Weekly*, 5:333–35; Link, *The Road to the White House*, p. 41; "The Committee of Fifty of Princeton University," c. Feb. 18, 1905, *PWW*, 16:3–5.

18. ERW to MWW and JWW, Apr. 2, 1905, FBS Papers.

19. EAW to Anna Harris, Feb. 12, 1907, *PWW*, 17:34.

20. WW, Public Addresses and Lectures, ibid., 16:595–96.

21. WW to Robert Bridges, Apr. 28, 1905, ibid., p. 86 and n. 1; *Princeton Alumni Weekly*, 5:510; RSB memorandum of conversations with Stockton Axson, Feb. 8, 10, and 11, 1925, RSB Coll.

22. Diary of Mary Celestine Mitchell Brown, Apr. 26 and 27, 1905, Marjorie Brown King Papers; *Princeton Alumni Weekly*, 5:510.

23. EAW to Anna Harris, Feb. 12, 1907, *PWW*, 17:34.

24. Elliott, *My Aunt Louisa and WW*, p. 209.

25. McAdoo, *The Priceless Gift*, p. 240; McAdoo, *The Woodrow Wilsons*, p. 87; Stockton Axson, "Mr. Wilson as Seen by One of His Family Circle," p. 3; ERW to MWW and JWW, May 15, 1905, FBS Papers.

26. EAW to JWW, May 19, 1905, FBS Papers.

27. John G. Hibben to WW, July 14, 1905, *PWW*, 16:155; Jenny D. Hibben to WW, July 19 and Aug. 15, 1905, ibid., pp. 158, 180.

28. Florence S. Hoyt to WW, Sept. 14, 1914, ibid., 31:29.

29. John G. Hibben to WW, July 14, 1905, ibid., 16:155.

30. WW to Williamson U. Vreeland, July 10, 1905, ibid., pp. 154 n. 1, 155.

31. Jenny D. Hibben to WW, July 19, 1905, ibid., p. 158.

32. Stockton Axson stated that after the summer in Lyme in 1905, Ellen's "health was soon restored," Axson Memoir; EAW to Louisa H. Brown, Nov. 8, 1905, Wilson Coll.

33. Elliott, *My Aunt Louisa and WW*, pp. 209–10.

34. EAW to Louisa H. Brown, Nov. 8, 1905, Wilson Coll.

35. Martha Berry to WW, Nov. 19, 1914, Wilson Papers; *New York Times*, Jan. 25, 1914, Sec. 3, p. 3.

36. RSB memorandum of conversations with Stockton Axson, Sept. 4, 5, and 6, 1931, p. 2, RSB Coll.; McAdoo, *The Woodrow Wilsons*, p. 41; Florence S. Hoyt to WW, Sept. 12, 1914, *PWW*, 31:28.

37. McAdoo, *The Priceless Gift*, p. 240.

38. EAW to Florence S. Hoyt, May 22, 1905, Wilson Papers.

Chapter 20

1. EAW to John B. Van Meter, Feb. 25, 1905, Goucher College alumnae records.

2. EAW to John B. Van Meter, May 4, 1905, ibid.

3. Carolynn Q. McIlnay, Registrar, Peabody Conservatory of Music, to author, Apr. 13, 1981.

4. MWW to JWW, Aug. 1 and Sept. 18, 1905, FBS Papers.

5. EAW to John B. Van Meter, Oct. 13, 1905, Goucher College alumnae records.

6. EAW to Anna Harris, Feb. 12, 1907, *PWW*, 17:34.

7. WW to Arthur W. Tedcastle, Apr. 10, 1906, ibid., 16:357.

8. WW to Frederic and Emily Chapman Yates, Nov. 6, 1906, ibid., p. 482; EAW to JWW, Oct. 28, 1906, FBS Papers.

9. WW to Theodore Roosevelt, Aug. 8, 1905, *PWW*, 16:172–73.

10. Elliott, *My Aunt Louisa and WW*, p. 221.

11. Ibid., pp. 221–23.

12. WW, Public Addresses and Lectures, *PWW*, 16:596–97.

13. The suggestion that this incident was another in a series of strokes that WW experienced prior to his major stroke in Oct. 1919 was first offered by Weinstein (Weinstein, "WW's Neurological Illnesses," *JAH*, 57:334–37). Weinstein has since expanded his treatment of the idea (Weinstein, *WW: A Medical and Psychological Biography*, pp. 18, 127, 141–48, 158–61, 164, 165, 216). The editors of *PWW*, in annotating their material, express agreement with Weinstein's diagnoses. (*PWW*, 9:507 n. 2; ibid., 10:3 n. 3; ibid., 11:137 n. 2, 601; ibid., 16:412 n. 1; ibid., 17:550 n. 1, 643; ibid., 18:345 n. 3, 669; ibid., 19:193 n. 6, 781.) However, this interpretation of the medical evidence has become the subject of a vigorous discussion in the literature. (See, e.g., Weinstein, Anderson, and Link, "WW's Political Personality: A Reappraisal," *Political Science Quarterly*, 93:585–98; George and George, "WW and Colonal House: A Reply to Weinstein, Anderson and Link," *Political Science Quarterly*, 96:641–65; Marmor, "Wilson, Strokes, and Zebras," *New England Journal of Medicine*, 307:528–35; Post, "WW Re-examined: The Mind-Body Controversy Redux and Other Disputations," *Political Psychology*, 4:289–306; George and George, "Comments on 'WW Re-examined: The Mind-Body Controversy Redux and Other Disputations,'" *Political Psychology*, 4:307–12; Weinstein, "Comments on 'WW Re-examined: The Mind-Body Controversy Redux and Other Disputations,'" *Political Psychology*, 4:313–24; Marmor, "Comments on 'WW Re-examined: The Mind-Body Controversy Redux and Other Disputations,'" *Political Psychology*, 4:325–27; Post, "Reply to the Three Comments on 'WW Re-examined: The Mind-Body Controversy Redux and Other Disputations,'" *Political Psychology*, 4:329–331; George, Marmor, and George, "Issues in Wilson Scholarship: References to Early 'Strokes' in the *Papers of WW*," *JAH*, 70:845–53; Link et al., letter to the editor in "Communications," *JAH*, 70:945–55; and George, Marmor, and George, letter to the editor in "Communications," *JAH*, 71:198–212.)

14. EAW to Mary E. Hoyt, June 12, 1906, *PWW*, 16:423–24. The "seven women" were Madge, Margaret, Jessie, Nell, Ellen, Annie Howe, and Annie's daughter.

15. WW to the Class of 1906, June 10, 1906, ibid., p. 420 and n. 1.

16. Ibid., p. 412 n. 1.

17. EAW to Florence S. Hoyt, June 27, 1906, ibid., pp. 429–30.

18. McAdoo, *The Woodrow Wilsons*, pp. 94–95; *PWW*, 16:437 n. 1; WW to Annie W. Howe, Aug. 2, 1906, *PWW*, 16:432.

19. WW to EAW, Aug. 23, 1906, *PWW*, 16:437, 438 n. 1; EAW to William Macbeth, Mar. 16, 1907, Macbeth Gallery Papers, Archives of American Art (hereafter cited as Macbeth Papers). The Yates portrait now hangs in Whig Hall on the campus of Princeton University.

20. McAdoo, *The Priceless Gift*, pp. 241–42. Signed in 1906 by Yates near EAW's left shoulder, the portrait shows, on the lower left, a second signature by

Yates dated "1911." In December 1910, EAW invited Yates, then in the USA to paint portraits of the Vanderlip family in New York, to spend Christmas at Prospect. (*PWW*, 22:187 n. 2; EAW to Frederic Yates, Dec. 20, 1910, ibid., p. 234.) During that visit, Yates could have added the second signature and date, possibly because he may have touched up EAW's portrait. On the lower right, there appears the notation, "Sidney Lanier," in WW's handwriting, which WW must have added at a later date when he incorrectly attributed to Lanier the inspiration for EAW's "lovely expression" that, in fact, came as a result of WW's reading to her from Robert Browning's "Saul." Just below the "Sidney" there appears Yates's drawing of Saul hanging from his cross as described by EWM (McAdoo, *The Woodrow Wilsons*, p. 95). The original portrait can be seen in the WW House, 2340 S Street, N.W., Washington, D.C.

21. WW to Annie W. Howe, Aug. 2, 1906, *PWW*, 16:432.

22. WW to EAW, Aug. 22, 24, 25, and 31, 1906, ibid., pp. 436, 438, 439, 444, 445 n. 3. EAW's letters to WW written during this side-trip have not been found.

23. WW to EAW, Sept. 1 and 2, 1906, ibid., pp. 445, 445–46.

24. WW to Cleveland H. Dodge, Sept. 16, 1906, ibid., p. 453.

25. WW to Frederic and Emily C. Yates, Nov. 6, 1906, ibid., p. 481; Margaret R. Axson to JWW, July 5 and 30, Aug. 26, Sept. 12 and 27, 1906, FBS Papers.

26. McNeely DuBose, who served as rector of St. Mary's School from 1903 through 1907, returned to the pastorate as rector of Grace Episcopal Church, Morganton, North Carolina.

27. ERW to JWW, Oct. 26, 1906, FBS Papers; MWW to JWW, c. mid-Oct. 1906, ibid.

28. ERW to JWW, Oct. 21 and 26, 1906, ibid.

29. EAW to JWW, Nov. 11, 1906, ibid.

30. McAdoo, *The Woodrow Wilsons*, p. 150; Agnes Tedcastle to RSB, Mar. 28, 1925, RSB Coll.; Goucher College alumnae records, 1905–1908; Mary E. Hoyt, "Jessie Wilson Sayre," pp. 11, 21, FBS Papers; Academic Report of JWW, 1905–1906, ibid.; MWW to JWW, c. Nov. 3, 1906, ibid.

31. EAW to JWW, Nov. 4 and Dec. 17, 1906, FBS Papers; ERW to JWW, Dec. 4, 1906, ibid.; MWW to JWW, Dec. 10, 1906, ibid.; Mary E. Hoyt, "Jessie Wilson Sayre," p. 21, ibid.

32. McAdoo, *The Woodrow Wilsons*, p. 95; Helen Bones to Jessie Bones Brower, c. May 3, 1913, *PWW*, 29:558; WW to MAH, May 10, 1914, *PWW*, 30:12–13.

33. WW to Frederic and Emily C. Yates, Nov. 6, 1906, *PWW*, 16:482; EAW to JWW, Nov. 2, 1906, FBS Papers; Carolynn Q. McIlnay, Registrar, Peabody Conservatory of Music, to author, Apr. 20, 1981.

34. EAW to JWW, Oct. 28, 1906; MWW to JWW, c. mid-Oct. 1906, FBS Papers. Margaret's beaux, G. D. Kellogg and Herring Winship, had apartments at 10 Nassau Street.

35. Mulder, *WW: The Years of Preparation*, pp. 112–13; minutes of the session of the Second Presbyterian Church of Princeton, N.J., Nov. 25, 1905, Speer

Library, Princeton Theological Seminary.

36. EAW to JWW, Oct. 28, 1906, FBS Papers; MWW to JWW, Oct. 29, 1906, ibid.

37. EAW to JWW, Nov. 11, 1906, ibid.

38. A News Report, Dec. 8, 1906, *PWW*, 16:497–503; Leitch, *A Princeton Companion*, p. 82.

39. MWW to JWW, Dec. 10, 1906, FBS Papers.

40. EAW to JWW, Nov. 11, 1906, ibid.

41. The peregrinations of William Dearing Hoyt, M.D., are in the Family Collection of W. Dana Hoyt.

42. EAW to JWW, Dec. 12 and 17, 1906, FBS Papers.

43. EAW to JWW, Dec. 12, 1906, ibid.

44. EAW to Anna Harris, Feb. 12, 1907, *PWW*, 17:33; McAdoo, *The Woodrow Wilsons*, pp. 91–92.

45. EAW to JWW, Jan. 28, 1907, FBS Papers.

46. WW to Moses T. Pyne, Jan. 10, 1907, *PWW*, 16:553–54.

Chapter 21

1. EAW to JWW, Feb. 3, 1907, FBS Papers.

2. WW to EAW, Jan. 27, 1907, *PWW*, 17:22; From the Diary of William Starr Myers, Feb. 12, 1907, ibid., p. 35.

3. MWW to JWW, c. Jan. 19, 1907, FBS Papers.

4. MWW to JWW, c. Feb. 4, 1907, ibid.

5. *PWW*, 11:200 n. 1; Elliott, *My Aunt Louisa and WW*, pp. 105–6.

6. MWW to JWW, c. May 21, 1907, FBS Papers.

7. EAW to JWW, Feb. 20, 1907, ibid.

8. EAW to JWW, Feb. 18, 1907, ibid.

9. EAW to JWW, Feb. 18, 1907, ibid.; MWW to JWW, Mar. 4, 1907, ibid.

10. EAW to JWW, Apr. 12 and 29, 1907, ibid.; MWW to JWW, Apr. 22, 1907, ibid.

11. EAW to William Macbeth, Mar. 16, 1907, Macbeth Papers. There is no record of a Yates exhibit having been held at the Macbeth Gallery.

12. EAW to JWW, Jan. 28, 1907, ibid.

13. From Woodrow Wilson's Diary, Jan. 25, 1904, *PWW*, 15:140 and n. 1; EAW to WW, May 11, 1904, ibid., p. 321.

14. EAW to Anna Harris, May 5, 1907, ibid., 17:137; EAW to Ben Palmer Axson, May 25, 1907, Georgia Historical Society, Savannah.

15. EAW to JWW, May 25, 1907, FBS Papers; Elliott, *My Aunt Louisa and WW*, pp. 188–89.

16. EAW to JWW, May 27, 1907, FBS Papers; McAdoo, *The Woodrow Wilsons*, p. 63. Cleveland H. Dodge to WW, Dec. 19, 1906, *PWW*, 16:534–35. The window was removed and placed in storage in 1933 when Harold Willis Dodds, fifteenth president of Princeton University, moved into Prospect. Allegedly sold to an antiques dealer, the window is now the property of the owner of a restaurant, "Charley's Other Brother," in Mount Holly, N.J. Wickham and

Stone also designed three Tiffany memorial windows for the chapel of St. Mary's College in Raleigh, N.C. (*St. Mary's Muse*, 11[3]:19, 11[6]:9, 16). The memorial window to Gertrude Sullivan is the only one of the three which is signed by Stone and Wickham.

Chapter 22

1. Link, *The Road to the White House*, p. 43.

2. A Supplementary Report to the Board of Trustees of Princeton University, c. Dec. 13, 1906, *PWW*, 16:519, 523.

3. Ibid., pp. 519–25.

4. A Report to the Board of Trustees of Princeton University, c. June 6, 1907, ibid., 17:185.

5. Editorial Note, ibid., 12:291.

6. Andrew F. West to the Board of Trustees' Committee on the Graduate School, May 13, 1907, ibid., 17:142–46, 142 n. 1; William M. Sloane et al. to the Board of Trustees of Princeton University, Oct. 15, 1906, ibid., 16:458; A Resolution, c. Oct. 20, 1906, ibid., p. 467.

7. To the Board of Trustees' Committee on the Graduate School, ibid., 17:164–68.

8. For a fuller discussion of the quadrangle and the graduate school controversies, see Link, *The Road to the White House*, pp. 45–90; however, Link has since qualified his treatment of the West-Wilson controversy (Weinstein et al., "Woodrow Wilson's Political Personality: A Reappraisal," *Political Science Quarterly*, 93:596 n. 30).

9. EAW to JWW, Apr. 12, 1907, FBS Papers.

10. EAW to JWW, Jan. 28, 1907, ibid.

11. WW to Andrew C. Imbrie, July 10, 1907, *PWW*, 17:270.

12. John G. Hibben to WW, July 8, 1907, ibid., pp. 263–64.

13. WW to John G. Hibben, July 10, 1907, ibid., pp. 268–69.

14. Interview with Eleanor Marquand Delanoy, Feb. 20, 1981; Elliott, *My Aunt Louisa and WW*, pp. 225–32.

15. Elliott, *My Aunt Louisa and WW*, pp. 228–31; John G. Hibben to EAW, Sept. 4, 1907, *PWW*, 17:372.

16. RSB memorandum of a talk with Stockton Axson, Mar. 15 and 16, 1927, RSB Coll.

17. EAW to JWW, Sept. 27, 1907, FBS Papers; ERW to JWW, Sept. 28, 1907, ibid.; McAdoo, *The Woodrow Wilsons*, p. 99.

18. From the Minutes of the Princeton University Faculty, Sept. 26, 1907, *PWW*, 17:402; excerpt from the Diary of William Starr Myers, Sept. 26, 1907, ibid., p. 403.

19. EAW to JWW, Sept. 27 and Oct. 3, 1907, FBS Papers.

20. From the Minutes of the Board of Trustees of Princeton University, Oct. 17, 1907, *PWW*, 17:441–42.

21. EAW to JWW, Oct. 19, 1907, FBS Papers.

22. WW to Melancthon W. Jacobus, Oct. 23, 1907, *PWW*, 17:451.

23. RSB memorandum of a talk with Stockton Axson, Mar. 15 and 16, 1927, RSB Coll.; Stockton Axson memorandum to RSB, Sept. 6, 1931, ibid.; Stockton Axson memorandum to RSB, Aug. 27, 1928, ibid.; Winthrop M. Daniels to John G. Hibben, Aug. 9, 1907, *PWW*, 17:342–43.

24. EAW to JWW, Oct. 19, 1907, FBS Papers.

25. WW to JWW, Sept. 26, 1907, ibid.

26. EAW to JWW, May 3, 1908, ibid.; Mary E. Hoyt, "Jessie Wilson Sayre," p. 22, ibid.

27. MWW to JWW, Nov. 16, 1907, ibid.

28. EAW to JWW, Nov. 16, 1907, ibid.

29. Stockton Axson to JWW, Nov. 9 and 13, 1907, ibid.

30. EAW to JWW, Nov. 16, 1907, ibid.

31. EAW to Agnes Tedcastle, Dec. 12, 1907, Wilson Papers.

32. EAW to JWW, Dec. 14, 1907, FBS Papers. The editors of *PWW* state that Wilson had "unquestionably" suffered a slight stroke (*PWW*, 17:550 n. 1).

33. From the Minutes of the Board of Trustees of Princeton University, Jan. 9, 1908, *PWW*, 17:595.

34. EAW to JWW, Jan. 14, 1908, FBS Papers.

35. EAW to JWW, Jan. 19, 1908, ibid.

36. EAW to JWW, Jan. 14, 1908, ibid.

37. ERW to EAW, Jan. 6, 1908, Wilson-McAdoo Coll.

38. EAW to Agnes Tedcastle, Dec. 12, 1907, Wilson Papers; EAW to JWW, Jan. 19, 1908, FBS Papers.

39. EAW to Mary C. M. Brown, Feb. 20, 1908, from Marjorie B. King. Ellen sometimes spelled the nickname for Mary C. Brown, "Meemee," "Maymee," or "Mimi."

Chapter 23

1. WW to EAW, Jan. 30, 1907, *PWW*, 17:26.

2. Hulbert, *The Story of Mrs. Peck*, p. 158.

3. WW to MAHP, Feb. 6, 1907, *PWW*, 17:29.

4. WW to EAW, Jan. 26, 1908, ibid., p. 607.

5. Ibid., p. 29 n. 1; ibid., 20:127 n. 2; Hulbert, *The Story of Mrs. Peck*, pp. 13–125; MAHP to WW, Feb. 10, 1910, *PWW*, 20:118.

6. WW to EAW, Jan. 26, 1908, ibid., 17:608.

7. WW to EAW, Feb. 4, 1908, ibid., p. 612.

8. A Salutation, c. Feb. 1, 1908, ibid., p. 611.

9. EAW to JWW, Mar. 14, 1908, FBS Papers.

10. Henry B. Thompson et al. to the Board of Trustees of Princeton University, Apr. 8, 1908, *PWW*, 18:236–41; Link, *The Road to the White House*, p. 57.

11. ERW to EAW, Apr. 29, 1908, Wilson-McAdoo Coll.; EAW to JWW, Apr. 25, 1908, FBS Papers.

12. EAW to JWW, May 6, 1908, ibid.

13. ERW to EAW, May 15, 1908, Wilson-McAdoo Coll.; ERW to JWW, May 22, 1908, FBS Papers.

14. EAW to B. M. King, Mar. 13, 1912, Wilson Coll.

15. *The St. Mary's Muse: The Yearbook of the Students of St. Mary's School, Raleigh, N.C.,* 10 (1907–8): 91.

16. A News Report of a Commencement Address to the Woman's College of Baltimore, June 4, 1908, *PWW*, 18:320.

17. A News Report, June 10, 1908, ibid., p. 335.

18. EAW to JWW, Apr. 25, 1908, FBS Papers.

19. EAW to JWW, May 6, 1908, ibid.

20. ERW to EAW, May 15, 1908, Wilson-McAdoo Coll.

21. ERW to EAW, Dec. 10, 1907, Wilson-McAdoo Coll.; EAW to Agnes Tedcastle, Dec. 12, 1907, Wilson Papers; EAW to JWW, Dec. 14, 1907, FBS Papers; WW to Andrew F. West, July 23, 1908, *PWW*, 18:373.

22. WW to Cleveland H. Dodge, June 18, 1908, *PWW*, 18:337–38.

23. WW to EAW, July 20, 1908, ibid., pp. 371–72.

24. Ibid., p. 372 n. 8. Stockton Axson alludes to WW's "second breakdown in 1908" (RSB interview with Stockton Axson, Mar. 15 and 16, 1927, RSB Coll.); Mulder and Baker attribute WW's vacation in England to reasons of health (Mulder, *WW: The Years of Preparation,* pp. 202–3; Baker, *L and L,* 2:270–71). Weinstein states that "there was a confrontation over Mrs. Peck" (Weinstein, *Woodrow Wilson,* p. 185).

25. WW to EAW, Aug. 3, 1908, *PWW*, 18:387.

26. WW to EAW, Aug. 18, 1908, ibid., p. 403.

27. WW to EAW, June 26 and Aug. 30, 1908, ibid., pp. 343, 415.

28. WW to EAW, Feb. 4, 1908, ibid., 17:613.

29. WW to EAW, July 30, 1908, ibid., 18:383–84.

30. WW to EAW, Aug. 3, 1908, ibid., p. 387.

31. WW to EAW, July 13, Aug. 27 and 30, 1908, ibid., pp. 363, 413, 414–15.

32. WW to EAW, July 10, 30, and Aug. 24, 1908, ibid., pp. 357, 382, 412.

33. EAW to Margaret Calloway Axson, Aug. 22, 1908, Wilson Coll.

34. *Connecticut and American Impressionism,* pp. 130–31, 172.

35. Heming, *Miss Florence and the Artists of Old Lyme,* p. 26.

36. *Connecticut and American Impressionism,* p. 123.

37. Ibid., pp. 43, 54 n. 67, 162, 168, 175.

38. The curatorial records of the Florence Griswold Museum contain a listing of all of the members of the Old Lyme art colony who exhibited there from 1902 through 1917. Ellen Wilson is not among them.

39. EAW to Margaret Calloway Axson, Aug. 22, 1908, Wilson Coll.

40. WW to EAW, Aug. 20, 1908, *PWW*, 18:408.

41. WW to Frederic Yates, Sept. 25, 1908, ibid., p. 422.

42. WW, Public Addresses and Lectures, ibid., pp. 670–71.

43. WW to MAHP, Oct. 19, 1908, ibid., pp. 466–67, 468 n. 1.

44. Mary L. G. Hinsdale to WW, Oct. 8, 1908, ibid., p. 440; WW to MAHP, Sept. 30, 1908, ibid., pp. 423–24.

45. WW to MAHP, Nov. 2, 1908, ibid., p. 480.

46. For a discussion of Wilson's political growth, see Link, *The Road to the White House,* pp. 122–32.

47. EAW to Emily C. Yates, Feb. 15, 1909, Wilson Coll.

48. Mary E. Hoyt, "Jessie Wilson Sayre," pp. 23, 25, FBS Papers; JWW to Alice Appenzeller, Oct. 20, 1908, family letters in possession of Woodrow Wilson Sayre (hereafter cited as WWS Papers).

49. McAdoo, *The Woodrow Wilsons*, p. 150.

50. EAW to Emily C. Yates, Feb. 15, 1909, Wilson Coll.; McAdoo, *The Woodrow Wilsons*, p. 113.

51. MWW to JWW, c. mid-Oct. 1906 and Mar. 20, 1907, FBS Papers.

52. EAW to Emily C. Yates, Feb. 15, 1909, Wilson Coll.

53. Edward G. Elliott to WW, Jan. 12, 1909, *PWW*, 18:612.

54. EAW to Emily C. Yates, Feb. 15, 1909, Wilson Coll.; *Connecticut and American Impressionism*, pp. 167–68.

55. EAW to Emily C. Yates, Feb. 15, 1909, Wilson Coll.

56. Ibid.

57. *50th Anniversary of Dial Lodge*, Princeton University Archives.

58. EAW to Emily C. Yates, Feb. 15, 1909, Wilson Coll.

59. The Wilsons' library is now housed in the Library of Congress from which a listing is available. The books shelved in the S Street House were collected by Edith Bolling Wilson.

Chapter 24

1. WW to MAHP, Apr. 13, 1909, *PWW*, 19:162.

2. Ibid., p. 125 n. 1; WW to Cyrus H. McCormick, May 15, 1909, ibid., pp. 196–97. For a full discussion of these events, see Thorp et al., *The Princeton Graduate School, A History*.

3. EAW to Emily C. Yates, Oct. 1, 1909, Wilson Coll. Ellen's acceptance in the Lyme colony was not usual; many of the artists "jealously felt that their ranks were being invaded by lowly students and amateurs" (*Connecticut and American Impressionism*, p. 130).

4. WW to MAHP, June 19, July 11 and 18, 1909, *PWW*, 19:262, 308, 313–14.

5. Heming, *Miss Florence*, pp. 24–25.

6. WW to MAHP, Sept. 5, 1909, *PWW*, 19:357–58, 359 n. 1.

7. *Connecticut and American Impressionism*, pp. 121–23.

8. EAW to Emily C. Yates, Oct. 1, 1909, Wilson Coll.

9. Heming, *Miss Florence*, p. 26.

10. EAW to Agnes Tedcastle, Sept. 28, 1909, Wilson Papers.

11. From the Minutes of the Board of Trustees of Princeton University, Oct. 21, 1908, *PWW*, 19:437–39.

12. WW to MAHP, Oct. 24, 1909, ibid., p. 443.

13. WW to Cleveland H. Dodge, Dec. 27, 1909, ibid., p. 631.

14. EAW to Florence S. Hoyt, Feb. 24, 1910, Wilson Papers.

15. Bragdon, *Woodrow Wilson: The Academic Years*, p. 372; McAdoo, *The Woodrow Wilsons*, p. 99.

16. Daggett, "Woodrow Wilson's Wife," *Good Housekeeping*, 56:318.

17. WW to MAHP, Oct. 24, 1909, *PWW*, 19:443.

18. Stockton Axson memorandum to RSB, Sept. 6, 1931, RSB Coll.

19. MAHP to WW, Feb. 19, 1910, *PWW*, 20:118.

20. WW to MAHP, Apr. 13, 1909, ibid., 19:160.

21. Hulbert, *The Story of Mrs. Peck*, pp. 219–20.

22. WW to MAHP, Apr. 13, 1909, *PWW*, 19:160.

23. Mulder, *WW: The Years of Preparation*, pp. 247, 258.

24. Moses T. Pyne to Joseph B. Shea, Dec. 18, 1909, *PWW*, 19:608; Moses T. Pyne to WW, Dec. 20, 1909, ibid., p. 610.

25. WW to MAHP, Oct. 24 and 25, 1909, ibid., pp. 442–43, 446.

26. Editorial Note, ibid., 20:6–9.

27. WW to Cleveland H. Dodge, ibid., p. 83.

28. The Pennsylvania Academy of the Fine Arts, Archives.

29. WW to MAHP, Feb. 12, 1910, *PWW*, 20:122.

30. WW to EAW, Feb. 20 and 21, 1910, ibid., pp. 144, 146.

31. WW to MAHP, Feb. 18, 25, and 28, 1910, ibid., pp. 141, 178, 185–86.

32. MAHP to WW, Feb. 18, 22, and 25, 1910, ibid., pp. 142, 156, 181.

33. EAW to WW, Feb. 17, 1910, ibid., pp. 134–36.

34. WW to Edith B. Galt, Sept. 19 and 21, 1915, ibid., 34:491, 497. Edwin A. Weinstein suggests that the few months of madness were Nov. and Dec. 1909, and Jan. 1910, when the graduate college controversy was most intense (Weinstein, *WW*, p. 207).

35. An Admission, c. Sept. 20, 1915, *PWW*, 34:496–97.

36. Diary of Breckinridge Long, Jan. 11, 1924, Breckinridge Long Papers, Library of Congress.

37. WW to EAW, Feb. 14, 1889, *PWW*, 6:92–93.

38. EAW to WW, Aug. 2, 1913, ibid., 28:103; Helen W. Bones to Arthur Walworth, Jan. 19, 1950, Walworth Papers, Yale University Library.

39. Stockton Axson memorandum to RSB, Sept. 6, 1931, RSB Coll.

40. Ibid.

41. In a conversation with Arthur and Margaret Link in 1962 in Washington, Eleanor W. McAdoo was adamant that MAHP was a friend of the Wilson family (Margaret D. Link to author, Apr. 14, 1981).

42. WW to MAHP, Aug. 19, 1911, *PWW*, 23:283; EAW to JWW, May 8, 1910, FBS Papers; EAW to MAH, May 5, 1913, Wilson Papers.

43. For a fuller discussion of the Wilson-Hulbert affair, see Saunders, "Love and Guilt: WW and Mary Hulbert," *American Heritage*, 30(3):68–77.

44. EAW to WW, Feb. 24, 1910, *PWW*, 20:172.

45. EAW to WW, Feb. 28, 1910, ibid., pp. 189–90.

46. News Report, Apr. 17, 1910, ibid., p. 367.

47. Link, *The Road to the White House*, p. 84.

48. EAW to Florence S. Hoyt, Feb. 24, 1910, Wilson Papers.

49. EAW to Agnes Tedcastle, Apr. 10, 1910, ibid.

50. Harris Kirk to EAW, Feb. 23, 1910, ibid.

51. EAW to JWW, Apr. 28, 1910, FBS Papers.

52. EAW to Mary C. M. Brown, June 3, 1910, from Marjorie B. King.

53. John M. Raymond and Andrew F. West to WW, May 22, 1910, *PWW*,

20:464 and nn. 2, 3. The Wyman bequest was about six hundred thousand dollars.

54. McAdoo, *The Woodrow Wilsons*, p. 101.

55. WW to MAHP, June 5 and 17, 1910, *PWW*, 20:501 and n. 1, 535–36.

56. From the Minutes of the Board of Trustees of Princeton University, June 9, 1910, ibid., pp. 509–11.

57. WW to MAHP, Oct. 12, 1908, ibid., 18:449.

58. EAW to Agnes Tedcastle, Apr. 10, 1910, Wilson Papers.

59. EAW to William Macbeth, telegram, Apr. 11, 1910, Macbeth Papers; EAW to William Macbeth, Apr. 11 and 23, 1910, ibid. The Ryder painting is in the possession of Ellen Wilson's grandson, Woodrow Wilson Sayre.

60. EAW to JWW, July 1, 1910, FBS Papers.

61. ERW to JWW, July 11, 1910, ibid.

62. EAW to Agnes Tedcastle, Aug. 7, 1910, Wilson Papers.

63. Edward G. Elliott to WW, July 14, 1910, *PWW*, 20:580.

64. EAW to Mary C. M. Brown, Oct. 25, 1910, from Marjorie B. King.

65. EAW to Agnes Tedcastle, Aug. 7, 1910, Wilson Papers.

66. EAW to Mary C. M. Brown, Oct. 25, 1910, from Marjorie B. King.

Chapter 25

1. Col. Harvey's Speech, Feb. 3, 1906, *PWW*, 16:300.

2. Memorandum of Stockton Axson for RSB, Mar. 15 and 16, 1927, RSB Coll.

3. Link, *The Road to the White House*, p. 120.

4. Ibid., p. 112.

5. Ibid., p. 142.

6. Ibid., p. 145.

7. McAdoo, *The Woodrow Wilsons*, pp. 108–9; Mulder, *WW: The Years of Preparation*, p. 266; A Statement, July 15, 1910, *PWW*, 20:581.

8. Link, *The Road to the White House*, p. 167.

9. EAW to WW, Sept. 16, 1910, telegram, *PWW*, 21:101.

10. From the Minutes of the Board of Trustees of Princeton University, Oct. 20, 1910, ibid., p. 364; To the Board of Trustees of Princeton University, Oct. 20, 1910, ibid., p. 362 and n. 1.

11. Trustee Minutes, Oct. 20, 1910, ibid., p. 365; Charles W. McAlpin to WW, Nov. 3, 1910, ibid., p. 539.

12. Henry G. Duffield to WW, Dec. 13, 1910, ibid., 22:186–87; Princeton University Treasurer's Account Book, Ledger D, Aug. 1907–July 1911, Princeton University Archives.

13. Link, *The Road to the White House*, pp. 142, 173, 217, 224.

14. ELA to WW, Mar. 1, 1885, *PWW*, 4:320–21.

15. Cloe Arnold, "The Governor's Lady," *Delineator*, 80:18.

16. EAW to Robert Bridges, Oct. 15, 1910, Wilson Papers; Robert Bridges to EAW, Oct. 18, 1910, ibid.

17. Henry B. Thompson to EAW, Nov. 1, 1910, Princeton University Archives.

18. Henry B. Thompson to Andrew C. Imbrie, Nov. 1, 1910, ibid.

19. Rich, "Prospect: The Search for a Garden," *The Princeton University Library Chronicle*, 42:15.

20. *PWW*, 21:608 n. 2.

21. EAW to George B. M. Harvey, Nov. 12, 1910, Wilson Papers.

22. EAW to Mary C. M. Brown, Nov. 14, 1910, Wilson Coll.

23. EAW to Frederic Yates, Dec. 20, 1910, *PWW*, 22:187 n. 2, 234 and n. 1.

24. WW to Frederic Yates, Dec. 14, 1910, ibid., p. 187; ERW to JWW, c. Dec. 14, 1910, FBS Papers. Stockton was surely at the Hartford Retreat (now the Institute for Living), but their records do not list a "Stockton Axson" as a patient in December 1910. Because of the confidentiality assured him by Dr. Pritchard, Stockton could have been registered under an alias (John H. Houck, M.D., to author, May 1 and Aug. 7, 1981).

25. Memorandum of Stockton Axson to RSB, Aug. 27, 1928, RSB Coll.; Stockton Axson to JWW, Nov. 15, 1913, family letters in possession of Eleanor Axson Sayre (hereafter cited as EAS Papers).

26. EAW to Mary C. M. Brown, Feb. 8, 1911, Wilson Coll.

27. ERW to JWW, c. Dec. 14, 1910, FBS Papers. Patient records at the Institute for Living are confidential, therefore Stockton Axson's diagnosis was not available for inspection.

28. EAW to WW, May 25, 1911, *PWW*, 23:82.

29. EAW to Mary C. M. Brown, Feb. 8, 1911, Wilson Coll.; Stockton Axson to EAW, Feb. 27, 1911, note on a news clipping, Wilson Papers.

30. EAW to Mary C. M. Brown, Feb. 8, 1911, Wilson Coll.

31. ERW to JWW, c. Dec. 14, 1910, FBS Papers.

32. McAdoo, *The Woodrow Wilsons*, pp. 116–17.

33. WW to MAHP, Jan. 13, 1911, *PWW*, 22:329; EAW to Adele Williams, Feb. 3, 1911, Adele Williams Papers, in possession of Catherine Williams Bayliss, Richmond, Va.; McAdoo, *The Woodrow Wilsons*, p. 116.

34. EAW to Adele Williams, Feb. 3, 1911, Adele Williams Papers.

35. Bowman, *The Present Day Club, 1898–1948*, p. 10.

36. EAW to Mary C. M. Brown, Nov. 14, 1910, Wilson Coll.; McAdoo, *The Woodrow Wilsons*, pp. 120–21.

37. EAW to WW, May 11, 1911, *PWW*, 23:30 and n. 1.

38. EAW to Anna Harris, Mar. 20, 1911, Wilson Coll.

39. EAW to Mary C. M. Brown, Oct. 25, 1910, ibid.

40. WW to MAHP, Mar. 12, 1911, *PWW*, 22:500–501, 503 n. 2; McAdoo, *The Woodrow Wilsons*, p. 123.

41. Mrs. McNeely DuBose McDowell to author, Mar. 12, 1979.

42. Hirst, *WW: Reform Governor*, pp. 177–94.

43. EAW to Mary C. M. Brown, Feb. 8, 1911, Wilson Coll.

44. Stockton Axson memorandum to RSB, Aug. 27, 1928, RSB Coll.

45. Link, *The Road to the White House*, pp. 318–27.

Chapter 26

1. McAdoo, *The Woodrow Wilsons*, p. 128; EAW to WW, May 11, 1911, *PWW*, 23:30.

2. A News Report, May 8, 1911, *PWW*, 23:21–22.

3. EAW to WW, May 15 and 22, 1911, ibid., pp. 52, 53 n. 1, 81.

4. EAW to WW, May 11, 1911, ibid., pp. 31, 32 n. 7.

5. EAW to WW, May 22, 1911, ibid., p. 81.

6. WW to Cleveland H. Dodge, June 9, 1911, ibid., p. 139; WW to MAHP, June 25 and July 16, 1911, ibid., pp. 174, 213; McAdoo, *The Woodrow Wilsons*, p. 130.

7. WW to MAHP, July 30, 1911, *PWW*, 23:240; McAdoo, *The Woodrow Wilsons*, p. 129.

8. McAdoo, *The Woodrow Wilsons*, p. 129.

9. WW to MAHP, Sept. 17, 1911, *PWW*, 23:330.

10. WW to MAHP, Aug. 19 and Oct. 29, 1911, ibid., pp. 283, 424.

11. McAdoo, *The Woodrow Wilsons*, p. 131.

12. An Announcement, *Trenton Evening Times*, Aug. 23, 1911, *PWW*, 23:290; Daggett, "Woodrow Wilson's Wife," *Good Housekeeping*, 56:321.

13. WW to MAHP, Oct. 8, 1911, *PWW*, 23:424–25.

14. McAdoo, *The Woodrow Wilsons*, p. 127. The Cleveland Lane house is now a privately owned dwelling.

15. Ibid.; Lucy and Mary Smith are listed in the Princeton City (Borough) Directory, issued in Dec. 1911, as residents at 25 Cleveland Lane.

16. Link, *The Road to the White House*, pp. 171, 313, 314, 333; *PWW*, 23:136 n. 3.

17. William G. McAdoo to WW and EAW, Dec. 25, 1911, telegram, Wilson Papers.

18. EAW to ERW, Dec. 25, 1911, Wilson-McAdoo Coll.

19. McAdoo, *The Woodrow Wilsons*, pp. 134–35; interview with Marjorie Brown King, Jan. 24, 1981; ERW to MWW, c. Jan. 2, 1912, Wilson-McAdoo Coll.

20. H. J. Simmons to WW, Feb. 21, 1912, telegram, Wilson Papers; WW to MAHP, Feb. 28, 1912, *PWW*, 24:218.

21. EAW to B. M. King, Mar. 13 and Sept. 28, 1912, Wilson Coll.

22. McAdoo, *The Woodrow Wilsons*, p. 137; Stockton Axson to Lucy Smith, Mar. 17, 1916, from Marjorie Brown King; EAW to B. M. King, Sept. 9, 1912, Wilson Coll.; interview with Marjorie Brown King, Jan. 24, 1981.

23. EAW to B. M. King, Sept. 9 and 28, 1912, Wilson Coll.; Alumni Records, Princeton University Library.

24. EAW to B. M. King, Sept. 28, 1912, Wilson Coll.

25. EAW to B. M. King, Sept. 9, 1912, ibid.

26. EAW to John W. Wescott, Feb. 23, 1912, *PWW*, 24:189–90. "Dr. Stengal" was Dr. Alfred Stengal.

27. Link, *The Road to the White House*, pp. 122–32.

28. Ibid., pp. 359–68, 376; EAW to Robert Ewing, Jan. 12, 1912, *PWW*, 24:40–42.

29. EAW to Richard H. Dabney, Feb. 9, 1912, *PWW*, 24:147–49.

30. Link, *The Road to the White House*, p. 350.

31. Ibid., p. 347.

32. WW to William Jay Gaynor, Mar. 11, 1912, *PWW*, 24:240.

33. JWW to MWW, c. Feb. 25 and mid-Apr., 1912, Wilson-McAdoo Coll.

34. EAW to John G. Hibben, Feb. 10, 1912, *PWW*, 24:149–50.

35. Florence S. Hoyt to WW, Sept. 12, 1914, ibid., 31:29.

36. RSB memorandum of an interview with Stockton Axson, Mar. 15 and 16, 1927, RSB Coll.

37. EAW to Nancy S. Toy, Aug. 20, 1912, Wilson Papers.

38. A News Report, Apr. 17, 1912, *PWW*, 24:333–34; A News Report, Apr. 17, 1912, ibid., p. 335.

39. *Savannah Morning News*, Apr. 12 and 20, 1912; *Savannah Evening Press*, Apr. 20, 1912.

40. A Report of Remarks to College Students in Macon, Ga., Apr. 21, 1912, *PWW*, 24:354–55.

41. JWS to RSB, Dec. 1, 1925, RSB Coll.; Mary E. Hoyt, "Jessie Wilson Sayre," pp. 28, 49, FBS Papers.

42. Lunardini and Knock, "WW and Woman Suffrage: A New Look," *Political Science Quarterly*, 95:655–71.

43. Stockton Axson memorandum to RSB, Aug. 27, 1928, RSB Coll.

Chapter 27

1. Daggett, "Woodrow Wilson's Wife," p. 317.

2. McAdoo, *The Woodrow Wilsons*, p. 153; WW to MAHP, June 17, 1912, *PWW*, 24:481–82.

3. Axson Memoir.

4. McAdoo, *The Woodrow Wilsons*, pp. 148–49.

5. Ibid., p. 156; A News Report, June 29, 1912, *PWW*, 24:409; A News Report, July 2, 1912, *PWW*, pp. 523, 585 n. 2; Stockton Axson memorandum to RSB, Aug. 27, 1928, RSB Coll.

6. A News Report, July 2, 1912, *PWW*, 24:523–24.

7. Link, *The Road to the White House*, p. 451; Stockton Axson memorandum to RSB, Aug. 27, 1928, and Sept. 6, 1931, RSB Coll.

8. A News Report, June 30 and July 1, 1912, *PWW*, 24:514, 516.

9. McAdoo, *The Woodrow Wilsons*, p. 161.

10. A News Report, July 2, 1912, *PWW*, 24:522–27.

11. McAdoo, *The Woodrow Wilsons*, p. 165.

12. A News Report, July 3, 1912, *PWW*, 24:528; Link, *The Road to the White House*, pp. 470–71, 488.

13. WW to MAH, July 28, 1912, *PWW*, 24:572; Link, *The Road to the White House*, p. 472.

14. WW to MAH, Aug. 25, 1912, *PWW*, 25:55–56.

15. A News Report, Aug. 2, 1912, ibid., 24:583.

16. McAdoo, *The Woodrow Wilsons*, pp. 166–67; Oilliams, "Will Uncle Sam's Hostesses Be Three Bachelor Maids?," *Today's*, 8:11.

17. Daggett, "Woodrow Wilson's Wife," p. 320.

18. Ibid.

19. Ellen Axson Wilson's Description of Her Husband, July 28, 1912, *PWW*, 24:573.

20. J. M. Sare to EAW, Oct. 8, 1912, Wilson Papers.

21. EAW to MAH, Sept. 23, 1912, ibid.; EAW to Nancy S. Toy, Sept. 23, 1912, ibid.; EAW to Anna Harris, Oct. 21, 1912, ibid.

22. WW to MAH, Dec. 22, 1912, *PWW*, 25:616.

23. Two News Reports, Oct. 15, 1912, ibid., pp. 418–19.

24. From the Diary of Colonel House, Oct. 20, 1912, ibid., p. 448.

25. McAdoo, *The Woodrow Wilsons*, pp. 176, 178–79; Link, *The Road to the White House*, pp. 521–22.

26. Link, *The Road to the White House*, p. 523; Two News Reports, Nov. 5, 1912, *PWW*, 25:518–19; McAdoo, *The Woodrow Wilsons*, p. 180.

27. Remarks to Princeton Students and Neighbors, Nov. 5, 1912, *PWW*, 25:520 and n. 1; McAdoo, *The Woodrow Wilsons*, p. 181.

28. Interview with Eleanor Marquand Delanoy, Feb. 20, 1981.

29. John G. Hibben to WW, Nov. 5, 1912, *PWW*, 25:522; WW to John G. Hibben, ibid., p. 534.

30. JWW to Alice Appenzeller, Dec. 5, 1912, WWS Papers.

31. *Trenton Evening Times*, Dec. 9, 1912, p. 1.

32. JWW to Alice Appenzeller, Dec. 5, 1912, WWS Papers.

33. *New York Times*, Dec. 22, 1912, p. 1.

34. EAW to Florence S. Hoyt, Jan. 3, 1913, Wilson Papers.

35. An Address at Mary Baldwin Seminary, Staunton, Va., Dec. 28, 1912, *PWW*, 25:626–27 and n. 1.

36. Stockton Axson memorandum to RSB, Sept. 6, 1931, RSB Coll.

37. McAdoo, *The Woodrow Wilsons*, p. 196.

38. McAdoo, *Crowded Years*, p. 272.

39. Henrietta Ricketts and R. H. Casey to Josephine P. Morgan, Jan. 10 and 16, 1913, from A. Perry Morgan, Jr.

40. McAdoo, *The Woodrow Wilsons*, pp. 198–99; EAW to WW, Sept. 25, 1913, *PWW*, 28:328.

41. Jaffray, *Secrets of the White House*, pp. 36–38; William H. Taft to EAW, Jan. 3, 1913, *PWW*, 27:12, 13 n. 2; WW to William H. Taft, Jan. 2, 1913, *PWW*, 27:5.

42. William H. Taft to EAW, Jan. 6, 1913, *PWW*, 27:16–17.

43. EAW to William H. Taft, Jan. 10, 1913, ibid., p. 28.

44. WW to William H. Taft, Jan. 8, 1913, ibid., pp. 18–19; EAW to Helen Herron Taft, Feb. 26, 1913, ibid., p. 138.

45. *Ladies Home Journal*, 30 (Apr.): 28–29; ibid. (May): 18–19.

46. *Harper's Weekly*, 57 (Mar. 8, 1913): 12; ibid. (Apr. 19, 1913): 15.

47. *Review of Reviews*, 47:273; *Literary Digest*, 46:558; *Independent*, 73:73.

48. Gordon, "The Tact of Mrs. Woodrow Wilson," *Collier's*, 50 (Mar. 8, 1913): 13.

49. *Current Opinion*, 54 (Mar. 1, 1913): 195–96.

50. Hosford, "The New Ladies of the White House," *Independent*, 73:1161; Hosford, "The Lady of the White House," ibid., 74:870.

51. Rhodes and Hopkins, *The Economy Administration Cook Book*. A copy is in the library at the Woodrow Wilson birthplace, Staunton, Va.

52. McAdoo, *The Woodrow Wilsons*, p. 197; *New York Times*, Jan. 18, 1913, p. 22; *New York Herald*, Mar. 1, 1913, p. 9.

Chapter 28

1. WW to MAH, Mar. 2, 1913, *PWW*, 27:146.

2. *New York Times*, Mar. 2, 1913, p. 1.

3. Helen W. Bones to Jessie W. Bones Brower, Mar. 1, 1913, *PWW*, 29:556.

4. *New York Times*, Mar. 3, 1913, p. 3; *Church Calendar*, week beginning Sunday, Mar. 2, 1913, First Presbyterian Church, Princeton, N.J.; Record of Accessions by Examination and Letter, Dismissions, Ordinations, Deaths, Suspended, etc. (1909–1924), First Presbyterian Church, Princeton, N.J., Speer Library, Princeton Theological Seminary; WW to James H. Taylor, Apr. 23, 1913, *PWW*, 27:147. The Woodrow Wilson family pew, number 57 in the Princeton church sanctuary, is marked with a small brass plaque.

5. *Princeton Alumni Weekly*, 13:418–19; McAdoo, *The Woodrow Wilsons*, p. 199.

6. McAdoo, *The Woodrow Wilsons*, pp. 200–202.

7. William H. Taft to WW, Jan. 6, 1913, *PWW*, 27:17–18. The Wilsons took two personal maids, Margaret Norton and Anna Goodwin, from Princeton (*New York Times*, Mar. 4, 1913, p. 4).

8. *Washington Herald*, Mar. 5, 1913, p. 4.

9. Stockton Axson memorandum to RSB, undated, RSB Coll.; McAdoo, *The Woodrow Wilsons*, p. 205.

10. Frederic Yates to Emily C. Yates, Mar. 5, 1913, *PWW*, 27:155.

11. McAdoo, *The Woodrow Wilsons*, p. 211; Frederic Yates to Emily C. Yates, Mar. 5, 1913, *PWW*, 27:155–56.

12. Hoover, "Diary kept by the Head Usher at the White House," Mar. 4, 1913–Mar. 4, 1921, pp. 1–12, passim (hereafter cited as Hoover, Head Usher's Diary).

13. Ibid., pp. 2–30, passim.

14. Ibid., pp. 1–12, passim. Mary Scott was the daughter of William Berryman Scott, Blair Professor of Geology; Sarah Elizabeth Duffield, the daughter of Henry Green Duffield, treasurer of Princeton University.

15. *Washington Post*, Mar. 16, 1913, p. 2.

16. MWW to RSB, July 8 and Sept. 15, 1931, RSB Coll. EAW's inaugural gown was designed by a firm in Paterson, N.J., said to be the "original American silk manufacturers." Made of pale green silk brocade, rose pattern, the gown was lace trimmed down the front of the skirt, with a draping of lace at

the bodice that fell in a butterfly shape in front. Bead work repeated the butterfly motif on the sleeves (*New York Times*, Mar. 3, 1913, p. 3).

17. A News Report, Jan. 17, 1913, *PWW*, 27:59.

18. McAdoo, *The Woodrow Wilsons*, pp. 228, 230.

19. Hoover, Head Usher's Diary, pp. 1–13, passim.

20. Helen W. Bones to Jessie W. Bones Brower, June 1, 1913, *PWW*, 29:561.

21. Hoover, Head Usher's Diary, pp. 2–13, passim.

22. Morris, *Edith Kermit Roosevelt*, pp. 238–39, 241–42; records of the Office of the Curator, the White House.

23. McAdoo, *The Woodrow Wilsons*, pp. 214–17; records of the Office of the Curator, the White House. MWW's Steinway piano, built in 1891, had two previous owners before its purchase in February 1906 by the Wilsons. Returned to Steinway and Sons in New York in 1921, the piano was subsequently the property of Mary M. L. (Mrs. Albert) Simpler and, in 1975, of William C. and Janice K. Archbold, who gave it to the Woodrow Wilson House, 2340 S Street, Washington, D.C. (Records, WW House).

24. Records of the Office of the Curator, the White House.

25. *Washington Post*, Feb. 15, 1914, p. 9.

26. McAdoo, *The Woodrow Wilsons*, p. 218.

27. Records of the Office of the Curator, the White House; Morris, *Edith Kermit Roosevelt*, p. 253.

28. Helen W. Bones to Mrs. W. U. Vreeland, Mar. 17, 1913, Wilson Papers.

29. EAW to Emily C. Yates, June 10, 1913, ibid.; see, e.g., *New York World*, Mar. 1913.

30. *Washington Post*, Mar. 18, 1913, p. 5.

31. Florence S. Hoyt memorandum to RSB, c. Apr. 1926, RSB Coll.

32. Hoover, Head Usher's Diary, p. 4.

33. Charlotte E. W. Hopkins to WW, June 21, 1915, *PWW*, 33:430, 432 n. 1; Bicknell, "The Homemaker of the White House," *Survey*, 33 (Oct. 3, 1914): 19.

34. Bicknell, "The Homemaker of the White House," pp. 19–22.

35. Ibid., p. 21.

36. From the Diary of Colonel House, Oct. 30, 1913, *PWW*, 28:476.

37. *New York Times*, Nov. 1, 1913, p. 3.

38. In her book, *The Secret City*, Constance Green writes that Ellen Wilson supplied some of the impetus for segregation of government workers because of her "shocked disapproval . . . at seeing colored men and white women working in the same room in the Post Office Department" (Green, *The Secret City*, pp. 172–73). A person who did communicate shocked disapproval at nonsegregated government employees was Thomas Dixon, Jr. (see Thomas Dixon, Jr., to WW, July 27, 1913, *PWW*, 28:88–89). There is no evidence for Green's assertion. Rayford W. Logan, who also believed that Ellen Wilson influenced President Wilson's expansion of segregation, says that his statements are based solely on his recollections "at the time" and these recollections were supported "by similar belief" of his contemporaries (Rayford W. Logan to the author, Nov. 29, 1978). Green's footnotes on pp. 172–73, to which Logan also alludes,

refer to the *Washington Bee, Crisis, Washington Post, New York Times, Nation,*
and to official documents and reports, none of which mention Ellen Wilson.

Segregation of employees in public buildings, e.g., the Bureau of Engraving
and Printing, Treasury, and Post Office, had begun—indeed, was completed by
late July 1913—before Ellen's intervention began in October. (May Childs Ner-
ney to Oswald G. Villard, Sept. 30, 1913, *PWW,* 28:402–10. For a discussion of
the segregation issue in 1913, see Lunardini, "Standing Firm: William Monroe
Trotter's Meetings with Woodrow Wilson, 1913–1914," *Journal of Negro History,*
64:244–54.)

Snobbery and bigotry were totally out of character for Ellen Wilson. In 1884,
she enrolled at the Art Students League, where neither sexual nor racial barriers
existed; and where, indeed, a young black artist, George Alexander Bickles, was
a student shortly after she left (Lawrence Campbell to author, Sept. 3, 1980).
That she went to New York fully aware of the league's liberal admissions policies is unquestionable. In 1888, after John Franklin Jameson, professor of history at Brown University, visited the Wilsons in Middletown, he sent Ellen a
booklet by George Washington Cable, entitled *The Negro Question,* a reasoned
defense of civil, educational, and political rights for blacks. Jameson, Woodrow's friend and colleague, would not have sent this to Ellen had he thought
that the contents might offend her (John F. Jameson to WW, Nov. 20, 1888,
PWW, 6:23–24).

She had received Booker T. Washington at Prospect in 1902 and ignored
Sadie (Mrs. Thomas A.) Hoyt's outraged disapproval. Jessie stated, however,
that her mother "felt much more strongly about the color line" than did her
father, and that she had "far more of the old southern feeling, with its curious
paradox of a warm personal liking for the Negroes, combined with an instinc-
tive hostility to certain assumptions of equality" (memorandum of an interview
with Jessie W. Sayre, Dec. 1, 1925, RSB Coll.). But Ellen never wavered when a
principle was at stake, even an issue unpopular with politicians and Washington
society—the eradication of slum neighborhoods and improvement of the environment of government employees (Stockton Axson memorandum to RSB,
Sept. 6, 1931, RSB Coll.).

Constance Green states that even the blacks "who recognized the importance
of slum clearance as a weapon against disease and hopelessness" found Ellen
Wilson's "brand of philanthropy intolerably patronizing" (Green, *The Secret
City,* p. 175). Ellen's "brand of philanthropy" required direct intervention rather
than simple endorsement of prospective legislation.

39. Link, *The New Freedom,* pp. 243–49; William M. Trotter's Address to the
President, Nov. 6, 1913, *PWW,* 28:491 and n. 1, 498 n. 1.

40. *Washington Bee,* Apr. 1 and 15, 1916; *PWW,* 28:498 n. 1.

41. EAW to WW, July 2, 1913, *PWW,* 28:21.

42. McAdoo, *The Woodrow Wilsons,* pp. 236–37; Baker, *L and L,* 4:469;
Stockton Axson memoranda to RSB, Aug. 27, 1928 and undated, RSB Coll.

43. EAW to May M. Fine, Mar. 16, 1913, Wilson Coll.

44. Margaret G. Elliott to EAW, Apr. 3 and May 7, 1913, Wilson Papers.

45. Marie Bayliss to J. R. Tumulty, Dec. 31, 1912, ibid.

46. Helen S. Davis to EAW, Mar. 20, 1914, ibid.; Hoover, Head Usher's Diary, p. 31.

47. McAdoo, *Crowded Years*, p. 285.

48. Ibid., pp. 285, 512.

49. Hoover, Head Usher's Diary, pp. 6, 13; McAdoo, *The Woodrow Wilsons*, pp. 246–48.

50. *New York Times*, June 21, 1913, p. 1.

51. Baker, *L and L*, 4:16.

Chapter 29

1. EAW to Arthur W. Tedcastle, Mar. 16, 1913, Wilson Papers.

2. WW to MAH, Mar. 16, 1913, *PWW*, 27:189.

3. EAW to Arthur W. Tedcastle, Apr. 3, 1913, Wilson Papers.

4. Ibid.

5. EAW to WW, July 12, 1883, *PWW*, 2:384.

6. Sayre, *Glad Adventure*, pp. 4–5, 7, 9, 35–37, 41.

7. The original plaster cast, discovered a decade ago in an antique shop in Philadelphia, was presented by Pendleton Herring, President of the WW Foundation, to the S Street House in Washington, D.C.

8. Sayre, *Glad Adventure*, pp. 40–41; McAdoo, *The Woodrow Wilsons*, p. 150.

9. Hoyt, "Jessie Wilson Sayre," p. 53; Sayre, *Glad Adventure*, p. 42; McAdoo, *The Woodrow Wilsons*, p. 254.

10. EAW to WW, July 24 and Aug. 5, 1913, *PWW*, 28:81, 120.

11. Hoover, Head Usher's Diary, pp. 13–14, 18.

12. WW to EAW, July 27, 1913, *PWW*, 28:85.

13. EAW to WW, July 18 and Aug. 2, 1913, ibid., pp. 43 and n. 7, 103.

14. EAW to WW, Aug. 19, 1913, ibid., pp. 194–95.

15. EAW to WW, July 18 and 20, 1913, ibid., pp. 43, 55. The Vonnoh portrait hangs in the Woodrow Wilson House, 2340 S Street, N.W., Washington, D.C.

16. EAW to WW, Aug. 19, 1913, ibid., p. 195.

17. EAW to WW, Aug. 6, 1913, ibid., pp. 126–27.

18. EAW to WW, July 2 and 29, 1913, ibid., pp. 21, 96.

19. EAW to WW, July 20, 1913, ibid., p. 55.

20. WW to EAW, July 20, 1913, ibid., p. 45.

21. EAW to WW, July 24, 1913, ibid., p. 81.

22. Ibid.

23. EAW to WW, July 30, 1913, ibid., p. 99.

24. EAW to WW, Aug. 19, 1913, ibid., p. 195.

25. See Link, *The New Freedom*, pp. 347–77, for a discussion of the Mexican crisis, and pp. 331–46 for the Nicaraguan problem.

26. EAW to WW, Sept. 10, 1913, *PWW*, 28:273.

27. WW to EAW, Aug. 17, 1913, ibid., p. 179.

28. EAW to WW, Aug. 3, 1913, ibid., p. 109.

29. WW to EAW, Aug. 5, 1913, ibid., pp. 113–14.

30. EAW to WW, Aug. 20, 1913, ibid., p. 199.

31. Hoover, Head Usher's Diary, pp. 16–17; Stockton Axson memorandum to RSB, Sept. 6, 1931, RSB Coll.; *PWW*, 10:381 nn. 1, 3.

32. WW to EAW, Sept. 3, 1913, *PWW*, 28:249.

33. EAW to WW, Sept. 4, 1913, ibid., p. 256.

34. EAW to WW, Sept. 25, 1913, ibid., pp. 327–28; from the Diary of Colonel House, Dec. 22, 1913, ibid., 29:56.

35. EAW to WW, Aug. 10, 1913, ibid., 28:138.

36. EAW to WW, Sept. 5 and 7, 1913, ibid., pp. 259 and n. 1, 264–65.

37. EAW to WW, Sept. 8 and 9, 1913, ibid., pp. 266–67, 269–70.

38. EAW to WW, Sept. 20 and 26, 1913, ibid., pp. 308, 331. In 1921, Martha M. Berry gave a life-size, unsigned oil portrait of EAW to the Carnegie Library, Rome, Georgia. According to Inez Henry, Berry's former secretary who was director of the Martha Berry Museum, President Wilson had sent the painting, allegedly done by EAW herself, to the Berry School sometime after EAW's death in 1914. There are no records of the gift in the Berry School archives, nor is there any mention of it in the correspondence between Woodrow Wilson and Martha Berry (thirteen letters from November 21, 1914 to May 5, 1923, Wilson Papers).

The painting, a replica of EAW's official first lady photograph taken by Harris and Ewing in March 1913, had to be executed after that date. EAW could possibly have done this work in the summer of 1913 in Cornish, New Hampshire; but had she done so, she surely would have referred to such an effort in her frequent, detailed letters to Woodrow. Eleanor Axson Sayre believes that the style of the painting is unlike that of her grandmother and that for EAW to work on such a large canvas was atypical.

Restored by Walter P. Frobos of Athens, Georgia, the portrait was hung in the Carnegie Library in Rome after a dedication ceremony on October 1, 1972. It has been reproduced in color in the *Rome Tribune-Herald*, entertainment section, September 29, 1972, and in Margaret Brown Klapthor's *The First Ladies*, White House Historical Association in cooperation with the National Geographic Society, 1975, p. 62.

39. "W. Wilson" to William Macbeth, Nov. 29, 1911, Macbeth Papers. The letter which accompanied the "Edward Wilson" painting was filed by the Macbeth Gallery in the folder of correspondence labeled "Ellen A. Wilson."

40. EAW to William Macbeth, May 25, 1912, Macbeth Papers.

41. William Macbeth to EAW, June 3, 1912, ibid.

42. EAW to William Macbeth, June 21, 1912, ibid.

43. William Macbeth to EAW, June 22, 1912, ibid.

44. *Trenton Evening Times*, Jan. 8, 1913, p. 11; *The Art Institute of Chicago Catalog of the Twenty-fifth Annual Exhibition of American Oil Paintings and Sculpture . . . Nov. 5 to Dec. 8, 1912*, Mrs. Woodrow Wilson, entry 300; Art Association of Indianapolis, 28th Annual Exhibition of Oil Paintings by American Artists, Dec. 17, 1912, to Feb. 3, 1913, Mrs. Woodrow Wilson, entry 85.

45. *Catalog of the 108th Annual Exhibition, Feb. 9 to March 30, 1913*, The Pennsylvania Academy of the Fine Arts, Ellen A. Wilson, entries 483, 487.

46. Shirley Maxfield, executive secretary, Pen and Brush, Inc., to author, Apr. 7, 1982; *New York Times*, Nov. 22, 1913, p. 1; Archives, National Association of Women Artists.

47. *New York Herald*, Feb. 20, 1913, p. 13. The Arts and Crafts Guild, founded in 1906 to encourage and support art in craftsmanship, sponsored exhibits chosen by a jury.

48. *New York Times*, Feb. 20, 1913, p. 5.

49. *Ashtabula Beacon*, Apr. 23, 1913, p. 1. James Smith left his entire estate in trust to the Smith Home for Aged Women, where Ellen's painting now hangs.

50. *Trenton Evening Times*, Jan. 8, 1913, p. 11.

51. Helen W. Bones to William Macbeth, Jan. 11, 1913, Macbeth Papers.

52. Sayre, "Dedicatory Remarks," Oct. 1, 1972, MS copy, Wilson File, Carnegie Library, Rome, Ga.

53. EAW to William Macbeth, June 21 and Dec. 13, 1912, Macbeth Papers; A. Catherine Tack, Carnegie Library of Pittsburgh, to author, Dec. 11, 1981; Brown, *American Painting*, p. 4.

54. Brown, *American Painting*, p. 63; EAW's entries were numbers 299, *Near Princeton, New Jersey*, and 307, *Old Wagon Road*. The *New York Times* makes no mention of EAW's paintings in the preview on Dec. 20, 1913, nor in the review on Dec. 21, 1913, of the academy exhibition.

55. EAW to William Macbeth, Nov. 30, 1912, Macbeth Papers. The catalog of the Cleveland Art Loan Exposition lists "William Macbeth, New York City," as one who lent works of art, but does not show Ellen Wilson as an individual participant.

56. *New York Times*, Nov. 14, 15, and 22, 1913, pp. 20, 11, 1.

57. EAW to WW, Sept. 28, Oct. 6 and 8, 1913, *PWW*, 28:338, 368, 375.

58. EAW to WW, Sept. 29 and Oct. 12, 1913, ibid., pp. 345, 399.

59. EAW to WW, Oct. 5, 1913, ibid., pp. 363–64.

60. EAW to WW, Oct. 13, 1913, ibid., p. 400.

61. WW to EAW, Aug. 17 and Oct. 12, 1913, ibid., pp. 180, 393–94.

Chapter 30

1. EAW to WW, July 2 and 27, 1913, *PWW*, 28:20, 21 n. 1, 88.

2. EAW to WW, Oct. 10 and 12, 1913, ibid., pp. 387, 398; WW to Annie W. Howe, Oct. 12, 1913, ibid., p. 397.

3. Walter H. Page to WW, July 20, 1913, ibid., pp. 52–53.

4. EAW to WW, Sept. 5, 1913, ibid., p. 259; WW to Walter H. Page, Sept. 11, 1913, ibid., p. 274.

5. Alice D. W. Garrett to JWW, Oct. 28 and Nov. 5, 1913, EAS Papers.

6. EAW to WW, July 22–Oct. 13, 1913, *PWW*, 28:63–400, passim.

7. Hoover, Head Usher's Diary, pp. 20–21.

8. EAW to Stockton Axson, Nov. 17, 1913, Axson Papers, Rice University.

9. JWS's Bride's Record Book, FBS Papers.

10. Ibid., gift number 302; interview with Eleanor Axson Sayre, Jan. 18, 1981.

11. McAdoo, *The Woodrow Wilsons*, pp. 261–62.

12. *Washington Post*, Nov. 26, 1913, p. 1; McAdoo, *The Woodrow Wilsons*, p. 262.

13. Mary C. M. Brown to Mrs. H. S. Mitchell, Nov. 26, 1913, Marjorie B. King Papers.

14. Ibid.; McAdoo, *The Woodrow Wilsons*, p. 264.

15. EAW to JWS, Dec. 4, 1913, EAS Papers.

16. Hoover, Head Usher's Diary, p. 23.

17. EAW to JWS, Dec. 4, 1913, EAS Papers; Hoover, Head Usher's Diary, p. 23; EAW to Stockton Axson, Dec. 5, 1913, Axson Papers, Rice University.

18. Cecil Spring Rice to EAW, Dec. 3, 1913, Wilson Papers; Cecil Spring Rice to WW, Nov. 25, 1913, EAS Papers.

19. EAW to JWS, Dec. 4, 1913, EAS Papers. Mrs. Robert Garrett was the treasurer, National Association Opposed to Woman Suffrage (Mrs. Arthur Dodge to WW, Mar. 17, 1913, Wilson Papers).

20. Hoover, Head Usher's Diary, p. 24; EAW to JWS, Dec. 11, 1913, EAS Papers.

21. EAW to Stockton Axson, Dec. 22, 1913, Axson Papers, Rice University.

22. EAW to JWS, Dec. 19, 1913, EAS Papers.

23. EAW to Mary C. M. Brown, Dec. 22, 1913, RSB Coll.

24. WW to JWS, Dec. 8, 1913, EAS Papers.

25. EAW to JWS, Dec. 19, 1913, ibid.

26. Stockton Axson to JWW, Nov. 15, 1913, ibid.

27. ERW to JWS, Dec. 28 and 31, 1913, ibid.

Chapter 31

1. Hoover, Head Usher's Diary, p. 26.

2. EAW to Stockton Axson, Jan. 24, 1914, Axson Papers, Rice University.

3. Henlock and Norris, "Flowers for First Ladies," p. 81; Hoover, Head Usher's Diary, pp. 26–27; EAW to Stockton Axson, Jan. 24, 1914, Axson Papers, Rice University.

4. EAW to Stockton Axson, Jan. 24, 1914, Axson Papers, Rice University.

5. EAW to JWS, Feb. 6, 1914, EAS Papers.

6. *New York Times*, Feb. 9, 1914, p. 7; EAW to JWS, Feb. 6, 1914, EAS Papers; *Washington Post*, Feb. 13, 1914, p. 2, and Feb. 15, 1914, Sec. 2, p. 9.

7. EAW to JWS, Feb. 20, 1914, EAS Papers.

8. Hoover, Head Usher's Diary, p. 28; EAW to JWS, Feb. 20, 1914, EAS Papers. The identity of Forster and the location of the portrait are not known.

9. EAW to Cleveland H. Dodge, Feb. 5, 1914, Wilson Coll.; EAW to JWS, Feb. 20, 1914, ibid.

10. Henlock and Norris, "Flowers for First Ladies," p. 81; records of the Office of the Curator, the White House; McAdoo, *The Woodrow Wilsons*, p. 237.

11. Hoover, Head Usher's Diary, pp. 28–29.

12. MWW to JWS, Mar. 19, 1914, EAS Papers.

13. Mary E. Hoyt memorandum for RSB, Oct. 1926, RSB Coll.; *New York Times*, Feb. 18, 1914, p. 2.

14. MWW to JWS, July 6, 1914, EAS Papers; *Musical Advance*, Aug. 1916, p. 5.

15. *Washington Post*, Nov. 1, 1913, p. 5.

16. EAW to WW, Sept. 18, 1913, *PWW*, 28:291.

17. Ibid., pp. 498–500 n. 1.

18. MWW to JWS, Dec. 29, 1913, EAS Papers.

19. ERW to Ben M. King, Feb. 28, 1914, Wilson Coll. Later, Ben King and Marjorie Brown fell in love and were married in Washington, D.C., on the morning of Dec. 28, 1920. The bride and groom then had lunch with President Wilson at the White House (interview with Marjorie Brown King, June 28, 1982).

20. McAdoo, *The Woodrow Wilsons*, p. 273.

21. EAW to JWS, Feb. 20, 1914, EAS Papers.

22. *New York Times*, Mar. 13 and 14, 1914, p. 1.

23. EAW to B. M. King, Sept. 9 and 28, 1912, Jan. 11, 1913, and Jan. 28, 1914, Wilson Coll.; Stockton Axson to B. M. King, Feb. 23 and Mar. 15, 1914, ibid.; MWW to B. M. King, Apr. 15, 1914, ibid.

24. McAdoo, *The Woodrow Wilsons*, p. 275.

25. EAW to JWS, Feb. 20, 1914, EAS Papers.

26. WW to B. M. King, Mar. 22, 1914, *PWW*, 29:370–71.

27. Hoover, Head Usher's Diary, pp. 30, 31.

28. Helen W. Bones to Margaret C. Axson, June 25, 1914, Georgia Historical Society, Savannah; Hoover, Head Usher's Diary, p. 30; ERW to JWS, c. Mar. 20, 1914, EAS Papers.

29. WW to Edward M. House, Apr. 2, 1914, *PWW*, 29:395.

30. Hoover, Head Usher's Diary, pp. 32, 33.

31. Ibid., pp. 33, 34; *Washington Post*, May 1, 1914, p. 4.

32. EAW to Arthur W. Tedcastle, Feb. 13, 1914, Wilson Papers.

33. J. R. Bowie to WW, Mar. 21, 1914, ibid.; *Rome Tribune-Herald*, Dec. 10, 1914, p. 1.

34. ERW to JWS, c. Mar. 20, 1915, EAS Papers.

35. Hoover, Head Usher's Diary, p. 35; *Washington Post*, May 7, 1914, p. 3.

36. *Washington Post*, May 8, 1914, pp. 1, 13.

37. McAdoo, *The Woodrow Wilsons*, pp. 287–88.

Chapter 32

1. EAW to Kate W. Wilson, May 14, 1914, Wilson Papers.

2. Ibid.

3. Helen W. Bones to Margaret C. Axson, June 25, 1914, Georgia Historical Society, Savannah; Hoover, Head Usher's Diary, p. 38; McAdoo, *The Woodrow Wilsons*, pp. 290–91.

4. Helen W. Bones to JWS, June 28, 1914, EAS Papers.

5. Helen W. Bones to JWS, July 4, 1914, ibid.

6. Henlock and Norris, "Flowers for First Ladies," p. 81.

7. WW to Cleveland H. Dodge, July 12, 1914, *PWW*, 30:278.

8. EWM to JWS, July 6, 1914, EAS Papers.

9. MWW to JWS, Mar. 1, 1914, ibid.

10. McAdoo, *The Woodrow Wilsons*, p. 296; Hoover, Head Usher's Diary, pp. 40, 41.

11. EAW to JWS, July 6, 1914, EAS Papers.

12. Helen W. Bones to JWS, July 10, 1914, ibid. The child, born in the White House on Jan. 17, 1915, was named Francis Bowes Sayre, Jr.

13. Helen W. Bones to JWS, July 13 and 24, 1914, ibid.

14. WW to MAH, Aug. 2, 1914, *PWW*, 30:328.

15. WW to Edward M. House, Aug. 3, 1914, ibid., p. 336.

16. Hoover, Head Usher's Diary, p. 42.

17. WW to Stockton Axson, Aug. 5, 1914, *PWW*, 30:345.

18. Edward G. Elliott to WW, Aug. 6, 1914, Wilson Papers.

19. *Washington Post*, Aug. 6, 1914, p. 1; Hoover, Head Usher's Diary, p. 42; RSB interview with Edward P. Davis, RSB Coll.

20. *Washington Post*, Aug. 7, 1914, p. 1; *New York Times*, Aug. 7, 1914, p. 1.

21. JWS to B. M. King, c. Sept. 1914, Wilson Coll.

22. RSB memorandum of interview with Cary T. Grayson, Feb. 18 and 19, 1926, RSB Coll.

23. Interview with Marjorie B. King, Aug. 15, 1981.

24. *New York Times*, Aug. 11, 1914, p. 9.

25. Hoover, Head Usher's Diary, p. 43.

26. Baker, *L and L*, 4:480; *Rome Tribune-Herald*, Aug. 11, 1914, p. 1.

27. *Washington Post*, Aug. 10, 1914, p. 4; *Rome Tribune-Herald*, Aug. 7, 10, and 11, 1914. Anna Harris attended Ellen's funeral services, but Rosalie DuBose did not.

28. Stockton Axson to Margaret A. Elliott, Aug. 12, 1914, Wilson Papers.

29. WW to EAW, Feb. 8, 1895, *PWW*, 9:180.

30. After Ellen's death, Woodrow met and fell in love with Edith Bolling Galt, a Virginia-born widow who was sixteen years younger than he. A friend of Helen W. Bones and Cary T. Grayson, Edith Galt soon helped to assuage the lonely president's grief. They were married on December 18, 1915, at her home in Washington. Edith was a devoted wife and constant companion throughout her husband's second term, and during his last three years as a private citizen in their home on S Street in Washington. Woodrow Wilson died there on February 3, 1924. Edith lived on at the S Street house until her death on December 28, 1961. The home is now a National Trust property and is open to the public.

Margaret Wilson never married and continued to pursue her interests in music and social causes. After extensive tours overseas during the First World War to sing for the servicemen, Margaret strained her voice and gave up further plans for a career in music. She later became a devotee of the teachings of Sri Aurobindo, a Hindu mystic, and, in 1938, moved to Aurobindo's ashram at Pondicherry, India. She died there of uremia on February 11, 1944, and was buried in the Christian cemetery at Pondicherry.

After her first son's birth in the White House in January 1915, Jessie Wilson Sayre had two more children: Eleanor Axson Sayre, in March 1916, and Woodrow Wilson Sayre, in February 1919. Francis Sayre, Jr., became an Episcopal clergyman and served as dean of the National Cathedral in Washington from 1951 until his retirement in 1978. Eleanor Sayre, a Bryn Mawr graduate, is now curator of prints and drawings at the Boston Museum of Fine Arts. Woodrow Sayre, who became a college teacher and writer after receiving his doctorate from Harvard University, is now retired. In January 1933, Jessie Sayre died suddenly in Cambridge, Massachusetts, after surgery, and is buried in the Sayre plot in Bethlehem, Pennsylvania.

Eleanor Wilson McAdoo had two daughters, Ellen Axson, born in May 1915, and Mary Faith in April 1920. Divorced from William G. McAdoo in July 1934, Eleanor spent most of her last years in California writing and compiling material about the Wilson family. She died on April 5, 1967, in Santa Barbara. Her daughter, Ellen, is now deceased; Mary Faith McAdoo Bush lives in California.

Ellen Axson Wilson has six great-grandchildren, four of whom (two sons and two daughters) are the children of Francis and Harriet Hart Sayre, and two (both sons) the children of Ellen McAdoo Hinshaw.

Stockton Axson, who was professor of English Literature and later head of the English Department at Rice University, never married. He died in Houston in February 1935 and was interred in the Myrtle Hill Cemetery beside Ellen. Margaret A. and Edward G. Elliott returned to the East in 1947, the year of Egie's death. Madge made her home in Princeton until her death in April 1958. The Elliotts lie in a plot in Princeton cemetery with Eddie, Florence, and their infant son, Edward Stockton.

Bibliography

Manuscripts and Archival Sources

AUGUSTA, GA.
St. Paul's Episcopal Church, Parish Register.
BALTIMORE, MD.
Goucher College, Alumnae Records.
CAMBRIDGE, MASS.
Eleanor Axson Sayre Family Papers, in possession of E. A. Sayre.
CHICAGO, ILL.
Art Institute of Chicago, Archives.
CLEVELAND, OHIO.
Cleveland Museum of Art, Archives.
GREENSBORO, N.C.
Erwin and Adams Family Papers, in possession of Elizabeth Erwin Hutchins
   and Rebecca Bond Jeffress Barney.
HENDERSON, N.C.
DuBose Family Papers, in possession of Dorothy K. MacDowell.
HOUSTON, TEX.
Rice University, Fondren Library.
   Stockton Axson Papers.
INDIANAPOLIS, IND.
Indianapolis Museum of Art, Archives.
MARTHA'S VINEYARD, MASS.
Francis Bowes Sayre, Jr., Family Papers, in possession of F. B. Sayre, Jr.
Woodrow Wilson Sayre Family Papers, in possession of W. W. Sayre.
MILLEDGEVILLE, GA.
Central State Hospital.
   Georgia State Archives, admission records.
MONTREAT, N.C.
Historical Foundation of the Presbyterian and Reformed Churches.
   Charleston Presbytery Records, 1859, 1865.
   Presbytery of Cherokee Records, 1866, 1867.
   First Presbyterian Church, Rome, Ga., Minutes of the session, 1866–1884.
   Stoney Creek Independent Presbyterian Church, Minutes of the session,
      1860, 1861, 1862, 1865.
MORGANTON, N.C.
Erwin and Adams Family Papers, in possession of Elizabeth Erwin Hutchins.

NEW HAVEN, CONN.
Yale University Library.
  Arthur Walworth Papers.
NEW MARKET, VA.
Marjorie Brown King Papers, in possession of M. B. King.
NEW YORK, N.Y.
National Academy of Design, Records.
National Association of Women Artists, Archives.
Pen and Brush, Inc., Archives.
PHILADELPHIA, PENN.
The Pennsylvania Academy of the Fine Arts, Archives.
PRINCETON, N.J.
Borough Hall, Records.
MacMillan Building, Princeton University, Records.
Junius Spencer Morgan Papers, in possession of A. Perry Morgan, Jr.
Princeton Theological Seminary Library.
  Accessions by Examination and Letter, Dismissions, Ordinations, Deaths,
    Suspended, etc. First Presbyterian Church, Princeton, N.J.
  First Presbyterian Church, Princeton, N.J., Records.
  Second Presbyterian Church of Princeton, N.J., Minutes of the session.
Princeton University Library.
  Woodrow Wilson Collection.
  May, Mary Tyndall, "Isaac Randolph, A Brief Sketch of His Life." (Hand-
    written manuscript, bound, 1948.)
  University Archives.
RALEIGH, N.C.
Library, St. Mary's College
RICHMOND, VA.
Adele Williams Papers, in possession of C. W. Bayliss.
ROCKPORT, MASS.
Family Collection, in possession of W. D. Hoyt.
ROME, GA.
Carnegie Library.
  Woodrow Wilson File.
First Presbyterian Church Library.
Floyd County Superior Court, Records.
SANTA BARBARA, CAL.
Library of the University of California.
  Wilson-McAdoo Collection.
SAVANNAH, GA.
Georgia Historical Society.
  Axson Family Genealogy.
  Ben Palmer Axson Papers.
Independent Presbyterian Church, Archives.
TRENTON, N.J.
Mercer County Court House, Records.

WASHINGTON, D.C.
Archives of American Art.
Library of Congress.
  Diary of Edward William Axson, Wilson Papers.
  Samuel Edward Axson Sermons.
  Ray Stannard Baker Papers.
  Diary kept by Head Usher of the White House, March 4, 1913–August 10, 1914, Wilson Papers.
  Diary of Breckinridge Long, Breckinridge Long Papers.
  Woodrow Wilson Papers.
Records of the Office of the Curator, the White House.
Woodrow Wilson House, Records.

Interviews

Ben Palmer Axson, 1979.
Mary Faith McAdoo Bush, 1981.
Eleanor Marquand Delanoy, 1979, 1981.
Margaret Murray Dodds, 1981.
Sara Fahy, 1979.
Inez Henry, 1978.
William Dana Hoyt, 1980, 1981, 1982.
Caroline C. Hunt, 1980.
Marjorie Brown King, 1981, 1982.
Eleanor Axson Sayre, 1981.
Francis Bowes Sayre, Jr., 1980.

Collected Works and Biographies

Baker, Ray Stannard. *Woodrow Wilson, Life and Letters*. 8 vols. Garden City, N.Y.: Doubleday, Page, 1927–1939.
Dobkin, Marjorie Housepian, ed. *The Making of a Feminist*. Kent, Ohio: Kent State University Press, 1979.
Hirst, David W. *Woodrow Wilson: Reform Governor*. Princeton, N.J.: Van Nostrand, 1965.
Klapthor, Margaret Brown. *The First Ladies*. Washington: National Geographic Society, 1974.
Link, Arthur S. *Wilson: The Road to the White House*. Princeton, N.J.: Princeton University Press, 1947.
_____. *Wilson: The New Freedom*. Princeton, N.J.: Princeton University Press, 1956.
Link, Arthur S.; Hirst, David W.; and Little, John, et al., eds. *The Papers of Woodrow Wilson*. 48 vols. to date. Princeton, N.J.: Princeton University Press, 1966–.
McAdoo, Eleanor, ed. *The Priceless Gift*. New York: McGraw-Hill, 1962.

Myers, Robert Manson, ed. *The Children of Pride*. New Haven, Conn.: Yale University Press, 1972.

Memoirs

Axson, Stockton. "Memoir of Woodrow Wilson." Typed manuscript in possession of Arthur S. Link.

_____. "Mr. Wilson as Seen by One of His Family Circle." *New York Times*, Magazine Section, Oct. 8, 1916, p. 6.

_____. "Woodrow Wilson As Man of Letters." *The Rice Institute Pamphlet*, 22 (Oct. 1935): 199–270.

Bragdon, Henry W. *Woodrow Wilson: The Academic Years*. Cambridge: Harvard University Press, 1967.

Elliott, Margaret Axson. *My Aunt Louisa and Woodrow Wilson*. Chapel Hill, N.C.: University of North Carolina Press, 1944.

Harbin, Edith Lester. "Oft-told Tales." Typed manuscript in possession of Jane Griffin Dix.

Heming, Arthur. *Miss Florence and the Artists of Old Lyme*. Essex, Conn.: Pequot Press, 1971.

Hoyt, Mary Eloise. "Jessie Wilson Sayre." Typed manuscript in possession of F. B. Sayre, Jr.

Hulbert, Mary Allen. *The Story of Mrs. Peck*. New York: Milton, Balch & Co., 1933.

Jaffray, Elizabeth. *Secrets of the White House*. New York: Cosmopolitan, 1926.

McAdoo, Eleanor Wilson. *The Woodrow Wilsons*. New York: Macmillan, 1937.

McAdoo, William Gibbs. *Crowded Years: The Reminiscences of William Gibbs McAdoo*. Boston: Houghton Mifflin, 1931.

Myers, William Starr, ed. *Woodrow Wilson: Some Princeton Memories*. Princeton, N.J.: Princeton University Press, 1946.

Patterson, Archibald W. *Personal Recollections of Woodrow Wilson and Some Recollections Upon His Life and Character*. Richmond, Va.: Whittet and Shepperson, 1929.

Perry, Bliss. *And Gladly Teach*. Boston: Houghton Mifflin, 1935.

Reid, Edith Gittings. *Woodrow Wilson: The Caricature, the Myth and the Man*. New York: Oxford University Press, 1934.

Sayre, Francis Bowes. *Glad Adventure*. New York: Macmillan, 1957.

Newspapers

Ashtabula (Ohio) *Beacon*, 1913.
Charlotte Observer, 1928.
Daily Princetonian, 1892, 1898, 1903, 1907, 1910, 1912.
Nashville Banner, c. 1913.
New York Herald, 1913.
New York Times, 1912, 1913, 1914, 1916.
New York World, 1910, 1913.

Philadelphia Evening Bulletin, 1911.
Rome (Ga.) *Courier,* 1878, 1881, 1884, 1885.
Rome (Ga.) *Tribune-Herald,* 1914, 1972.
Savannah Evening Press, 1912.
Savannah Morning News, 1912.
The State (Columbia, S.C.), 1957.
Trenton Evening Times, 1912, 1913.
Washington Bee, 1916.
Washington Herald, 1913.
Washington Post, 1913, 1914.

Periodicals

Collier's, 1913.
Country Life in America, 1913.
Current Opinion, 1913.
Delineator, 1912.
Good Housekeeping, 1913.
Harper's Weekly, 1913.
Independent, 1912, 1913.
Ladies Home Journal, 1913.
Literary Digest, 1913.
Musical Advance, 1916.
Princeton Alumni Weekly, 1893, 1902, 1903, 1904, 1905, 1910, 1913, 1944.
Review of Reviews, 1913.
Saturday Evening Post, 1931.
Savannah Life Magazine, 1947.
Southern Presbyterian, 1873.
Survey, 1914.
Today's, 1912.

Signed Contemporary Articles

Arnold, Cloe. "The Governor's Lady." *Delineator,* July 1912, p. 18.
Bicknell, Grace Vawter (Mrs. Ernest P.). "The Homemaker of the White House." *Survey,* Oct. 3, 1914, pp. 19–22.
Daggett, Mabel P. "Woodrow Wilson's Wife." *Good Housekeeping,* Mar. 1913, pp. 316–23.
Gordon, Frances McGregor. "The Tact of Mrs. Woodrow Wilson." *Collier's,* Mar. 8, 1913, p. 13.
Hawley, Sherwin. "The Wilson Garden at Princeton." *Country Life in America,* Sept. 1913, pp. 44–45.
Hosford, Hester."The Lady of the White House." *Independent,* Apr. 17, 1913, pp. 866–70.
———. "The New Ladies of the White House." *Independent,* Nov. 21, 1912, pp. 1159–65.

Oilliams, Leslie E. "Will Uncle Sam's Hostesses Be Three Bachelor Maids?" *Today's*, Nov. 1912, p. 11.

Unsigned Contemporary Articles and Photographs

"The Happiest Lady in Washington" (photograph). *Literary Digest*, Mar. 15, 1913, p. 558.

The Lane and *The River* by Mrs. Woodrow Wilson (color reproductions of her paintings). *Ladies Home Journal*, May 1913, pp. 18–19.

"Mrs. Woodrow Wilson" (A. G. Learned etching). *Harper's Weekly*, Apr. 19, 1913, p. 15.

"Mrs. Woodrow Wilson" (Davis and Sanford photograph). *Independent*, July 11, 1912, p. 73.

"The New Mistress of the White House." *Current Opinion*, Mar. 1, 1913, pp. 195–96.

"The New Mistress of the White House: Mrs. Woodrow Wilson" (photograph). *Review of Reviews*, Mar. 1913, p. 273.

"Personally Selected American-Designed Fashions by Mrs. Woodrow Wilson." *Ladies Home Journal*, Apr. 1913, p. 28.

"Personally Selected American-Designed Fashions by the Misses Wilson." *Ladies Home Journal*, Apr. 1913, p. 29.

Wilson Family Photographs. *Harper's Weekly*, Mar. 8, 1913, pp. 12–13.

Secondary Works and Articles

Axley, Lowry. *Holding Aloft the Torch*. Savannah, Ga.: Pigeonhole Press, 1958.

Axson, Samuel Edward. *Twelve Years of Church Work in the Rome Presbyterian Church*. Rome, Ga.: Alvin Omberg Printer, 1878.

Aycock, Roger. *All Roads to Rome*. Roswell, Ga.: W. H. Wolfe Associates, 1981.

Bancroft, Hubert Howe. *The Book of the Fair*. New York: Bounty Books, 1894.

Battey, George Magruder, Jr. *A History of Rome and Floyd County*. Atlanta: Webb and Vary, 1922.

Bowman, Eleanor. *The Present Day Club*. Princeton, N.J.: Privately printed, 1948.

Brown, Milton W. *American Painting from the Armory Show to the Depression*. Princeton, N.J.: Princeton University Press, 1955.

Campbell, Lawrence, ed. *The Art Students League of New York*. New York: Art Students League of New York, 1975.

Catalogue of the College of New Jersey at Princeton, 1890–1891. Princeton University Library.

Christian, Louise Aymar, and FitzRandolph, Howard Stella. *The Descendants of Edward FitzRandolph and Elizabeth Blossom, 1630–1950*. Privately printed, 1950.

Connecticut and American Impressionism. Catalog of a cooperative exhibition at the William Benton Museum of Art, Hurlbutt Gallery, and Lyme Historical Society. Storrs, Conn.: The William Benton Museum, 1980.

Cormack, Malcolm. *A Catalogue of Drawings and Watercolours in the Fitzwilliam Museum*. Cambridge: Cambridge University Press, 1975.

Cothran, Walter C. "A History of the First Presbyterian Church of Rome, Georgia." Typed manuscript, 1948, First Presbyterian Church Library, Rome, Ga.

50th Anniversary of Dial Lodge (1907–1957). Seeley Mudd Library, Princeton University.

Fiftieth Anniversary of the Art Students League of New York. New York: Art Students League, 1925.

Finch, Edith. *Carey Thomas of Bryn Mawr*. New York: Harper, 1947.

George, Juliette L., and George, Alexander L. "Comments on 'Woodrow Wilson Re-examined: The Mind-Body Controversy Redux and Other Disputations.'" *Political Psychology* 4 (June 1983): 307–12.

———. "Woodrow Wilson and Colonel House: A Reply to Weinstein, Anderson, and Link." *Political Science Quarterly* 96 (Winter 1981–82): 641–65.

George, Juliette L.; Marmor, Michael F.; and George, Alexander L. "Issues in Wilson Scholarship: References to Early 'Strokes' in the *Papers of Woodrow Wilson*." *The Journal of American History* 70 (March 1984): 845–53.

———. Letter to the editor in "Communications." *The Journal of American History* 71 (June 1984): 198–212.

Godley, Margaret. "Savannah's Most Famous June Wedding." *Savannah Life Magazine* (June 1947): 4–5, 12.

Green, Constance McLaughlin. *The Secret City*. Princeton, N.J.: Princeton University Press, 1967.

Hageman, John Frelinghuysen. *History of Princeton and Its Institutions*. 2 vols. Philadelphia: J. B. Lippincott, 1879.

Harris, John L. "Proposed Parsonages." Typed manuscript, First Presbyterian Church Library, Rome, Ga.

———. "Rome First Presbyterian Church, a Critical Period." Typed manuscript, First Presbyterian Church Library, Rome, Ga.

Henlock, Charles, and Norris, Margaret. "Flowers for First Ladies." *Saturday Evening Post* (Nov. 28, 1931): 12–13, 81–83.

Hennig, Helen Kohn, ed. *Columbia 1786–1936, A Mid-Century Supplement, 1936–1966*. Columbia, S.C.: R. L. Bryan Co., 1936.

Hicky, Louise McHenry. *Rambles Through Morgan County*. Madison, Ga.: Morgan County Historical Society, 1971.

Hoyt, David W. *A Genealogical History of the Hoyt, Haight, Hight Families*. Boston: Providence Press, 1871.

Landgren, Marchal E. *Years of Art: The Story of the Art Students League of New York*. New York: McBride, 1940.

Leitch, Alexander. *A Princeton Companion*. Princeton, N.J.: Princeton University Press, 1978.

Leyburn, Edward R. *Historical Sketch of the First Presbyterian Church, Rome, Georgia* (1845–1921). Rome, Ga.: Privately printed, 1921.

Link, Arthur S.; Hirst, David W.; Davidson, John Wells; and Little, John E.

Letter to the editor in "Communications." *The Journal of American History* 70 (March 1984): 945–55.

Lunardini, Christine A. "Standing Firm: William Monroe Trotter's Meetings with Woodrow Wilson, 1913–1914." *Journal of Negro History* 64 (Summer 1979): 244–54.

Lunardini, Christine A., and Knock, Thomas J. "Woodrow Wilson and Woman Suffrage: A New Look." *Political Science Quarterly* 95 (Winter 1980–81): 655–71.

Marmor, Michael F. "Comments on 'Woodrow Wilson Re-examined: The Mind-Body Controversy Redux and Other Disputations.'" *Political Psychology* 4 (June 1983): 325–27.

———. "Wilson, Strokes, and Zebras." *New England Journal of Medicine* 307 (Aug. 26, 1982): 528–35.

Minutes of the General Assembly of the Presbyterian Church in the Confederate States of America. Augusta, Ga., 1861, 1862; Columbia, S.C., 1863, 1864.

Minutes of the General Assembly of the Presbyterian Church in the United States. Augusta, Ga., 1865; Columbia, S.C., 1866–71; Richmond, Va., 1872–76; Wilmington, N.C., 1877–84.

Minutes of the Synod of Georgia, October 28th–November 2nd, 1885. Atlanta: Dodson's Printing Office, 1885.

Miss Fine's School: The Past and the Present. Princeton, N.J.: Privately printed, 1950.

Morris, Sylvia Jukes. *Edith Kermit Roosevelt.* New York: Coward, McCann, & Geoghegan, 1980.

Mulder, John M. *Woodrow Wilson: The Years of Preparation.* Princeton, N.J.: Princeton University Press, 1978.

Post, Jerrold M. "Reply to the Three Comments on 'Woodrow Wilson Re-examined: The Mind-Body Controversy Redux and Other Disputations.'" *Political Psychology* 4 (June 1983): 329–31.

———. "Woodrow Wilson Re-examined: The Mind-Body Controversy Redux and Other Disputations." *Political Psychology* 4 (June 1983): 290–306.

Princeton City Directory, 1906, 1908, 1911. Princeton University Library.

Rhodes, Susie Root, and Hopkins, Grace Porter. *The Economy Administration Cook Book.* New York: Syndicate Publishing Company, 1913.

Rice, Thaddeus Brackett, and Williams, Carolyn White, eds. *History of Greene County Georgia 1786–1886.* Macon, Ga.: J. W. Burke, 1961.

Rich, Frederic C. "Prospect: The Search for a Garden." *The Princeton University Library Chronicle* 48 (Autumn 1980): 9–15.

The St. Mary's Muse: The Yearbook of the Students of St. Mary's School, Raleigh, N.C. 10 (1907–8); 11 (Nov. 1906): 19; and (Jan. 1907): 9, 16.

Saunders, Frances W. "Love and Guilt: Woodrow Wilson and Mary Hulbert." *American Heritage* 30 (Apr./May 1979): 68–77.

Smith-Rosenberg, Carroll. "The Female World of Love and Ritual: Relations Between Women in Nineteenth-Century America." *Signs* 1 (Autumn 1975): 1–29.

Stacy, James. *History of the Midway Congregational Church, Liberty County, Georgia*. Newnan, Ga.: S. W. Murray, 1903.

Thomas, Albert Sidney. *An Historical Account of the Protestant Episcopal Church in South Carolina*. Columbia, S.C.: R. L. Bryan Co., 1957.

Thorp, Willard; Meyers, Minor, Jr.; and Finch, Jeremiah. *The Princeton Graduate School, A History*. Princeton, N.J.: Princeton University Graduate School, 1978; printed by Princeton University Press.

Washington, Ida H., and Washington, Paul A. *Carleton's Raid*. Canaan, N.H.: Phoenix Publishing, 1977.

Weinstein, Edwin A. "Comments on 'Woodrow Wilson Re-examined: The Mind-Body Controversy Redux and Other Disputations.'" *Political Psychology* 4 (June 1983): 313–24.

———. *Woodrow Wilson: A Medical and Psychological Biography*. Princeton, N.J.: Princeton University Press, 1981.

———. "Woodrow Wilson's Neurological Illnesses." *The Journal of American History* 57 (Sept. 1970): 334–37.

Weinstein, Edwin A.; Anderson, James William; and Link, Arthur S. "Woodrow Wilson's Political Personality: A Reappraisal." *Political Science Quarterly* 93 (Winter 1978): 585–98.

Wilkerson, Ethel. *Rome's Remarkable History*. Rome, Ga.: Privately printed, 1968.

Index

Publication of Supplementary Volumes to *The Papers of Woodrow Wilson* is assisted from time to time by the Woodrow Wilson Foundation in order to encourage scholarly work about Woodrow Wilson and his time. All volumes have passed the review procedures of the publishers and the Editor and the Editorial Advisory Committee of *The Papers of Woodrow Wilson*. Inquiries about the Series should be addressed to The Editor, Papers of Woodrow Wilson, Firestone Library, Princeton University, Princeton, N.J. 08540.

Inga Floto, *Colonel House in Paris: A Study of American Policy at the Paris Peace Conference 1919* (Princeton University Press 1981)

Raymond B. Fosdick, *Letters on the League of Nations. From the Files of Raymond B. Fosdick* (Princeton University Press 1966)

Wilton B. Fowler, *British-American Relations, 1917–1918: The Role of Sir William Wiseman* (Princeton University Press 1969)

John M. Mulder, *Woodrow Wilson: The Years of Preparation* (Princeton University Press 1978)

George Egerton, *Great Britain and the Creation of the League of Nations* (University of North Carolina Press 1978)

Stephen L. Vaughn, *Holding Fast the Inner Lines: Democracy, Nationalism, and the Committee on Public Information* (University of North Carolina Press 1980)

Robert C. Hilderbrand, *Power and the People: Executive Management of Public Opinion in Foreign Affairs, 1897–1921* (University of North Carolina Press 1980)

Edwin A. Weinstein, *Woodrow Wilson: A Medical and Psychological Biography* (Princeton University Press 1981)

Arthur S. Link, editor, *Woodrow Wilson and the Revolutionary World, 1913–1921* (University of North Carolina Press 1982)

Valerie Jean Conner, *The National War Labor Board: Stability, Social Justice, and the Voluntary State in World War I* (University of North Carolina Press, 1983)

Klaus Schwabe, *Woodrow Wilson, Revolutionary Germany, and Peacemaking, 1918–1919: Missionary Diplomacy and the Realities of Power* (University of North Carolina Press, 1985)

Frances Wright Saunders, *Ellen Axson Wilson: First Lady Between Two Worlds* (University of North Carolina Press, 1985)

DATE LOANED

GAYLORD 3563			PRINTED IN U.S.A.